EU TRADE AND INVESTMENT TREATY-MAKING POST-LISBON

This book offers the first thorough legal analysis of the practice of mixity since the Lisbon Treaty, providing the perspectives of international, EU, and national law.

It sets out a detailed theoretical understanding of mixity, the common commercial policy and the recent case law of the EU Court of Justice. It assesses recent practice and current challenges, such as the non-ratification of mixed agreements, ensuring parliamentary participation in EU treaty-making, the new architecture for concluding EU trade and investment agreements, as well as the new trade agreement between the EU and the UK post-Brexit. In so doing, the author argues that in the field of trade and investment, mixity is no longer a procedural technique to overcome legal uncertainties about competence allocations between the EU and the Member States. Instead, mixity has become a deliberate substantive design choice. This brings a fresh and innovative perspective to a key tenet of EU external relations law.

Volume 123 in the Series Modern Studies in European Law

Modern Studies in European Law

Recent titles in this series:

EU Criminal Law, Second Edition
Valsamis Mitsilegas

The EU as a Global Digital Actor: Institutionalising Global Data Protection, Trade, and Cybersecurity
Elaine Fahey

Exporting the European Convention on Human Rights
Maria-Louiza Deftou

Judicial Authority in EU Internal Market Law: Implications for the Balance of Competences and Powers
Vilija Velyvyte

The Changing European Union: A Critical View on the Role of Law and the Courts
Edited by Tamara Capeta, Iris Goldner Lang and Tamara Perisin

The Structural Transformation of European Private Law: A Critique of Juridical Hermeneutic
Leone Niglia

The Future of EU Constitutionalism
Edited by Matej Avbelj

The Changing Role of Citizens in EU Democratic Governance
Edited by Davor Jancic

The EU and the Baltic Sea Area
Edited by Allan Rosas and Henrik Ringbom

The Evolving Governance of EU Competition Law in a Time of Disruptions: A Constitutional Perspective
Edited by Carlo Maria Colombo, Kathryn Wright and Mariolina Eliantonio

The European Integrated Border Management: Frontex, Human Rights, and International Responsibility
Giulia Raimondo

Private Autonomy in EU Internal Market Law: Parameters of its Protection and Limitation
Rufat Babayev

Free Movement and Welfare Access in the European Union: Re-Balancing Conflicting Interests in Citizenship Jurisprudence
Victoria Hooton

EU Trade and Investment Treaty-Making Post-Lisbon: Moving Beyond Mixity
Gesa Kübek

For the complete list of titles in this series see www.bloomsbury.com/uk/series/modern-studies-in-european-law/

EU Trade and Investment Treaty-Making Post-Lisbon

Moving Beyond Mixity

Gesa Kübek

•HART•
OXFORD • LONDON • NEW YORK • NEW DELHI • SYDNEY

HART PUBLISHING

Bloomsbury Publishing Plc

Kemp House, Chawley Park, Cumnor Hill, Oxford, OX2 9PH, UK

1385 Broadway, New York, NY 10018, USA

29 Earlsfort Terrace, Dublin 2, Ireland

HART PUBLISHING, the Hart/Stag logo, BLOOMSBURY and the Diana logo are trademarks of Bloomsbury Publishing Plc

First published in Great Britain 2024

A catalogue record for this book is available from the British Library.

Library of Congress Cataloging-in-Publication data

ISBN: HB: 978-1-50996-463-5
ePDF: 978-1-50996-465-9
ePub: 978-1-50996-464-2

Typeset by Compuscript Ltd, Shannon

ACKNOWLEDGEMENTS

This book is a revised and updated version of my doctoral thesis, which I defended at the University of Passau in 2021. I am indebted to my supervisor, Christoph Herrmann, for his trust, guidance and continued support over the years. He played a crucial role in finding the topic of this book, and his expertise, eye for detail and challenges to my ideas have helped me enormously during the writing process. I am grateful to my first examiner, Jörg Philipp Terhechte, from whom I learned a lot about the academic profession during my time in Lüneburg. The broader discussions we had on EU integration have been very helpful for refining the narrative of this book. I am also grateful to my second examiner, Marise Cremona, for supporting my research stay at the European University Institute and for her invaluable comments and suggestions. They have been instrumental in preparing this book. I owe a special thanks to Ramses Wessel. His enthusiastic teaching inspired me to study EU external relations law all these years ago and I continue to learn a great deal from him about the discipline today.

Several chapters of this book were revised and/or written during a research stay at the University College London, which would have not been possible without the help of Piet Eeckhout, Gracia Marín Durán and Despoina Mantzari. I also thank Piet Eeckhout for invaluable comments and suggestions.

Navigating academia as an early-career researcher has not always been easy. Yet, I have had the great luck of encountering many colleagues along the way who provided encouragement, opportunities, new insights and/or constructive feedback. Aside from those already mentioned, and from among the many interlocutors and collaborators who have enriched my ideas and knowledge, I would especially like to thank Joni Heliskoski, Isabelle Van Damme, Yuliya Kaspiarovich, Judith Crämer, Isabella Mancini, Luca Pantaleo, Thomas Verellen, Graham Butler, Merijn Chamon, Luigi Lonardo, Christian J Tams, Jelena Bäumler, Anne Thies, Sofia Ranchordás, Viktor Szép and Aurélie Villanueva. A special thank you is due to Marijke Hoekstra for her assistance in conducting the research for Chapter 5 of this book.

This book has benefited from the practical insights offered by officials from the Commission, Council, and Parliament. I thank them for their time. To Jon Lloyd, I am grateful for fantastic editorial support. To Sinead Moloney and her team at Hart Publishing, I am grateful for the immense help and assistance during the publication process.

To my partner, Jed: thank you for supporting all my projects and dreams, as big or small as they may be, with a perfect mix of enthusiasm, patience and humour. Thanks to you, the last years of this journey have been by far the most joyful ones. To my parents, Doerte and Rainer, and my brother, Arne: Danke für das unerschütterliche Fundament. Ohne Euch wäre ich weder wo ich bin noch wer ich bin. Dieses Buch ist für Euch.

CONTENTS

PART III
THE INTERRELATIONSHIP BETWEEN TREATY-MAKING POWER AND PROCEDURE

TERMS AND ABBREVIATIONS

Act on EU Cooperation I	Gesetz über die Zusammenarbeit von Bundesregierung und Deutschem Bundestag in Angelegenheiten der Europäischen Union (Act on Cooperation between the Federal Government and the German Federal Parliament in Matters Concerning the European Union)
Act on EU Cooperation II	Gesetz über die Zusammenarbeit von Bund und Ländern in Angelegenheiten der Europäischen Union (Act on Cooperation between the Federation and the Länder in Matters Concerning the European Union)
ACTA	Anti-Counterfeiting Trade Agreement
Berne Convention	Berne Convention for the Protection of Literary and Artistic Works
Bijzondere Wet tot Hervorming der Instelling (Belgium)	Special Law on Constitutional Reform
BITs	Bilateral Investment Treaties
BGBl	Bundesgesetzblatt (Federal Law Gazette) (Germany)
Deutscher Bundesrat	German Federal Council
Deutscher Bundestag	German Federal Parliament
Bundesverfassungsgericht	German Federal Constitutional Court
Canberra Convention	Convention on the Conservation of Antarctic Marine Living Resources
CARIFORUM	Caribbean Forum
CCAMLR	Commission for the Conservation of Antarctic Marine Living Resources
CCP	Common Commercial Policy

CETA	Comprehensive Economic and Trade Agreement
CFSP	Common Foreign and Security Policy
CJEU	Court of Justice of the European Union
CLS	Council Legal Service
Conditional Access Convention	European Convention on the Legal Protection of Services based on, or consisting of, Conditional Access
Conseil constitutionnel	French Constitutional Council
Cooperation Agreement Belgian Mixity	Samenwerkingsakkoord van 8 maart 1994 tussen de federale overheid, de Gemeenschappen en de Gewesten over de nadere regelen voor het sluiten van gemengde verdragen (Cooperation agreement of 8 March 1994 between the Federal Government, the Communities, and the Regions on arrangements for concluding mixed agreements)
COREPER	Comité des representants permanents (Committee of the Permanent Representatives of the Governments of the Member States to the European Union)
COTIF	Convention Concerning International Carriage by Rail
Criteria voor de beoordeling van verdragen (First Chamber of the Dutch Parliament)	Assessment Criteria of the First Chamber
DG	Directorate General
DGE	Directorate General for European Affairs and Coordination (Belgium)
EAEC	European Atomic Energy Community
EC	European Community
ECB	European Central Bank
ECHR	European Convention on Human Rights
ECI	European Citizenship Initiative
ECT	Energy Charter Treaty
ECOWAS	Economic Community of West African States

EEA	European Economic Area
EEC	European Economic Community
Eerste Kamer der Staten-Generaal	First Chamber of the Dutch Parliament
EFTA	European Free Trade Area
Erg.-Lfg.	Ergänzungslieferung (supplementary issue)
EP	European Parliament
EPA	Economic Partnership Agreement
ERTA	European Road Transport Agreement
EU Cooperation Agreement	Samewerkingsakkoord tussen de Federale Staat, de Gemeenschappen en de Gewesten, met betrekking tot de vertegenwoordiging van het Koninkrijk België in de Ministerraad van de Europese Unie (Cooperation Agreement between the Federal State, the Communities and the Regions regarding the Representation of the Kingdom of Belgium in the Council of Ministers of the European Union)
EUI	European University Institute
EUSFTA	European Union-Singapore Free Trade Agreement
EUSIPA	European Union-Singapore Investment Protection Agreement
EUSPCA	European Union-Singapore Partnership and Cooperation Agreement
EUVFTA	European Union-Vietnam Free Trade Agreement
EUVIPA	European Union-Vietnam Investment Partnership Agreement
EUVPCA	European Union-Vietnam Partnership and Cooperation Agreement
FTA	Free Trade Agreement
Folketinget	Danish Parliament
GATS	General Agreement on Trade in Services
	General Agreement on Tariffs and Trade
	Government Procurement Agreement

Højesteret	Danish Constitutional Court
ILO	International Labour Organization
INTA	Committee on International Trade of the European Parliament
Integrationsverantwortungsgesetz (Germany)	Responsibility for Integration Act
IPA	Investment Protection Agreement
IPRs	Intellectual Property Rights
ISDS	Investor-State Dispute Settlement
Istanbul Convention	Council of Europe Convention on Preventing and Combating Violence against Women and Domestic Violence
ITA	Information Technology Agreement
Kingdom Law	Rijkswet goedkeuring en bekendmaking verdragen (Kingdom Law on the Approval and Publication of Treaties) (the Netherlands)
Marrakesh Treaty	Marrakesh Treaty to Facilitate Access to Published Works for Persons Who are Blind, Visually Impaired or Otherwise Print Disabled
Mercosur	Mercado Común de Sur (Southern Common Market)
MIC	Multilateral Investment Court
NAFTA	North American Free Trade Agreement
New York Convention	Convention on the Recognition and Enforcement of Foreign Arbitral Awards
OJ	Official Journal of the European Union
OTIF	Intergovernmental Organisation for International Carriage by Rail
Paris Agreement	Paris Agreement on Climate Change
Paris Convention	Paris Convention for the Protection of Industrial Property
PCA	Partnership and Cooperation Agreement
QMV	Qualified Majority Voting
Raad van State	Council of States (Belgium, the Netherland
REIO	Regional Economic Integration Organ

SIA	Sustainable Impact Assessment
SPA	Strategic Partnership Agreement
Stb	Staatsblad (State Law Gazette) (Belgium, the Netherlands)
SWIFT	Society for Worldwide Interbank Financial Telecommunication
TCA	Trade and Cooperation Agreement
TEU	Treaty on European Union
TFEU	Treaty on the Functioning of the European Union
TPC	Trade Policy Committee
Treaty-Making Guide	Ministère de l'Europe et des Affaires Étrangères, Guide des bonnes pratiques en matière de négociation et de conclusion des engagements internationaux de la France
Trb	Tractatenblad (Treaty Law Gazette) (the Netherlands)
TRIPS	Agreement on Trade-Related Aspects of Intellectual Property Rights
TSD	Trade and Sustainable Development
TTIP	Transatlantic Trade and Investment Partnership
Tweede Kamer der Staten-Generaal	Second Chamber of the Dutch Parliament
UEMOA	Union Economique et Monétaire Ouest Africaine (West African Economic and Monetary Union)
UNCITRAL	United Nations Commission on International Trade
UNCLOS	United Nations Convention on the Law of the Sea
UNTS	United Nations Treaty Series
USMCA	United States-Mexico-Canada Agreement
VCLT	Vienna Convention on the Law of Treaties
VCLTIO	Vienna Convention on the Law of Treaties between States and International Organizations

Withdrawal Agreement	Agreement on the Withdrawal of the United Kingdom of Great Britain and Northern Ireland from the European Union and European Atomic Energy Community
WIPO	World Intellectual Property Organization
WTO	World Trade Organization

TABLE OF FIGURES

TABLE OF CASES

Chronologically, by date of delivery

1. International Courts and Tribunals

2. Court of Justice of the European Union

3. National Constitutional Courts

TABLE OF TREATIES, LEGISLATION, AND PRACTICE

Chronologically, by year (of publication)

1. EU Founding Treaties

2. Member State Constitutions

3. International Treaties

4. EU Legislation and Practice

4.1 Regulations

4.2 Directives

4.3 European Council Conclusions

4.4 Proposed/Recommended Council Decisions

4.5 Council Decisions

4.6 European Parliament Resolutions

4.7 Selected Practice

5. Member State Legislation and Practice

5.1 Decisions of Member States Meeting within the Council

5.2 Member State Legislation

Denmark

Belgium

5.3 National Parliament Proposals, Resolutions, and Notes

Denmark

Belgium

France

Germany

The Netherlands

5.4 Selected Practice

Denmark

Belgium

France

Germany

The Netherlands

1

Introduction

I. Mixity

Mixity is one of the most challenging and intricate practices in European Union (EU) external relations law. It epitomises the parallel existence of the EU and its constitutive, yet still sovereign, Member States on the international plane. As such, mixity is a 'defining characteristi[c] of the constitutional life of the European Union'[1] that presents a 'telling illustration of the specific character of the European Union integration project'.[2]

The notion of mixity refers to the practice of the EU and the Member States making international agreements jointly.[3] The resulting mixed agreements include among their contracting parties not only the EU but also all or some of its Member States. In other words, the EU and the Member States express their wish to be bound vis-a-vis third parties in one and the same legal instrument.[4] As a consequence, the mixed procedure requires that international agreements are ratified not only by the EU but also by the Member States in accordance with their respective national constitutional obligations. The mixed ratification of international agreements therefore necessitates the participation of (sub-)national parliaments and, depending on each agreement's substantive content, may lead to national referenda. Mixity thus elevates the role of national governments, parliaments, citizens and constitutional courts in the treaty ratification process. Simultaneously, however, mixity increases the duration and legal complexity of a treaty's ratification process and clouds its entry into force with considerable uncertainty.[5]

Mixity raises questions about power, procedure and public participation. These legal and political questions have intensified in recent years. The entry into force of the Lisbon Treaty changed the power balance between the EU and the Member States, questioning the legal rationale for mixity in some areas. This is particularly the case

[1] C Hillion and P Koutrakos (eds), *Mixed Agreements Revisited: The EU and its Member States in the World* (Hart Publishing, 2010) xix.

[2] A Rosas, 'Mixity Past, Present and Future' in M Chamon and I Govaere (eds), *EU External Relations Law Post-Lisbon: The Law and Practice of Facultative Mixity* (Brill/Nijhoff, 2020) 8.

[3] For an early definition, see P Pescatore, 'Les relations extérieures des Communautés européennes. Contribution à la doctrine de la personnalité des organisations internationales' (1961) 103 *Collected Courses of the Hague Academy of International Law* 1, 104. See also J Heliskoski, *Mixed Agreements as a Technique for Organizing the International Relations of the European Community and its Member States* (Kluwer Law International, 2001) 1.

[4] M Maresceau, 'A Typology of Mixed Bilateral Agreements' in Hillion and Koutrakos (n 1) 11, 12.

[5] D O'Keeffe and HG Schermers (eds), *Mixed Agreements* (Kluwer, 1983) x.

for the EU's trade policy, a traditional beacon of EU external relations power.[6] At the same time, the challenges associated with mixity became more frequent and complex with the politicisation of EU trade and investment policy.[7] The near-rejection of the EU-Canada Comprehensive Economic and Trade Agreement (CETA) by the Walloon Parliament sparked debates about the need to better involve national parliaments and citizens in EU trade policy, on the one hand, and about the risk of political blackmail and paralysis inherent to the allocation of numerous veto rights, on the other hand.[8] After the Court of Justice of the European Union (CJEU) provided a broad interpretation of the EU's post-Lisbon external trade competence, the EU began to *move beyond mixity*, including for the conclusion of its most important trade agreement in recent times, the Trade and Cooperation Agreement (TCA) with the United Kingdom (UK).

In light of the recent developments in law and practice, this book analyses the operation of mixity in the post-Lisbon era, with a particular focus on the EU's trade and investment policy. Through an in-depth study of treaty-making law and practice on the international, EU and national planes, the book lays bare the complex and interwoven relations between power and procedure in EU external relations. It argues that in the field of trade and investment, mixity is no longer a procedural technique to overcome uncertainties about competence allocations between the EU and the Member States. Instead, mixity has become a deliberate substantive design choice. Consequentially, the decision to opt for mixity in EU trade and investment policy should no longer be made as a matter of principle, but should be based on a careful balancing exercise conducted at the outset of the treaty-making process. For the making of bilateral EU trade and investment liberalisation agreements, it is arguably time to *move beyond mixity* and to find new ways of integrating (sub-)national actors in EU external decision-making, both at the EU and at the national level.

II. Mixity and the EU's Bilateral Trade Agenda

Bilateral trade and investment agreements may have never been as important as they are today.[9] The World Trade Organization (WTO) Doha Round negotiations have been

[6] See further M Bungenberg and C Herrmann (eds), *Common Commercial Policy after Lisbon*, Special Issue, *European Yearbook of International Economic Law* (Springer, 2013).

[7] On the politicisation of the EU's trade policy, see S Meunier and R Czesana, 'From Back Rooms to the Street? A Research Agenda for Explaining Variation in the Public Salience of Trade Policy-Making in Europe' (2019) 26 *Journal of European Public Policy* 1847; F De Ville and G Siles-Brügge, *TTIP: The Truth about the Transatlantic Trade and Investment Partnership* (Polity Press, 2016). On the CCP and recent challenges, see C Herrmann (ed), *Die Gemeinsame Handelspolitik im europäischen Verfassungsverbund* (Nomos, 2020).

[8] On the former see, eg, C Eckes, *EU Powers under External Pressure: How the EU's External Actions Alter its Internal Structures* (Oxford University Press, 2019) 32; on the latter, see D Kleimann and G Kübek, 'The Signing, Provisional Application, and Conclusion of Trade and Investment Agreements in the EU: The Case of CETA and *Opinion 2/15*' (2018) 45 *Legal Issues of Economic Integration* 13, 44.

[9] Terhechte is even speaking about a new era for bilateral agreements ('neues Zeitalter für bilaterale Verträge'). See JP Terhechte, 'Im Dienste der Demokratie? Das institutionelle Gleichgewicht in der Gemeinsamen Handelspolitik der EU' in Herrmann (n 7) 153. For a critical account of this development, see C Herrmann, 'Bilateral and Regional Trade Agreements as a Challenge to the Multilateral Trading System' (2008) 63 *Aussenwirtschaft: Schweizerische Zeitschrift für internationale Wirtschaftsbeziehungen* 263.

deadlocked for more than a decade.[10] Moreover, the WTO's jurisdictional effectiveness has been systemically dismantled by the United States' (US) blockage of Appellate Body member appointments.[11] In the resulting 'new world of tit-for-tat threats, divide-and-rule attempts and plain coercion', states increasingly rely on unilateral trading measures.[12] In the face of declining multilateralism and growing unilateralism, bilateral agreements have become essential for ensuring that trade and investment relations continue to be governed by international law. Moreover, the EU's broad network of bilateral trade agreements has become an expression of its external trade power, which the EU increasingly uses as a lever to achieve wider policy objectives, such as in the domains of security (eg, economic sanctions)[13] or sustainability (eg, trade and sustainable development chapters in EU trade and investment agreements).[14] By providing a platform 'for enhanced cooperation pursuing [EU] values and interests', bilateral trade and investment agreements facilitate the fulfilment of the EU's 'geopolitical ambitions globally' at a time of rising geopolitical instability.[15]

The EU has concluded bilateral trade agreements since the early 1970s.[16] As the second-largest exporter and importer of goods, and the largest exporter and importer of services worldwide,[17] it is 'as an active player in the global market that the Union has played its first and still most-high profile role'.[18] Since 2006, the EU has shown a clear preference for developing bilateral trade relations with the wider world.[19] In a strategic move that was largely viewed as a reaction to the stagnated WTO reform

[10] See further PC Mavroidis, 'Doha, Dohalf, or Dohaha? The WTO Licks its Wounds' (2011) 3 *Trade, Law and Development* 367.

[11] On WTO dispute settlement, see, eg, I Van Damme, *Treaty Interpretation by the WTO Appellate Body* (Oxford University Press, 2009) 3. On the Appellate Body crisis, see, eg, B Hoekman and PC Mavroidis, 'Burning Down the House? The Appellate Body in the Centre of the WTO Crisis' (2019) 56 *EUI Working Paper RSCAS*.

[12] S Meunier, 'The End of Naivety: Assertiveness and New Instruments in EU Trade and Investment Policy (2022) 55 *Policy Brief, EUI Global Governance Programme*.

[13] Most recently, the EU has used its trade power to impose sanctions against Russia in response to Russia's war of aggression against Ukraine. See further L Lonardo, *Russia's 2022 War against Ukraine and the EU's Foreign Policy Reaction: Context, Diplomacy, and Law* (Palgrave Macmillan, 2022); and V Szép and K Chawla, 'The EU's 2022 Sanctions against Russia: External Shocks Altering EU Restrictive Measure Practices?' (2023) 16 *Hungarian Yearbook of International Law and European Law* 196.

[14] See, eg, WT Douma, 'The Promotion of Sustainable Development through EU Trade Instruments' (2017) *European Business Law Review* 197.

[15] European Commission, Trade Policy Review: An Open, Sustainable and Assertive Trade Policy [2021] COM (2021) 66 final, 9. On earlier initiatives, see Editorial Comments, 'Playing by the Rules: Free and Fair Trade' (2018) 55 *Common Market Law Review* 373.

[16] A consistently updated overview of the EU's bilateral trade agenda is available via the website of the Directorate-General for Trade (DG Trade): https://policy.trade.ec.europa.eu/eu-trade-relationships-country-and-region/negotiations-and-agreements_en.

[17] European Commission, DG Trade Statistical Guide [2022].

[18] M Cremona, 'The Union as a Global Actor: Roles, Models, Identity' (2004) 41 *Common Market Law Review* 553, 555.

[19] On the EU's post-Lisbon bilateral trade agenda and the substantive design of such agreements see further, BA Melo Araujo, *The EU Deep Trade Agenda: Law and Policy* (Oxford University Press, 2016); M Cremona, 'The European Union and Regional Trade Agreements' in C Herrmann and JP Terhechte (eds), *European Yearbook of International Economic Law 2010* (Springer, 2010) 245; F Hoffmeister, 'Bilateral Developments in EU Trade Policy Seven Years after Lisbon: A Look into the Spaghetti-Bowl à la Bruxelloise (2010–2016)' in M Bungenberg et al (eds), *European Yearbook of International Economic Law 2017* (Springer, 2017) 411; and W Weiß, 'Vertragliche Handelspolitik der EU' in in A von Arnauld and M Bungenberg (eds), *Europäische Außenbeziehungen*, Enzyklopädie Europarecht, vol 12, 2nd edn (Nomos, 2020) 759, 795.

and the bilateral trade agenda of the US,[20] the European Commission announced that it will initiate a 'new generation of carefully selected and prioritised [Free Trade Agreements (FTAs)]'.[21] The first new generation EU trade agreement was the FTA with South Korea, which was signed in 2009 and entered into force in 2015.[22] Since then, the EU has negotiated, signed and/or concluded new generation trade and investment agreements with, amongst others, Canada,[23] Japan,[24] Singapore,[25] Vietnam[26] and New Zealand.[27] In addition, it concluded several Association Agreements including deep and comprehensive free trade areas (DCFTAs) with, amongst others, Ukraine,[28] Georgia,[29] Moldova[30] and the UK.[31]

Mixity has historically played a big role in the making of EU trade agreements, despite being counterintuitive in the field of trade policy. The conclusion of tariff and trade agreements, as part of the Common Commercial Policy (CCP), has always been an exclusive competence of the EU.[32] Agreements that fully fall within EU exclusive competence must be concluded by the EU alone as a matter of law (EU-only agreements).[33] Conversely, mixity is legally required if the envisaged agreement falls partially within the Member States' exclusive competence (mandatory mixed agreements). Mixity is optional if the envisaged agreement falls within a competence shared by the EU and the Member States (facultative mixed agreements). In light of the exclusive nature of the CCP, one could thus expect that EU FTAs are generally concluded as EU-only agreements. The same presumption could be made about Association Agreements. As third states are associated with the EU and not with the individual Member States,[34] one could expect a higher prevalence of EU-only Association Agreements. Yet, Association

[20] M Cremona, 'Guest Editorial: Negotiating the Transatlantic Trade and Investment Partnership (TTIP)' (2015) 52 *Common Market Law Review* 351. See also JN Bhagwati, 'US Trade Policy: The Infatuation with FTAs' (1995) 726 *Colombia University Discussion Paper Series*.

[21] Communication from the Commission to the Council, the European Parliament, the European Economic and Social Committee and the Committee of the Regions 'Global Europe: Competing in the World' [2006] COM (2006) 567 final, 15.

[22] Free Trade Agreement between the European Union and its Member States, of the one part, and the Republic of Korea, of the other part [2011] OJ L127/6.

[23] Comprehensive Economic and Trade Agreement (CETA) between Canada, of the one part, and the European Union and its Member States, of the other part [2017] OJ L11/2.

[24] Agreement between the European Union and Japan for an Economic Partnership [2018] OJ L330/3.

[25] Free Trade Agreement between the European Union and the Republic of Singapore [2019] OJ L294/3.

[26] Free Trade Agreement between the European Union and the Socialist Republic of Viet Nam [2020] OJ L186/3.

[27] Council Decision (EU) 2023/1323 of 27 June 2023 on the signing, on behalf of the Union, of the Free Trade Agreement between the European Union and New Zealand [2023] OJ L166/48.

[28] Association Agreement between the European Union and its Member States, of the one part, and Ukraine, of the other part [2014] OJ L161/3.

[29] Association Agreement between the European Union and the European Atomic Energy Community and their Member States, of the one part, and Georgia, of the other part [2014] OJ L260/4.

[30] Association Agreement between the European Union and the European Atomic Energy Community and their Member States, of the one part, and the Republic of Moldova, of the other part [2014] OJ L260/4.

[31] Trade and Cooperation Agreement between the European Union and the European Atomic Energy Community, of the one part, and the United Kingdom of Great Britain and Northern Ireland, of the other part [2021] OJ L149/10.

[32] Opinion 1/75, *Local Cost Standard*, EU:C:1975:145. See now Article 3(1)(e) in conjunction with Article 207(1) of the Consolidated Version of the Treaty on the Functioning of the European Union [2012] OJ C326/47 (hereinafter 'TFEU').

[33] Article 2(1) TFEU. See further Chapter 2, section II.

[34] See further Chapter 8, section III.A.

Agreements are typically concluded as mixed agreements, while trade agreements have only been concluded by the EU alone from 2017 onwards (see Figure 1.1 below).

Against this background, the following sections will take a look back and explain the evolution of mixity in EU trade and investment policy, as well as recent developments that marked the start of the *move beyond mixity.*

III. The Evolution of Mixity in EU Trade and Investment Policy

So far, the choice for or against mixity has rarely been made on a case-by-case basis.[35] Mixity has proven to be path-dependent. In practice, the decision to opt for mixity was often made out of principle and not for pressing legal or political reasons.[36] Only significant events, such as primary law amendments, new case law or specific political circumstances, led the EU institutions to divert from a well-trodden path. The default treaty-making procedure varies by policy field and/or type of agreement. For example, Association Agreements and – until recently – FTAs were almost always concluded as mixed agreements, whereas agreements in the area of the Area of Freedom Security and Justice (AFSJ)[37] or the Common Foreign and Security Policy (CFSP)[38] are usually concluded by the EU alone. The fact that mixity is prevalent in the area of trade and for

Figure 1.1 The evolution of mixity in EU trade and investment policy

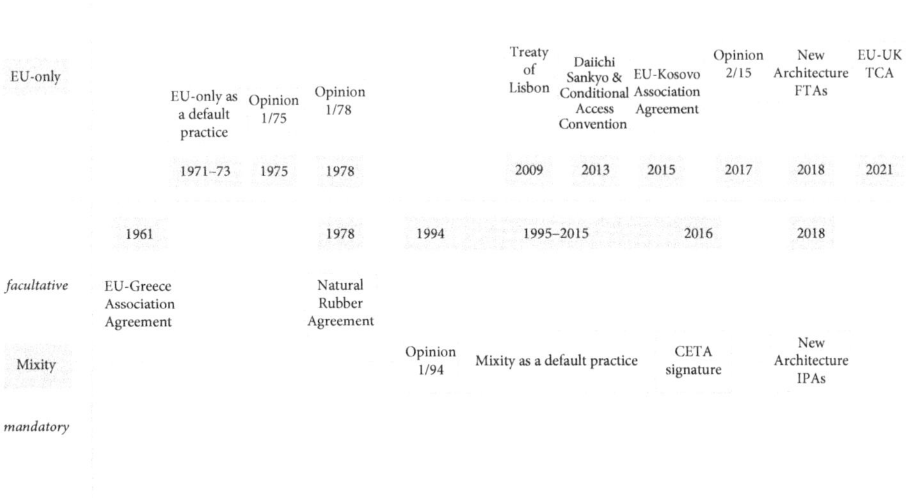

[35] The TCA is a notable exception. See further Chapter 8.
[36] Interview with a Commission official, 9 November 2018.
[37] Most notably readmission agreements. See especially C Matera and M Gatti, 'Facultative Mixity in the Area of Freedom, Security and Justice' in Chamon and Govaere (n 2) 187.
[38] See especially P Van Elsuwege, 'Old Habits Die Hard: Questions of Facultative Mixity in Relation to the Common Foreign and Security Policy' in Chamon and Govaere (n 2) 169.

forming an association with the EU but virtually absent in the area of security underlines that the choice of treaty-making procedure does not always purely follow the logic of competence allocations.

Figure 1.1 illustrates the evolution of mixity in EU trade and investment policy, which the following sections explain chronologically.[39]

A. The Pre-Lisbon Era and the Rise of Mixity

The CCP has long been recognised by the CJEU as an a priori exclusive external competence of the EU. The scope of the CCP was initially confined to the conclusion of tariff and trade agreements, as well as to the adoption of measures on liberalisation, export policy and trade defence (Article 113(1) of the European Economic Community (EEC) Treaty). In *Opinion 1/75*, the CJEU concluded that it would be 'impossible' for Member States to exercise concurrent powers in areas covered by Article 113(1) EEC. It held that if the Member States were to adopt a different position from the Community in the field of the CCP, they 'would thereby distort the institutional framework, call into question the mutual trust within the [then] Community and prevent the latter from fulfilling its task in the defence of the common interest'.[40] Furthermore, in *Opinion 1/78*, the CJEU concluded that the reach of Article 113 EEC had to be interpreted dynamically in light of the developments in international economic law and policy.[41] Therefore, the scope of the CCP cannot be perceived as static.

As a consequence, the Community's first bilateral trade agreements with, respectively, Switzerland, Austria, Iceland and Norway in the early 1970s were concluded by the Community alone using Article 113 EEC as a single substantive legal basis.[42] In addition, the 1990 customs agreement with Andorra and the 1997 agreement on trade in goods between the Community, the Government of Denmark and the Home Government of the Faroe Islands fell within the scope of the CCP.[43] Therefore, these

[39] An earlier version of sections III.A – III.C has previously been published in G Kübek and I Van Damme, 'Facultative Mixity and the European Union's Trade and Investment Agreements' in Chamon and Govaere (n 2) 137, 140 et seq.

[40] Opinion 1/75 (n 32) 1364.

[41] Opinion 1/78, *International Agreement on Rubber*, EU:C:1979:224. On the importance of Opinions 1/75 and 1/78 for the evolution of mixity, see JHH Weiler, *The Constitution of Europe: 'Do the New Clothes Have an Emperor?' and Other Essays on European Integration* (Cambridge University Press, 1999) 173–74.

[42] Regulation (EEC) No 2842/72 of the Council of 19 December 1972 concluding an Agreement between the European Economic Community and the Republic of Iceland and adopting provisions for its implementation [1972] OJ L301/2; Regulation (EEC) No 2836/72 of the Council of 19 December 1972 concluding an Agreement between the European Economic Community and the Republic of Austria and adopting provisions for their implementation [1972] OJ L300/1; Regulation (EEC) No 2840/72 of the Council of 19 December 1972 concluding an Agreement between the European Economic Community and the Swiss Confederation and adopting provisions for its implementation and concluding an additional Agreement concerning the validity for the Principality of Liechtenstein, of the Agreement between the European Economic Community and the Swiss Confederation of 22 July 1972 [1972] OJ L300/188; Regulation (EEC) No 1691/73 of the Council of 25 June 1973 concluding an Agreement between the European Economic Community and the Kingdom of Norway and adopting provisions for its implementation [1973] OJ L171/1.

[43] Agreement in the form of an exchange of letters between the European Economic Community and the Principality of Andorra [1990] OJ L374/14; Agreement between the European Community, of the one part, and the Government of Denmark and the Home Government of the Faroe Islands, of the other part [1997] OJ L53/2.

agreements were concluded as mandatory Community-only agreements. Moreover, the Community's Association Agreements with Malta and Cyprus were concluded without the participation of the Member States.[44] Multilaterally, the CJEU considered in *International Fruit Company* that the Community had superseded the Member States in their external commitments as regards the 1947 General Agreement on Tariffs and Trade (GATT),[45] rendering the 1947 GATT binding on the Community notwithstanding the lack of formal membership.[46]

Mixity was already well established in practice at this stage. The EEC concluded its first mixed agreement, the Association Agreement with Greece, in 1961.[47] The CJEU also recognised the possibility of mixed agreements at the time. For example, the CJEU decided in *Opinion 1/78* that the Member States were allowed to become contracting parties to the International Rubber Agreement, although the agreement fell squarely within the scope of the CCP. Mixity was optional for the conclusion of the International Rubber Agreement because the Member States ensured the financing of buffer stock in their own capacity.[48] Nevertheless, mixity remained an exception in the area of trade until the mid-1990s.

As a result of the Uruguay Round and the establishment of the WTO, a deeper trade agenda emerged[49] covering not only trade in goods but also trade in services and trade-related intellectual property rights (IPRs). Thus, the scope of international trade agreements began to exceed the scope the CCP pre-Maastricht, which was, as already discussed, at the time already an a priori EU exclusive competence.

In *Opinion 1/94*, the CJEU was asked by the Commission to clarify whether the (then) Community had 'the competence to conclude all parts of [the Agreements establishing the WTO] alone'.[50] However, the CJEU interpreted the Commission's request in *Opinion 1/94* as relating solely to the scope of the Community's exclusive competence.[51] Hence, the CJEU did not further qualify whether the competence for trade in services and commercial aspects of IPRs was shared between the Community and the Member States or whether the Member States alone remained competent in those areas. As a result, the CJEU did not address whether or not the Community could conclude the WTO Agreements alone.[52]

Given that the precise nature of the Community's competence with respect to trade in services and commercial aspects of IPRs was not clarified by *Opinion 1/94*, some Member States claimed that they remained competent in these areas, meaning

[44] Agreement establishing an association between the European Economic Community and Malta [1971] OJ L61/2; Agreement establishing an Association between the European Economic Community and the Republic of Cyprus [1973] OJ L133/2.
[45] Annex 1A of the Marrakesh Agreement Establishing the World Trade Organization [1995] UNTS Vol. 1867, 3.
[46] Joined Cases 21 to 24/72, *International Fruit Company*, EU:C:1972:115.
[47] Accord créant une association entre la Communauté économique européenne et la Grèce [1963] OJ 26/294, no longer in force.
[48] Opinion 1/78 (n 41) para 60.
[49] Or re-emerged, if compared to the Havana Charter.
[50] Opinion 1/94, *WTO Agreements*, EU:C:1994:384, para 6. See also C Herrmann and T Streinz, 'Die EU als Mitglied der WTO' in von Arnauld and Bungenberg (n 19) 853, 879 et seq.
[51] ibid para 1.
[52] Critically, Editorial Comments, 'The Aftermath of Opinion 1/94 or How to Ensure Unity of Representation for Joint Competences' (1995) 32 *Common Market Law Review* 386.

that they considered that the conclusion of the WTO Agreements required mixity.[53] Furthermore, the CJEU's conclusion that the Community and the Member States were 'jointly competent' to sign and ratify the General Agreement on Trade in Services (GATS)[54] and the Agreement on Trade Related Aspects of Intellectual Property Rights (TRIPS Agreement)[55] was understood by certain stakeholders as referring to the need for a mixed agreement, even though, in fact, the CJEU did not take a position on who should or could sign the WTO Agreements.[56] Its conclusions were limited to the question of competence. They did not address the exercise of that competence.

As a result of *Opinion 1/94*, trade agreements were no longer concluded as mandatory Community-only agreements (and only exceptionally jointly with the Member States). Mixity became the practical default for concluding trade agreements after 1994.[57] Between 1994 and 2018, almost all of the EU's trade and investment agreements were concluded as (facultative) mixed agreements.

B. The Early Post-Lisbon Years

The Lisbon Treaty significantly widened the definition of the CCP. Pursuant to Article 207(1) of the Treaty on the Functioning of the European Union (TFEU), that policy now covers 'changes in tariff rates, the conclusion of tariff and trade agreements relating to trade in goods and services, and the commercial aspects of intellectual property, foreign direct investment, the achievement of uniformity in measures of liberalisation, export policy and measures to protect trade such as those to be taken in the event of dumping or subsidies'. Article 3(1)(e) TFEU states that the EU enjoys exclusive competence for those matters. In *Daiichi Sankyo* and *Conditional Access Convention*, the CJEU concluded that the TRIPS Agreement and the GATS principally fall within the scope of the CCP post-Lisbon. In that regard, *Opinion 1/94* is no longer good law.[58]

Despite the expansion of the CCP by the Lisbon Treaty, mixity remained 'sticky' in practice. The first trade and investment agreement concluded by the EU post-Lisbon, ie, the FTA with Korea, comprises a protocol on cultural cooperation that falls squarely outside the EU's exclusive competence,[59] justifying the recourse to mixity. The next FTA,

[53] For a view supporting mandatory mixity for the WTO conclusion, see, eg, A Dashwood, 'Why Continue to Have Mixed Agreements at All?' in JHJ Bourgeois, J-L Dewost and M-A Gaiffe (eds), *La Communauté européenne et les accords mixtes: Quelles perspectives?* (PIE-Peter Lang, 1997) 94 et seq. Contra, see, eg, P Gilsdorf, 'Die Außenkompetenzen der EG im Wandel' (1995) 30 *Zeitschrift Europarecht* 145, 156–57.

[54] Annex 1B of the Marrakesh Agreement Establishing the World Trade Organization [1995] UNTS Vol 1867, 3.

[55] Annex 1C of the Marrakesh Agreement Establishing the World Trade Organization [1995] UNTS Vol 1867, 3.

[56] Opinion 1/94 (n 50) paras 98 and 105, respectively. Contra, see T Tridimas and P Eeckhout, 'The External Competence of the Community and the Case-Law of the Court of Justice: Principle versus Pragmatism' (1994) 14 *Yearbook of European Law* 143, 175, especially fn 122.

[57] See also Case C-53/96, *Hermès*, EU:C:1998:292; Joined Cases C-300 and 392/98, *Dior and Others*, EU:C:2000:688.

[58] Case C-414/11, *Daiichi Sankyo*, EU:C:2013:520; and Case C-137/12, *Commission v Council (Conditional Access Convention)*, EU:C:2013:675. See further Chapter 3, section III.A.

[59] EU-Korea FTA, Protocol on Cultural Cooperation [2011] OJ L127/1418. See further Chapter 2, section III.B; and Chapter 4, section III.D.

concluded with Peru and Colombia, did not cover cultural and audiovisual services.[60] The Commission therefore proposed the signature and conclusion of the FTA with Peru and Colombia as an 'EU-only' agreement, given that '[a]ll the areas covered by the trade agreement fall within the competence of the EU and, more particularly, within the scope of Articles 91, 100(2) and 207 TFEU'.[61] However, the Council unanimously decided to alter the proposal, with the result that the agreement became mixed.[62] The only exception to the default of mixity at the time was the Stabilisation and Association Agreement with Kosovo. As some Member States do not recognise Kosovo as a state under public international law, they preferred the conclusion of the Stabilisation and Association Agreement by the EU alone for political reasons.[63]

In the meantime, the scope of EU trade and investment agreements expanded. Originally envisaged as a cornerstone of the Transatlantic Trade and Investment Partnership (TTIP) with the US, a comprehensive investment protection chapter, including investor-state dispute settlement, became a design feature of new generation EU FTAs. For this reason, amongst others, the Council and the Member States insisted that new generation trade and investment agreements had to be concluded as mixed agreements as a matter of law and not 'just' for political reasons. After the failure of the TTIP, CETA became the first EU trade and investment agreement that included a component on substantive investment protection and investor-state dispute settlement. Contrary to the Council and the Member States' views, the Commission contented that the EU could conclude CETA alone as a matter of law.[64] In an unprecedented decision initiated by its Secretary-General at the time, Martin Selmayr, the Commission ultimately caved in to the political pressure from the Council and the Member States and proposed the signature of CETA as a mixed agreement.[65] As mentioned above, the backtrack to the mixed procedure resulted in an anti-climax of unprecedented scale with the Walloon government's near-rejection of CETA at the signature stage. Ultimately, however, a solution was found and CETA was signed on 30 October 2018.[66]

[60] Trade Agreement between the European Union and its Member States, of the one part, and Colombia and Peru, of the other part [2012] OJ L354/3.

[61] Proposal for a Council Decision on the conclusion of the Trade Agreement between the European Union and Colombia and Peru [2011] COM/2011/0569 final.

[62] Council Decision (EU) 2012/735 of 31 May 2012 on the signing, on behalf of the Union, and provisional application of the Trade Agreement between the European Union *and its Member States*, of the one part, and Colombia and Peru, of the other part [2012] OJ L354/1 (emphasis added).

[63] Stabilisation and Association Agreement between the European Union and the European Atomic Energy Community, of the one part, and Kosovo, of the other part [2016] OJ L71/3. Cyprus, Greece, Romania, Slovakia and Spain do not recognise Kosovo. The use of the EU-only procedure was a way to circumvent an indirect positioning of (some) Member States on Kosovo. This reasoning is inter alia evident in the report of the House of Commons, 'The EU and Kosovo: Stabilisation and Association Agreement (SAA)' (2019). See also P Van Elsuwege, 'Legal Creativity in EU External Relations: The Stabilisation and Association Agreement between the EU and Kosovo' (2017) 22 *European Foreign Affairs Review* 393.

[64] The (then) Commissioner Malmström stated: 'From a strict legal standpoint, the Commission considers this agreement to fall under exclusive EU competence. However, the political situation in the Council is clear, and we understand the need for proposing it as a 'mixed' agreement, in order to allow for a speedy signature.' See European Commission, 'Press Release: European Commission Proposes Signature and Conclusion of EU-Canada Trade Deal' [2016] IP/16/2371.

[65] Interview with a Council official, 7 November 2018. See further Proposal for a Council Decision on the signing on behalf of the European Union of the Comprehensive Economic and Trade Agreement between Canada of the one part, and the European Union and its Member States, of the other part [2016] COM/2016/0444 final.

[66] See Chapter 6.

C. *Opinion 2/15* and the Decline of Mixity

The intense discussions between the Commission, other EU institutions and the Member States regarding whether CETA should be a mixed agreement took place at a time when the Commission had already requested from the CJEU an opinion on the allocation of competences between the EU and the Member States as regards the EU-Singapore FTA (EUSFTA).[67] The EUSFTA (at the time) contained, similar to CETA, a substantive investment protection component and an investor-state dispute settlement mechanism. In the *Opinion 2/15* proceedings, the Commission argued that the EU enjoyed exclusive competence for the entire EUSFTA. In the alternative, the Commission asked the CJEU to conclude that the EUSFTA fell, for certain parts, within the EU's shared competences and for all other parts within its exclusive competence. According to the Commission, under either position, it would be possible for the EU to conclude alone the EUSFTA. In fact, the main question in *Opinion 2/15* put to the CJEU was whether the EU had the '*requisite* competence' to conclude the EUSFTA alone.[68] The Commission argued that the competence for concluding an EU-only agreement may be 'exclusive and/or shared'.[69] The other part of the Commission's request asked the CJEU to specify what parts of the agreement fell within the EU's exclusive or shared competence and possibly within the Member States' competence only.

According to Advocate General Sharpston, the EUSFTA could be concluded only by the EU and the Member States acting jointly, given that part of the agreement covered a matter for which the EU had no competence whatsoever (namely the termination of existing bilateral investment agreements concluded between individual Member States and Singapore).[70] In her view, the EUSFTA provisions on internal waterway, maritime and air transport services[71] did not affect or alter EU secondary legislation within the meaning of the third sentence of Article 3(2) TFEU (the 'ERTA test').[72] Consequently, the EU's competence for those transport services would remain shared.[73] Furthermore, Advocate General Sharpston considered that the EU shared competence with the Member States for the provisions of the EUSFTA governing investments other than foreign direct investments (ie, foreign non-direct investments)[74] and trade and sustainable development, insofar as the latter provisions concerned labour, environmental and social standards.[75] Although those conclusions did not necessarily imply that, as

[67] Opinion 2/15, *FTA with Singapore*, EU:C:2017:376.

[68] Request for an opinion submitted by the European Commission pursuant to Article 218(11) TFEU [2015] OJ C 363/18 (emphasis added).

[69] Written Observations of the Commission in *Opinion 2/15*, Ref Ares(2015)3942621 [2015], document on file with the author. The European Parliament (EP) supported the Commission's argument in favour of the EU's capacity to exercise shared external competence alone without further developing it (interview with an EP official, 7 November 2018).

[70] Opinion of Advocate General Sharpston, Opinion 2/15, *FTA with Singapore*, EU:C:2016:992, para 570. See further H Lenk 'Mixity in EU Foreign Trade Policy is Here to Stay: Advocate General Sharpston on the Allocation of Competence for the Conclusion of the EU-Singapore Free Trade Agreement' (2017) 2 *European Papers* 357.

[71] Transport services are explicitly carved-out from the scope of the CCP by Article 207(5) TFEU.

[72] See further Chapter 3, sections II.E and III.E.

[73] Opinion of Advocate General Sharpston, Opinion 2/15 (n 67) paras 208–19.

[74] ibid paras 361, 362–70.

[75] ibid paras 497–504.

a matter of law, the EUSFTA had to be mixed, the fact that in her view the EU had no competence to terminate bilateral investment agreements concluded between some Member States and Singapore[76] led the Advocate General to conclude that the agreement must be mixed.

Unlike the Advocate General, the CJEU did not discuss the distinction between facultative and mandatory mixity in the context of the EUSFTA. The Commission's main question in *Opinion 2/15* regarding the 'requisite competence of the European Union to conclude alone the [EUSFTA]' was not answered by the operative part of the *Opinion*. That part was limited to the CJEU's conclusions on the allocation of competences. With regard to the allocation of competence, the CJEU provided a very broad interpretation of the reach of Article 207(1) TFEU, concluding that all components of new generation FTAs except foreign non-direct investments and investor-state-dispute settlement fall within exclusive EU competence. FTAs that (deliberately) exclude these investment protection disciplines must therefore be concluded under the EU-only procedure.

On 31 August 2017, only three months after the delivery of *Opinion 2/15*, the Commission publicly circulated a proposal for a 'new architecture for splitting EU FTAs and EU investment agreements' that was generally approved by the Council on 8 May 2018.[77] Accordingly, FTAs and IPAs will be negotiated and ratified separately, the former under the EU-only procedure and the latter under the mixed procedure. The EU institutions have since applied the new architecture to all FTAs under negotiation or ratification. However, the Council decided that Association Agreements should in principle remain mixed agreements.[78] A notable exception to the Council's principled opinion is the TCA with the UK, which qualifies as an Association Agreement, but has nevertheless been concluded under the EU-only procedure.[79]

The new architecture has come at a cost for the EU's external investment policy. So far, the EU has only signed two stand-alone IPAs, with Singapore and Vietnam, as mixed agreements. Negotiations for a stand-alone IPA with China were concluded in 2020, but the agreement will probably never reach the ratification stage for political reasons.[80] The majority of the EU's (envisaged) new generation trade agreements, including those with Japan, Mercosur,[81] the UK, New Zealand, Australia and India, do not cover investment protection disciplines. The reasons underpinning that choice may be more political than legal. The CJEU, in an Opinion procedure initiated by Belgium, confirmed the compatibility of the newly developed investment court system (ICS) enshrined in CETA with EU law (*Opinion 1/17*).[82] Politically, investment dispute resolution nonetheless remains contested, including within the EU. A prominent example

[76] ibid paras 376–98. See also Opinion 1/76, *Inland Waterways*, EU:C:1977:63.

[77] Council of the European Union, *Draft Council Conclusions on the Negotiation and Conclusion of EU Trade Agreements – Adoption* [2018] 8622/18. See further Chapter 7.

[78] See Chapter 7, section II.

[79] See further Chapter 8.

[80] Recommendation for a Council Decision authorising the Commission to open negotiations on an investment agreement between the European Union and the People's Republic of China [2013] COM (2013)297 final, partly declassified in February 2016.

[81] However, the FTA with Mercosur has been designed as part of a wider Association Agreement. See further New EU-Mercosur Trade Agreement, Agreement in Principle reached 1 July 2019, not yet published in the OJ.

[82] Opinion 1/17, *Comprehensive Economic and Trade Agreement with Canada*, EU:C:2019:341.

is the recent announcement of the intended exit of EU and some Member States from the Energy Charter Treaty (ECT).[83] However, the EU and its Member States remain supportive of the establishment of a multilateral investment court (MIC).

IV. The Rationale for Mixity

Opinions 2/15 and *1/17* and the new architecture inaugurated a new era for EU trade and investment treaty-making. Some stakeholders were required to adjust to that perceived 'brave new world'.[84] In this world, mixity will certainly remain relevant, but less so. The legal certainty provided by *Opinion 2/15* about the vertical allocation of trade and investment competence within the EU changed the rationale for mixity. So far, mixity has been generally understood as a procedural technique that is used to overcome an uncertain division of competences between the EU and the Member States during the ratification of international agreements (see section IV.A). *Opinion 2/15* did away with that uncertainty by providing an *ex ante* attribution of treaty-making power between the EU and the Member States in the field of trade and investment. As a result, the choice for or against mixity can be made deliberately during the negotiations of an EU trade and investment agreement through careful substantive treaty design (section IV.B).

A. Mixity as a Procedural Gap-Filler

With no procedural legal basis in the EU Treaties and virtually no precedent in international law, mixed agreements were aptly described as being 'somehow ill-fitted both to the [EU's] legal system and to the traditional conceptual scheme of general internal law'.[85] In view of this conceptual uneasiness, it is not surprising that the legal explanation of and justification for mixity in scholarly literature changed over time.

Early writings appeared to approach mixed agreements with doctrinal scepticism, limiting the legal justification for making mixed agreements to the limited scope of EU competence and thus legally mandatory situations.[86] In reaction to the increasing practical recourse to mixity without compelling legal reasons, scholars began to view the nature of competence – and the growing number of non-exclusive external EU competences – as the main explanation for mixed agreements,[87] although without

[83] Non-paper from the European Commission, 'Next Steps as Regards the EU, Euratom and Member States' Membership in the Energy Charter Treaty', leaked via Euroactive, https://www.euractiv.com/wp-content/uploads/sites/2/2023/02/Non-paper_ECT_nextsteps.pdf.

[84] Interview with a Council official, 7 November 2018.

[85] Heliskoski (n 3) 3.

[86] See, eg, P Pescatore, 'External Relations in the Case-Law of the Court of Justice of the European Communities' (1979) 16 *Common Market Law Review* 615, 624, 642; KD Stein, *Der gemischte Vertrag im Recht der Außenbeziehungen der Europäischen Wirtschaftsgemeinschaft* (Duncker & Humblot, 1986) 23 et seq; and A Bleckmann, 'The Mixed Agreements of the EEC in Public International Law' in O'Keeffe and Schermers (n 5) 155.

[87] Dashwood (n 53) 93–99; A Dashwood and J Heliskoski, 'The Classic Authorities Revisited' in A Dashwood and C Hillion (eds), *The General Law of EC External Relations* (Sweet & Maxwell, 2000) 3, 17; A Rosas,

abandoning the overall critical outlook on mixity.[88] Barav aptly captured the prevailing zeitgeist: 'mixed agreements are probably a necessary evil, part of the integration process, but nobody would like to see any more of them'.[89]

By looking predominantly at the practice of making mixed agreements, Heliskoski's pioneering work advanced a practice-driven understanding of mixity as a move from substance to procedure.[90] In view of the lack of a concrete attribution of competence between the EU and the Member States, Heliskoski argued that the choice of the mixed procedure allowed legal flexibility rather than strict judicial demarcation in areas of great political sensitivity. At a time when the EU's founding treaties were more frequently amended, Heliskoski considered an *ex ante* account of attribution extremely difficult and unnecessary, as mixity enabled the EU and the Member States to enter into treaty negotiations without lengthy discussions about the precise vertical allocation of treaty-making power. Persisting questions about competence allocations between the EU and the Member States could be addressed through an *ex post facto* determination of responsibility at the implementation stage.[91] Heliskoski found that in doing so, mixity creates an 'enabling effect' as it 'postpones disputes about the issues of competence to a stage – that of the implementation of the agreement – where they can be circumvented … by procedural solutions'.[92]

The enabling effect of mixity on the EU's and the Member States' external relations has since been widely recognised. The recognition of that rationale for mixity did not change the fact that mixed agreements continued to create problems in practice.[93] However, it meant that these problems could in part be justified on procedural grounds.

B. Mixity as a Substantive Design Choice

In the field of trade and investment, the rationale of using mixity as a 'procedural gap-filler' changed in the post-Lisbon era. In 2017, the year in which *Opinion 2/15* was

'The European Union and Mixed Agreements' in A Dashwood and C Hillion (eds), *The General Law of EC External Relations* (Sweet & Maxwell, 2000) 200.

[88] See especially C-D Ehlermann, 'Mixed Agreements: A List of Problems' in O'Keeffe and Schermers (n 5) 3; and Rosas (n 87).

[89] A Barav, 'The Division of External Relations Power between the European Economic Community and the Member States in the Case Law of the Court of Justice' in CWA Timmermans and ELM Völker (eds), *Division of Powers between the European Communities and Their Member States in the Field of External Relations: Colloquium 30 and 31 May 1980, Amsterdam* (Kluwer, 1981) 144. Contra, modestly appraising mixity, see JHH Weiler, 'The External Legal Relations of Non-unitary Actors: Mixity and the Federal Principle' in O'Keeffe and Schermers (n 5) 35.

[90] See especially M Koskenniemi's foreword to Heliskoski (n 3) vii et seq.

[91] Heliskoski (n 3) 48 et seq, 95 et seq and 241 et seq.

[92] See A Dashwood's review of Heliskoski (n 3), back cover.

[93] See J Czuczai, 'Mixity in Practice: Some Problems and Their (Real or Possible) Solution' in Hillion and Koutrakos (n 1) 229; F Hoffmeister, 'Curse or Blessing? Mixed Agreements in the Recent Practice of the European Union and its Member States' in Hillion and Koutrakos (n 1) 249, 267; A Rosas, 'The Future of Mixity', in Hillion and Koutrakos (n 1) 367, 371. See also R Leal-Arcas, *Theory and Practice of EC External Trade Law and Policy* (Cameron May, 2008); P Eeckhout, *EU External Relations Law*, 2nd edn (Oxford University Press, 2011) 212 et seq; L Bollrath, *Die Vertragsschlusskompetenz der Europäischen Gemeinschaft auf dem Gebiet der Gemeinsamen Handelspolitik* (Nomos, 2008) 23 et seq; and F Kaiser, *Gemischte Abkommen im Lichte bundesstaatlicher Erfahrungen* (Mohr Siebeck, 2012) 3.

delivered, the Lisbon Treaty had been in force for almost 10 years. With no major treaty reform in sight, the dynamic evolution of the EU's external trade powers stagnated at the height of the CCP's expansion. Against that background, *Opinion 2/15* established an *ex ante* account of attribution in the field of trade and investment. Because of the resulting clarity over the division of treaty-making power between the EU and the Member States, there is no longer a need to use mixity as a technique to overcome competence disputes over trade and investment matters. Knowledge of the reach of the EU's exclusive competence, coupled with the broad scope of the CCP post-Lisbon, makes it possible to design EU-only FTAs with few material twists. Mixity will in particular be triggered by the inclusion of a component on substantive investment protection and investor-state dispute settlement. Facultative mixity can be created by widening the scope of the agreement to include more 'trade and …' matters, while excluding substantive investment protection disciplines.[94] Post-Lisbon, the question of mixity has thus become a substantive choice that is factored into the design of EU trade and investment agreements.

Recent events have also changed the justifications for using mixity. The 'enabling effect' described by Heliskoski no longer unfolds in the field of trade and investment. Not only is there no longer a need to overcome competence disputes between the EU and the Member States before concluding trade and investment agreements, but the emergence of the non-ratification crisis further demonstrated that not all problems of mixity can be postponed to the stage of treaty implementation. Instead, the opportunities and pitfalls of mixity must be carefully weighed and balanced at the outset of the treaty-making process. It is about weighing the substantive benefits of making a comprehensive trade and investment agreement against the procedural costs inherent to a more complex ratification process and the allocation of numerous veto rights. Moreover, and irrespective of the chosen treaty-making procedure, questions about public participation in EU trade and investment policy arise.

V. Objectives, Limitations and Structure

This book seeks to offer a thorough legal analysis of the practice of mixity in the field of trade and investment post-Lisbon. To do so, it examines the *interrelationship between treaty-making power and procedure* from the perspectives of international, EU and national constitutional law. Instead of considering the law merely in the abstract, this book seeks to combine a theoretical understanding of mixity with an in-depth assessment of (inter)institutional practice in the context of current challenges. Against that background, it suggests some solutions for striking a better balance between power, procedure and participation in future practice.

This book does not make a general case against mixity. It argues that the decision in favour or against mixity in the field of trade and investment should no longer be taken as a matter of principle, but deliberately, on the basis of a careful balancing exercise reflected in the substantive design of an agreement. Clarity about the allocation of

[94] A case in point is the TCA. See further Chapter 8.

trade power between the EU and the Member States enables them to consider the costs of mixity for the unity and effectiveness of EU external action against the benefits of their joint external presence. That balancing exercise arguably tilts in favour of EU-only action in areas that principally fall within the EU's exclusive competence, such as trade. In areas where the EU is less powerful, or simply for practicality,[95] mixity may be a more preferable (design) choice. Either way, questions about public participation in the formation of EU trade and investment policy arise, and this book seeks to provide some ideas for integrating national parliaments more closely in the process of making EU trade and investment agreements, particularly through their governments.

As indicated in its title, this book is about the making of EU trade and investment agreements. It therefore does not address questions that arise after a mixed agreement enters into force.[96] Moreover, as mentioned above, it focuses on the EU's bilateral trade and investment agenda. The focus on the process of making agreements in a distinct policy context enables this book to bring to light the actual practice of mixity, as well as issues that have clear practical consequences. At the same time, the choice not to consider mixity as a general phenomenon in other policy fields may come at the cost of generalisability. While the general theoretical insights on mixity offered by this book are largely transferrable to other policy areas and types of agreements, the specific conclusions drawn in the context of the EU's trade and investment policy may not be. This is all so more so for material areas where the division of competence between the EU and the Member States remains largely unclear. As a result, generalisability beyond the field of trade and investment is not a goal of this book.

The book is structured as follows: Chapters 2 and 3 focus on the determination and effects of *treaty-making power*. Chapter 2 explains how the division of competence between the EU and the Member States impacts the character of EU agreements. It distinguishes between three main types of agreements: mandatory EU-only; mandatory mixed; and facultative agreements. Chapter 3 analyses the reach and limits of the EU's competence over trade and investment matters in light of the CJEU's recent case law. In doing so, it outlines the reduced scope for mixity in the field of trade and investment post-Lisbon. Taken together, Chapters 2 and 3 demonstrate that the EU has become a more powerful trade actor post-Lisbon and that the clarity and pragmatism inherent in

[95] See, eg, the case of the European Convention on the Legal Protection of Services based on, or consisting of, Conditional Access [2003] Council of Europe Treaty No 178, discussed further in Chapter 2, section II.B.

[96] The implementation and enforcement of mixed EU agreements has been extensively discussed in the literature, especially with regard to the assumption of international responsibility by the EU and/or the Member States in the context of multilateral agreements. See, eg, Heliskoski (n 3) 157 et seq; M Cremona, 'External Relations of the EU and the Member States: Competence, Mixed Agreements, International Responsibility, and Effects of International Law' (2006) 22 *EUI Working Paper Law* 15 et seq; PJ Kuijper, 'International Responsibility for Mixed Agreements' in Hillion and Koutrakos (n 1) 208; A Thies, *International Trade Disputes and EU Liability* (Cambridge University Press, 2013); A Delgado Casteleiro, *The International Responsibility of the European Union: From Competence to Normative Control* (Cambridge University Press, 2016); E Neframi, *Les accords mixtes de la Communauté européenne* (Bruylant, 2007) 523 et seq; PT Stegmann, *Responsibility of the EU and the Member States under EU International Investment Protection Agreements: Between Traditional Rules, Proceduralisation and Federalisation* (Springer, 2019); E Leinarte, *Functional Responsibility of International Organizations: The European Union and International Economic Law* (Cambridge University Press, 2021). On the administrative implementation, see JP Terhechte, 'Common Commercial Policy and External Trade' in HCH Hofmann et al (eds), *Specialized Administrative Law of the European Union: A Sectoral Review* (Oxford University Press, 2018) 64.

the CJEU's recent case law allow it to assert power alone, leading to more unified and effective EU external action. The chapters also show that there is nevertheless scope for mixity, resulting both from the limits to exclusivity and the Council's discretion to make a political choice for mixity in certain situations. As the substantive triggers of (facultative) mixity in the field of trade and investment are known, it is ultimately up to the Commission, as the EU negotiator, and the third state, to include or exclude room for mixity in the treaty design. Such a decision should arguably be based on a careful analysis of the costs and benefits of mixity, conducted at the outset of the negotiation process.

Chapters 4 and 5 turn to the *treaty-making procedure*. By examining the law and practice of negotiating, signing, provisionally applying and concluding an international agreement, they provide an overview of the lifespan of EU trade and investment agreements up to the point of their entry into force. Chapter 4 takes an international and EU law perspective. Chapter 5 turns to national constitutional law and the role of national parliaments. The chapters show that irrespective of the character of EU agreements, be they mixed or EU-only, treaty-making is a multi-level affair which includes international, EU as well as national players. However, a procedural shift from mixity to EU-only treaty-making challenges the EU and the Member States to adjust their political and institutional cooperation to the vertical situation presented by the EU-only mode. A substantive design choice away from mixity therefore needs to be coupled with new ways for (sub-)national actors to engage in the EU decision-making process. This can, on the one hand, be achieved by establishing direct information and cooperation channels between the EU institutions and national parliaments during the negotiations of EU trade and investment agreements (Chapter 4). On the other hand, there are various ways to enhance the control of national parliaments over EU trade policy on the basis of national constitutional law and practice (Chapter 5).

Chapters 6, 7 and 8 discuss the *interrelationship between treaty-making power and procedure* in the context of recent events and challenges, namely the non-ratification of bilateral mixed trade and investment agreements (Chapter 6), the new architecture (Chapter 7) and the making of the EU-UK TCA (Chapter 8). These chapters shed light on new problems of mixity and show what solutions may be used to address these problems in light of recent practice. Overall, they make a case for carefully balancing the benefits and costs of mixity and for limiting mixity in fields of EU exclusive competence such as trade. Moreover, they highlight the growing awareness of the EU and the Member States of the 'built-in' flexibility of facultative mixity and argue that a choice in favour or against mixity in such a scenario should no longer be made as a matter of principle, but on a case-by-case basis, in view of the specific legal, economic and political circumstances at hand.

Chapter 9 brings the main themes and findings of the previous chapters together. Ultimately, it links back to the title of this book by recapitulating to what extent and how EU trade and investment treaty-making has *moved beyond mixity*.

PART I

Treaty-Making Power

2

The Character of EU International Agreements

I. Introduction

The choice for or against mixity entails costs and benefits. As explained in Chapter 1, mixity provides a technique for bridging legal gaps over the vertical allocation of competence within the EU, so that the EU and the Member States may enter into treaty negotiations without lengthy political quarrels or even litigation. Mixity is also the most inclusive decision-making modality available to the EU legislature, equipping around 40 (sub-)national players with a decisive voice.[1] Needless to say, that inclusiveness comes at a high price: mixity not only prolongs the decision-making process, it also lowers the threshold for individual rent-seeking capable of paralysing the EU's external relations capacity.[2] This price is particularly high for agreements that are largely covered by exclusive EU competences, such as trade and investment agreements. Advocate General Kokott argued that mixity is 'out of place in the common commercial policy', basing her argument predominantly on pragmatic reasons:

> The more players there are on the European side at international level, the more difficult it will be to represent effectively the interests of the Community and its Member States outwardly, in particular vis à vis significant trading partners. Even if the Commission acts as the joint spokesperson of the Community and the Member States in negotiations, this will be preceded by considerable work on coordination, together with de facto pressure for unanimity if, in addition to the Community, all the Member States act individually in dealings involving international law.
>
> In addition, there is a risk that individual Member States may, to the detriment of the common interest, obstruct or protract negotiations with non-member countries in order to secure concessions for themselves. Conversely, for non-member countries it may be sufficient, in negotiations 'with Europe', to apply pressure to individual Member States in order circuitously to force concessions from the Community as a whole.[3]

[1] The precise number of sub-parliamentary actors is difficult to determine. See further Chapter 5, section I.

[2] D Kleimann and G Kübek, 'The Signing, Provisional Application, and Conclusion of Trade and Investment Agreements in the EU: The Case of CETA and Opinion 2/15' (2018) 45 *Legal Issues of Economic Integration* 13, 44–45.

[3] Opinion of Advocate General Kokott, Case C-13/07, *WTO Accession of Vietnam*, case withdrawn, EU:C:2009:190, paras 72–73.

Despite such obvious hurdles brought about by the recourse to mixity, the character of agreements concluded by the EU is not merely a practical or political choice, but follows from the frontiers set out in EU primary law. As was highlighted by Advocate General Sharpston:

> A ratification process involving all the Member States alongside the European Union is of necessity likely to be both cumbersome and complex. It may also involve the risk that the outcome of lengthy negotiations may be blocked by a few Member States or even by a single Member State. That might undermine the efficiency of EU external action and have negative consequences for the European Union's relations with the third State(s) concerned.
>
> However, the need for unity and rapidity of EU external action and the difficulties which might arise if the European Union and the Member States have to participate jointly in the conclusion and implementation of an international agreement cannot affect the question who has competence to conclude it. That question is to be resolved exclusively on the basis of the Treaties.[4]

In other words, the decision to include (sub-)national actors in EU treaty-making must be made in accordance with the boundaries set by EU primary law, irrespective of the practical impact of that choice on the unity, effectiveness or inclusiveness of EU treaty-making.[5]

Against this background, this chapter explains how the allocation of competence between the EU and its Member States determines the treaty-making procedure and hence the resulting character of an EU international agreement. In doing so, it shows how the EU institutions, and especially the Commission, can predetermine the character of trade and investment agreements through their substantive design. This chapter further outlines how much scope the law leaves for the EU institutions, and especially the Member States in the European Council, to make a political decision about mixity. It argues that for agreements where mixity remains a political choice in the Council, that choice should be made deliberately, on the basis of a careful analysis for the specific case at hand, rather than opting for mixity as a matter of principle.

This chapter does not provide an elaborate typology of mixed agreements, which has been done elsewhere.[6] Instead, it focuses on the three main characters of EU international agreements: mandatory EU-only agreements (section II), mandatory mixed agreements (section III) and facultative mixity (sections IV and V). Section VI concludes.

[4] Opinion of Advocate General Sharpston, Opinion 2/15, *FTA with Singapore*, EU:C:2016:992, paras 565–66. See also Opinion 1/94, *WTO Agreements*, EU:C:1994:384, para 107; Opinion 2/00, *Cartagena Protocol*, EU:C:2001:664, para 41; Opinion 1/08, *GATS Schedules of Commitments*, EU:C:2009:739, para 127.

[5] See also Kleimann and Kübek (n 2) 17 et seq, 43.

[6] HG Schermers, 'A Typology of Mixed Agreements' in D O'Keeffe and HG Schermers (eds), *Mixed Agreements* (Kluwer, 1983) 23; A Rosas, 'The European Union and Mixed Agreements' in A Dashwood and C Hillion (eds), *The General Law of EC External Relations* (Sweet & Maxwell, 2000) 200 205 et seq; M Maresceau, 'Typology of Bilateral Mixed Agreements' in C Hillion and P Koutrakos (eds), *Mixed Agreements Revisited: The EU and its Member States in the World* (Hart Publishing, 2010) 11; AJ Kumin and P Bittner, 'Die "gemischten" Abkommen zwischen der Europäischen Union und ihren Mitgliedstaaten einerseits und dritten Völkerrechtssubjekten andererseits' in W Oberwexer (ed), *Die Europäische Union im Völkerrecht* (Nomos, 2012) 75, 77–79; J Heliskoski and G Kübek, 'A Typology of EU Mixed Agreements Revisited' in N Levrat et al (eds), *The EU and its Member States' Joint Participation in International Agreements* (Hart Publishing, 2022) 23.

II. Mandatory EU-Only Agreements

Exclusivity entails a full transfer of power from the Member State to the EU level. For the field of EU external relations, exclusivity implies that the Member States may not conduct foreign relations in their own right.[7] As a result, agreements covering EU exclusive competence must be concluded by the EU alone.

A. Law

EU-only action is required, as a matter of law, in fields that fall within EU exclusive competence. Pursuant to Article 2(1) TFEU, 'only the Union may legislate and adopt legally binding acts [in areas of EU exclusive competence], the Member States being able to do so themselves only if so empowered by the Union or for the implementation of Union acts'. Article 2(1) TFEU applies to both internal and external EU action.[8] Agreements that fully fall within the EU's exclusive competence must therefore be concluded by the EU alone (mandatory EU-only agreements).

By way of exception, the Member States may legally become contracting parties to agreements that classify as mandatory EU-only agreements in three main instances. The first of these are multilateral agreements or conventions which only states may conclude or accede to. However, in such instances, the Member States must act as trustees of the EU's interests, ie, act by means of a concerted position agreed at the EU level.[9]

Second, the EU may re-delegate exclusive competence back to the Member State level for practical reasons. An example for such a re-delegation of power is Regulation 1219/2012 (the 'grandfathering regulation'), which establishes transitional arrangements for bilateral investment agreements between Member States and third countries.[10] As will be further explained in Chapter 3, the Treaty of Lisbon shifted the competence over foreign direct investment (FDI) into the exclusive realm of the CCP.[11] Pre-Lisbon, FDI qualified as a shared competence and was exercised by the Member States. Amongst others, the Member States concluded bilateral investment agreements (BITs) with third states in their own right. Regulation 1219/2012 pragmatically reacts to the (pre-)existence of Member State agreements in the field of what is (now) an exclusive EU

[7] See further, eg, A Rosas, 'Exclusive, Shared and National Competence in the Area of EU External Relations: Do Such Distinctions Matter?' in I Govaere et al (eds), *The European Union in the World: Essays in Honour of Professor Marc Maresceau* (Brill/Nijhoff, 2014) 17; and P Eeckhout, 'Exclusive External Competences: Constructing the EU as an International Actor' in *The Court of Justice and the Construction of Europe: Analyses and Perspectives on Sixty Years of Case-Law* (TMC Asser Press, 2013) 613. For exclusivity and the CCP, see further also Chapter 3, section II.A.

[8] See especially Case 22/70, *ERTA*, EU:C:1971:32, para 19; and now Article 3(1) in conjunction with Article 216(1) TFEU. See further Chapter 3, section II.E.

[9] Case C-45/07, *IMO I*, EU:C:2009:81, para 28. See especially Marise Cremona, 'Member States as Trustees of the Community Interest: Participating in International Agreements on Behalf of the European Community' (2009) 17 *EUI Working Paper Law*.

[10] Regulation (EU) No 1219/2012 of 12 December 2012 establishing transitional arrangements for bilateral investment agreements between Member States and third countries [2012] OJ L351/40. See further M Keller and M Schmitt, '120. Verordnung 1219/2012' in HG Krenzler, C Herrmann and M Niestedt (eds), *EU-Außenwirtschafts- und Zollrecht*, 21st edn (CH Beck, 2023).

[11] See Chapter 3, section II.B.

competence. It re-delegates powers back to the Member States, allowing them to maintain, amend or make BITs as long as the EU has not concluded its own BIT with that third state. Eventually, the EU envisages to 'grandfather' the Member States' BITs with a new generation of IPAs.

A third instance where the Member States become part of agreements that qualify as EU-only agreements are so-called false mixed agreements.[12] Conceptually, false mixed agreements remain difficult to grasp, as the EU does not re-delegate the competence to act in a certain material area fully back to the Member States. Instead, exclusivity continues to exist at the EU level, but the EU – as it were – delegates *part* of the capacity to exercise that power to the Member State level. Consequentially, the Member States become contracting parties to an agreement for which they have no material power. This may be best explained by the well-known example of the International Coffee Agreement.[13] The Member States were expressly authorised to sign and conclude the International Coffee Agreement for practical reasons alongside the (then) Community, 'notwithstanding the exclusive Community competence in this matter'.[14]

B. Trade Practice

As was mentioned in Chapter 1, the CCP is an exclusive competence of the EU.[15] Nevertheless, few mandatory EU-only trade agreements existed before the move to the new architecture in 2018.[16] In addition to the EU's early trade agreements with Iceland, Austria, Switzerland and Norway that were highlighted in Chapter 1,[17] some 'trade and …' agreements qualified as mandatory EU-only agreements because they still fell within the exclusive scope of the CCP.[18] Some agreements amending or complementing the WTO Agreements were concluded by the EU alone,[19] such as the Protocol amending the TRIPS Agreement,[20] the Agreement on Trade Facilitation (ATF),[21] the Expansion of the Information Technology Agreement (ITA)[22] and the Protocol Amending the

[12] On false mixity, see especially Schermers (n 6) 27.

[13] See further P Koutrakos, *EU International Relations Law*, 2nd edn (Hart Publishing, 2015) 164.

[14] Council Decision (EC) 2001/877 of 24 September 2001 on the signing and conclusion on behalf of the European Community of the International Coffee Agreement 2001 [2001] OJ L326/22, fifth recital.

[15] Article 3(1)(e) in conjunction with Article 207(1) TFEU.

[16] Chapter 1, especially sections III.A and III.B. On the new architecture, see Chapter 7.

[17] Chapter 1, section III.A.

[18] For example, the Energy Star Agreement subject to Case C-281/01, *Energy Star Agreement*, EU:C:2002:761.

[19] See further R Kampf, 'Zwangslizenz-VO vor Art. 1 Erwägungsgründe' in Krenzler et al (n 10) paras 27 et seq.

[20] Council Decision (EC) 2007/768 of 19 November 2007 on the acceptance, on behalf of the European Community, of the Protocol amending the TRIPS Agreement, done at Geneva on 6 December 2005 [2007] OJ L311/35.

[21] Council Decision (EU) 2015/1947 of 1 October 2015 on the conclusion, on behalf of the European Union, of the Protocol Amending the Marrakesh Agreement establishing the World Trade Organisation [2015] OJ L284/1.

[22] Council Decision (EU) 2016/971 of 17 June 2016 on the conclusion, on behalf of the European Union, of an agreement in the form of the Declaration on the Expansion of Trade in Information Technology Products (ITA) [2016] OJ L161/2. Notably, the original Ministerial Declaration WT/MIN(96)/16 of 13 December 1996 already listed only the European Communities and not the Member States in their own right.

Government Procurement Agreement (GPA).[23] Exceptionally, Association Agreements were concluded by the EU alone, including the EU-UK TCA discussed in Chapter 8, but the use of the EU-only procedure for making Association Agreements has been a political choice rather than a legal requirement (see further section IV.C). The EU-only procedure is required as a matter of law for agreements governing a Member State's withdrawal from the EU, including the Brexit Withdrawal Agreement.

Yet, as will be further elaborated upon in Chapter 7, the EU-only mode will be the default option for making EU FTAs under the new architecture. By deliberately carving out material issue areas that fall outside the EU's exclusive competence, the Commission has begun to avoid mixity through a careful substantive design of new generation FTAs. The EU-Japan Economic Partnership Agreement marked the first mandatory EU-only FTA post-Lisbon and now serves as a procedural and substantive blueprint for designing such agreements.

Before the new architecture, mixity was often artificially created by the Member States in the Council. Yet, the impetus for moving away from the EU-only mode did not always come from the Member States in the Council alone. In order to legally justify the political choice for mixity made as part of a broader inter-institutional compromise, it was at times the Commission that insisted on the insertion of exclusive Member State competence in the scope of prima facie EU-only agreements.[24] Until recently, the EU-only procedure was therefore rarely deployed in areas of express exclusive competence because agreements were intentionally designed to exceed the scope of the EU's expressly defined exclusive competence.[25] If concluded, EU-only agreements usually resulted from either political desire (facultative EU-only agreement) or the effects of the ERTA doctrine,[26] but not from express exclusivity alone.

In view of the increased clarity of the allocation of competence between the EU and the Member States post-Lisbon – especially in the field of trade – it will become harder to justify the artificial design of mixed agreements. However, false mixity might remain a viable option for political and practical reasons. Two recent examples of this are the Conditional Access Convention[27] and the Marrakesh Treaty.[28] With regard to the former, the CJEU found in *Conditional Access Convention* that the EU has exclusive competence to conclude the Conditional Access Convention.[29] Yet, in contrast to other EU Member States,[30] France, the Netherlands and Romania did not denounce

[23] The GPA has been adopted by the EU 'with regard to its 27 Member States', all of which form one party. See wto.org/english/tratop_e/gproc_e/memobs_e.htm. See also Council Decision (EU) 2014/115 of 2 December 2013 on the conclusion of the Protocol Amending the Agreement on Government Procurement [2014] OJ L68/1. The 1994 GPA, by contrast, was adopted as an incomplete mixed agreement. See further Heliskoski and Kübek (n 6) 38.

[24] Rosas (n 6) 218.

[25] With the exception of fishery agreements. See, eg, Agreement on a Sustainable Fisheries Partnership between the European Union and the Republic of Senegal [2014] OJ L304/3.

[26] Article 3(2) third indent TFEU. See further Chapter 3, section II.E.

[27] European Convention on the Legal Protection of Services based on, or consisting of, Conditional Access [2001] Council of Europe Treaty No 178.

[28] Marrakesh Treaty to Facilitate Access to Published Works for Persons Who are Blind, Visually Impaired, or Otherwise Print Disabled [2013] WIPO Lex No TRT/MARRAKESH/001.

[29] Case C-137/12, *Conditional Access Convention*, EU:C:2013:441.

[30] Bulgaria, Romania and Cyprus.

the Conditional Access Convention after the CJEU gave its judgment.[31] Pursuant to Article 9(2) of the Conditional Access Convention, 'the European Community shall exercise its right to vote and cast a number of votes equal to the number of its member States that are Parties to the Convention'. Accordingly, the EU would have no votes in the framework of the Conditional Access Convention without (some of) its Member States. Mixity is therefore a practical necessity. The story is somewhat similar for the second example, ie, the Marrakesh Treaty. The Marrakesh Treaty was originally signed by all the Member States and the EU. However, in *Opinion 3/15*, the CJEU found that the Marrakesh Treaty falls fully within the realm of exclusive EU competence.[32] As a consequence, the Marrakesh Treaty was eventually ratified by the EU alone. At the point of its conclusion, the Marrakesh Treaty thus classified as a mandatory EU-only agreement. Nevertheless, the Member States continue to be listed as signatory parties. It remains to be seen if the Member States will denounce the Marrakesh Treaty, remain eternal signatories in vain or finalise the 'false mixed' ratification process after obtaining EU authorisation. In the latter case, the Member States would become contracting parties without having any material or practical powers in their own right with regard to the substance of the agreement or within its decision-making framework.[33]

III. Mandatory Mixed Agreements

According to Article 47 of the Treaty on European Union (TEU), the EU shall have legal personality.[34] However, the EU's capacity to act remains confined to the scope of its conferred powers (Article 5 TEU). In areas where the Member States have conferred no power whatsoever to the EU level, the Member States retain exclusive power and capacity to act, both internally and externally. As a consequence, the EU's legal personality exists alongside the sovereignty and international capacity of its Member States. Mandatory mixity therefore results from the co-existence of exclusive EU and exclusive Member State competence.[35] Both the Union and the Member States are legally required to become contracting parties to an international agreement in their own right so as to assume the legal obligations that fall within their respective exclusive prerogatives.

Mandatory mixity remedies the limitations of the EU's international power and capacity for agreements that partially fall within the exclusive prerogatives of the Member States without simultaneously constraining the Member States' capacity to act independently. Mixity is – and remains – a procedural tool. It must therefore be

[31] Article 17 of the Conditional Access Convention (n 27).

[32] See further G Kübek, 'The Concept of (Non-)Commerciality and the ERTA Doctrine Post-Lisbon: Opinion 3/15, Marrakesh Treaty', in G Butler and RA Wessel (eds), *EU External Relations Law: The Cases in Context* (Hart Publishing, 2022) 851.

[33] See also G Kübek, 'Redefining the Boundaries of the Common Commercial Policy and the ERTA Doctrine: Opinion 3/15, Marrakesh Treaty' (2018) 55 *Common Market Law Review* 883, 899.

[34] On the concept of legal personality, see further RA Wessel, 'Revisiting the International Legal Status of the EU' (2000) 5 *European Foreign Affairs Review* 507, 509 et seq.

[35] The term 'co-existent competence' was introduced by Rosas (n 6) 204; it was subsequently used by Advocate General Wahl, Opinion 3/15, *Marrakesh Treaty*, EU:C:2016:657, para 122.

distinguished from the 'flexibility clause' enshrined in Article 352(1) TFEU.[36] Article 352(1) TFEU essentially seeks to equip the EU, through a one-off delegation, with necessary power in an area where such power is not foreseen by the Treaties, subject to specific procedural rules (unanimity voting in the Council etc). By contrast, mandatory mixity does not shift power to the EU level. Instead, it enables the EU and the Member States to 'join forces', ie, exercise their respective exclusive competence alongside each other, without re-allocating such competence. Politically, mixity is therefore the most feasible tool for the EU and the Member States to conclude international agreements in areas where neither one of them has the capacity to act alone.

Normally, all the Member States become individual contracting parties to mixed agreements. However, there may be circumstances where the individual participation of only some Member States is required or desired. A mixed agreement concluded by the EU and only some of the Member States is called an 'incomplete mixed agreement'. In *Opinion 1/19*, the CJEU recognised the practice of incomplete mixity and confirmed that this practice can be used for mandatory and facultative mixed agreements alike.[37]

A. Law

The EU's constitutive Treaties largely remained silent on mixity. In fact, the term 'mixed agreement' has never been mentioned in EU primary law. The Treaty establishing the European Atomic Economic Energy Community (EAEC) had foreseen '[a]greements … to which, in addition to the Community, one or more Member States are parties' (Article 102 EAEC). In *Ruling 1/78*, the CJEU confirmed that there were 'strong grounds for using the procedure envisaged by Article 102 [EAEC]' where 'it appears that the subject-matter of an agreement or convention falls in part within the power and jurisdiction of the Community and in part within that of the Member States'.[38]

The EEC Treaty did away with a general reference to agreements to which the (then) Community and the Member States may become parties. And despite pleas from

[36] On the flexibility clause, see G Butler, 'The EU's Flexibility Clause: Past, Present, and Future' in A Bakardjieva-Engelbrekt and X Groussot (eds), *The Future of Europe: Legal and Political Integration beyond Brexit* (Hart Publishing, 2019) 63.

[37] Opinion 1/19, *Istanbul Convention*, EU:C:2021:832. As has been argued elsewhere, the fact that the CJEU appeared to treat mandatory and facultative incomplete mixed agreement interchangeably is problematic. The 'incompleteness' of mandatory mixed agreements might imply that the EU has to assume international responsibility in areas where it has no competence whatsoever. See further G Kübek, 'Facing and Embracing the Consequences of Mixity: Opinion 1/19, Istanbul Convention' (2022) 59 *Common Market Law Review* 1465, 1482.

[38] Ruling 1/78, *Draft Convention of the International Atomic Energy Agency*, EU:C:1978:202, para 9. On Ruling 1/78 and mandatory mixity, see also JHH Weiler, 'The External Legal Relations of Non-unitary Actors: Mixity and the Federal Principle' in O'Keeffe and Schermers (n 6) 35, 75; J Heliskoski, *Mixed Agreements as a Technique for Organizing the International Relations of the European Community and its Member States* (Kluwer Law International, 2001) 32–33; and A Barav, 'The Division of External Relations Power between the European Economic Community and the Member States in the Case Law of the Court of Justice' in CWA Timmermans and ELM Völker (eds), *Division of Powers between the European Communities and Their Member States in the Field of External Relations: Colloquium 30 and 31 May 1980, Amsterdam* (Kluwer, 1981) 51.

academia,[39] a procedural legal basis governing the negotiation, signature, provisional application, conclusion and implementation of mixed agreements (ie, a 'mixed' counterpart of what is now Article 218 TFEU) was never inserted into the primary law of the then Community and now Union. That mixity exists against Treaty silence is not a sign of its legal invalidity; on the contrary, mandatory mixity begins by definition where the scope of EU primary law ends. It is a logical consequence of the principle of conferred powers.

Notwithstanding the EEC Treaty's silence, questions pertaining to the practice of mixity continued to preoccupy the CJEU. The first instance was *Opinion 1/76.* As was explained above, the CJEU concluded that the Community had implied external competence for the conclusion of the Inland Waterway Transport Agreement. Yet, it noted that a 'special problem' arose from the fact that the entry into force of the Inland Waterway Transport Agreement required amending two prior agreements on the same subject matter to which six Member States alone were contracting parties.[40] The CJEU concluded that the legal requirement for certain Member States to amend their pre-existing agreements 'explain[ed] and justifie[d] the participation in the [Inland Waterway Transport] Agreement, together with the Community, of the six abovementioned States'.[41] The Inland Waterway Transport Agreement was accordingly concluded as an incomplete mixed agreement by the Community and some of its Member States.[42] However, the CJEU also noted that 'except for the special undertaking mentioned above, the legal effects of the agreement with regard to the Member States result … exclusively from the conclusion of the latter by the Community'.[43] The CJEU refrained from clarifying whether the Member States' participation in the Inland Waterway Transport was merely 'justified' or in fact legally required. As a result, *Opinion 1/76* left open the question of whether the Member States' need to amend their pre-existing international agreements triggered mandatory mixity. This question resurfaced in the context of *Opinion 2/15* and is further discussed below.

A few years later, in *Portugal v Council*, the applicant claimed that the conclusion of some provisions of the Cooperation Agreement with India fell within the Member States' exclusive competence and, as a result, that the Member States would have been legally required to conclude the agreement jointly with the Community.[44] In that context, the CJEU formally recognised the legal requirement for the Member States to participate independently in agreements that fall partially outside the Community's competence for the first time with regard to the Community. Yet, the CJEU concluded that mandatory mixity was not required for the conclusion of the Cooperation Agreement with India.[45]

As was mentioned in Chapter 1, some stakeholders claimed that *Opinion 1/94* legally prescribed the conclusion of the GATT and the GATS as mixed agreements.[46]

[39] See especially A Dashwood, 'External Relations Provisions of the Amsterdam Treaty' (1998) 35 *Common Market Law Review* 1019, 1043; and Heliskoski (n 38) 111 et seq.

[40] Opinion 1/76, *Inland Waterways*, EU:C:1977:63, para 6. See further especially G De Baere, *Constitutional Principles of EU External Relations Law* (Oxford University Press, 2008) 232.

[41] Opinion 1/76 (n 40) para 7.

[42] See also Heliskoski and Kübek (n 6) 36.

[43] Opinion 1/76 (n 40) para 7.

[44] Case C-268/94, *Portugal v Council*, EU:C:1996:461, para 31.

[45] ibid para 68. See also Heliskoski (n 38) 34.

[46] Chapter 1, section III.A.

Proponents of mandatory mixity drew on the CJEU's conclusion that 'the chapters on the right of establishment and on freedom to provide services [of the EC Treaty] do not contain any provision expressly extending the competence of the Community to "relationships arising from international law"'.[47] In view of that conclusion, they argued that the Community had no competence whatsoever to conclude agreements that liberalise access to the Member States' service markets by nationals of third states (here WTO members).[48] The CJEU never took a position as to whether mixity was mandatory or facultative for the conclusion of the WTO Agreements. However, it held that 'it does not follow that the Community institutions are prohibited from using the powers conferred on them in that field in order to specify the treatment which is to be accorded to nationals of non-member countries'.[49] It thus appears that, at the time, Community competence existed, but had not yet been exercised, so that exclusivity could not be implied. As a result, the mixed conclusion of the GATS and the TRIPS Agreements was arguably facultative and not mandatory.

The Amsterdam Treaty principally aimed at doing away with the shared competence caveats of the CCP identified in *Opinion 1/94*. According to Article 133(5) EC of the Amsterdam Treaty, it was ultimately for the Member States in the Council to unanimously decide whether or not to extend the scope of the CCP to agreements on services and commercial aspects of IPRs.[50] The reach of the CCP over trade in services and commercial aspects of IPRs was therefore left to the Council's (political) discretion. However, the Nice Treaty re-introduced some of the shared competence caveats.[51] In particular, it introduced a provision that required mixity, as a matter of law, for the conclusion of trade agreements that included certain specific service sectors. Pursuant to Article 133(6) second indent EC, agreements relating to trade in cultural, audiovisual, educational, social and human health services:

> [S]hall fall within the shared competence of the Community and its Member States. Consequently, in addition to a Community decision … the negotiation of such agreements *shall require the common accord of the Member States*. Agreements thus negotiated *shall be concluded jointly by the Community and the Member States*. (Emphasis added)

The recourse to the mixed procedure for agreements that covered trade in cultural, audiovisual, educational, social or human health services was therefore not a political choice, but a legal requirement. *Opinion 1/08* confirmed that reading.[52] Here, the CJEU was inter alia asked to determine whether the (then) Community had exclusive competence under the Nice Treaty to conclude agreements modifying the Schedules of

[47] Opinion 1/94 (n 4) para 81.

[48] A Dashwood, 'The Attribution of External Relations Competence' in Dashwood and Hillion (n 6) 115, 130.

[49] Opinion 1/94 (n 4) para 90.

[50] For a critical view, see Dashwood (n 39) 1020–23; and HG Krenzler, 'Die Reichweite der gemeinsamen Handelspolitik nach dem Vertrag von Amsterdam – eine Debatte ohne Ende?' (1998) 33 *Zeitschrift Europarecht* 223.

[51] See further C Herrmann, 'Vom misslungenen Versuch der Neufassung der gemeinsamen Handelspolitik durch den Vertrag von Nizza' (2001) 12 *Europäische Zeitschrift für Wirtschaftsrecht* 269; C Herrmann, 'Common Commercial Policy after Nice: Sisyphus Would Have Done a Better Job' (2002) 39 *Common Market Law Review* 7; and M Cremona, 'A Policy of Bits and Pieces? The Common Commercial Policy after Nice' (2001) 4 *Cambridge Yearbook of European Legal Studies* 61.

[52] See further M Cremona, 'Balancing Union and Member State Interests: Opinion 1/2008, Choice of Legal Basis and the Common Commercial Policy under the Treaty of Lisbon' (2010) 35 *European Law Review* 678.

Specific Commitments of the Community and the Member States under the GATS.[53] In general, the CJEU found that the Community had acquired exclusive competence for trade in services modes 1–4, which were formerly situated outside the scope of the CCP (*cf Opinion 1/94*) through the Amsterdam and Nice Treaty reforms.[54] Yet, the CJEU found that the GATS Schedules of Commitments touched inter alia on educational services and hence on Article 133(6) second indent EC.[55] It held that 'in contrast to the agreements relating to trade in services which do not concern the services identified in the second indent of Article 133(6) EC, agreements which relate to those services cannot be concluded by the Community acting alone, such conclusion requiring the joint participation of the Community and the Member States'.[56] Consequently, the amendments to the GATS Schedules of Commitments were concluded as a mandatory mixed agreement by the (then) Community and the Member States.

Article 133(6) second indent EC expressly denoted the Community's competence over cultural, audiovisual, educational, social and human health services as 'shared'. The French version of Article 133(6)(2) EC likewise referred to 'compétence *partagée* entre la Communauté et ses États membres' (emphasis added). However, the legal requirement for mixity at the time did not result from the non-exclusive nature of the Community's power over these service sectors. Instead, mixity was a specific procedural requirement that arose only when using Article 133(6) second indent EC as a legal basis. Indeed, the German version of Article 133(6) second indent EC refers to *gemischte* ('mixed') and not *geteilte* ('shared') competence, indicating that the requirement for mixity was a procedural and not a substantive safeguard. Despite the unfortunate reference to 'shared' competence in the English and French versions of Article 133(6) second indent EC, the provision arguably did not imply that, at the time, all agreements that fell within shared competence had to be made under the mixed procedure as a matter of law. As will be further explained below, mixity is generally not a legal requirement in areas of shared competence, but rather a political choice (see section IV).

The Treaty of Lisbon no longer requires agreements covering sensitive service sectors to be concluded jointly by the EU and the Member States. There is hence no longer a procedural legal requirement for mixity in the field of the CCP, although the conclusion of EU trade agreements falling within the scope of what is now Article 207(5) TFEU remains subject to unanimity voting in the Council.[57] The only case where the Lisbon Treaty procedurally foresees mixity is the ratification of the accession agreement to the European Convention on Human Rights (ECHR),[58] which is in practice somewhat irrelevant as the Member States, in any event, would have to ratify the agreement in their own right as ECHR members.

Notwithstanding the absence of a legal requirement for mixity in the field of trade and investment, the debate about mandatory mixity in the field of trade and investment re-emerged in *Opinion 2/15*. The EUSFTA automatically supersedes the Member States'

[53] Opinion 1/08 (n 4) para 1.
[54] ibid para 119. On the modes of services, see further Article I:2 GATS.
[55] ibid paras 148–49.
[56] ibid para 134.
[57] See further Chapter 4, sections III.C and III.D.
[58] Article 218(8) TFEU.

BITs with Singapore.[59] The Council – supported by all Member States – contended that 'these provisions presuppose that the Member States concerned (and Singapore) consent to [them]. The Union does not have the power to suspend or terminate these bilateral agreements'.[60] Advocate General Sharpston supported the Council's view. She concluded that the Member States enjoy exclusive competence to terminate their pre-existing BITs with Singapore.[61] Therefore, in her view, the EUSFTA could 'be concluded only by the European Union and the Member States acting jointly'.[62] According to her, the EUSFTA thus constituted a mandatory mixed agreement. However, the CJEU did not follow her view on this point. It found that 'the line of argument that a provision [on the termination of existing agreements] of the envisaged agreement cannot be included in an agreement concluded by the European Union since it falls within a competence of the Member States alone cannot succeed'.[63] In this regard, the CJEU appeared to depart from its earlier conclusions in *Opinion 1/76*, as it did not consider that the need of the Member States to terminate their pre-existing agreements alone 'explained' or 'justified' mixity.[64] Instead, it held that the competence to suspend or terminate the Member States' BITs is ancillary to the substantive provisions on investment, ie, exclusive for FDI and shared for foreign non-direct investments.[65] The doctrine of succession[66] thus enabled the EU to terminate pre-existing Member State agreements – at least in the fields of exclusive EU competence.[67]

Lastly, the issue of mandatory mixity arose in *Opinion 1/19*. In this case, it was not disputed that the EU lacks the competence to conclude certain parts of the Istanbul Convention concerning substantive criminal law. The CJEU therefore held that it 'is common ground between the parties … that the Istanbul Convention is, assuming it is concluded, to be a mixed agreement'.[68] In doing so, the CJEU, albeit implicitly, re-affirmed mandatory mixity.

[59] Originally Article 9.10(1) EUSFTA and the related footnote; now Article 4.12(3)(a) EUSIPA.

[60] Written Observations of the Council in Opinion 2/15, SGS16/00027, on file with the author, 92.

[61] Opinion of Advocate General Sharpston, Opinion 2/15 (n 4) paras 378–98.

[62] ibid para 570.

[63] Opinion 2/15, *FTA with Singapore*, EU:C:2017:376, para 251.

[64] Opinion 1/76 (n 40) para 7. Opinion 2/15 might therefore be read as an indication that mixity was not legally required after all for the conclusion of the Inland Waterways Agreement.

[65] Opinion 2/15 (n 63) paras 247–56.

[66] As established in Joined Cases 21 to 24/72, *International Fruit Company*, EU:C:1972:115; and confirmed in Case 38/75, *Nederlandse Spoorwegen*, EU:C:1975:154. See further A Petti and J Scott, 'International Agreements in the EU Legal Order: International Fruit' in Butler and Wessel (n 32) 21; G Butler, 'EU Customs Union, International Agreements of Member States and the Doctrine of Substitution: Nederlandse Spoorwegen' in Butler and Wessel (n 32) 57; and, more broadly, RA Wessel, 'Dissolution and Succession: The Transmigration of the Soul of International Organizations' in J Klabbers and Å Wallendahl (eds), *Research Handbook on the Law of International Organisations* (Edward Elgar, 2001) 342.

[67] The CJEU did not further elaborate whether the EU could terminate agreements on behalf of the Member States in a facultative scenario. This would constitute an expansive approach of the doctrine of succession, which has so far only applied once competence was exclusively transferred to the EU. While theoretically challenging, this question is of little practical significance under the new architecture. The treaty termination clause is part of the stand-alone IPAs, which will be mixed agreements. See further Chapter 7, section II.

[68] Opinion 1/19 (n 37) para 239. The case confirms that in some (albeit very few) areas, exclusive Member State competence is indeed still a thing. See further B de Witte, 'Exclusive Member State Competences: Is There Such a Thing?' in S Garben and I Govaere (eds), *The Division of Competences between the EU and the Member States: Reflections on the Past, the Present and the Future* (Hart Publishing, 2017) 59.

B. Trade Practice

Advocate General Kokott's famous 'pastis metaphor' is one of the most-cited explanatory accounts of mandatory mixity. Accordingly:

> Individual aspects of an agreement for which the Community has no competence internally 'infect' the agreement as a whole and make it dependent on the common accord of the Member States ... Just as a little drop of pastis can turn a glass of water milky, individual provisions, however secondary, in an international agreement ... can make it necessary to conclude a shared agreement.[69]

In other words, Advocate General Kokott considered that the insertion of a single provision falling within exclusive Member State competence into the scope of an international agreement of the EU triggers mandatory mixity. Other Advocates General have disagreed with her legal Opinion, arguing that international agreements of the EU can only be 'infected' with mixity if the part falling within exclusive Member State competence is not ancillary to that agreement's main objective and content (the so-called 'centre of gravity' test).[70] According to Advocate General Wahl, who was supported by Advocate General Szpunar,

> [A] mixed agreement would be required, generally, where an international agreement concerns coexistent competences: that is, it includes a part which falls under the exclusive competence of the Union and a part which falls under the exclusive competence of the Member States, *without any of those parts being ancillary to the other.* (Emphasis added)[71]

Advocates General Wahl and Szpunar therefore argue that the 'centre of gravity' test is also applicable for agreements that fall partially outside the EU's competence. Exclusive Member State competence may, according to this view, be absorbed by an agreement's main aim and content. Advocate General Kokott soon countered the legal Opinions of her colleagues. Building on the inherent logic of her 'pastis metaphor', she argued that:

> [The] centre of gravity approach may not result *vertically* in an extension of the Union's competences compared with the Member States; otherwise the principle of conferral would be undermined (Article 5(1), first sentence, and (2) TEU, in conjunction with Article 4(1) TEU). However, that centre of gravity approach is readily applicable *horizontally*, that is to say, where it is clear that the Union has competences for all the components of its envisaged act and it is merely necessary to make the correct choice between those powers. (Emphasis in original)[72]

Legally, Advocate General Kokott is arguably correct. Besides the fact that the absorption of an exclusive Member State prerogative under a material area falling within the EU's competence would result in an unlawful expansion of the scope of the Treaties,[73]

[69] Opinion of Advocate General Kokott, *WTO Accession of Vietnam* (n 3) para 121.

[70] The centre of gravity test is further explained in Chapter 3, sections II.C and II.D.

[71] Opinion of Advocate General Wahl, Opinion 3/15 (n 35) para 122, emphasis added. See also Opinion of Advocate General Szpunar, Case C-600/14, *COTIF I*, EU:C:2017:296, para 85.

[72] Opinion of Advocate General Kokott, Joined Cases C-626/15 and C-659/16, *Antarctic MPAs*, EU:C:2018:362, para 82. See also Opinion of Advocate General Kokott, Case C-244/17, *Kazakhstan Cooperation Agreement*, EU:C:2018:364, para 59.

[73] Article 5 of the Consolidated Version of the Treaty on European Union [2012] OJ C326/13 (hereinafter 'TEU'). The EU can only expand its competence vertically – internally or externally – by using the 'flexibility clause' and the special procedures set out therein (Article 352(1) TFEU). Otherwise, that provision would lose its purpose and function.

the EU could also not assume obligations under international law vis-a-vis third parties in areas where it has no internal competence whatsoever. Under EU law, the legal basis of the decision concluding an international agreement and of the internal act implementing that agreement must not necessarily be the same.[74] Hence, even when assuming that the 'centre of gravity' test could be used to bring exclusive Member State competence under the umbrella of existing EU powers in the decision on the conclusion of an international agreement, the EU would still lack the internal power to subsequently implement that agreement (even through the Member States) for the parts in which it has no competence.[75] Therefore, mixity is mandatory as soon as an international agreement covers a single material area that falls within exclusive Member State competence. Otherwise, the EU risks breaching international law, because it might not be able to respect the entirety of the legal obligations it assumed vis-a-vis its treaty partner(s).

The fact that the insertion of a single treaty clause falling within exclusive Member State competence turns the entire agreement mixed as a matter of law may be (ab)used politically to generate 'mixity at all costs'.[76] Prior to the entry into force of the Lisbon Treaty, Rosas listed several practical examples where the Member States artificially designed mixed agreements through the inclusion of a 'second pillar' CFSP clause on political dialogue into the scope of pre-Lisbon trade agreements.[77] As the CFSP was formally situated outside the powers of the (then) Community, political dialogue clauses served as viable 'poisoned pills' in practice.[78] According to Kuijper, the infection of trade agreements with political dialogue clauses was a means of legalising 'a genuine compromise between Commission and Council, in which the Council gave away its own exclusive power to conclude a "mixed" trade agreement in part to the Member States'.[79] However, in the post-Lisbon era, the CFSP is rooted firmly within the scope of the Treaties. The insertion of CFSP clauses into the scope of trade and investment agreements therefore no longer triggers mandatory mixity. In *Kazakhstan Cooperation Agreement*, the CJEU clarified that Article 218 TFEU applies to the conclusion and implementation of CFSP treaties, and that the centre of gravity test may be used with regard to CFSP and non-CFSP treaty components.[80] Political dialogue clauses can thus no longer be used to 'infect' trade agreements with mixity.

[74] The EU could, for example, implement an agreement by means of more than one legal act. By doing so, the objective and content of each implementing act may be different than that of the agreement as a whole.

[75] See further also M Chamon, 'Constitutional Limits to the Political Choice for Mixity' in E Neframi and M Gatti (eds), *Constitutional Issues of EU External Relations Law* (Nomos, 2018) 137, 146.

[76] A Rosas, 'Mixed Union: Mixed Agreements' in M Koskenniemi (ed), *International Law Aspects of the European Union* (Kluwer Law International, 1998) 125, 145.

[77] Rosas (n 6) 204 et seq. See also Maresceau (n 6) 20 et seq. On the resulting 'cross-pillar' mixed agreements, see further RA Wessel, 'Cross-Pillar Mixity: Combining Competences in the Conclusion of the EU International Agreements' in Hillion and Koutrakos (n 6) 30.

[78] PJ Kuijper, 'Case C-244/17 – *Commission v Council*: The Centre of Gravity Test Revisited in the Context of Article 218 (9) TFEU', *European Law Blog*, 26 November 2018, europeanlawblog.eu/2018/11/26/case-c-244-17-commission-v-council-the-centre-of-gravity-test-revisited-in-the-context-of-article-218-9-tfeu/.

[79] PJ Kuijper, 'Post-CETA: How We Got There and How to Go On' (2017) 53 *Revue trimestrielle de droit européen* 181.

[80] Case C-244/17, *Kazakhstan Cooperation Agreement*, EU:C:2018:662, paras 44 et seq. See further G Butler, *Constitutional Law of the EU's Common Foreign and Security Policy: Competence and Institutions in External Relations* (Hart Publishing, 2019) 214.

Nevertheless, several provisions in new generation EU trade and investment agreements suggest that the attempts to generate 'mixity at all costs' have been ongoing post-Lisbon. The EU-Korea FTA, for example, includes a Protocol on Cultural Cooperation,[81] ie, an area of competence where the EU may solely support and coordinate Member State action. The Protocol expressly encourages one or several Member States to implement or make new co-production agreements with Korea and thus requires the Member States to make use of their independent treaty-making capacity.[82]

In the *Opinion 2/15* proceedings, the Council and the Member States claimed that new generation trade and investment agreements contain various individual provisions that in themselves would turn these agreements into mixed agreements. For example, the Council contended that the EU was not competent to conclude Article 12.3(3) and (4) of the EUSFTA alone. The provision stipulates that the parties commit to respecting, promoting, and implementing specifically the freedom of association and to ratifying and/or implementing the related fundamental Conventions of the International Labour Organization (ILO). The Council argued that the conclusion of this specific provision by the EU would lead to an unlawful harmonisation of national laws (Article 153(5) in conjunction with Article 207(6) TFEU).[83] Some of the Member States further maintained that although they are all members of the fundamental ILO Conventions (and therefore would not assume additional legal obligations through the EUSFTA), the implementation of these agreements would be an exclusive national competence.[84] Another example is what is now Article 3.23 of the EU-Singapore Investment Protection Agreement (EUSIPA), which in the Council's view fell within exclusive national competence. This provision stipulates that neither party shall grant diplomatic protection to an investor that has agreed to participate in dispute resolution under the ICS. The Council contended that the right to grant diplomatic protection falls within the Member States' prerogatives under public international law.[85] As was explained in the previous section, the Council, the Member States and Advocate General Sharpston also opined that what is now Article 4.12(3)(a) EUSIPA concerning the termination of the Member States' individual BITs triggered mixity as a matter of law. However, the CJEU decided in *Opinion 2/15* that the EUSFTA merely re-states existing international legal norms and does not levy any new rights and obligations on the Member States, and, in contrast to Advocate General Sharpston, did not find that an individual provision of the EUSFTA triggered mandatory mixity. Any attempts to generate 'mixity at all costs' in recent practice have therefore been unsuccessful.

IV. Facultative Mixity

Facultative mixity was first defined by Rosas in 2000. According to Rosas, 'where the competence of the [EU to conclude an international agreement] is non-exclusive, but there are no competences reserved for the Member States either, mixity becomes

[81] EU-Korea FTA, Protocol on Cultural Cooperation [2011] OJ L127/1418.

[82] For example, Article 5(2) of the EU-Korea Protocol on Cultural Cooperation.

[83] Written Observations of the Council (n 60) 106–08.

[84] See also J Heliskoski, 'Mixed Agreements: The EU Law Fundamentals' in R Schütze and T Tridimas (eds), *Oxford Principles of European Union Law*, vol I (Oxford University Press, 2018) 1174, 1176–77.

[85] Written Observations of the Council (n 60) 92–93.

facultative'.[86] Hence, agreements falling within shared competence do not, as a matter of law, need to be agreements to which both the EU and the Member States are parties. That decision is taken in the Council. If the Council decides to exercise the shared competence, the EU alone concludes the agreement (a facultative EU-only agreement). Conversely, if the Council decides not to exercise (part of) the shared competence, the Member States may exercise the competence and consequently become parties to a mixed agreement. In those circumstances, a mixed agreement is an option, but not a legal requirement (facultative mixity).[87] The choice in favour of mixity is therefore not always mandatory as a matter of law (see section III above). In certain circumstances, mixity is a political choice of the Member States in the Council. In this book, facultative mixity is not understood as meaning that the Council has already chosen *not* to exercise shared competences and to conclude a mixed agreement. Instead, it is understood as describing *the possibility to make a choice* for or against mixity in areas of shared competence. It does not imply that that choice has already been made.[88]

A. Law

Although facultative mixity lies within the political discretion of the Council, its conception is rooted in law, more specifically Article 2(2) TFEU. Pursuant to the second and third sentences of Article 2(2) TFEU, in areas of shared competence, '[t]he Member States shall exercise their competence to the extent that the Union has not exercised its competence. The Member States shall again exercise their competence to the extent that the Union has decided to cease exercising its competence.'[89] Although that article principally concerns the internal exercise of competence, Advocate General Sharpston has observed that its principles and logic 'must be respected in all action taken by the European Union, whether internal or external'.[90] According to her:

> If the European Union does not choose to exercise [its right of pre-emption under Article 2(2) TFEU], external competence – like internal competence – will remain with the Member States and it follows that they (and not the European Union) will be competent to negotiate, sign and conclude an international agreement whose subject matter falls within that area of shared competence.[91]

Likewise, Advocate General Wahl has argued that:

> [T]he choice between a mixed agreement or an EU-only agreement, when the subject matter of the agreement falls within an area of shared competence … is generally a matter for the discretion of the EU legislature.[92]

[86] Rosas (n 6) 206. See also A Rosas, 'Mixity Past, Present and Future: Some Observations' in M Chamon and I Govaere (eds), *EU External Relations Law Post-Lisbon: The Law and Practice of Facultative Mixity* (Brill/Nijhoff, 2020) 8.
[87] G Kübek and I Van Damme, 'Facultative Mixity and the European Union's Trade and Investment Agreements' in Chamon and Govaere (n 86) 137.
[88] ibid 137–38.
[89] See further, eg, CWA Timmermans, 'ECJ Doctrines on Competence' in L Azoulai (ed), *The Question of Competence in the European Union* (Oxford University Press, 2014) 155, 162.
[90] Opinion of Advocate General Sharpston, Opinion 2/15 (n 4) para 73.
[91] ibid.
[92] Opinion of Advocate General Wahl, Opinion 3/15 (n 35) para 119.

Therefore, as Advocate General Szpunar pointed out:

> [T]he issue of competence ... must not be conflated with that of a mixed agreement.[93]

Facultative mixity thus results from an external reading of Article 2(2) TFEU.[94] The provision gives the EU a choice about exercising shared competence and thus its right of pre-emption, both internally and externally. Ultimately, that choice is made in the Council. Pursuant to Article 218(5) and (6) TFEU, the decisions to sign and conclude an international agreement are authorised by the Council on the basis of a Commission proposal. Pursuant to Article 293(1) TFEU, the Council may amend the Commission's proposals on the signature and conclusion of an agreement unanimously. The Council, acting unanimously, therefore has the final say over the exercise of shared competence and thus about whether or not to sign and conclude a mixed agreement. Irrespective of whether the EU or the Member States exercise the shared competence, the CJEU has the jurisdiction to review the resulting agreement.[95] As the CJEU pointed out in *Demirel*, the Member States, by concluding a facultative mixed agreement, not only fulfil an obligation in relation to the third party but also 'within the [EU] system, an obligation in relation to the [EU]' for the due performance of the agreement, which in turn justifies and requires CJEU oversight.[96]

B. Law and Logic

The previous section showed that facultative mixity results from applying Article 2(2) TFEU – which primarily concerns the exercise of internal competence – analogously to the external decision-making of the EU. Yet, the internal and external application of Article 2(2) TFEU may not necessarily follow the same logic.

Internally, the decision of the Council to cease exercising shared competence may result in 27 different national regulatory regimes in a given field. If the internal exercise of shared competence is left with the Member States, each Member State may regulate a material issue *individually* in accordance with its respective national law. As long as the EU has not exercised shared internal competence, the Member States may thus make their own rules. By inference, it may be argued that the existing *internal* competence must be exercised by the EU if the Member States in the Council want to regulate a material issue *collectively*.[97] In other words: common internal EU rules can only be established by secondary EU law, which, if based on a shared competence-conferring Treaty provision, can trigger pre-emption.

[93] Opinion of Advocate General Szpunar, *COTIF I* (n 71) para 81. See also Opinion of Advocate General Kokott, *Antarctic MPAs* (n 72) paras 112–13.

[94] See also J Heliskoski, 'The Exercise of Non-exclusive Competence of the EU and the Conclusion of International Agreements' in K Lenaerts et al (eds), *An Ever-Changing Union? Perspectives on the Future of EU Law in Honour of Allan Rosas* (Hart Publishing, 2019) 293, 295 et seq.

[95] Case 12/86, *Demirel*, EU:C:1987:400, para 10.

[96] ibid paras 10–11.

[97] See also C Herrmann and H Rosenfeld, 'Europarechtliche Grundlagen und Grenzen der Errichtung eines einheitlichen Bankenabwicklungsmechanismus (SRM)', *Gutachten im Auftrag der Bundestagsfraktion Bündnis90/Die Grünen* (2014) 25.

However, in the external realm, the collective exercise of shared competence by Member States does not appear to necessitate recourse to the existing competence-conferring Treaty provision. Mixed agreements stipulate rules that are applicable in the same way to its contracting parties. And usually that includes all EU Member States. When concluding a mixed agreement, the Member States therefore collectively make common rules through that mixed agreement in areas of shared competence. Externally, the Council's decision to cease exercising shared competence pursuant to Article 2(2) TFEU may therefore lead to a situation where the Member States exercise shared competence without using the applicable shared competence-conferring Treaty provision as a legal basis.[98] The Member States do not use EU law as a legal basis because mixity implies that it is not the Council but the Member States that exercise the shared competence.

Can Member States make common external rules in areas of shared competence *collectively*, with each Member State acting in its own right? Or would the Member States be required – as they are internally – to use the respective shared competence-conferring Treaty provision as a legal basis and, as a result, act collectively through the Council? As the following section will show, the CJEU has generally accepted facultative mixity as a result of an external reading of Article 2(2) TFEU and has not been concerned about the collective exercise of shared competence by Member States acting in their own right in the context of mixed agreements. It therefore appears that the Member States have greater leverage to act externally than internally in fields of shared competence.

C. Judicial Recognition

In practice, the Council usually resorts to mixed agreements in areas of shared competence. The Member States generally prefer mixed agreements over EU-only agreements because mixity gives them an opportunity to remain visible external actors, equips their national parliaments with veto powers and therefore de facto (re-)instates unanimity in the Council.[99] Indeed, as was explained in Chapter 1, between 1994 and 2018 almost all EU trade and investment agreements were concluded as mixed agreements.[100] In practice, therefore, the distinction between mandatory and facultative mixity has so far not played a defining role for the conclusion of EU trade and investment agreements, as mixity was used out of principle as soon as an agreement fell partially outside the scope of the EU's exclusive competence. There were two main exceptions. First, the Stabilisation and Association Agreement with Kosovo was concluded as a facultative EU-only agreement for political reasons because not all of the Member States recognise Kosovo as a sovereign state under public international law. The Member States in the Council therefore agreed *not* to be listed as independent contracting parties to an

[98] See also P Eeckhout, *EU External Relations Law*, 2nd edn (Oxford University Press, 2011) 217.

[99] See, eg, C-D Ehlermann, 'Mixed Agreements: A List of Problems' in O'Keeffe and Schermers (n 6); and Maresceau (n 6).

[100] See in more detail Chapter 1, section III.A.

agreement with Kosovo.[101] Second, the EU-UK TCA was concluded as a facultative EU-only agreement, amongst other reasons to increase the speed of the ratification process in view of the stringent Brexit timelines (see further Chapter 8).

Because (almost) all agreements falling (partially) within shared competence were concluded as mixed agreements in practice, facultative mixity became legally disputed. Rosas noted at the time that the distinction between mandatory and facultative mixity 'is not always recognised in practice'[102] because it was in the Council 'almost always taken for granted that the lack of exclusive Community competence of necessity requires mixity'.[103]

In the run-up to the signature of CETA, the common (mis)perception that mixity is required as a matter of law in areas of shared competence regained prominence.[104] Although the CJEU had in its pre-Lisbon case law recognised the recourse to mixity in areas of shared competence, it never explicitly stated that mixity, in that context, is a political choice rather than a legal requirement.[105] The request for *Opinion 2/15* granted the CJEU an opportunity to confirm the existence of facultative mixity. The main question in *Opinion 2/15* put to the CJEU was whether the EU had the '*requisite* competence' to conclude the EUSFTA alone.[106] Essentially, the CJEU was therefore also (albeit implicitly) asked to qualify whether shared competence equips the EU with the 'requisite' treaty-making power to conclude the EUSFTA alone. Indeed, the Commission argued in its written observations that the competence for concluding an 'EU-only' agreement may be 'exclusive and/or shared'.[107]

Advocate General Sharpston found that 'the text of Article 2(2) TFEU can be read as permitting the European Union to exercise its right of pre-emption in relation to both external and internal competence'.[108] She thus acknowledged facultative mixity, although, as previously explained, she found that a single provision in the EUSFTA, namely the termination of the Member States' BITs, triggered mandatory mixity.[109]

The CJEU, unlike Advocate General Sharpston, did not discuss the distinction between facultative and mandatory mixity. The operative part of *Opinion 2/15* exclusively relates to the allocation of competence between the EU and the Member States for concluding the EUSFTA. The Commission's main question regarding the 'requisite' treaty-making power of the EU to conclude the EUSFTA without the Member States was not answered by the CJEU. Yet, as will be discussed further in Chapter 3,[110]

[101] See also Chapter 1, section III.B; and P Van Elsuwege, 'Legal Creativity in EU External Relations: The Stabilisation and Association Agreement between the EU and Kosovo' (2017) 22 *European Foreign Affairs Review* 393.

[102] Rosas (n 6) 206.

[103] ibid fn 37. This legal view was, at least pre-Lisbon, not limited to the Council and the Member States. See similarly E Neframi, *Les accords mixtes de la Communauté européenne: aspects communautaires et internationaux* (Bruylant, 2007) 107–11.

[104] See especially W Weiß, 'The Reception of EU Facultative Mixity in Germany's Constitutional Order' in Chamon and Govaere (n 86) 363.

[105] On the CJEU's recognition of mixity pre-Lisbon, see especially Heliskoski (n 38) 25 et seq.

[106] Request for an opinion submitted by the European Commission pursuant to Article 218(11) TFEU [2015] OJ C311/18 (emphasis added).

[107] Written Observations of the Commission in *Opinion 2/15*, Ref Ares(2015)3942621 [2015], on file with the author, 8. See further also Kübek and Van Damme (n 87) 147 et seq.

[108] Opinion of Advocate General Sharpston, Opinion 2/15 (n 4) para 73.

[109] See above, section III.A.

[110] See Chapter 3, sections IV.A and IV.B.

the CJEU concluded that the EUSFTA 'cannot be approved by the European Union alone'[111] because the EU shares competence for foreign non-direct investments and investor-state dispute settlement (ISDS) with the Member States. A literal reading of that statement suggested that mixity is legally required for agreements falling within shared competences and that therefore facultative mixity was no longer possible.[112] This ostensible rejection of facultative mixity by the CJEU was heavily criticised by early commentators, who pointed to the existence of shared external competence pursuant to Article 216(1) TFEU, the EU's capacity to exercise shared competence pursuant to Article 2(2) TFEU and the legality of existing facultative 'EU-only' agreements.[113]

The *COTIF I* case provided an opportunity for the CJEU to promptly correct its apparent erroneous statement that the EU 'cannot' conclude agreements in areas of shared competences alone.[114] The case concerned the EU's capacity to exercise shared competence alone within the framework of the Revision Committee of the Convention concerning International Carriage by Rail (COTIF). Both the Member States and the EU are parties to COTIF. Article 6(2) of the EU accession agreement to COTIF stipulates that: 'For decisions in matters where the Union shares competence with its Member States, either the Union or its Member States shall vote.' Accordingly, the Member States in the Council adopted per qualified majority voting (QMV) a Council Decision establishing a concerted EU position in the Revision Committee of the Intergovernmental Organisation for International Carriage by Rail (OTIF) as regards certain amendments to the Convention.[115] Germany subsequently asked the CJEU to partially annul that Council decision, claiming that the EU cannot exercise external competence alone in areas of shared competence.

The CJEU found that the EU had shared external competence for the rail transport issues covered by the contested decision by virtue of Article 91(1) in conjunction with Article 216(1) TFEU,[116] dismissing Germany's argument that the EU has 'no external competence' in areas outside Article 3(2) TFEU.[117] Thereafter, the CJEU clarified that the Council's decision to exercise shared external competence pursuant to Article 2(2) TFEU pre-empts the Member States from acting independently.[118] As a consequence, the CJEU concluded that the concerted action in the OTIF Revision Committee could be adopted by the EU alone. In that context, the CJEU noted that:

> Admittedly, the Court found, in paragraph 244 of [*Opinion 2/15*], that the relevant provisions of the agreement concerned, relating to indirect foreign investment, which fall within the shared competence of the European Union and its Member States, could not be approved by

[111] Opinion 2/15 (n 65) paras 244, 279, 282, 292 and 304.

[112] See also Kübek and Van Damme (n 87) 147 et seq.

[113] See, eg, Kleimann and Kübek (n 2) 38; M Cremona, 'Shaping EU Trade Policy Post-Lisbon: Opinion 2/15 of 16 May 2017' (2018) 14 *European Constitutional Law Review* 231; H Lenk, 'More Trade and Less Investment for Future EU Trade and Investment Policy: CJEU, Opinion 2/15, Free Trade Agreement between the European Union and Singapore, 16 May 2017, EU:C:2017:376' (2018) 19 *Journal of World Investment and Trade* 305, 316; and D Thym, 'Mixity after Opinion 2/15: Judicial Confusion over Shared Competences' *Verfassungsblog*, 31 May 2017, verfassungsblog.de/mixity-after-opinion-215-judicial-confusion-over-shared-competences.

[114] Case C-600/14, *COTIF I*, EU:C:2017:935. See also Heliskoski (n 94) 297 et seq.

[115] Council Decision (EU) 2014/699 of 24 June 2014 establishing the position to be adopted on behalf of the European Union at the 25th session of the OTIF Revision Committee as regards certain amendments to the Convention concerning International Carriage by Rail (COTIF) and to the Appendices thereto [2014] OJ L293/26.

[116] *COTIF I* (n 114) paras 52–59.

[117] ibid para 38.

[118] ibid paras 66–67.

> the Union alone. However, in making that finding, the Court did no more than acknowledge the fact that, as stated by the Council in the course of the proceedings relating to that Opinion, there was no possibility of the required majority being obtained within the Council for the Union to be able to exercise alone the external competence that it shares with the Member States in this area.[119]

The need to clarify a landmark decision such as *Opinion 2/15* is unfortunate to say the least. If the CJEU follows non-legal concerns, such as institutional decision-making preferences, the dividing lines between legal procedural possibilities and political realities arguably require separate analyses.[120] It may further be noted that the CJEU's clarification of *Opinion 2/15* in paragraph 68 of the *COTIF I* judgment was 'somewhat premature'.[121] The Commission had only proposed the signature of the EUSFTA in April 2018, ie, approximately one year after *Opinion 2/15* was delivered. As a result, the Council had not formally decided to sign or conclude the EUSFTA as a mixed agreement at the time.[122]

The CJEU's clarification in *COTIF I* is explicitly confined to the part of *Opinion 2/15* concerning foreign non-direct investments. It does not concern ISDS. Consequentially, there is legal doubt about whether mixity for agreements containing ISDS is mandatory or facultative, irrespective of the shared competence of the EU in that field.[123] A subsequent statement of Koen Lenaerts suggests that there is an element of political choice during the ratification of agreements containing ISDS/ICS.[124] Yet, that has not been confirmed by the CJEU as an institution.

In its judgment in *COTIF I*, the CJEU finally recognised facultative mixity. It underlined that mixity in areas of shared competence is not required as a matter of law, but follows from the political choice taken in the Council. The CJEU did not question the legality of the Council's choice either in favour of mixity (*Opinion 2/15*) or in favour of the EU-only procedure (*COTIF I*). In doing so, it highlighted that there is no general legal obligation incumbent on the Council either to exercise shared competence or, alternatively, to leave such exercise with the Member States.[125]

V. Limits to Facultative Mixity

Facultative mixity is generally at the discretion of the Member States in the Council. Yet, there might be a situation where the Council's political choice in favour or against mixity

[119] ibid para 68.

[120] G Kübek, 'The European Union's External Trade and Investment Policy Post-Lisbon: Competence, Procedure and Scope of Action' in M Andenas et al (eds), *The European Union as an Actor in International Economic Law* (TMC Asser Press, 2020) 93, 111.

[121] Interview with a Council official, 7 November 2018.

[122] ibid.

[123] See further Chapter 3, section IV.B; and Kübek and Van Damme (n 87) 148 et seq.

[124] K Lenaerts, 'Modernising Trade Whilst Safeguarding the EU Constitutional Framework: An Insight into the Balanced Approach of Opinion 1/17', Seminar on Opinion 1/17, Belgian Ministry of Foreign Affairs, 6 September 2019. See further Chapter 3, IV.B.

[125] See Heliskoski (n 84). See also T Verellen, 'Convergence and Divergence in EU External Action: The Very Slowly Emergent Doctrine of Shared Competence' in M Sahadžić et al (eds), *Accommodating Diversity in Multilevel Constitutional Orders: Legal Mechanisms of Divergence and Converge* (Routledge, 2023) 112, 124.

in areas of shared competence is constrained by law. In other words, some circumstances arguably legally require the making of EU-only agreements in areas of shared competence. Other circumstances may legally require the making of mixed agreements in areas of shared competence. Legal limits to facultative mixity are therefore emerging.

A. Loyal Cooperation and Unity

Pursuant to Article 4(3) TEU, both the EU and the Member States are under a duty to cooperate loyally.[126] That duty weighs generally more heavily on the Member States than it does on the EU. Pursuant to the third sentence of Article 4(3) TEU, '[t]he Member States shall facilitate the achievement of the Union's tasks and refrain from any measure which could jeopardise the attainment of the Union's objectives'. The duty of loyal cooperation may thus result in a duty of abstention for the Member States. In particular, the CJEU found in *PFOS* that Article 4(3) third sentence TEU may result in a legal obligation of the Member States to refrain from action in areas of shared competence if a common EU strategy to act exists.[127]

The CJEU underlined that the duty of loyal cooperation is relevant to the making of mixed agreements. Article 4(3) TEU applies to the entire 'life cycle' of mixed agreements,[128] ie, their negotiations,[129] signature and conclusion,[130] and implementation.[131] However, it is not clear whether the duty of loyal cooperation also applies *before* the life cycle of a mixed agreement begins, ie, to the decision to make a mixed agreement in the first place. Does Article 4(3) TEU in any way constrain the choice to use the mixed procedure, especially in areas of shared competence?

Eeckhout has argued that: 'Where an agreement falls wholly within the EU's non-exclusive external competences, and the EU concludes the agreement, there is no legal justification for mixity. The requirement of unity in the international representation of the EU demands pure EU agreements in such cases.'[132] Since mixity inevitably brings about devolution; it might, in certain situations, pose a serious challenge to the

[126] On loyal cooperation in EU external relations, see, eg, A Delgado Casteleiro and J Larik, 'The Duty to Remain Silent: Limitless Loyalty in EU External Relations?' (2004) 36 *European Law Review* 522; A Hatje, *Loyalität als Rechtsprinzip in der Europäischen Union* (Nomos, 2001); E Neframi, 'The Duty of Loyalty: Rethinking its Scope through its Application in the Field of EU External Relations' (2010) 54 *Common Market Law Review* 323; M Klamert, *The Principle of Loyalty in EU Law* (Oxford University Press, 2014); J Larik, '*Pars Pro Toto*: The Member States' Obligations of Sincere Cooperation, Solidarity and Unity' in M Cremona (ed), *Structural Principles in EU External Relations Law* (Hart Publishing, 2018) 175; C Eckes, *EU Powers Under External Pressure: How the EU's External Actions Alter its Internal Structures* (Oxford University Press, 2019) 45 et seq. In the context of mixity, see specifically C Hillion, 'Mixity and Coherence in EU External Relations: The Significance of the "Duty of Cooperation"' in Hillion and Koutrakos (n 6) 87; M Demper, *Kooperationsstrukturen und Kooperationsvereinbarungen zwischen der EU und den Mitgliedstaaten im Rahmen gemischter Abkommen* (Nomos, 2018); and C Hillion and M Chamon, 'Facultative Mixity and Sincere Cooperation' in Chamon and Govaere (n 86) 86.

[127] Case C-246/07, *PFOS*, EU:C:2010:203.

[128] Eeckhout (n 98) 193.

[129] Case C-433/03, *Commission v Germany*, EU:C:2005:462; see also (although not addressed by the CJEU) the second plea in law in Case C-114/12, *Neighbouring Rights*, EU:C:2014:2151, para 43.

[130] Opinion 2/91, *ILO Convention No 170*, EU:C:1993:106, para 38; Opinion 1/94 (n 4) para 109.

[131] eg, Case C-246/07 (n 129) paras 89 et seq; Case C-620/16, *COTIF II*, EU:C:2019:256, para 100.

[132] Eeckhout (n 98) 217.

principle of unity in the EU's external representation. The CJEU has consistently linked Article 4(3) TEU to the (judge-made) duty to ensure 'unity and consistency of the EU's external action'.[133] In *COTIF II*, the CJEU further qualified the requirements of unity in the context of Article 4(3) TEU. Accordingly, unity is called into question by Member State action jeapordising 'the effectiveness of the international action of the European Union, as well as the latter's credibility and reputation on the international stage'.[134] In *COTIF II*, the respective Member State's actions (here Germany) were found to be in breach of Article 4(3) TEU.[135]

Nevertheless, as Hillion and Chamon argue, Article 4(3) TEU cannot be stretched to imply that Member States always have to refrain from exercising shared external competence and from becoming contracting parties to facultative mixed agreements in their own right.[136] The duty of loyal cooperation does not impose a general legal obligation incumbent on the Council to make EU-only agreements in areas of shared competence. The CJEU found in *Hybrid Acts* that the duty of loyal cooperation does not 'justify the Council setting itself free from compliance with … Article 218 TFEU'.[137] Likewise, Article 4(3) TEU cannot affect the allocation of power and capacity prescribed by Articles 3–6 TFEU.[138] However, Article 4(3) TEU may affect the *exercise* of shared competence by the EU institutions and/or the Member States. Therefore, Article 4(3) TEU could arguably exceptionally function as a limit to facultative mixity, namely where the exercise of shared external competence by the Member States would evidently call into question the unity, consistency, effectiveness, credibility and reputation of the EU's external action.[139]

Advocate General Wahl held that although facultative mixity 'is predominantly political in nature', the decision to make a mixed agreement in that context should be subject to 'limited judicial review', namely where such a decision is 'inappropriate having regard to the objective which the competent institution is seeking to pursue'.[140] The Advocate General viewed that to be the case:

> [W]here a decision to conclude a mixed agreement might, because of the urgency of the situation and the time required for the 28 [now 27] ratification procedures at national level, seriously risk compromising the objective pursued, or cause the Union to breach the principle *pacta sunt servanda*.[141]

As the *pacta sunt servanda* principle applies only after a treaty has been concluded, it does not affect the making of mixed agreements. It might become relevant with regard to EU decision-making within the framework of existing mixed agreements. However, in circumstances that require urgent international action, the decision to make a mixed agreement might, as the Advocate General points out, seriously threaten

[133] Opinion 1/94 (n 4) para 108; Case C-266/03, *Commission v Luxembourg*, EU:C:2005:341, para 60; *Commission v Germany* (n 129) para 66; *PFOS* (n 127) para 73; *COTIF II* (n 131) para 45.
[134] *COTIF II* (n 131) para 98.
[135] ibid para 100.
[136] Hillion and Chamon (n 126) 102.
[137] Case C-28/12, *Hybrid Acts*, EU:C:2015:282, paras 54–55. See also Opinion 1/19 (n 37) para 242.
[138] *Commission v Germany* (n 129) para 58.
[139] See also, albeit more cautiously, Hillion and Chamon (n 126) 102.
[140] Opinion of Advocate General Wahl, Opinion 3/15 (n 35) para 120.
[141] ibid para 121.

the EU's capacity to act in a unified and timely manner. The Council's decision to make a mixed agreement in areas of shared competence could in this instance risk jeopardising the attainment of the EU's objective within the meaning of the third sentence of Article 4(3) TEU. In such a scenario, loyal cooperation may prevent facultative mixity.[142]

B. Hybridity

Facultative mixed agreements are made on the premise that (part of the) shared competences are exercised by the Member States in their own right, while the remaining (shared or exclusive) competences are exercised by the EU. Facultative mixity thus presupposes that an agreement has multiple components: one of which falls within powers exercised by the EU and one of which falls within powers exercised by Member States. Conversely, facultative mixity is difficult to realise if an agreement or decision only has a single purpose or component and thus uses a single legal basis.

Article 2(2) TFEU specifies that *either* the Member States *or* the EU exercise shared competence; it does not provide for *joint action* by the EU *and* the Member States in the case of the exercise of shared competences. Similarly, the exercise of a parallel competence within the meaning of Article 4(3) and (4) TFEU by the EU in the context of an international agreement always implies that the EU assumes the legal rights and obligations of that agreement in full. Although Article 4(3) and (4) TFEU precludes pre-emption, it does not provide a basis for the EU and the Member States to divide, as it were, the exercise of a single parallel competence as between them.[143]

In *Hybrid Acts*, the CJEU held that so-called 'hybrid decisions' (ie, decisions adopted simultaneously by both the Council and the Governments of the Member States) infringe EU law.[144] In *Opinion 1/19* the CJEU confirmed that hybridity may not only emerge from two separate decisions – one being the result of a consensus between Member States and the other one adopted by the EU – being brought together in a single decision.[145] An established practice is incompatible with EU law as soon as it amounts to a 'hybrid decision-making process', for example, by making EU decision-making contingent on the consensus of the Member States where such a consensus is not foreseen by the Treaties.[146]

The joint adoption of an international agreement or a decision that concerns a single subject matter falling within a competence shared with the Member States arguably

[142] Scholars further considered whether the principle of subsidiarity could have an impact on the Council's decision (not) to exercise shared external competence. See especially I Bosse-Platière and M Cremona, 'Facultative Mixity in Light of the Principle of Subsidiarity' in Chamon and Govaere (n 86) 49. For bilateral agreements, the principle of subsidiary mainly applies to the EU's decision to make an agreement at all. As bilateral mixed agreements cannot be concluded by the Member States without the EU, the question whether Member States should act instead of the EU does not arise (Article 5(3) TEU). As Bosse-Platière and Cremona argue, the principle of subsidiary does thus 'not govern the decision as to whether the Member should also be parties, that is the decision on mixity' (at 83).

[143] Interview with a Commission official, 9 November 2018.

[144] *Hybrid Acts* (n 137) paras 49–57.

[145] Opinion 1/19 (n 37) para 244.

[146] ibid para 246. See further Kübek (n 37) 1480.

has a similar effect to a hybrid decision-making process.[147] If an agreement or an external decision concerns a single shared competence-conferring Treaty provision, it logically follows from Article 2(2) TFEU that *either* the EU *or* the Member States must exercise that competence. The EU and the Member States cannot simultaneously exercise a shared competence. Otherwise, this would lead to a double (or hybrid) exercise of the same shared competence. Advocate General Sharpston observed that the EU and the Member States cannot jointly exercise a shared competence within the meaning of Article 2(2) TFEU. In her view:

> Pre-emption under Article 2(2) TFEU is expressly stated to be reversible. If the European Union ceases to act in respect of a particular part of a particular shared competence, that competence reverts to the Member States. And the parts must always add up to a whole – every competence exercised in a shared area is *either* exercised by the European Union *or* exercised by the Member States. It cannot be in limbo between the two. (Emphasis in original)[148]

If an agreement or an external decision concerns a single subject matter falling within shared competence and either the EU or the Member States (but not both) may exercise competence, the following question arises: who should exercise that shared competence?

Advocate General Kokott addressed this question in her Opinion in *Antarctic MPAs*.[149] In that case, the Commission had asked the CJEU to annul two decisions (hereinafter 'the decisions') regarding the submission of positions 'by the European Union *and* the Member States' to the Commission for the Conservation of Antarctic Marine Living Resources (CCAMLR). The CCAMLR is a decision-making body established within the framework of the Convention on the Conservation of Antarctic Marine Living Resources (the Canberra Convention).[150] The Advocate General came to the conclusion that the decisions fell within a shared competence, namely the EU's competence on environmental policy (Article 192 TFEU).[151] Notwithstanding the prevalence of shared competence, Advocate General Kokott held that the decisions should have been adopted by the EU alone and not by the EU *and* the Member States jointly. In her view, the Council had 'erroneously summarily equated shared competences and mixed action'.[152] The need for mixity would only arise if the 'Union itself does not have sufficient exclusive *and* shared competence' (emphasis added).[153] Yet, she found 'no objective evidence amenable to review in this case that the Council exercised the Union's environmental competences … only partially for political reasons'.[154] In particular, it would not be 'apparent anywhere in the contested decisions that the Union refrained from exercising its powers in environmental policy … or wished to

[147] See also Kübek and Van Damme (n 87) 157.

[148] Opinion of Advocate General Sharpston, Opinion 2/15 (n 4) para 61. For an analysis, see also Kübek and Van Damme (n 87) 154 et seq.

[149] Opinion of Advocate General Kokott, *Antarctic MPAs* (n 74).

[150] Convention on the Conservation of Antarctic Marine Living Resources ('Canberra Convention') [1980] UNTS Vol 1329, 47.

[151] ibid para 100; subsequently confirmed by the CJEU in Joined Cases C-626/15 and C-659/16, *Antarctic MPAs*, EU:C:2018:925, paras 99 et seq.

[152] Opinion of Advocate General Kokott, *Antarctic MPAs* (n 74) para 116.

[153] ibid para 108.

[154] ibid para 114.

leave those measures in the responsibility of the Member States'.[155] Therefore, in the Advocate General's view, the decision would not leave 'sufficient scope for voluntary participation by … Member States'.[156]

The crux of the *Antarctic MPAs* case was arguably that the Advocate General – and subsequently the CJEU (see below) – found that the contested decisions concerned a single shared competence area, namely environmental policy. The adoption of the decisions by the EU *and* the Member States therefore led to a double (or hybrid) exercise of a single shared competence. This appears to be why Advocate General Kokott concluded that there is no space for voluntary participation of the Member States, unless mixity can be objectively justified. Indeed, the simultaneous (or hybrid) exercise of a single shared competence by both the EU and the Member States appears to be only plausible in cases where mixity can be justified for overriding legal, (geo)political, or practical reasons. The justification would, as it were, 'de-activate' the principle of pre-emption inherent in Article 2(2) TFEU, and exceptionally allow the joint exercise of power by the EU and the Member States. Without such a justification, the wording of Article 2(2) TFEU suggests that the joint exercise of a single shared competence by the EU and the Member States is not possible.

C. International Law

Like Advocate General Kokott, the CJEU concluded that the decisions at issue fell within a single shared competence field, namely the environment. Yet, the CJEU did not further address the issues raised by the Advocate General with regard to hybridity. Instead, it established a different limit to facultative mixity: international law. In doing so, it recognised for the first time that the political discretion of the Council over the exercise of shared external competence is not unfettered, but is subject to legal constraints.

Despite finding that the competence at issue was shared, and in sharp contrast to the Advocate General, the Court found that mixity was mandatory. In the specific system set out by the Antarctic Treaty,[157] of which the Canberra Convention forms part, the 'exercise by the European Union of the external competence … that excludes the Member States would be incompatible with international law'.[158] Mixity can therefore be mandatory for reasons relating to international law, regardless of the vertical allocation of competence laid down in the Treaties.

The CJEU's conclusions were based on two central arguments. First, it noted that the Canberra Convention's clause on regional economic integration organisations (the REIO clause) makes the EU's membership dependent on the membership of its Member States. Thus, the Canberra Convention did not equip REIOs 'with fully autonomous status within the CCAMLR'.[159] Second, the Court underlined that only the Member

[155] ibid para 115.
[156] ibid, paras 110–11, Point (b).
[157] The Antarctic Treaty [1961] UNTS Vol. 402, 71.
[158] *Antarctic MPAs* (n 151) para 128. See further M Chamon, 'Verplicht gemengd optreden van de Unie en de lidstaten binnen de Canberra Conventie ondanks het bestaan van een gedeelde bevoegdheid' (2019) 67 *SEW: Tijdschrift voor Europees en economisch recht* 250.
[159] *Antarctic MPAs* (n 151) para 130.

States, and not the EU, are parties to the overarching Antarctic Treaty, as the latter is only open to states. In light of Article V of the Canberra Convention, which provides that parties to the Convention that are not part of the overarching Antarctic Treaty, such as the EU, must recognise the special responsibilities and position of the consulting parties to the Antarctic Treaty, the CJEU concluded that:

> [T]o permit the European Union to have recourse, within the CCAMLR, to the power which it has to act without the participation of its Member States in an area of shared competence, when, unlike it, some of them have the status of Antarctic Treaty consultative parties, might ... undermine the responsibilities and rights of those consultative parties – which could weaken the coherence of that system of agreements.[160]

Chamon and Cremona have argued that the CJEU's reasoning is inconsistent with both EU and public international law.[161] Their excellent arguments will not be repeated here. Within the scope of the present chapter, it suffices to note that the CJEU, unlike Advocate General Kokott, was not concerned with the fact that the requirement for mixity in the case at hand led to a joint exercise of a single shared competence by the EU and the Member States that is not foreseen in Article 2(2) TFEU. The CJEU's conclusions were principally focused on the question whether the EU's membership in an international agreement depends on the parallel membership of the Member States in the same agreement. Taken at face value, the case suggests that the exercise of shared competence by the EU alone is only possible if the EU qualifies as a 'fully autonomous' member of the international organisation within whose framework it acts.

The CJEU's conclusions in *Antarctic MPAs* should have no repercussions in the field of trade. Trade agreements fall within the EU's exclusive competence and the EU is a fully autonomous member of the WTO.[162] The situation could be different in the field of investment. The EU's most recent investment agreements, such as CETA, refer to and apply the rules of overarching dispute settlement regimes, such as the International Centre for Settlement of Investment Disputes (ICSID), the United Nations (UN) Commission on International Trade Law (UNCITRAL) or the Convention on the Recognition and Enforcement of Foreign Arbitral Awards (the New York Convention).[163] Yet, only the Member States, and not the EU, can become members of ICSID,[164] UNCITRAL[165] and the New York Convention.[166] An analogous application of the CJEU's conclusion in *Antarctic MPAs* would therefore imply that the EU must exercise its shared external investment competence jointly with the Member

[160] ibid para 133.

[161] M Chamon and M Cremona, 'The Representation of the EU and its Member States in Multilateral Fora: The AMP Antarctique Effect' in Levrat et al (n 6) 97.

[162] Article XI(1) of the Marrakesh Agreement Establishing the World Trade Organization [1995] UNTS Vol 1867, 3.

[163] Convention on the Recognition and Enforcement of Foreign Arbitral Awards ('New York Convention') [1959] UNTS Vol 330, 3.

[164] Article IX of the Convention on the Settlement of Investment Disputes between States and Nationals of Other States [1965] UNTS Vol 575, 159.

[165] UNCITRAL is composed of UN General Assembly members that are elected on a rotating basis (Article II(1) of the General Assembly Resolution 2205(XXI) of 17 December 1966). The EU cannot become a UN member (Article 4 of the Charter of the United Nations (1945)).

[166] Article IX of the New York Convention.

States so as to ensure 'the coherence of that system of agreements'[167] and, ultimately, compliance with international law.[168] However, the extent to which the *Antarctic MPAs* case has precedential value is questionable.[169] The CJEU appears to limit the reach of its own judgment by underlining the 'specific context' and 'circumstances' of the Antarctic Treaty system.[170] It therefore remains doubtful whether the 'international law limit' to facultative mixity can be transferred to the field of trade and investment.

VI. Conclusion

Competences are determinants of the procedure for making EU international agreements. The choice between mixity and EU-only treaty-making is therefore, first and foremost, a legal one – irrespective of the practical impact of that choice on the unity, effectiveness, inclusivity, credibility and reputation of EU external action. Provided that the material content of an agreement falls fully within the realm of EU exclusive competence, it must legally be concluded by the EU alone. Conversely, if an agreement includes an area that falls within national prerogatives, the Member States are required to become contracting parties to that agreement in their own right as a matter of law. In areas of shared competence, mixity is generally facultative. Facultative mixity means that the Member States in the Council have a political choice to decide for or against mixity. However, the notion does not suggest that that choice has already been made. Nevertheless, facultative mixity broadens the scope for mixity because the Member States in the Council can bend the choice of procedure to their political preferences for mixity. Indeed, in the past, mixity was used out of principle as soon as an agreement fell partially outside the scope of the EU's exclusive competence, watering down the distinction between mandatory and facultative mixity. In view of the judicial recognition of the element of choice inherent in facultative mixity, the procedure for treaty-making – be that mixed or EU-only – should arguably become more considerate and deliberate on a case-by-case basis. This is particularly the case for trade and investment agreements, where the allocation of external competence between the EU and the Member States is sufficiently clear. As a result, the EU institutions can balance the costs and benefits of using the mixed procedure at the point of designing such agreements and/or when making political choices about the character of 'trade and …' agreements falling within shared competence. Chapter 8 further argues that the TCA is a case in point for the latter, exemplifying that the Council has begun to evaluate the costs of mixity and – at least in special situations – make a choice *beyond mixity* in the facultative scenario for the benefit of procedural effectiveness.

The present chapter has discussed the character of EU agreements in the field of trade and investment. Although the CCP has been an exclusive EU competence ever since its inception in the Treaty of Rome, there have historically been few mandatory

[167] *Antarctic MPAs* (n 151) para 133.
[168] See also Kübek and Van Damme (n 87) 166–67.
[169] See also Chamon and Cremona (n 161).
[170] *Antarctic MPAs* (n 151) paras 128 and 132.

EU-only trade agreements. The majority of trade agreements of the EU were concluded as mixed agreements. The prevalence of mixity resulted from the legal uncertainty about the precise nature of competence for trade in services and IPRs *Opinion 1/94* brought about, as well as the general political preference of the Member States to resort to mixity as soon as an agreement partially fell outside the reach of the CCP. In certain circumstances, 'false mixity' has also proven to be beneficial for the EU and the Member States for procedural or practical reasons. For example, some Member States did not denounce the Conditional Access Convention after the CJEU confirmed the EU's exclusive treaty-making powers because the EU would not have any voting rights within the framework of the Convention without its Member States. Aside from such specific circumstances, the recourse to mixity in the field of trade and investment was overhauled in 2018 with the introduction of the new architecture.[171] Accordingly, the substance of EU trade and investment agreements is adjusted to the scope of the EU's exclusive competence in order to generate mandatory EU-only FTAs. In doing so, the EU will be able to act in a more unified, effective and credible manner on the external economic plane.

As a matter of law, the vast majority of EU trade and investment agreements did not have to be concluded as mixed agreements. During the Nice era, key exceptions were trade agreements covering sensitive commercial service sectors, such as cultural and audiovisual services (Article 133(6)(2) EC). The Schedules of Specific Commitments annexed to the GATS Agreement were a case in point (*Opinion 1/08*). Moreover, it was at the time common practice to 'infect' trade agreements with third pillar political dialogue clauses to render mixity necessary as a matter of law, since the CFSP was formally situated outside the (then) Community. In the post-Lisbon era, trade and investment agreements can no longer be 'infected' with CFSP provisions because the pillar structure was abolished and, as a result, CFSP provisions may be absorbed under a treaty's predominant purpose and subjected to the procedural rules of Article 218 TFEU. This was recently confirmed by the CJEU in *Kazakhstan Cooperation Agreement*. Attempted 'triggers of mixity', ie, minuscular provisions that may be claimed to fall within national prerogatives, nevertheless remain visible in the design of new generation EU trade and investment agreements. *Opinion 2/15* largely silenced such claims over exclusive national trade and investment prerogatives. In particular, the CJEU also rejected Advocate General Sharpston's argument that one aspect of new generation trade and investment agreements, namely the termination of the Member States' BITs, falls within the exclusive competence of the Member States and that mixity was therefore required as a matter of law. In the future, the *ex ante* competence review provided by the CJEU in *Opinion 2/15* will make political and institutional attempts to generate mandatory mixity 'at all costs' significantly more difficult.

Facultative mixity has been – and certainly continues to be – the most contentious technique for making EU agreements. Facultative mixity logically flows from an external reading of Article 2(2) TFEU. If the Council decides to cease exercising shared external competence, the Member States become independent parties to a mixed agreement. Conversely, if the Council decides to exercise shared external competence, the EU concludes the resulting agreement alone. The CJEU's conclusion in *Opinion 2/15*

[171] See further Chapter 7.

that the EUSFTA cannot be approved by the EU alone because it contains areas falling within shared competence caused some doubts about the legality of facultative mixity. However, shortly afterwards, the CJEU corrected its apparent error in *COTIF I* and clarified that the Council generally has political discretion about the choice of treaty-making procedure in areas of shared competence. The CJEU's conclusion in *COTIF I* only concerned foreign non-direct investments. The CJEU did not correct *Opinion 2/15* with regard to ISDS.

The extent to which facultative mixity can be constrained by law is unclear. However, the notion that the political choice inherent in facultative mixity is subject to legal limits is uncontested. The CJEU concluded in *Antarctic MPAs* that mixity may be legally required for reasons relating to international law, regardless of the vertical division of competences set out in the Treaties. In that case, the CJEU found that mixity was required because the EU is not a fully autonomous member of the international agreement and body at issue or relevant agreements forming their context. If this criterion were to be applied analogously to the making of EU investment agreements containing the ICS, it would suggest that mixity is mandatory because the EU is not a fully autonomous member of ICSID, UNCITRAL or the New York Convention. Yet, the precedential value of the *Antarctic MPAs* case is questionable.

Likewise, the EU is arguably legally required to make EU-only agreements in areas of shared competence in certain circumstances. The principle of loyal cooperation set out in Article 4(3) TEU may exceptionally prescribe facultative EU-only action, namely where the exercise of shared external competence by Member States would evidently call into question the unity, consistency, effectiveness and reputation of the EU's external action. Moreover, facultative mixity may be limited in cases where the envisioned external act concerns a single shared competence. Arguably, the joint exercise of a single shared competence by the EU and the Member States is contrary to the wording of Article 2(2) TFEU and has a similar effect to hybrid decision-making. The joint exercise of a single shared competence by the EU and the Member States, that is, the 'de-activation' of the principle of pre-emption inherent in Article 2(2) TFEU, may only exceptionally be possible for overriding legal, political or practical reasons, as was the case, for example, in *Antarctic MPAs*. In view of the persisting institutional and political contestation about facultative mixity, it will be interesting to see whether the CJEU will (be asked to) further demarcate legal procedural limits to the Council's political choices.

3

Allocation of EU Trade and Investment Competence

I. Introduction

In any type of multi-level governance system, the allocation of competence determines the degree of dispersion of authority. In case of the EU, the vertical allocation of competence determines when the EU has the authority to act alone, when the Member States have the authority to act as sovereign states and when the authority to act is shared between the EU and the Member States. As Advocate General Sharpston highlighted:

> Competences are conferred on the Union essentially for the purpose of enabling it to legislate in various areas of policy and economic activity within the territory of the European Union. It is an EU-centric view of the world (rather than a 'Weltanschauung'). It is about striking the desired balance between unifying (supranational) central authority set up under the Treaty and the European Union's constituent, still sovereign, Member States (the 'Herren der Verträge').[1]

When it comes to the EU's external trade and investment policy, the desired balance between unifying and de-centralising treaty-making authority is essentially struck by the interplay of two interrelated developments: first, the scope of the EU's trade and investment competences; and, second, the scope of international economic law and policy.[2] History has shown that the latter tends to evolve more rapidly than the former, leaving the Member States, as drafters of the Treaties, with the task of matching the scope of the EU's external trade powers with their external trade ambitions.[3] The CCP post-Lisbon has been adjusted to reflect the scope of the WTO and now covers trade in goods, services, commercial aspects of IPRs, and FDI (Article 207(1) TFEU). Nevertheless, the comprehensive and deep scope of new generation trade and investment agreements has, in some fields, evolved beyond the reach of the EU's exclusive

[1] Opinion of Advocate General Sharpston, Opinion 2/15, *FTA with Singapore*, EU:C:2016:992, para 57. See further P Craig, 'Competence: Clarity, Conferral, Containment and Consideration' (2004) 29 *European Law Review* 323; or A von Bogdandy and J Bast, 'The Federal Order of Competences' in A von Bogdandy and J Bast (eds), *Principles of European Constitutional Law*, 2nd edn (Hart, CH Beck, Nomos, 2009) 275.

[2] See also G Kübek, 'The European Union's External Trade and Investment Policy Post-Lisbon: Competence, Procedure and Scope of Action' in M Andenas et al (eds), *EU External Action in International Economic Law: Recent Trends and Developments* (TMC Asser Press, 2020) 93.

[3] *cf* Figure 1.1 in Chapter 1.

CCP powers post-Lisbon, allowing for Member State participation in an otherwise EU-only policy domain.[4] The desired balance between supranational and national sovereign authority in the EU's external trade policy therefore remains contentious and subject to individual institutional or national preferences.

Chapter 1 outlined that clarity about the post-Lisbon scope of the EU's exclusive trade powers has turned mixity into a substantive treaty design choice. Chapter 2 explained the key procedural options, namely (facultative) EU-only treaty-making or (facultative) mixity, that now feed into the substantive design of new generation EU trade and investment agreements. This chapter, in turn, analyses the substantive reach and limits of EU competence in the field of trade and investment. It illustrates which parts of EU trade and investment agreements can be concluded by the EU alone and which parts (may) trigger mixity. In doing so, it explains to what extent the choice between EU-only and mixity in the field of trade and investment has become a substantive design choice and what that choice precisely entails.

The chapter is structured as follows. As a background for discussion and for readers that are not specialists in EU (external relations) law, section II provides a brief overview of the instruments used for determining the correct choice of legal basis and the nature of EU external competence. Section III highlights the reach of the EU's exclusive external competence over trade and investment, taking particular account of the methods used by the CJEU for deriving (implied) exclusive EU competence in its post-Lisbon case law. Section IV outlines the limits of the EU's exclusive competence over investment matters. Section V concludes.

II. Categorising and Delimitating Trade and Investment Competence

As was mentioned in the previous chapters, the CCP has been an exclusive competence of the EU since its inception by the Treaty of Rome. Exclusivity in the field of external trade is a necessary corollary of the creation of the (then) Community as a customs union (section II.A). Today, the objectives of the CCP (Articles 205 and 206 TFEU) and its scope (Article 207 TFEU) are expressly codified in EU primary law (section II.B). Provided that an international agreement fully falls within the exclusive scope of Article 207 TFEU, it must be concluded by the EU alone. To determine whether Article 207 TFEU qualifies as the main substantive legal basis of an agreement, the CJEU uses the so-called centre of gravity test (section II.C), which has been modified for the CCP (section II.D). Should the centre of gravity test reveal that the agreement in question falls (partially) within shared competence, it is also relevant to determine whether exclusive EU competence can nevertheless be implied. The most important test in this regard is the so-called ERTA test (section II.E).

[4] *cf* Chapter 1, section III. For a concise overview of the scope of new generation EU trade and investment agreements, see F Hoffmeister, 'The EU's Trade and Investment Agreements: European Convergence with World Trade Law?' in E Fahey (ed), *Framing Convergence with the Global Legal Order* (Hart Publishing, 2020) 25.

A. The Express Exclusive Nature of the CCP

The Treaty of Rome did not explicitly specify the nature of the Community's competence. However, in *Opinion 1/75*, the CJEU confirmed that only the Community may act in the field of the CCP and that the Member States must generally refrain from acting in their own right.[5] In doing so, the CJEU established the concept of external exclusivity. The exclusive nature of the CCP is now enshrined in Article 3(1)(e) TFEU. The rationale for exclusivity that emerged from the CJEU's reasoning is the coherent and effective operation of the EU's institutional framework in its external commercial relations. Internally, the EU and the Member States may share the competence for improving the functioning of the single market as potential conflicts can be addressed through a conflict resolution mechanism based on pre-emption and thus the primacy of EU law. Conversely, distortions in the sphere of the CCP may only be eliminated by 'strict uniformity' of EU action.[6] As a result, the 'freedom to which the Member States could lay claim by invoking a concurrent power, so as to ensure that their interests were separately satisfied in external relations' is 'incompatible' with the very conception of a *common* commercial policy.[7]

Indeed, the construction of a common EU market without internal frontiers such as customs or rules of origins coupled with a common external tariff logically excludes the making of individual trade agreements by Member States. Pursuant to Articles XXIV:5 and XXIV:8 GATT, the European Economic Community could have either been established as a customs union or as a free trade area.[8] The founding Member States chose the former option, which necessitated the establishment of a common commercial policy to make trade agreements with third states.[9] The exclusive nature of the CCP is thus an inevitable consequence of the Community's creation as a customs union under the pre-existing rules of the GATT 1947.[10] In this respect, the (now) EU differs from

[5] Opinion 1/75, *Local Cost Standard*, EU:C:1975:145, 1364. See further especially M Cremona, 'EU External Competence: Rationales for Exclusivity' in S Garben and I Govaere (eds), *The Division of Competences Between the EU and the Member States: Reflections on the Past, the Present and the Future* (Hart Publishing, 2017) 133.

[6] Opinion 1/75 (n 5) 1364. Cremona noted that the CJEU has cautioned the use of 'uniformity' as a justification for exclusivity in its later case law. See M Cremona, 'EU External Relations: Unity and Conferral of Powers' in L Azoulai (ed), *The Question of Competence in the European Union* (Oxford University Press, 2014) 65. See also G De Baere, *Constitutional Principles of EU External Relations* (Oxford University Press, 2008) 38 et seq.

[7] Opinion 1/75 (n 5) 1364.

[8] See further C Herrmann and T Streinz, 'Die EU als Mitglied der WTO' in A von Arnauld and M Bungenberg (eds), *Europäische Außenbeziehungen*, Enzyklopädie Europarecht, vol 12, 2nd edn (Nomos, 2022) 853, 876 et seq; and T Cottier, 'Towards a Common External Economic Policy of the European Union' in M Bungenberg and C Herrmann (eds), *Common Commercial Policy after Lisbon*, Special Issue, *European Yearbook of International Economic Law* (Springer, 2013) 3. On the impact of the WTO on the design of the EEC, see further G de Búrca and J Scott, 'The Impact of the WTO on EU Decision-Making' in G de Búrca and J Scott (eds), *The EU and the WTO: Legal and Constitutional Issues* (Hart Publishing, 2001) 2; and J Larik, 'Much More Than Trade: The Common Commercial Policy in a Global Context' in MD Evans and P Koutrakos (eds), *Beyond the Established Legal Orders: Policy Interconnections Between the EU and the Rest of the World* (Hart Publishing, 2011) 13.

[9] Case C-41/76, *Donckerwolke*, EU:C:1976:182, para 25. See further P Eeckhout, 'Linking Internal and External Trade in a Perfect Customs Union: *Donderwolcke*' in G Butler and RA Wessel (eds), *EU External Relations Law: The Cases in Context* (Hart Publishing, 2022) 90.

[10] That this is not only a theoretical construction may be exemplified by the well-known trade conflict stories on banana imports or Japanese cars. See P Eeckhout, *EU External Relations Law*, 2nd edn (Oxford University Press, 2011) 443 et seq.

other free trade areas, such as the European Free Trade Area (EFTA), the European Economic Area (EEA) or the North Atlantic free trade area (the United States-Mexico-Canada Agreement (USMCA), formerly the North American Free Trade Agreement (NAFTA)), where the members maintain their individual trade policy because there is no common external tariff.

B. The Express Scope and Objectives of the CCP

Today, the CCP is situated in Title II of Part V of the TFEU on '[t]he Union's external action'. Article 205 TFEU firmly embeds the CCP in the overall structure of the EU's external action. Accordingly, EU action taken under Title II of Part V of the TFEU 'shall be guided by the principles, pursue the objectives and be conducted in accordance with the general provisions laid down in Chapter 1 of Title V of the Treaty on European Union'. Article 205 TFEU thus links the substantive treaty provisions on EU trade policy to the EU's external relations objectives[11] contained in Articles 3(5) and 21 TEU, which include amongst others peace and security,[12] human rights and democracy,[13] the strict observance of international law and the promotion of good global governance,[14] the eradication of poverty,[15] environmental and sustainable development[16] and free and fair trade.[17] The CCP itself is composed of two provisions: Article 206 TFEU, which sets out the objectives of the CCP, and Article 207 TFEU, which defines the CCP's material scope, instruments and procedural rules.

Article 206 stipulates that 'the Union shall contribute, in the common interest, to the harmonious development of world trade, the progressive abolition of restrictions on international trade and on foreign direct investment, and the lowering of customs and other barriers'. In contrast to its predecessors ('the *Member States* aim to contribute to'), the Lisbon Treaty made the pursuit of the goals stipulated in Article 206 TFEU *obligatory* for the *Union* ('*shall* contribute to').[18] Read together with Article 205 TFEU, the provision underlines that although the CCP externally follows the internal 'principle of an open market economy with free competition',[19] it is not about trade liberalisation alone. Trade liberalisation under the CCP has to be achieved gradually, and the effects of trade liberalisation must be balanced against and within the overall system of the

[11] See further J Larik, *Foreign Policy Objectives in European Constitutional Law* (Oxford University Press, 2016); JP Terhechte, *Europäische Verfassungsstudien* (Nomos, 2020) 261 et seq; M Cremona, 'Values in EU Foreign Policy' in M Evans and P Koutrakos (eds), *Beyond the Established Legal Orders: Policy Interconnections between the EU and the Rest of the World* (Hart Publishing, 2011) 275; Y Kaspiarovich and RA Wessel, 'The Role of Values in EU External Relations: A Legal Assessment of the EU as a "Good" Global Actor' in E Fahey and I Mancini (eds), *The EU as a Good Global Actor* (Edward Elgar, 2021) 92; and E Neframi, 'Vertical Division of Competences and the Objectives of the European Union's External Action' in M Cremona and A Thies (eds), *The European Court of Justice and External Relations Law* (Hart Publishing, 2014) 73.

[12] Articles 3(5) and 21(a), (c) TEU.

[13] ibid Articles 3(5) and 21(b).

[14] ibid Articles 3(5) and 21(c), (h).

[15] ibid Articles 3(5) and 21(d).

[16] ibid Articles 3(5), 11 and 21(d), (f).

[17] ibid Articles 3(5) and 21(e).

[18] T Cottier and L Trinberg, 'Artikel 206 AEUV' in H von der Groeben et al (eds), *Europäisches Unionsrecht: EUV, AEUV, GRC*, 7th edn (Nomos, 2015) para 9.

[19] Articles 119(1), (2), 120, and 127(1) TFEU.

EU's external relations goals and actions. According to settled case law, 'the objective of contributing to the progressive abolition of restrictions on international trade cannot compel the institutions to liberalise imports from non-member countries where to do so would be contrary to the interest of the [Union]'.[20]

The scope of the CCP is set out in Article 207(1) TFEU. Although that paragraph does not provide a general definition of 'commercial policy', it defines the four main components of the CCP: trade in goods, services, commercial aspects of IPRs, and FDI. The notion of 'trade in goods' comprises all types of goods, also including agricultural goods, energy carriers, such as gas or natural oil,[21] and dual-use goods.[22] However, truly military goods are excluded from the scope of the CCP.[23] The notion of 'trade in services' comprises the four modes of supply of services[24] as classified in Article I:2 GATS.[25] Pursuant to Article 207(5) TFEU, transport services are carved out from the CCP. Agreements covering transport services therefore require recourse to additional legal bases (Articles 91 and 100 TFEU). Moreover, the making of trade agreements covering cultural and audiovisual services (Article 207(4)(a) TFEU) or social, education and health services (Article 207(4)(b) TFEU) may require unanimity in the Council.[26] The notion of 'commercial aspects of intellectual property rights' draws closely on the Title of the Agreement on Trade-Related Aspects of Intellectual Property Rights, implying that scope of the CCP encompasses the TRIPS Agreement in its entirety.[27]

The integration of FDI into the scope of the CCP was a novelty of the Lisbon Treaty.[28] Article 207(1) TFEU refers specifically to 'foreign direct investment' and thus

[20] eg, Case C-150/94, *United Kingdom v Council of the European Union*, EU:C:1998:547, para 67. See further, eg, Cottier and Trinberg (n 18) 8; M Hahn, 'Artikel 207 AEUV' in C Calliess and M Ruffert (eds), *EUV/AEUV: Das Verfassungsrecht der Europäischen Union mit Europäischer Grundrechtecharta, Kommentar*, 6th edn (CH Beck, 2022) para 6.

[21] Without prejudice to Article 4(2)(i) and 194 TFEU. See further Hahn (n 20) para 19; and M Hahn, 'Auswärtige Annexkompetenzen interner Politiken' in A von Arnauld and M Bungenberg (eds), *Europäische Außenbeziehungen*, Enzyklopädie Europarecht, vol 12, 2nd edn (Nomos, 2020) 1031, 1079.

[22] Opinion 1/94, *WTO Agreements*, EU:C:1994:384, para 27. See further, eg, M Nettesheim, 'Artikel 207 AEUV' in R Streinz (ed), *EUV/AEUV: Vertrag über die Europäische Union, Vertrag über die Arbeitsweise der Europäischen Union, Charta der Grundrechte der Europäischen Union*, 3rd edn (CH Beck, 2018) para 12.

[23] Article 346(1)(b) second indent TFEU.

[24] The four modes of supply defined in Article 1:2 GATS are: the supply of a service from the territory of one party into the territory of another party ('cross border trade' (mode 1)), the supply of a service in the territory of one party to the consumer of another party ('consumption abroad' (mode 2)), the supply of a service by a service provider of one party through commercial presence in the territory of another party ('commercial presence' (mode 3)) and the supply of a service by a service provider of one party through presence of natural persons of that party in the territory of another party ('presence of natural persons' (mode 4)).

[25] Opinion 1/08, *GATS Schedules of Commitments*, EU:C:2009:739, paras 4, 118–19. See also Opinion 2/15, *FTA with Singapore*, EU:C:2017:376, paras 54–55.

[26] See further Chapter 4, sections 4.3.3 and 4.3.4.

[27] As noted and confirmed by the Court in Case C-414/11, *Daiichi Sankyo*, EU:C:2013:520, para 55. See further below, section III.A.

[28] See further, eg, A Dimopoulos, *EU Foreign Investment Law* (Oxford University Press, 2011); C Herrmann, 'Die Zukunft der mitgliedstaatlichen Investitionspolitik nach dem Vertrag von Lissabon' (2010) 21 *Europäische Zeitschrift für Wirtschaftsrecht* 207; J Wouters et al, 'The European Union's External Relations after the Lisbon Treaty' in S Griller and J Ziller (eds), *The Lisbon Treaty: EU Constitutionalism without a Constitutional Treaty?* (Springer, 2008) 143, 171–72.

not to all types of foreign investments (ie, direct and non-direct foreign investments). The term 'FDI' is not further defined in the FEU Treaty. Article 64(1)–(2) TFEU on the free movement of capital between Member States and third countries also refers to 'direct investment', suggesting that the term must be interpreted alike for both provisions.[29] In that context, the CJEU has acknowledged the indicative value of the nomenclature of movements of capital set out in Annex I to Council Directive 88/361/EEC.[30] Accordingly, direct investments are 'investments of all kinds by natural persons or commercial, industrial or financial undertakings, and which serve to establish or to maintain lasting and direct links between the person providing the capital and the entrepreneur to whom or the undertaking to which the capital is made available in order to carry on an economic activity'. Conversely, foreign non-direct investments 'may, inter alia, take place in the form of the acquisition of company securities with the intention of making a financial investment without any intention to influence the management and control of the undertaking ("portfolio" investments).'[31] Foreign non-direct investments involve capital movements or payments and therefore generally fall within the scope of Article 63 TFEU.

C. The General Centre of Gravity Test

The previous chapter explained that agreements falling within the scope of the CCP must be concluded by the EU alone as a matter of law (mandatory EU-only agreements).[32] To put it in slightly more technical terms, if Article 207 TFEU qualifies as the only substantive legal basis of an EU trade and investment agreement, that agreement must be concluded under the EU-only procedure. By inference, if an EU trade and investment agreement requires recourse to other, non-exclusive legal bases, mixity becomes facultative or mandatory. Therefore, as the CJEU recalled in *Opinion 1/08*, the nature of a competence, whether exclusive or not, and the choice of legal basis 'are two questions which are closely linked': the answer to the former depends on the choice of the latter.[33]

The choice of legal basis of an EU act is determined by the so-called centre of gravity test.[34] The centre of gravity test is a judge-made test, which seeks to ensure that

[29] See, eg, Nettesheim (n 22) para 21.

[30] Council Directive 88/361/EEC of 24 June 1988 for the implementation of Article 67 of the Treaty [1988] OJ L178/5. See further Case C-446/04, *Test Claimants in the FII Group Litigation*, EU:C:2006:774, paras 181–82; Case C-326/07, *Commission v Italy*, EU:C:2009:193, para 35; and Case C-464/14, *SECIL*, EU:C:2016:896, paras 75–76.

[31] Opinion 2/15 (n 25) para 227. See also Joined Cases C-282/04 and C-283/04, *Commission v The Netherlands*, EU:C:2006:608, para 19; Case C–171/08, *Commission v Portugal*, EU:C:2010:412, para 49; Case C-81/09, *Idryma Typou*, EU:C:2010:622, para 4; and Case C-212/09, *Commission v Portugal*, EU:C:2011:717, para 47.

[32] See further Chapter 2, section II.

[33] Opinion 1/08 (n 25) para 111. See also Case C-370/07, *CITES*, EU:C:2009:590, paras 47–49.

[34] In the context of EU external relations, see also S Adam, 'The Legal Basis of International Agreements of the European Union in the Post-Lisbon Era' in Inge Govaere et al (eds), *The European Union in the World: Essays in Honour of Professor Marc Maresceau* (Brill/Nijhoff, 2014) 65; and G Butler, 'Pinpointing the Appropriate Legal Basis for External Action' (2015) 6 *European Journal of Risk Regulation* 323.

the choice of legal basis does 'not simply depend on an institution's conviction', but is based 'on objective factors amenable to judicial review'.[35] Accordingly:

> If examination of a [Union] measure reveals that it pursues a twofold purpose or that it has a twofold component and if one of those is identifiable as the main or predominant purpose or component, whereas the other is merely incidental, the act must be based on a single legal basis, namely that required by the main or predominant purpose or component.[36]

In other words, the 'incidental' purpose or component of an EU measure may be absorbed under the legal basis of the 'predominant' purpose (or aim) or component of that measure. The absorption is not general; it occurs on a case-by-case basis for a specific instrument. The legal basis of other, similar EU legal acts is irrelevant. The legal basis of each EU act must be determined solely on the basis of that act's own aim and content.[37] Advocate General Wahl underlined that 'the interpreter should strive to identify, where possible, only one or, failing that, the absolute minimum number of legal bases'.[38] However, this statement also highlights that the recourse to a single legal basis may not always be possible in practice. Indeed, the CJEU also accounted for the possibility of using multiple legal bases, provided that they are not procedurally incompatible:[39]

> Exceptionally, if on the other hand it is established that the act simultaneously pursues a number of objectives or has several components that are indissociably linked, without one being secondary and indirect in relation to the other, such an act will have to be founded on the various corresponding legal bases.[40]

In order to determine which substantive element of an envisaged measure is the 'predominant purpose or component' and which one is merely 'incidental', the CJEU has regard to the *context*, *aim* and *content* pursued by that measure.[41]

The *context* in which the measure is adopted is specifically relevant for international agreements that do not entail a statement of intent such as a preamble. Indeed, '[i]n the absence of an express statement of that kind', the CJEU generally assesses the agreement at issue 'in the light of the international agreements forming its context'.[42] The analysis of the context of an agreement may therefore be viewed as a prelude or, at times, additional

[35] See, eg, Case 45/86, *Commission v Council*, EU:C:1987:163, para 11; Case C-411/06, *Shipments of Waste*, EU:C:2009:518, para 45; Case C–155/07, *Parliament v Council*, EU:C:2008:605, para 34.

[36] See, eg, *Shipments of Waste* (n 35) paras 46–47; Case C-211/01, *Commission v Council*, EU:C:2003:452, paras 38–39; and Case C-178/03, *Commission v Parliament and Council*, EU:C:2006:4, paras 41–42.

[37] Case C-81/13, *United Kingdom v Council*, EU:C:2014:2449, para 36.

[38] Opinion of Advocate General Wahl, Opinion 3/15, *Marrakesh Treaty*, EU:C:2016:657, para 34.

[39] This is generally the case for legal acts on the borderline between the CFSP and TFEU external relations. See especially Case C-300/89, *Titanium Dioxide*, EU:C:1991:244, paras 17 et seq. Notably, Article 218 TFEU can be used as an overarching procedure for 'mixed' CFSP and TFEU acts. See Case C-244/17, *Kazakhstan Cooperation Agreement*, EU:C:2018:662, paras 44 et seq.

[40] See, eg, *Shipments of Waste* (n 35) para 47; *Commission v Council* (n 36) para 40; and *Commission v Parliament and Council* (n 36) para 43. For a recent example, see Opinion 1/15, *EU-Canada PNR*, EU:C:2017:592, para 94.

[41] See, eg, Joined Cases C-626/15 and C-659/16, *Antarctica Treaty*, EU:C:2018:925, para 76.

[42] Case C-389/15, *Revised Lisbon Agreement*, EU:C:2017:798, para 53. For an example, see *United Kingdom v Council* (n 37) paras 60 et seq; or Opinion 2/00, *Cartagena Protocol*, EU:C:2001:664, paras 24–28. The CJEU sometimes examines the context criteria in addition to and in light of the agreement's stated aims. See, eg, Opinion 1/91, *EEA I*, EU:C:1991:490, para 19.

information before assessing its aim and the content. To determine the *aim* of a measure, the CJEU generally pursues a textual analysis with a view to distilling its 'ends' (the 'why' question). In doing so, it identifies whether the measure in question indeed envisages two or more – potentially interlinked – ends or whether it predominantly intends to govern a single material issue.[43] In practice, the CJEU focuses on the preamble of a measure or any other express statements of intent.[44] Scholars have convincingly argued that the CJEU overly relied on the 'aims test' in past practice.[45] More reliability could be generated by focusing on the analysis of the *content* of the EU act at issue. This 'content test' concerns the substantive provisions of the instrument in question (the 'what' question). The link between aim and content is also important: does the substantive content of the relevant measure effectuates one or several of the pre-identified aims? Methodologically, the CJEU proceeds by analysing the specific provisions contained in the instrument at hand and infers their practical effects.[46] In addition to that qualitative effort, the CJEU sometimes uses a quantitative approach: it counts the number of provisions relating to one aim of a treaty and contrasts them with the number of provisions relating to a conflicting aim of that treaty.[47]

The CJEU's complex methodology for choosing the correct legal basis generated scholarly criticism.[48] The 'context, aim, and content' criteria developed by the CJEU were viewed as being too broad and unspecific to fully rule out institutional bias. The Council acknowledged that:

> [S]ince the legal basis of an EU act determines the decision-making procedure that applies, it necessarily affects the balance of powers between the institutions as well. Disputes concerning the applicable legal basis therefore remain, by their very nature, of very great political significance and are potentially highly contentious.[49]

As will be further shown below, the recent conflicts about the vertical attribution of power in the field of trade and investment are indicative of just how politically charged and legally complex the choice of correct legal basis can become. Nevertheless, the recent case law also shows that the CJEU's methodological approach to the choice of legal basis has become more consistent. In its post-Lisbon case law on the EU's trade and investment policy, the CJEU applied its CCP-specific centre of gravity test like a mantra (see also below),[50] focusing more on an analytical and, at times, teleological interpretation

[43] See, eg, Case C-281/01, *Energy Star Agreement*, EU:C:2002:761, para 39.

[44] See especially *Shipments of Waste* (n 35) paras 50–54.

[45] See, eg, M Klamert, 'Conflicts of Legal Basis: No Legality and No Basis But a Bright Future under the Lisbon Treaty?' (2010) 35 *European Law Review* 497, 501 et seq.

[46] See, eg, Case C-94/03, *Rotterdam Convention*, EU:C:2006:2, paras 37 et seq; Opinion 3/15, *Marrakesh Treaty*, EU:C:2017:114, paras 71 et seq.

[47] See, eg, Opinion 2/00 (n 42) para 33; *Kazakhstan Cooperation Agreement* (n 39) paras 44 et seq.

[48] N Emiliou, 'Opening Pandora's Box: The Legal Basis of Community Measures before the Court of Justice' (1994) 19 *European Law Review* 488, 499; P Koutrakos, 'Legal Basis and Delimitation of Competences in EU External Relations' in M Cremona (ed), *EU Foreign Relations Law: Constitutional Fundamentals* (Hart Publishing, 2008) 171; D Kleimann, 'Reading *Opinion 2/15*: Standards of Analysis, the Court's Discretion, and the Legal View of the Advocate General', *EUI Working Paper RSCAS 2017/23*.

[49] Case C-350/12 P, *Council v Sophie in 't Veld*, EU:C:2014:2039, para 29. See further P Leino, 'The Politics of Efficient Compromise in the Adoption of EU Legal Acts' in M Cremona and C Kilpatrick (eds), *EU Legal Acts: Challenges and Transformations* (Oxford University Press, 2018) 30, 36.

[50] See, eg, Opinion 3/15 (n 46), paras 71 et seq, paras 91 et seq; Opinion 2/15 (n 25), eg, paras 88 et seq. (on FDI), paras 113 et seq (on IPRs), paras 136 et seq (on competition) or paras 149 et seq (on trade and sustainable development); and *Revised Lisbon Agreement* (n 42) paras 66 et seq.

of a treaty's content in addition to a textual analysis of its stated aims, rather than purely or predominantly relying on the latter.[51] However, given the political, substantive and procedural implications of the choice of legal basis, that choice will remain subject to institutional bias and will continue to generate new case law.

D. The CCP-Specific Centre of Gravity Test

Due to its exclusive nature, the general requirement to use QMV, as well as the strong role of the Commission, the CCP has been one of the most contentious policy areas with regard to legal basis conflicts, including before the CJEU. In *Opinion 1/78*, the CJEU provided a dynamic conception of the CCP, equipping it with the ability to adapt to the growing international governance of economic policy.[52] Yet, the principle of conferral prohibits an 'endless' dynamic conception of the reach of the CCP that would effectively render all other competence-conferring Treaty provisions nugatory.

In light of the political and institutional sensitivity of the matter, and perhaps with the aim of strengthening the objectivity and reliability of its general approach, the CJEU developed an adapted version of the centre of gravity test in the sphere of the CCP. Building on the general centre of gravity test and its distinction between 'predominant' and 'incidental' purposes or components, the CCP-specific test is used to clarify whether a measure's 'predominant purpose' is indeed the CCP. The origin of the 'CCP-specific' test dates back to *Opinion 1/94*, although, at the time, the CJEU did not apply it consistently throughout the Opinion.[53] First mentioned as an analytical formula to establish the CCP as the 'centre of gravity' of the EC-Hungary Agreement on wines in *ERSA*,[54] the CCP-specific test has become the standard method for solving competence disputes about international trade matters post-Lisbon. Accordingly:

> It is settled case law that the mere fact that an act of the European Union is liable to have implications for international trade is not enough for it to be concluded that the act must be classified as falling within the common commercial policy. On the other hand, a European Union act falls within the common commercial policy if it relates specifically to international trade in that it is essentially intended to promote, facilitate or govern trade and has direct and immediate effects on trade.[55]

In other words, the CCP is the 'predominant purpose' of a measure if it interrelates specifically with international trade. Such a specific relationship to trade is – as for the general centre of gravity test – ascertained or denied by establishing, first, the intent of the measure (the aim, which may also be inferred through the measure's context) and, second, its direct and immediate effects in practice (the content). The logic and approach of the original centre of gravity test has therefore been maintained for

[51] See further sections II.D, III.B and III.C.

[52] Opinion 1/78, *International Agreement on Rubber*, EU:C:1979:224, para 44.

[53] The use of the CCP-specific test in *Opinion 1/94* was confined to the matter of IPRs. See Opinion 1/94 (n 22) para 57. The limited use of the test in selected areas continued in Opinion 2/00 (n 42) para 40; and *Energy Star Agreement* (n 43) paras 40–41.

[54] Case C-347/03, *ERSA*, EU:C:2005:285, para 75.

[55] See, eg, *Daiichi Sankyo* (n 27) para 51.

the CCP. Yet, the CCP-specific test further qualifies the 'context, aim, and content' criteria by predetermining precisely what aim a CCP-directed measure needs to intend (ie, the promotion, facilitation or governance of trade) and what its substantive content must effectuate in practice (ie, it must effect trade directly and immediately). In addition, the CCP-specific test qualifies the attributes of a measure that relates merely indirectly or incidentally to trade (ie, it is liable to have merely 'implications' on trade, instead of having 'direct and immediate effects').

E. Implied Exclusivity and the ERTA Doctrine

If the centre of gravity test reveals that a commercial agreement (partially) falls outside the CCP and requires (additional) recourse to shared competence-conferring Treaty provisions, it is also relevant to determine whether exclusivity can nonetheless be implied. Pursuant to Article 3(2) TFEU, the EU has not only exclusive competence where the Treaties so provide, but also for:

> [T]he conclusion of an international agreement when its conclusion is provided for in a legislative act of the Union or is necessary to enable the Union to exercise its internal competence, or in so far as its conclusion may affect common rules or alter their scope.

In contrast to express exclusive competences, these implied exclusive competences are actually shared competences, and arguably remain so.[56] It is the external exercise of shared competences by the Member States that is being pre-empted; their internal nature as such is not reversed. As will be shown below, despite the close resemblance between Articles 3(2) (exclusivity of external competence) and 216(1) TFEU (existence of external competence), the former provision does not effectuate that all implied external competences are automatically exclusive.[57]

In practice, implied exclusive competences result most frequently from an application of the third indent of Article 3(2) TFEU, which codifies the so-called ERTA doctrine.[58] In essence, the ERTA doctrine maintains that 'where common rules have

[56] The pre-emptive effect of implied exclusivity appears to be generally accepted. See, for example, Cremona (n 6) 69; Eeckhout (n 10) 626 et seq; G De Baere, *Constitutional Principles of EU External Relations* (Oxford University Press, 2008) 43 et seq; D O'Keeffe, 'Exclusive, Concurrent and Shared Competence' in C Hillion and P Koutrakos (eds), *Mixed Agreements Revisited: The EU and its Member States in the World* (Hart Publishing, 2010) 179, 192 et seq. *Contra*, making an explicit distinction between pre-emption (blocking effect) and Article 3(2) TFEU (exclusivity), see CWA Timmermans, 'ECJ Doctrines on Competence' in Azoulai (n 6) 155, 162 et seq.

[57] See further section IV.A.

[58] Case 22/70, *ERTA*, EU:C:1971:32. On implied powers, see also Joined Cases 3, 4 and 6/76, *Kramer*, EU:C:1976:114, 17 et seq, 30 et seq; Opinion 1/76, *Inland Waterways*, EU:C:1977:63; and Opinion 1/94 (n 22). See further M Cremona, 'A Constitutional Basis for Effective EU External Action? An Assessment of the Provisions on EU External Action in the Constitutional Treaty' (2006) 30 *EUI Working Paper Law*; Eeckhout (n 10) 71 et seq; A Dashwood and J Heliskoski, 'The Classic Authorities Revisited' in A Dashwood and C Hillion (eds), *The General Law of EC External Relations* (Sweet & Maxwell, 2000) 3; J Temple Lang, 'The ERTA Judgement and the Court's Case Law on Competence and Conflict' (1986) 6 *Yearbook of European Law* 183; P Koutrakos, *EU International Relations Law*, 2nd edn (Hart Publishing, 2015) 77 et seq; T Tridimas and P Eeckhout, 'The External Competence of the Community and the Case-Law of the Court of Justice: Principle versus Pragmatism' (1994) 14 *Yearbook of European Law* 143; A Ott, 'EU External Competence' in J Larik and RA Wessel (eds), *EU External Relations Law*, 2nd edn (Hart Publishing, 2020) 61, 63 et seq; T Verellen,

been adopted, the Member States no longer have the right, acting individually or collectively, to undertake obligations with non-member countries which affect those rules'.[59]

The resulting ERTA test has two tiers, which are applied cumulatively.[60] Under the first-tier ERTA test, the CJEU conducts a comprehensive and detailed analysis of the agreement at issue and common EU rules, with a view to determining if international and EU rules materially *overlap to a large extent*[61] (the 'area largely covered' criterion). The envisaged agreement and the EU law in force must not coincide fully, as the CJEU considers the nature and content as well as the future development of the EU's legal framework.[62] Legislative acts laying down minimum standards are per se insufficiently detailed to cover an international agreement to a large extent.[63] Moreover, as will be further explained below, the CJEU confirmed that the term 'common rules' only relates to secondary legislation and does not comprise EU primary law.[64]

Provided that the international agreement at issue largely overlaps with common rules, the CJEU will move on to the second-tier ERTA test and determine whether the conclusion of the envisioned international agreement would *affect or alter* the 'uniform and consistent application' of common rules and 'the proper functioning of the system which they establish in order to preserve the full effectiveness of [Union] law' (the 'alter or affect' criterion).[65] It is not necessary to show a contradiction between international and EU rules – in other words, adverse effects of the former on the latter.[66] Evidence of a potential effect of an international agreement on the meaning, scope and effectiveness of EU secondary law is sufficient to that effect.[67] However, if such potential effects could have been forestalled by concerted EU action, they cannot be considered as 'affecting'

'The ERTA Doctrine in the Post-Lisbon Era: Note under Judgment in *Commission v Council* (C-114/12) and Opinion 1/13' (2015) 21 *Columbia Journal of European Law* 383; M Chamon, 'Implied Exclusive Powers in the ECJ's Post-Lisbon Jurisprudence: The Continued Development of the ERTA Doctrine' (2018) 55 *Common Market Law Review* 1101. On the transformative effect of implied EU powers, see JHH Weiler, 'The Transformation of Europe' (1991) 100 *Yale Law Journal* 2405, 2415.

[59] Opinion 1/03, *Lugano Convention*, EU:C:2006:81, para 116. See also *ERTA* (n 58) paras 17, 20–21; Opinion 2/91, *ILO Convention No 170*, EU:C:1993:106, para 11; Case C-467/98, *Commission v Denmark*, EU:C:2002:625, para 111.

[60] Article 3(2)(3) TFEU provides only an incomplete codification of the CJEU's pre-Lisbon ERTA case law because it merely codifies the second tier of the ERTA test. Despite that incomplete codification, the CJEU continues to apply the original ERTA test post-Lisbon. For a critical view, see R Schütze, 'Lisbon and the Federal Order of Competences: A Prospective Analysis' (2008) 33 *European Law Review* 709, 714.

[61] See, eg, Opinion 2/91 (n 59) paras 25–26; Case C-239/03, *Commission v France*, EU:C:2004:598, paras 29–31; Case C-240/09, *Lesoochranárske zoskupenie*, EU:C:2011:125, para 36. The Court's analysis may include the examination of various EU legal instruments – to that extent, see Case C-114/12, *Neighbouring Rights*, EU:C:2014:2151, paras 81–82.

[62] See, eg, Opinion 1/13, *The Hague Convention on Child Abduction*, EU:C:2014:2303, para 74; and Case C-66/13, *Green Network*, EU:C:2014:2399, para 33.

[63] Opinion 2/91 (n 59) paras 21 et seq. See also Case C-459/03, *MOX Plant*, EU:C:2006:345, paras 102–05; and, most recently, Opinion 3/15 (n 46) paras 120–121.

[64] Opinion 2/15 (n 25) paras 230 et seq.

[65] See, eg, Opinion 1/13 (n 62) para 74; or Opinion 1/03 (n 59) para 128.

[66] eg, Opinion 2/91 (n 59) paras 25–26; *Commission v Denmark* (n 59) para 82; *Neighbouring Rights* (n 61) para 71.

[67] Opinion 1/13 (n 62) para 85. See further A Arena, 'Exercise of EU Competences and Pre-emption of Member States' Powers in the Internal and the External Sphere: Towards "Grand Unification"?' (2016) 35 *Yearbook of European Law* 28.

EU law in and of themselves. In such situations, the lack of common rules may serve as an indication that the field is not largely covered.[68]

In sum, the EU's power to conclude a trade and investment agreement alone depends on whether: (1) Article 207(1) TFEU qualifies as a centre of gravity of that agreement; and (2) an area falling outside the CCP's centre of gravity can be turned into an implied exclusive competence by the ERTA doctrine. The reach of the EU's express and implied exclusive competences – in contrast to shared competences – therefore stands at the centre of the wider debate about the character (EU-only versus mixity) of EU trade and investment agreements.

III. The Reach of EU Exclusivity Post-Lisbon

The Lisbon Treaty placed trade in services, commercial aspects of IPRs, and FDI on the same exclusive footing as trade in goods. Yet, as mentioned in the introduction, the EU's external trade ambitions, as reflected in its new generation trade and investment agreements, soon exceeded the express scope of the CCP. Questions about the post-Lisbon scope of the CCP therefore not only concerned the wording and definition of Article 207(1) TFEU. A recurring question, including before the CJEU, has been whether trade-related aspects governed by EU trade and investment agreements, such as competition policy, trade and sustainable development, or foreign non-direct investments, can either be subsumed under the CCP's 'centre of gravity' or be made subsequently exclusive by means of the ERTA doctrine. It was arguably the CJEU's broad interpretation of the CCP's centre of gravity (sections III.A, III.B and III.C) as well as its more lenient application of the ERTA-test (sections III.D and III.E) that facilitated the *move beyond mixity* in the field of trade post-Lisbon.

A. International Trade as a Centre of Gravity

As was explained above, the CCP-specific 'centre of gravity test' requires the establishment of specific links to *international* trade in order for a measure to fall within the scope of Article 207(1) TFEU.[69] However, international trade is conceptualised from an EU perspective: it is not about what is regarded as trade or investment policy in international relations (and is therefore covered by trade and investment agreements between

[68] See Opinion 1/94 (n 22) para 79. See further *Commission v Denmark* (n 59) paras 86–87; Case C-468/98, *Commission v Sweden*, EU:C:2002:626, para 81; Case C-469/98, *Commission v Finland*, EU:C:2002:627, paras 85–86; Case C-471/98, *Commission v Belgium*, EU:C:2002:628, paras 98–99; Case C-472/98, *Commission v Luxembourg*, EU:C:2002:629, paras 91–92; Case C-475/98, *Commission v Austria*, EU:C:2002:630, paras 100–01; and Case C-476/98, *Commission v Germany*, EU:C:2002:631, paras 111–12 On the operationalisation of the 'affect test' in these cases, see also F Hoffmeister, 'Commission v. United Kingdom, Commission v. Denmark, Commission v. Sweden, Commission v. Finland; Commission v. Belgium, Commission v. Luxembourg; Commission v. Austria, Commission v. Germany' (2004) 96 *American Journal of International Law* 567, 570.

[69] See section II.D.

the EU and third countries), but what constitutes external trade under EU law.[70] As soon as an international trade agreement predominantly affects trade within the EU's internal market, it cannot be concluded under the CCP alone. Conversely, if an agreement has direct and immediate effects on international trade, it falls within the scope of the CCP irrespective of whether the area in question internally falls within shared competence. This may, for example, occur for agreements on IPRs or services whose regulation is only partially harmonised within the internal market.[71]

In its pre-Lisbon case law, the CJEU was cautious about maintaining a clear distinction between shared internal and exclusive external EU trade powers. In *Opinion 2/92*, the CJEU found that 'the national treatment rule relates only partially to international trade with non-member countries: it affects internal trade to the same extent as international trade, if not more so'.[72] Similarly, in *Opinion 1/94*, the CJEU noted that there is '[a]dmittedly … a connection between intellectual property and trade in goods' because agreements governing intellectual property have 'effects on trade'.[73] The CJEU nonetheless concluded that the TRIPS Agreement fell outside the CCP at the time because it affected 'internal trade just as much as, if not more than, international trade'.[74]

In its post-Lisbon case law, the CJEU expanded the conception of 'international trade' under EU law and, with it, the 'absorption capacity' of the CCP. This was first apparent in *Daiichi Sankyo*. This case essentially raised the question whether the TRIPS Agreement was covered by the CCP post-Lisbon or continued to fall in an area where the Member States retain 'primary competence'.[75] The Commission had argued that *Opinion 1/94* was no longer material post-Lisbon and that the 'TRIPs Agreement as a whole relates to 'commercial aspects of intellectual property' within the meaning of Article 207(1) TFEU'.[76] Conversely, the intervening Member States had contested that 'the majority of the rules in the TRIPs Agreement … concern international trade only indirectly' and therefore continued to fall outside the scope of the CCP post-Lisbon.[77] Advocate General Cruz Villalón sought that Article 207(1) TFEU could not be read as encompassing the entire TRIPS Agreement, as this could lead to a 'deactivation' of the Member States' shared internal trade powers.[78] The CJEU did not follow his view. It emphasised that 'the FEU Treaty differs appreciably from the EC Treaty previously in force, in that it includes new aspects of contemporary international trade in that

[70] See also Opinion of Advocate General Sharpston, Opinion 2/15 (n 1) para 566. For an early example on how that distinction between internal and external trade materialises, see Case 270/80, *Polydor*, EU:C:1982:43, para 19. See also M Cremona, 'The Internal Market and External Economic Relations' in P Koutrakos and J Snell (eds), *Research Handbook on the Law of the EU's Internal Market* (Edward Elgar, 2017) 479.

[71] See also Kübek (n 2).

[72] Opinion 2/92, *Third Revised Decision of the OECD*, EU:C:1995:83, para 26.

[73] Opinion 1/94 (n 22) para 57. See also D Kleimann, 'Reading Opinion 2/15: Standards of Analysis, the Court's Discretion, and the Legal View of the Advocate General' (2017) 23 *EUI Working Paper RSCAS* 9.

[74] Opinion 1/94 (n 22) para 57.

[75] *Daiichi Sankyo* (n 27) paras 31–32. See further especially I Van Damme, 'Case C-414/11 Daiichi: The Impact of the Lisbon Treaty on the Competence of the European Union over the TRIPS Agreement' (2015) 4 *Cambridge Journal of International and Comparative Law* 73; and J Larik, 'No Mixed Feelings: The Post-Lisbon Common Commercial Policy in Daiichi Sankyo and Commission v. Council (Conditional Access Convention)' (2015) 52 *Common Market Law Review* 779.

[76] *Daiichi Sankyo* (n 27) para 43.

[77] ibid para 44.

[78] Opinion of Advocate General Cruz Villalón, Case C-414/11, *Daiichi Sankyo*, EU:C:2013:49, para 60.

policy'.[79] In the face of this 'significant development in primary law',[80] the CJEU apparently took a new look at the definition of 'international trade' under EU law. It found that the TRIPS Agreement now displays a specific link to international trade. The new classification of the TRIPS Agreement as part of the CCP was certainly facilitated by the wording of Article 207(1) TFEU, which, as the CJEU noted, 'correspond[s] almost literally to the very title of the TRIPs Agreement'.[81] The CJEU further underpinned this finding through the application of the CCP-specific centre of gravity test. Accordingly, the TRIPS Agreement facilitates international trade by standardising certain IPRs at a global level and, as part of the wider WTO system, has immediate effects on the governance of international trade. As a consequence, the CJEU concluded that the TRIPS Agreement falls within the scope of Article 207(1) TFEU and not within the internal market.[82] It further highlighted that, contrary to the Advocate General's view,[83] the EU's exclusive external and shared internal competence over intellectual property can co-exist. According to the CJEU, 'it remains altogether open to the European Union … to legislate on the subject of intellectual property by virtue of competence relating to the internal market'.[84] However, the resulting legislation would have to comply with any international commitment the EU has decided to uphold.

The CJEU further demarcated the boundaries between external and internal trade post-Lisbon in *Conditional Access Convention*, which was delivered only three months after *Daiichi Sankyo*.[85] The CJEU was asked to determine whether the instrument facilitating the EU's accession to the Conditional Access Convention could be adopted under Article 114 TFEU (the internal market) or, alternatively, Article 207 TFEU (the CCP). The intervening Member States argued that the Convention primarily aims to approximate the legislation of the contracting parties.[86] Conversely, the Commission argued that the Convention, from an EU perspective, primarily aims to ensure the protection of covered services in non-EU contracting parties, and that the approximation of laws within the EU was only a means to achieving that end.[87] The CJEU sided with the Commission. It found that the Convention was mainly about exporting the EU's internal acquis to third countries. Such an external harmonisation had 'a specific connection with international trade in those services, by dint of which it can legitimately be linked to the common commercial policy'.[88] The CJEU acknowledged that 'Articles 6 and 8 of the Convention are also supposed to improve the conditions for the functioning of the internal market'. Yet, that objective was 'purely incidental to the primary objective' of external harmonisation.[89] As it concerns 'the defence of the European Union's global interests', the Convention fell 'by its very nature within the ambit of the common

[79] *Daiichi Sankyo* (n 27) para 46. See also Opinion 2/15 (n 25) para 141.
[80] *Daiichi Sankyo* (n 27) para 48.
[81] ibid para 55.
[82] ibid paras 53–54, 58–59.
[83] Opinion of Advocate General Cruz Villalón, *Daiichi Sankyo* (n 78) para 74.
[84] *Daiichi Sankyo* (n 27) para 59.
[85] Case C-137/12, *Conditional Access Convention*, EU:C:2013:675.
[86] ibid para 44. *cf* also Articles 4, 6 and 8 of the European Convention on the Legal Protection of Services Based on, or Consisting of, Conditional Access [2001] European Treaty Series No 178.
[87] *Conditional Access Convention* (n 85) paras 36–37.
[88] ibid para 65.
[89] ibid para 71.

commercial policy'.[90] In doing so, the CJEU linked the centre of gravity of the CCP post-Lisbon back to its broad and dynamic origins in *Opinions 1/75* and *1/78*.[91]

B. *Opinion 2/15* and the CCP's Absorption Capacity

Together with the pre-Lisbon *Opinion 1/08*, the judgments in *Daiichi Sankyo* and *Conditional Access Convention* highlighted that large parts of the GATS (aside from transport services) and the TRIPS Agreement are fully encompassed by the CCP post-Lisbon. However, these judgments dealt with areas expressly listed in Article 207(1) TFEU (services and commercial aspects of IPRs). In *Opinion 2/15*, the CJEU dealt for the first time with a new generation trade and investment agreement, the EUSFTA, which governs several areas of international economic law and policy that are not expressly mentioned in Article 207(1) TFEU. Building on the broad understanding of what constitutes international trade as a 'centre of gravity' developed in *Daiichi Sankyo* and *Conditional Access Convention*, the Commission argued that all areas covered by the EUSFTA other than transport services and foreign non-direct investments could be 'absorbed' by the CCP's 'centre of gravity'.[92] The Council disagreed, arguing that the EUSFTA contained various fields that continue to fall within shared and/or exclusive Member State competence.[93]

Given the vast scope of the EUSFTA, the CJEU had to repeat its CCP-specific centre of gravity test numerous times. The outcome of the test evinced the broad absorption capacity of the CCP post-Lisbon that was already discernible in *Daiichi Sankyo* and *Conditional Access Convention*. The CJEU found that within the framework of the EUSFTA, the following areas have direct and immediate effects on trade: market access rules, including trade remedies in goods,[94] technical barriers to trade, and sanitary and phytosanitary measures,[95] customs and trade facilitation,[96] non-tariff barriers to trade and investment in renewable energy generation,[97] services, establishment and electronic commerce except for transport,[98] government procurement,[99] FDI protection,[100] the protection of IPRs,[101] competition[102] and sustainable development.[103] It thus largely sided with the Commission on these points.

[90] ibid para 69.
[91] *cf* Chapter 1, section III.A.
[92] Written Observations of the Commission in Opinion 2/15, Ref Ares(2015)3942621 [2015], on file with the author, 9.
[93] Written Observations of the Council in Opinion 2/15, SGS16/00027 [2016], on file with the author, 3.
[94] Opinion 2/15 (n 25) paras 40–43.
[95] ibid paras 44–45.
[96] ibid paras 46–48.
[97] ibid paras 72–74.
[98] ibid paras 49–55.
[99] ibid paras 75–77.
[100] ibid paras 87 et seq.
[101] ibid paras 111 et seq. See subsequently also *Revised Lisbon Agreement* (n 42) paras 52 et seq.
[102] Opinion 2/15 (n 25) paras 131 et seq.
[103] ibid paras 155 et seq. See further section III.C.

In its application of the CCP-specific centre of gravity test, the CJEU increasingly focused on the content of the individual provisions of the EUSFTA rather than on the stated intent of the agreement. The EU's competence over FDI protection is a case in point. The Council and the Member States had submitted observations to the CJEU that Article 207(1) TFEU solely relates to the admission, but not to the operation ('post-establishment') of foreign direct investments.[104] In their view, FDI protection largely fell within shared internal market competence or was exclusively preserved for the Member States. However, using its CCP-specific centre of gravity test, the CJEU came to the opposite conclusion. In contrast to previous case law – where the analysis was largely vested on a treaty's express statement of intent (ie, the 'aims test')[105] – the CJEU examined the provisions of the EUSFTA to demonstrate how the establishment of a legal framework for investment protection promotes, governs and facilitates trade between the EU and Singapore, and how the established legal guarantees for foreign investors in the EU and Singapore, respectively, affect international trade between the parties.[106] This 'content test' brought to light the external harmonisation achieved by the rules of the EUSFTA and their effects on trade between the parties. In that way, the CJEU's reasoning in *Opinion 2/15* follows the logic of Advocate General Kokott in *Conditional Access Convention*, who had argued that external harmonisation is the 'object of many modern trade agreements' because 'those agreements provide for the creation of uniform legal standards … for certain products, activities or sectors with a view to facilitating cross-border trade'.[107]

In addition to broadening the CCP's absorption capacity, the CJEU also widened the scope of 'incidental' or 'indirect' objectives in the context of trade agreements. In essence, the CJEU underlined that treaty provisions must have independent effects on the parties' trade relations to qualify as a main objective of a trade agreement. This was not the case for the EUSFTA's provisions on inland waterways transport and moral rights. With regard to inland waterways transport, the CJEU found that the EUSFTA's provisions were 'extremely limited in scope' and therefore incidental. The CJEU concluded that inland waterways transport is only governed by the EU's schedules of commitments for services annexed to the main text of the EUSFTA and therefore 'not liberalised' as such.[108] With regard to moral rights, the CJEU found that the mere reference to the Berne Convention 'is not sufficient … for that subject to be regarded, in its own right, as a component of [the EUSFTA], which does not mention moral rights'.[109]

[104] ibid para 85. See, in more detail, Written Observations of the Council (n 93) 62 et seq.
[105] Section II.D.
[106] Opinion 2/15 (n 25) paras 87–96.
[107] Opinion of Advocate General Kokott, Case C-137/12, *Conditional Access Convention*, EU:C:2013:441, para 67.
[108] Opinion 2/15 (n 25) para 214. This line of reasoning can be squared with the vertical division of competence because the CJEU did not subsume any material issue area that falls exclusively within the realm of Member State competence under the exclusive scope of the CCP.
[109] ibid para 129. It may be noted that the CJEU in Case C–13/00, *Commission v Ireland*, EU:C:2002:184 had previously held that the Berne Convention falls largely within the scope of the (then) Community's competence (para 16).

In sum, the CJEU thus broadened the CCP's absorption capacity by: (1) focusing its analysis on the content of EU trade and investment agreements and the degree and effects of the external harmonisation they bring about; and (2) advancing a broad understanding of 'incidental' objectives to trade. In a third step, the CJEU provided a teleological reading of the CCP, facilitating a value-driven design of EU trade policy instruments.

C. *Opinion 2/15* and the CCP's Integral Values

As was explained above, the Lisbon Treaty generated an explicit link between the substance of the CCP and the EU's external relations values stipulated in Articles 3(5) and 21 TEU.[110] In *Opinion 2/15*, the CJEU was essentially asked to what extent this nexus between substance and values demands a goal-driven interpretation and application of EU trade policy. The question arose in the context of determining the nature of the EU's competence for concluding the Trade and Sustainable Development (TSD) Chapter of the EUSFTA. The intervening Member States and the Council had argued that the TSD Chapter falls outside the scope of the CCP. The EU ratification instruments of the EUSFTA would thus require reference to the Treaty bases on environment, labour and social policy. In their view, the objective of rooting trade within a coherent and goal-driven external relations policy would not legally turn non-exclusive competence areas into trade policy.[111] Advocate General Sharpston largely agreed with this consideration. She considered that the link between Article 207(1) TFEU and Articles 3(5) and 21 TEU, as well as the 'sustainability mandate' set out in Article 11 TFEU, were 'not relevant for resolving the issue of competence' because objectives 'cannot affect the scope of the common commercial policy laid down in Article 207 TFEU'.[112]

The CJEU disagreed. Its conclusions largely built on the earlier *Philippines Framework Agreement* case, where it found that the nexus between substance (here development cooperation) and values prescribed by the Lisbon Treaty means that EU policy is not limited to the express confines of a given substantive legal basis (here Article 208 TFEU), but also pursues the objectives referred to in Articles 3(5) and 21 TEU.[113] In *Opinion 2/15*, it further developed this line of reasoning by concluding that the link between the substantive provisions of the CCP (Articles 206 and 207(1) TFEU) and the EU's external relations values (Articles 3(5) and 21 TEU), read in conjunction with Article 11 TFEU, implied that 'the objective of sustainable development … forms an integral part of the common commercial policy'.[114]

[110] Section III.B.

[111] Interview with a Council official, 7 November 2018. See also Written Observations of the Council (n 93) 94 et seq.

[112] Opinion of Advocate General Sharpston, Opinion 2/15 (n 1) para 495.

[113] Case C-377/12, *Philippines Framework Agreement*, EU:C:2014:1903, para 37. See further M Broberg and R Holdgaard, 'Demarcating the Union's Development Cooperation Policy after Lisbon: Commission v. Council (Philippines PCFA)' (2015) 52 *Common Market Law Review* 54.

[114] Opinion 2/15 (n 25) para 147. Pointing to the possibility of such a goal-driven reading of substantive EU law, see J Larik, 'From Speciality to a Constitutional Sense of Purpose: On the Changing Role of the Objectives of the European Union' (2014) 63 *International and Comparative Law Quarterly* 935.

The language used by the CJEU is noteworthy: sustainable development was not degraded as a 'secondary' or 'incidental' objective to trade, but was acknowledged as an 'integral part' thereof. As Cremona highlighted, the qualification of sustainable development as 'integral' instead of 'incidental' to trade shows that the CJEU is 'willing to take seriously the catalogue of general external objectives … as complementary to and capable of influencing the objective of trade liberalisation spelled out in Article 206 TFEU'.[115] Indeed, the CJEU's conclusions suggest that the pursuit of the EU's external trade policy *must* be value-driven. In the past, the CJEU had already set some normative *de minimis* standards in *Portugal v Council*[116] and *Front Polisario* (albeit more suggestively),[117] as these judgments prescribe realising the CCP in compliance with international (human rights) law.[118] *Opinion 2/15* further enjoins a value-based framing of the CCP. Notably, the CJEU declared that the express reference to the EU's general external relations objectives in Article 207(1) TFEU places an 'obligation on the European Union to integrate those objectives and principles into the conduct of its common commercial policy'.[119] The use of the word 'obligation' suggests that the value-based framing of the CCP is required as a matter of law and not a mere policy choice.[120] Notably, the CJEU drew a general link between EU trade policy (Articles 206 and 207 TFEU) and the EU's external relations objectives (Articles 3(5) and 21 TEU).[121] As a result, the mandate to pursue a value-based trade policy seemingly applies not only to sustainability but also to other external relations objectives listed in the Treaties, including human rights (eg, Article 21(1) TEU) and security (eg, Article 21(2)(a) TEU).

However, the CJEU underlined that the CCP's capacity to absorb its integral values remains conditional on meeting the threshold set out by the CCP-specific centre of gravity test. In *Opinion 2/15*, the CJEU concluded that the TSD Chapter of the EUSFTA met this threshold. In essence, the CJEU found that the TSD Chapter has direct and immediate effects on trade because it ensures: (1) that trade between the EU and Singapore does not reduce the level of environmental and social protection below the standards laid down by international commitments; and (2) that environmental and social standards are not applied in a protectionist manner.[122] By applying

[115] M Cremona, 'Shaping EU Trade Policy Post-Lisbon: Opinion 2/15 of 16 May 2017' (2018) 14 *European Constitutional Law Review* 231, 243. For a contextual legal analysis, see also M Cremona, 'Distinguished Essay: A Quiet Revolution – The Changing Nature of the EU's Common Commercial Policy' in M Bungenberg et al (eds), *European Yearbook of International Economic Law 2017* (Springer, 2017) 3.

[116] Case C-268/94, *Portugal v Council*, EU:C:1996:461, para 23. See further V Kube, 'The European Union's External Human Rights Commitment: What is the Legal Value of Article 21 TEU?' (2016) 10 *EUI Working Paper Law* 27.

[117] Case C-104/16 P, *Front Polisario*, EU:C:2016:973. Less suggestively, see Case T-512/12, *Front Polisario*, EU:T:2015:953. See further, eg, E Cannizzaro, 'In Defence of *Front Polisario*: The ECJ as a Global *Jus Cogens* Maker' (2018) 55 *Common Market Law Review* 569; J Odermatt, '*Council of the European Union v. Front Populaire pour la Libération de la Saguia-El-Hamra et Du Rio de Oro (Front Polisario)*' (2017) 111 *American Journal of International Law* 731.

[118] On the human rights obligations of the EU in the context of the CCP, see V Kube, *EU Human Rights, International Investment Law and Participation: Operationalizing the EU Foreign Policy Objective to Global Human Rights Protection* (Springer, 2019).

[119] Opinion 2/15 (n 25) para 143.

[120] See also Kübek (n 2); and G Gruni, 'Towards a Sustainable World Trade Law? The Commercial Policy of the European Union after Opinion 2/15 CJEU' (2018) 13 *Global Trade and Customs Journal* 4.

[121] Opinion 2/15 (n 25) paras 142–46.

[122] See Opinion 2/15 (n 25) paras 149–52.

the CCP-specific centre of gravity test also to measures pursuing an integral objective to trade, the CJEU forestalled an inflation of the scope of Article 207 TFEU through a conjoined reading with Articles 3(5) and 21 TEU that Advocate General Sharpston had warned against.[123] In the internal market context, the CJEU had previously followed a similar reasoning. In *Tobacco Advertising*, it held that a non-economic concern (here public health) may be integrated into a policy based on Article 114(2) TFEU. The CJEU found that the barriers to trade between Member States resulted precisely from that non-economic concern and therefore concluded that its pursuit did not shift the centre of gravity of the measure at issue, ie, its genuine aim to improve the functioning of the internal market.[124] Yet, the CJEU held that the EU legislature must ensure a high level of protection of non-economic concerns, including when pursued through internal market legislation.[125]

The CJEU's reasoning in *Opinion 2/15* raised two questions for the future reform of TSD Chapters. First, it remains unclear whether EU FTAs could still be concluded under the CCP alone if the parties were to raise the level of environmental and social protection beyond the standards of protection set in the relevant multilateral agreements. In *Opinion 2/15*, the CJEU considered that the TSD Chapter of the EUSFTA could be absorbed into the CCP because it generally refers to existing multilateral standards without turning them into independent commitments ('non-regression').[126] By inference, the CJEU noted that the EU cannot use its exclusive trade powers to make agreements that 'regulate the levels of social and environmental protection in the Parties' respective territory'.[127] This raises the question of when TSD commitments start having independent regulatory effect or, more broadly, when the objective to pursue sustainable development becomes substantial enough to become a treaty purpose in its own right. Second, it remains unclear whether EU FTAs could still be concluded under the CCP alone if TSD Chapters were to be integrated into the FTA's main dispute settlement mechanisms. In *Opinion 2/15*, the CJEU held that the EUSFTA's TSD Chapter can be absorbed under the CCP because it has its own (legally non-binding) dispute settlement mechanism, thereby safeguarding the application of the main mechanism for settling trade disputes.[128] This raises the question of whether using trade sanctions for enforcing TSD Chapters would imply that EU FTAs set independent environmental and social standards that regulate the levels of protection in the parties' territory and therefore require separate legal grounding. In practice, the EU has begun to use a sanctions-based approach, as a matter of last resort, to counter breaches of fundamental ILO principles or

[123] Opinion of Advocate General Sharpston, Opinion 2/15 (n 1) para 495.

[124] Case C-376/98, *Tobacco Advertising I*, EU:C:2000:544; Case C-380/03, *Tobacco Advertising II*, EU:2006:772.

[125] See further especially C Herrmann, 'Grenzen der Binnenmarktkompetenz in der Jüngeren Rechtsprechung des EuGH' in W Schroeder (ed), *Europarecht als Mehrebenensystem: Beiträge zum 7. Österreichischen Europarechtstag 2007* (Facultas, 2008) 141.

[126] Opinion 2/15 (n 25) paras 152, 155.

[127] ibid para 164.

[128] ibid para 154. In a surprising twist, the CJEU added that the parties may impose trade sanctions for a breach of TSD Chapter norms on the basis of Article 60 of the Vienna Convention on the Law of Treaties (VCLT). Yet, as Beaucillon has convincingly argued, this is an 'excessively broad appreciation of the customary rule'. See further C Beaucillon, 'Opinion 2/15: Sustainable Is the New Trade: Rethinking Coherence for the New Common Commercial Policy' (2017) 2 *European Papers* 819, 825.

of the object and purpose of the Paris Agreement.[129] However, as the EU and its trading partners are bound by ILO fundamental principles and the Paris Agreement in any case, this new enforcement practice may continue to be viewed as a 'non-regression' standard.

D. The Application of the ERTA Test Post-Lisbon

Aside from broadening the 'absorption capacity' of the CCP post-Lisbon, the CJEU has also expanded ERTA-type exclusivity. This section explains how the CJEU has gradually relaxed the two-stage ERTA test post-Lisbon, which forms the starting point of the recent case law on the reach of the EU's implied trade and investment competence, which is further explained in the next section.[130] Taken together, the broad absorption capacity of the CCP and the EU's implied exclusive trade powers enable the *move beyond mixity* in the field of trade.

In its post-Lisbon case law, the CJEU has relaxed both levels of the ERTA test. Regarding the first-level ERTA test (ie, 'the area largely covered' test), the CJEU has moved away from the idea that complete harmonisation[131] or, at the very least, a significant overlap between secondary EU law and an international treaty, is required to trigger ERTA effects.[132] Since its decision in *Opinion 1/03*, the CJEU has repeatedly held that the existence of residual Member State competence which 'could provide the basis for competence on the part of the Member States to conclude an international agreement' does not rule out findings of EU exclusivity.[133] In its post-Lisbon case law, the CJEU has further underlined that the Member States may be pre-empted from external EU action by means of Article 3(2) TFEU, despite possessing the internal capacity to legislate. A key judgment in this regard is *Green Network*.[134] In this case, the CJEU decided that the ERTA effect precluded the Member States from making international agreements in their own right regarding the production and certification of renewable energy, although the corresponding EU Directive equips the Member States with considerable legislative discretion.[135] The CJEU confirmed that 'considerable latitude' on the side of the Member States in the implementation of a Directive does not preclude a material area from being 'largely covered' by common EU rules.[136]

The CJEU has also applied the second-tier ERTA test, ie, the 'affect or alter criterion', more leniently post-Lisbon. This tendency was first apparent in *Neighbouring Rights*.

[129] Articles 26.16(2)(b) and 27.4(3) of the EU-New Zealand FTA.

[130] Section III.E.

[131] Opinion 1/94 (n 22) para 96.

[132] See also R Holdgaard, 'The European Community's Implied External Competence after the Open Skies Cases' (2003) 8 *European Foreign Affairs Review* 365, 388.

[133] Opinion 1/03 (n 59) para 149; R Schütze, *Foreign Affairs and the EU Constitution: Selected Essays* (Cambridge University Press, 2014) 291 et seq; P Mengozzi, 'The EC External Competencies: From the *ERTA* Case to the Opinion in the Lugano Convention' in P Poiares Maduro and L Azoulai (eds), *The Past and Future of EU Law: The Classics of EU Law Revisited on the 50th Anniversary of the Rome Treaty* (Hart Publishing, 2010) 213–17; N Lavranos, 'Opinion 1/03, Lugano Convention' (2006) 43 *Common Market Law Review* 1087, 1095 et seq.

[134] Case C-66/13, *Green Network*, EU:C:2014:2399, paras 54, 60.

[135] ibid para 60.

[136] ibid paras 54, 60.

In this case, the CJEU had to decide whether implied exclusive EU competence could be derived from the third indent of Article 3(2) TFEU for the negotiation and ratification of the Convention of the Council of Europe on the protection of the rights of broadcasting organisations. The Council and the Member States contended that the EU law in place did not cover new digital technologies and that in view of the Member States' retained competence in this field, the ERTA doctrine could not be applied.[137] However, instead of further analysing the precise scope of the material coverage of secondary EU law (the first-level ERTA test), the CJEU concluded that the ERTA effect came into being 'regardless' of whether common EU rules permitted the inclusion of digital technology broadcasters.[138] The inclusion of rules on digital technology broadcasters in the scope of an international agreement would in any event have 'a *horizontal effect* on the scope of the body of common EU rules relating to the protection of neighbouring rights of such organisations' (emphasis added).[139] That horizontal effect was sufficient for demonstrating that common rules are affected within the meaning of Article 3(2) TFEU (the second-level ERTA test), irrespective of the precise extent of the material overlap between internal and international rules (the first-level ERTA test). This finding shows that the broadening of the first-level ERTA test was matched with a less stringent cumulative application of the two-level ERTA test, making the 'effects on common rules' criterion decisive for deriving implied exclusive EU competence.

In sum, the post-Lisbon ERTA case law raised two questions with regard to the precise application of the two-level ERTA test: (1) 'when is an area sufficiently covered by EU rules to exclude Member States' competence to act externally …?';[140] and (2) what are (horizontal) effects on common rules and when are they sufficient for triggering Article 3(2) TFEU? These questions indicate that the more lenient application of the two-level ERTA test post-Lisbon has blurred the boundary between exclusive and shared external competence. It has become simpler to derive exclusive EU external competence by implication and less clear when common rules are insufficiently covered or not affected by the conclusion of an international agreement. The post-Lisbon case law concerning the EU's implied exclusive trade and investment powers must be read and understood in the context of these blurred boundaries between implied exclusive and shared competence, skewing in favour of the former.

E. Implied Exclusivity and the CCP Post-Lisbon

Two decisions by the CJEU affected the reach of the EU's implied exclusive competence over CCP matters: *Opinions 3/15* and *2/15*. The former Opinion concerned the EU's competence to conclude the Marrakesh Treaty alone.[141] The Marrakesh Treaty introduced two instruments, namely: (1) an exception to certain IPRs in order to make

[137] *Neighbouring Rights* (n 61) paras 44 et seq, 86.
[138] ibid para 87.
[139] ibid.
[140] Opinion of Advocate General Wahl, Opinion 3/15 (n 38) para 130, original emphasis removed.
[141] Marrakesh Treaty to Facilitate Access to Published Works for Persons Who are Blind, Visually Impaired, or Otherwise Print Disabled [2013] WIPO Lex No TRT/MARRAKESH/001. See also Chapter 2, section II.B.

accessible format copies more readily available for blind, visually impaired or print-disabled persons; and (2) certain obligations relating to the cross-border exchange of accessible format copies.[142] Although there was hence 'no doubt'[143] that the Marrakesh Treaty has implications on IPRs and the cross-border exchange of goods, the CJEU found that the Marrakesh Treaty primarily aims to improve the positions of blind, visually impaired or otherwise print-disabled persons.[144] In other words, the CJEU considered that the Marrakesh Treaty's 'centre of gravity' is non-commercial; as a result, it could not be concluded under the CCP.[145]

In a second step, the CJEU assessed whether the EU had nevertheless exclusive external competence to conclude the Marrakesh Treaty under the ERTA doctrine. The CJEU's reasoning with regard to the first-level ERTA test builds on and expands the logic of *Green Network*.[146] As in that case, the CJEU admitted that the 'EU legislature brought about only a *partial harmonisation* of copyright and related rights'.[147] In particular, the common EU rules in place left the introduction of exceptions to IPRs for the benefits of persons with a disability fully at the discretion of the Member States.[148] However, as in *Green Network*, the CJEU concluded that the incomplete harmonisation at the EU level 'cannot, in itself, be decisive'.[149] The Member States' retained legislative competence would result 'from the decision of the EU legislature to grant the Member States that option'.[150] The Member States would thus not be free to determine, in an unharmonised manner, the overall boundaries of their retained legislative capacity.[151] As a result, the CJEU found that the Marrakesh Treaty was 'largely covered' by EU secondary law, despite the apparent gaps with regard to the harmonisation of IPRs in the internal market. Because the conclusion of the Marrakesh Treaty required the EU to change (or alter) its common rules, the CJEU also found that the conditions of the second-level ERTA test were fulfilled. *Opinion 3/15* thus exemplified how the more lenient application of the ERTA test has expanded the scope of the EU's exclusive powers to conclude agreements that only indirectly relate to trade.

The reach of the EU's implied exclusive trade powers was further broadened by *Opinion 2/15*. Here, the question arose as to whether the EU could alone conclude the parts of the EUSFTA relating to maritime, road, and rail transport. As stated above, transport services fall outside the scope of the CCP pursuant to Article 207(5) TFEU and therefore principally qualify as a shared competence pursuant to Articles 90

[142] Articles 4, 5 and 6 of the Marrakesh Treaty.

[143] Opinion 3/15 (n 46) para 87.

[144] ibid para 89.

[145] See also G Kübek, 'The Concept of (Non-)Commerciality and the *ERTA* Doctrine Post-Lisbon: Opinion 3/15 (Marrakesh Treaty)' in Butler and Wessel (n 9) 851, 855–56.

[146] In addition, Opinion 3/15 affirmed a narrow reading of the 'minimum harmonisation' exception established in Opinion 2/91 (n 59). See further Kübek (n 145) 858; and T Verellen, 'Opinion 3/15 on the Marrakesh Treaty: ECJ Reaffirms Narrow "Minimum Harmonisation" Exception to *ERTA* Principle' (2017) 42 *Revista General de Derecho Europeo* 160.

[147] Opinion 3/15 (n 46) para 115.

[148] Articles 5(3)(b) and 5(4) of Directive 2001/29/EC of the European Parliament and of the Council of 22 May 2001 on the harmonisation of certain aspects of copyright and related rights in the information society [2001] OJ L167/10.

[149] Opinion 3/15 (n 46) para 117.

[150] ibia para 119.

[151] ibid paras 111–12, 121, 123.

and 100 TFEU.[152] In *Opinion 2/15*, however, the CJEU found that maritime, road and rail transport were 'largely covered' by EU secondary law and may alter or affect the secondary law in place.[153] Once again, the CJEU adopted a very lenient standard of review for the first-tier ERTA test, especially with regard to the EUSFTA's commitments on maritime transport. Within the EU, international maritime transport is governed by a single regulation that dates back to 1986 and has only nine articles.[154] Advocate General Sharpston's meticulous analysis showed that this regulation covers only cross-border trade in maritime services (modes 1 and 2). The EUSFTA further sets out rules regarding establishment (mode 3) and the presence of natural persons (mode 4) in the field of maritime transport. Advocate General Sharpston therefore concluded that the part of the EUSFTA relating to maritime transport services was not 'largely covered' by EU secondary law.[155] The CJEU came to a different conclusion. It found, first, that the EUSFTA does not require the parties to liberalise the supply of international maritime transport services by the presence of natural persons and therefore carved-out mode 4 from the 'area largely covered' test.[156] It further held that the EUSFTA's commitments under mode 3 are only limited.[157] The CJEU thus concluded that the EUSFTA's commitments on maritime transport services (modes 1–4) are 'largely covered' by EU law, even though the relevant EU secondary law does not cover modes 3 and 4.

The CJEU then turned to the second-level ERTA test. Its reasoning here resembled the logic of *Neighbouring Rights* because it did ultimately not pay much attention to its earlier finding that the EUSFTA's commitments on maritime transport were 'largely covered' by EU secondary law.[158] For the CJEU, the mere fact that '[t]he supply of maritime transport services … *is covered by* the common rules' (emphasis added)[159] was sufficient for deriving implied exclusivity because the EUSFTA would 'alter, even considerably … the scope of those common EU rules'.[160] Although the CJEU did not use the same terminology as in *Neighbouring Rights*, its conclusions suggest that the 'horizontal effects' created through the alternation of EU law by the EUSFTA were a sufficient criterion for triggering the ERTA effect.[161]

In the face of the CJEU's finding in *Opinion 2/15* regarding transport services, their carve-out from the exclusive scope of the CCP by Article 207(5) TFEU has lost (some of its) practical significance. The importance of the EU's derived exclusive competence over road, rail and maritime transport services – in addition to finding that the EUSFTA's commitments on inland waterways transport were merely incidental

[152] Section II.A.

[153] Opinion 2/15 (n 25) paras 182, 197, 206.

[154] Council Regulation (EEC) No 4055/86 of 22 December 1986 applying the principle of freedom to provide services to maritime transport between Member States and between Member States and third countries [1986] OJ L378/1.

[155] Opinion of Advocate General Sharpston, Opinion 2/15 (n 1) paras 238–41.

[156] Opinion 2/15 (n 25) para 178.

[157] ibid paras 179–180.

[158] See also J Heliskoski, 'The Exercise of Non-exclusive Competence of the EU and the Conclusion of International Agreements' in K Lenaerts et al (eds), *An Ever-Changing Union? Perspectives on the Future of EU Law in Honour of Allan Rosas* (Hart Publishing, 2019) 293, 302.

[159] Opinion 2/15 (n 25) para 188.

[160] ibid para 189.

[161] See further Cremona, 'Shaping EU Trade Policy Post-Lisbon' (n 115) 247; and Kübek (n 2).

to trade[162] – for the making of new generation EU trade and investment agreements can therefore not be overstated. One may nevertheless question whether the CJEU's broadening of the ERTA doctrine in *Opinion 2/15* has gone 'a bit too far'.[163] If a single regulation from the late 1980s with only nine articles can 'largely cover' a material field as complex as maritime transport services, one may indeed wonder if there is a boundary – and thus a methodological relevance – to the first-level ERTA test.

F. The Outlook on Future ERTA Case Law

In the aftermath of *Opinion 2/15*, the methodology of the ERTA test was further qualified in two cases that did not concern trade or investment policy. First, the CJEU highlighted in *Antarctic MPAs* that the burden of proof for establishing ERTA effects rests with the applicant. As the Commission failed to 'put forward evidence or arguments to establish that the exclusive nature of the external competence of the European Union on which it seeks to rely has been disregarded', the CJEU dismissed its claim for implied exclusivity.[164]

Second, Advocate General Szpunar applied a higher standard for passing the second-level ERTA test in *IMO II*. The Commission had brought a case before the CJEU about an agreement that was still under negotiation. Thus, the final text of the agreement did not exist, making it difficult to perform a 'comprehensive and detailed' analysis on the material overlap between the envisaged agreement and existing secondary EU law. The Advocate General nonetheless found that the future international agreement, in the form foreseen by the EU, concerns an area that is regulated to a large extent by EU law.[165] Yet, the Advocate General argued that the future agreement had no 'tangible effect' on the existing EU law.[166] Although the EU institutions could adapt the existing rules, there was no apparent obligation to do so.[167] By focusing on the criterion of 'tangible effects' capable of 'undermining the uniform and consistent application' of secondary EU laws, and not simply on the occurrence of 'horizontal effects', the Advocate General set a higher standard for fulfilling the second-level ERTA test than the CJEU in *Neighbouring Rights* and *Opinion 2/15*. However, the CJEU did not deal with the plea for ERTA-type exclusivity in *IMO II*. It remains to be seen whether the CJEU, in its future case law, will follow Advocate General Szpunar's suggestion to raise the bar for finding ERTA effects.

IV. Limits to EU Exclusivity Post-Lisbon

The previous sections showed that the express scope of the CCP post-Lisbon, coupled with a more lenient application of the 'centre of gravity' and the ERTA tests, allowed for

[162] See section III.B.
[163] Interview with a Council official, 7 November 2018. For a legal critique, see Chamon (n 58) 1140 et seq.
[164] *Antarctica Treaty* (n 41) paras 115–24.
[165] Opinion of Advocate General Szpunar, Case C-161/20, *IMO II*, EU:C:2021:957, para 142.
[166] ibid paras 118–19, 143–44.
[167] ibid para 152.

a broad reading of the EU's exclusive external trade powers post-Lisbon. Ultimately, the CJEU confirmed in *Opinion 2/15* that the EU has exclusive competence over all matters covered by new generation EU trade and investment agreements, except for foreign non-direct investments and ISDS. This section looks more closely into the rationale and implications of these 'last bastions' of Member State power in the field of trade and investment.

A. Foreign Non-direct Investments

Foreign non-direct investments relate, inter alia, to the acquisition of non-controlling company shares (portfolio investments), securities, short-term loans and other (im)material assets owned by private persons for personal use.[168] As mentioned above, Article 207(1) TFEU makes an express distinction between foreign direct and non-direct investments, thereby excluding the latter from the express scope of the CCP.[169] Foreign non-direct investments are covered by Article 63(1) TFEU, which provides that 'all restrictions on the movement of capital between Member States and between Member States and third countries shall be prohibited'.[170] Such an artificial distinction between foreign direct and non-direct investments is uncommon in international investment law. Modern investment agreements understand investments as 'every kind of asset which has the characteristics of an investment', irrespective of whether they are 'direct' or 'non-direct'.[171]

In *Opinion 2/15*, the question arose as to whether foreign non-direct investments can nevertheless be brought within the scope of the EU's exclusive external competence. Somewhat surprisingly, the Commission did not attempt to use the centre of gravity test to absorb foreign non-direct investments under the exclusive scope of the CCP, although it could be argued that the latter has direct and immediate effects on international trade and especially FDI. Instead, the Commission advanced a novel understanding of the ERTA doctrine, arguing that Article 63(1) TFEU should be understood as a 'common rule' that may be affected by the conclusion of the EUSFTA within the meaning of Article 3(2) TFEU.[172] Until then, common rules had always taken the form of secondary EU law, as primary law cannot be 'altered' within the meaning of Article 3(2) TFEU.[173] However, the Commission viewed Article 63(1) TFEU as a constitutional *Sonderfall* because the Treaties do not provide for a legal basis that authorises the adoption of secondary legislation on foreign non-direct investments. Indeed, Article 64(2) TFEU relates specifically to the movement of capital involving direct investments from or to third states, excluding (just like Article 207(1) TFEU)

[168] See also Council Directive 88/361/EEC (ie, the Nomenclature) (n 30) I-3, I-5; and *Test Claimants in the FII Group Litigation* (n 30) para 182.

[169] Section IV.A.

[170] The term 'capital movements' comprises non-direct investments included in new generation EU trade and investment agreements. See further *Commission v The Netherlands* (n 31) para 19; Opinion 2/15 (n 25) para 227.

[171] eg, Article 1.2(1) EUSIPA.

[172] Opinion 2/15 (n 25) para 229.

[173] As originally constructed in *ERTA* (n 58) paras 17–18.

non-direct investments from its scope. The Commission therefore contented that Article 63(1) TFEU – as the only fundamental freedom with an express external dimension – was designed to be self-sufficient, rendering the adoption of secondary legislation liberalising foreign non-direct investments unnecessary. As a consequence, it argued that Article 63(1) TFEU should be understood as a 'common rule' that may be 'affected' within the meaning of Article 3(2) TFEU.[174]

The CJEU largely followed Advocate General Sharpston's Opinion on this point and rejected the Commission's legal view. It began to interpret the notion of 'common rules' through the lens of its original ERTA case law, which concerned the legislative exercise of internal EU competence.[175] This line of reasoning is rather weak because the ERTA jurisprudence cannot constitutionally override Article 3(2) TFEU.[176] Indeed, the CJEU felt the need to support its reasoning by further noting that the hierarchy of norms within the EU's legal order, which places primary law above secondary law, logically precludes international agreements from 'altering' or 'affecting' the Treaties.[177] This rationale links to the Advocate General's central argument for rejecting the Commission's legal claim: if all primary law provisions were to be able to trigger ERTA effects, the distinction between the first and second paragraphs of Article 3 TFEU would be superfluous.[178]

Nevertheless, the CJEU found that the EU's external competence for foreign non-direct investments is shared in accordance with Article 63(1) TFEU in conjunction with the second indent of Article 216(1) TFEU.[179] This conclusion is a legal novelty. Although the CJEU recognised the existence of implied shared competence in *Opinion 1/03*,[180] it had never actually derived implied shared competence from Article 216(1) TFEU before. The almost identical wording of Article 3(2) TFEU (on the exclusive nature of external competence) and Article 216(1) TFEU (on the existence of external competence) has had the effect that implied competence almost automatically turned exclusive in past practice.[181] After *Opinion 2/15*, it has become clear that the majority of implied competences that are derived from the second indent of Article 216 TFEU will remain shared in nature, whereas implied competences that are derived

[174] Written Observations of the Commission (n 92) 107–10. See also F Ortino and P Eeckhout, 'Towards an EU Policy on Foreign Direct Investment' in A Biondi et al (eds), *EU Law after Lisbon* (Oxford University Press, 2012) 312, 317–18.

[175] Opinion 2/15 (n 25) paras 231–32. However, in doing so, the CJEU appears to contradict its own reasoning in Case C-370/12, *Pringle*, EU:C:2012:756, paras 104–07, where it considered applying Article 3(2) TFEU to a primary law provision, namely Article 122 TFEU.

[176] Similarly, see Cremona, 'Shaping EU Trade Policy Post-Lisbon' (n 115) 248; and Chamon (n 58) 1129.

[177] *Opinion 2/15* (n 25) para 235. In support of the CJEU's argument, Cremona, 'Shaping EU Trade Policy Post-Lisbon' (n 115) 248; *contra*, see Chamon (n 58) 1129; and T Verellen, 'Het Hof van Justitie en het EU-Singapore handelsakkoord, of de kunst van het koorddansen' (2018) *Tijdschrift voor Europees en Economisch Recht* 31, 31–33.

[178] Opinion of Advocate General Sharpston, Opinion 2/15 (n 1) para 358.

[179] Opinion 2/15 (n 25) paras 242–43.

[180] Opinion 1/03 (n 59) paras 114–15.

[181] For a critical view, see Cremona (n 58) 10–11; A Dashwood, 'The Relationship between the Member States and the European Union/European Community' in A McDonnell (ed), *A Review of Forty Years of Community Law: Legal Developments in the European Communities and the European Union* (Kluwer Law International, 2005) 37, 55 et seq; and M Klamert and N Mayell, 'Lost in Exclusivity: Implied Non-exclusive External Competences in Community Law' (2008) 13 *European Foreign Affairs Review* 493.

through the ERTA doctrine (Article 3(2) third indent TFEU) will become exclusive in nature. The latter is presumably also true where external competences are provided for in a legislative EU act (Article 3(2) first indent TFEU).

B. Investor-State Dispute Resolution

The original text of the EUSFTA contained an ISDS mechanism. In the face of fierce public and political critique, the Commission had afterwards reached agreement with Singapore to turn the ISDS mechanism into an ICS[182] at the stage of 'legal scrubbing'.[183] In *Opinion 2/15*, the CJEU was asked to clarify whether the original ISDS mechanism was covered by EU exclusive competence, shared competence or the exclusive competence of the Member States. The CJEU's conclusions can be fully transposed to the ICS.

The CJEU replied to this question in less than 10 paragraphs and its conclusions in this respect were – as has been argued elsewhere in more detail[184] – inadequate. It concluded that:

> Such a regime, which removes disputes from the jurisdiction of the courts of the Member States, cannot be of a purely ancillary nature … and cannot, therefore, be established without the Member States' consent.
>
> It follows that [the ISDS mechanism] of the envisaged agreement falls not within the exclusive competence of the European Union, but within a competence shared between the European Union and the Member States.[185]

There are three main flaws in the CJEU's logic. First, the CJEU based its conclusion on the understanding that ISDS 'removes disputes from the jurisdiction of the courts of Member States'. It extracted the criterion of removing disputes from Member State courts from its past case law on the compatibility of international agreements with the autonomy of the EU legal order.[186] Yet, *Opinion 2/15* did not concern the compatibility of the EUSFTA with EU law; it was about the division of competence between the

[182] For an evaluation of the ICS reform, see H Lenk, *The Investment Court System: A Viable Reform Initiative?* (Handelshögskolan vid Göteborgs Universitet, 2019). See also C Titi, 'International Investment Law and the European Union: Towards a New Generation of International Investment Agreements' (2015) 25 *European Journal of International Law* 639; J Bäumler, 'Should We Tame it, Cage it or Kill it? Past Criticisms, Present Developments, and Future Imperatives for Foreign Investment Protection in Light of the IPA-SA, TPP and CETA' (2016) 54 *Archiv des Völkerrechts* 261, 281 et seq; F Baetens, 'The European Union's Proposed Investment Court System: Addressing Criticisms of Investor-State Arbitration While Raising New Challenges' (2016) 43 *Legal Issues of Economic Integration* 367; L Pantaleo, *The Participation of the EU in International Dispute Settlement: Lessons from EU Investment Agreements* (TMC Asser Press, 2019) 69 et seq; S Schill, 'Authority, Legitimacy, and Fragmentation in the (Envisaged) Dispute Settlement Disciplines in Mega-Regionals' in S Griller et al (eds), *Mega-Regional Trade Agreements: CETA, TTIP, and TiSA: New Orientations for EU External Economic Relations* (Oxford University Press, 2017) 111.

[183] See further Chapter 4, section II.E.

[184] G Kübek and I Van Damme, 'Facultative Mixity and the European Union's Trade and Investment Agreements' in M Chamon and I Govaere (eds), *EU External Relations Law Post-Lisbon: The Law and Practice of Facultative Mixity* (Brill/Nijhoff, 2020) 137, 148 et seq.

[185] Opinion 2/15 (n 25) para 293.

[186] Opinion 1/09, *European Patent Court*, EU:C:2011:123; Opinion 2/13, *ECHR Accession II*, EU:C:2014:2454; Case C-284/16, *Achmea*, EU:C:2018:158. See already, albeit not as explicitly, Opinion 1/91 (n 42) paras 39–40; and Opinion 1/92, *EEA II*, EU:C:1992:189, para 19.

EU and the Member States for concluding the EUSFTA. Given that the criterion of removing disputes from Member State courts cannot be found in the Treaty rules on the existence and nature of competence, it is unclear why the CJEU in *Opinion 2/15* considered the criterion relevant for the allocation of competence between the EU and the Member States.[187]

Second, the CJEU found that the EU's competence for establishing an ISDS mechanism 'cannot be of a purely ancillary nature'. That finding breaks with the logic of prior case law relating to the EU's competence to anchor institutional rules and dispute settlement within the framework of international agreements. The CJEU itself remarked in *Opinion 2/15* that institutional provisions on mediation and dispute settlement principally 'fall within the same competence as the substantive provisions which they accompany'.[188] As a result, '[t]heir presence in the agreement has no effect on the nature of the competence to conclude [that agreement]'.[189] Consequently, Advocate General Sharpston had reasoned 'that the fact that the ISDS mechanism gives an investor of one Party the right to initiate arbitration proceedings against the other Party has *in itself* no bearing on the allocation of competences between the European Union and the Member States' (emphasis in original).[190] She thus concluded that the allocation of competence for ISDS is 'necessarily the same as for the substantive provisions [on investment]'.[191] The establishment of an ISDS mechanism would hence fall partly within the EU's exclusive competence (Article 207(1) TFEU for FDI) and partly within shared competence (Article 63(1) TFEU, read in conjunction with Article 216(1) TFEU, for non-direct foreign investments). By inference, the CJEU's conclusion that ISDS 'cannot be of a purely ancillary nature' implies that the EU's competence for establishing investor-state dispute resolution cannot be derived from the EU's competence for substantive investment protection (Articles 63(1) and 207(1) TFEU), but must be found elsewhere in the Treaties.

Third, it remains unclear what the legal basis for the 'shared' part of the Union competences could be. Other than Articles 207 and 63 TFEU (which cannot be used as legal bases because the EU's competence for ISDS is non-ancillary), there is no other shared competence-conferring Treaty provision that could be utilised.[192] There is also no provision in the TEU or the TFEU that specifically relates to the establishment of international investment courts by the EU or the latter's participation in such a dispute settlement system. Nor did the CJEU insist in *Opinion 2/15* that EU primary law had to be amended so as to include such a provision (as it did in *Opinion 2/94* regarding the

[187] Kübek and Van Damme (n 184) 151–52.

[188] Opinion 2/15 (n 25) para 276.

[189] ibid.

[190] Opinion of Advocate General Sharpston, Opinion 2/15 (n 1) para 526.

[191] ibid para 529. See also L Prete, 'Facultative Mixity after the Singapore Opinion: Clarity or Fresh Doubts' in Chamon and Govaere (n 184) 213, 216.

[192] It has been argued that Article 257 TFEU on the establishment of a European administration could be used as a legal basis for ISDS. However, that provision falls within the realm of supporting competence. It is also not clear whether the establishment of a 'European' administration could be stretched to include international dispute settlement mechanisms. See further Kübek and Van Damme (n 184) 151. On the original argument, see L Prete, 'Some Thoughts on Facultative and Obligatory Mixity after Singapore and COTIF, and before CETA', *Verfassungsblog*, 13 October 2018, verfassungsblog.de/some-thoughts-on-facultative-and-obligatory-mixity-after-singapore-and-cotif-and-before-ceta.

EU's accession to the ECHR, which was then codified in Article 6 TEU).[193] The CJEU did also not clarify the question of the 'shared' legal basis for ISDS/ICS in its conclusions in *COTIF I*, which was discussed in the previous chapter. The *COTIF I* case referred exclusively to paragraph 243 of *Opinion 2/15* and thus the CJEU's conclusions regarding foreign non-direct investments.[194]

In subsequent practice, different institutional understandings about the nature of the EU's competence over ISDS/ICS and about the character of EU IPAs have emerged. The Council Legal Service (CLS) believes that the:

> '[S]hared' competence to which the Court refers at [paragraph 293 of *Opinion 2/15*] means that the subject matter relates partially to matters for which the EU is competent, and partially to matters for which it has no competence whatsoever .... [T]he competence for portfolio investment can be exercised by the Union ... the competence for ISDS cannot (i.e., a case of 'obligatory mixity').[195]

Conversely, the Commission appears to accept such an understanding of shared competence for ISDS/ICS only 'to the extent that the Member States are required to act as respondents in certain disputes'.[196]

President Koen Lenaerts, albeit in his private capacity, noted that:

> Since there is no qualified majority in the Council to decide that the EU should exercise that competence alone, ISDS mechanisms in recently negotiated trade and investment agreements have to be accepted by the Union and all Member States.[197]

Contrary to the opinion of the CLS, the President's statement signals that ISDS falls within shared competence as such – otherwise the Council had no choice but to conclude a mixed agreement. Yet, the statement does not explain the absence of a shared competence-conferring provision authorising the EU to agree to ISDS. The precise allocation of competence between the EU and the Member States for establishing investor-state dispute resolution systems thus remains uncertain. In view of the diverging rationales for mixity used by the CLS and the Commission, the legal uncertainty about the precise nature of the competence for ISDS/ICS might cause future inter-institutional disputes and potentially new case law.

C. Designing Investment Protection Agreements

Opinion 2/15 concerned the division of competence between the EU and the Member States for concluding new generation trade and investment agreements. It did not

[193] Opinion 2/94, *ECHR Accession I*, EU:C:1996:140.
[194] Case 600/14, *COTIF I*, EU:C:2017:935, para 68. See further Chapter 2, section IV.C. See also D Colas, 'Retour sur la compétence externe partagée de l'Union: L'arrêt COTIF et les conditions de sa mise en application' in Chamon and Govaere (n 184) 384.
[195] Council Legal Service, 'CETA – draft joint decisions relating to ICS – adoption procedure' [2019] 12866/19, on file with the author, para 8.
[196] Recommendation for a Council Decision authorising the opening of negotiations for a Convention establishing a multilateral court for the settlement of investment disputes, COM (2017) 0493 final, 4.
[197] Speech by K Lenaerts, 'Modernising Trade Whilst Safeguarding the EU Constitutional Framework: An Insight into the Balanced Approach of Opinion 1/17', Seminar on Opinion 1/17, Belgian Ministry of Foreign Affairs, 6 September 2019.

concern the compatibility of such agreements with EU law. There had been some concerns about the compatibility of ISDS, and subsequently ICS, with the principle of autonomy of EU law.[198] The fact that the CJEU in *Opinion 2/15* extracted the 'removing disputes from Member States' courts' criterion from its case law on the compatibility of international agreements with EU law reinforced the existing doubts. Belgium eventually asked the CJEU for its Opinion on the compatibility of the ICS contained in CETA with EU law. The request by Belgium was part of a broader political compromise that eventually allowed Belgium to sign CETA after Wallonia's initial rejection of the agreement. In the resulting *Opinion 1/17*, the CJEU confirmed the compatibility of CETA's ICS with EU law.[199] In doing so, the CJEU paved the way for the making of stand-alone investment protection agreements by the EU that include investor-state dispute resolution, such as the envisaged Multilateral Investment Court.

The CJEU's conclusions in *Opinion 1/17* symbolise a new openness towards international (investment) law. The CJEU acknowledged EU and international law as separate legal systems whose interlinks are generally mutually beneficial. As this book is about mixity – and thus primarily about questions of external competence and procedure – the CJEU's reasoning about the compatibility of the ICS with EU primary law is outlined elsewhere.[200] It suffices to note that the CJEU in *Opinion 1/17* established conditions for the design of international (investment) courts or tribunals that could affect the way in which the EU and the Member States exercise their competence in the field of investment. To ensure compatibility with EU law, such agreements must, amongst other things, place the EU in a position to determine itself whether it wants to be the respondent in a dispute[201] and stipulate that investment tribunals may only read EU law 'as a matter of fact'.[202] They must also entail certain material guarantees with regard to the scope of the EU and the Member States to regulate in the public interest[203] and the position of small and medium enterprises.[204] By confirming that CETA fulfils these conditions, the CJEU turned CETA into a blueprint for the design of EU IPAs.

[198] See, eg, S Gáspár-Szilágyi, 'A Standing Investment Court under TTIP from the Perspective of the Court of Justice of the European Union' (2016) 28 *Journal of World Investment & Trade* 701; H Lenk, 'Prior Judicial Involvement in Investor-State Dispute Settlement: Lessons from the Court's Rhetoric in Opinion 2/15' (2018) 13 *Global Trade and Customs Journal* 19. *Contra*, see C Herrmann 'The Role of the Court of Justice of the European Union in the Emerging EU Investment Policy' (2014) 15 *Journal of World Investment & Trade* 570; P Koutrakos, 'The Autonomy of EU law and International Investment Arbitration' (2019) 88 *Nordic Journal of International Law* 41. For a broader contextual analysis of the internal and external dimensions of autonomy in the realm of investment, see Y Kaspiarovich, *L'UE et la protection des investissements internationaux: Une complexe articulation entre confiance mutuelle et réciprocité* (Schulthess, 2022).

[199] Opinion 1/17, *Comprehensive Economic and Trade Agreement with Canada*, EU:C:2019:341.

[200] G Kübek, 'Autonomy and International Investment Agreements after Opinion 1/17' (2020) *Europe and the World: A Law Review* 1.

[201] Article 8.21 CETA. See further C Contartese and L Pantaleo, 'Division of Competences, EU Autonomy and the Determination of the Respondent Party: Proceduralisation as a Possible Way-out?' in E Neframi and M Gatti (eds), *Constitutional Issues of EU External Relations Law* (Nomos, 2018) 409.

[202] Pursuant to Article 8.31(1), (2) CETA, the CETA Tribunal may only 'consider, as appropriate, the domestic law of a Party as a matter of fact'. It must follow the interpretation given to domestic law by the courts and authorities of the parties and not determine the domestic validity of the law.

[203] Opinion 1/17 (n 199) paras 150–59. Notably, the CJEU found that the ICS has no jurisdiction to declare EU policy measures necessary for safeguarding public security, public morals, public order as well as human, animal, plant life and health incompatible with IPA rules.

[204] ibid para 221.

The EU has indeed followed the CETA template in its ensuing IPAs. The Member States' BITs, by contrast, do not comply with most of the conditions the CJEU identified in *Opinion 1/17*.[205] It remains to be seen how the Member States and the Commission, in accordance with Regulation 1219/2012,[206] will react to the apparent need of the Member States to re-negotiate their external BITs, and whether *Opinion 1/17* might eventually incentivise the 'grandfathering' of Member State BITs with mixed EU IPAs that take due regard of the CJEU's conditions.

V. Conclusion

The EU is at the height of its conferred powers, especially in the field of trade and investment. Further substantial treaty change is unlikely in a political climate where discussions within the Member States frequently focus on disintegration rather than integration. The post-Lisbon allocation of competence between the EU and the Member States in the field of trade and investment appears to be in a stable equilibrium state. An authoritative interpretation of the reach and limits of the status quo of the EU's trade and investment powers by the CJEU therefore not only answers who is currently in charge to act (*ex post facto review*); it simultaneously determines who will be competent to act in the foreseeable future (*ex ante review*).

The CJEU's approach to the scope of the EU's exclusive trade powers post-Lisbon is expansive. The CJEU links the CCP back to its original construction: an external dimension of the internal market and customs union that is based on uniform principles, with no scope for unilateral action by the Member States. While the expansion of the EU's exclusive trade powers has been ignited by the Lisbon Treaty reform, it was catalysed by the CJEU's more lenient application of the centre of gravity test and the ERTA doctrine. The broad understanding of 'international trade' as a centre of gravity has allowed the absorption of areas that internally fall within shared competence and areas that pursue objectives that are 'integral' to trade under the exclusive scope of the CCP. The lenient application of the two-tier ERTA test by the CJEU has turned road, railway and maritime transport services into implied exclusive EU competences, while inland waterways transport was deemed to be only an incidental aspect of new generation EU trade and investment agreements. In that regard, the carve-out of transport services from the scope of the CCP prescribed by Article 207(5) TFEU has lost its practical significance. The more flexible framing of the CCP in light of its external effects and overarching goals may generally strengthen the consistency of EU external action. However, increased flexibility may come at the cost of reliability. It remains to be seen whether the CJEU will, in its future case law, further qualify its competence-deriving instruments.

The outcome of *Opinion 2/15* is highly pragmatic. It enables the EU to exercise its exclusive trade competence alone, as it is practically feasible to separate EU-only trade

[205] See further R Vidal Puig, 'Investment Arbitration in the EU Following *Achmea* and Opinion 1/17' (2019) 19 *ECB Legal Working Paper Series* 20, 24.

[206] Regulation (EU) No 1219/2012 of 12 December 2012 [2012] OJ L351/40 ('Grandfathering Regulation'). *cf* Chapter 2, section II.A.

from mixed investment protection agreements (see Chapter 7). The use of the EU-only procedure for making FTAs streamlines the treaty-making process and ensures that the resulting agreement cannot be vetoed by a (sub-)national actor (see Chapter 6). *Opinion 2/15* thus catalysed policy reform that has turned the EU into a more unified and effective external trade actor.

Yet, *Opinion 2/15* left some scope for mixity. The CJEU found that foreign non-direct investments and ISDS fall within a competence shared by the EU and the Member States. Clear limits to the reach of EU exclusivity therefore emerged in the field of investment. The previous chapter explained that the CJEU corrected its apparently erroneous conclusion that the parts of the EUSFTA falling within shared competence cannot be approved by the EU alone in *COTIF I*.[207] However, the relevant paragraph in the *COTIF I* judgment related only to foreign non-direct investments; it did not concern ISDS. It thus remains unclear whether the EU is capable of exercising its shared competence for ISDS alone or whether the Member States must become independent contracting parties to such agreements as a matter of law. The Council Legal Service considers agreements containing ISDS to be mandatory mixed agreements. Practice indicates that the Commission disagrees with that reading. The President of the CJEU, Koen Lenaerts, also signalled that EU IPAs qualify as facultative mixed agreements. Given the persisting legal uncertainty about the character of agreements including ISDS, they will likely be concluded as mixed agreements as a matter of principle. For most EU IPAs, mixity thus remains a procedural tool that is used to overcome legal uncertainty about the precise division of competence between the EU and the Member States.[208]

By pinpointing (potential) triggers of mixity, the CJEU has turned mixity into a substantive design choice in the field of trade and investment. The EU and the third state can balance the costs of mixity (eg, uncertainty of entry into force, political volatility) against the benefits of making comprehensive trade and investment agreements (eg, the reach and depths of the agreement). Moreover, the EU can consider the institutional consequences of its choice in favour or against mixity at the outset of the treaty-making process, in particular for national parliaments (see Chapters 4 and 5).

As will be further explained in Chapter 7, the EU has since *Opinion 2/15* generally opted in favour of *moving beyond mixity* by splitting EU FTAs and IPAs. The legality of IPAs that include an ICS was clarified by *Opinion 1/17*, where the CJEU confirmed the compatibility of CETA's ICS with EU primary law. In that decision, the CJEU underlined several conditions that agreements containing an ICS must meet in order to be compatible with EU law. While the EU's IPAs follow the 'CETA template', the Member States' individual BITs may have to be re-negotiated. It remains to be seen whether the apparent need of the Member States to re-negotiate their external BITs under the auspices of the Commission may eventually encourage the grandfathering of Member State BITs with EU IPAs. Although *Opinion 2/15* underlined that the CCP remains one of the most supranational policy fields set out in the Treaties, there thus remains room for further integration.

[207] See Chapter 2, section IV.C.
[208] See Chapter 1, section IV.A.

PART II

Treaty-Making Procedure

4

International and EU Law

I. Introduction

The making of international agreements is a multi-level affair.[1] It transcends (sub-)national borders and, consequently, legal orders. The making of international agreements by the EU – irrespective of whether such agreements are concluded under the EU-only or the mixed procedure – is subject to international, EU and national constitutional law. This chapter will highlight the international and EU law perspective, while Chapter 5 will analyse national constitutional legal orders of EU Member States.

Internationally, the making of agreements between states is governed by the 1969 Vienna Convention on the Law of Treaties (VCLT), which has been ratified by 116 parties to date.[2] All EU Member States except for France are parties to the VCLT. The EU itself cannot become a party because the VCLT only applies to states. There are nonetheless good reasons to apply the VCLT to the treaty-making practice of the EU.[3] First, the 1986 Vienna Convention on the Law of Treaties between States and International Organizations (VCLTIO) is unlikely to ever gain the 35 ratifications necessary for its entry into force.[4] Second, the EU has not signed the VCLTIO and generally applies the VCLT to its own practice.[5] Third, Article 3(b) VCLT clarifies that the rules of the

[1] The terms 'agreement' and 'treaty' are used synonymously in this book, in line with the broad definition of 'agreement' under EU law. According to the CJEU, the TEU and the TFEU use the 'expression [agreement] in a general sense to indicate any undertaking entered into by entities subject to international law which has binding force, whatever its formal designation' (Opinion 1/75, *Local Cost Standard*, EU:C:1975:145, at 1). The CJEU has also used the notion 'agreement' in the context of legally non-binding agreements (Case C-660/13, *Swiss MoU*, EU:C:2016:616). Yet, the procedure foreseen in Article 218 TFEU does not apply to the making of non-binding agreements (Case C-233/02, *France v Commission*, EU:C:2004:173).

[2] On the VCLT, see further especially O Dörr and K Schmalenbach (eds), *Vienna Convention on the Law of Treaties: A Commentary* (Springer, 2012); and O Corten and P Klein (eds), *The Vienna Conventions on the Law of Treaties: A Commentary* (Oxford University Press, 2011).

[3] See further J Odermatt, *International Law and the European Union* (Cambridge University Press, 2021) 63 et seq.

[4] See further, eg, GE do Nascimento e Silva, 'The 1986 Vienna Convention and the Treaty-Making Power of International Organizations' (1986) 29 *German Yearbook of International Law* 68; and for the (then) Community, see P Manin, 'The European Communities and the Vienna Convention on the Law of Treaties between States and International Organizations or between International Organizations' (1987) 24 *Common Market Law Review* 457. See generally M Fritzmaurice, 'Law of Treaties' in S Chesterman et al (eds), *The Oxford Handbook of United Nations Treaties* (Oxford University Press, 2019) 493, 507.

[5] Odermatt (n 3) 63 et seq. See, eg, Case C-327/91, *France v Commission*, EU:C:1994:305, para 25; Case C-416/96 *El-Yassini*, EU:C:1999:107, para 47; or Case C-162/96, *Racke*, EU:C:1998:293, para 25. Yet, the CJEU has rejected the idea that the VCLT applies to the EU's founding treaties due to their special character.

VCLT may be applied to non-state actors if they would be subject to these rules under international law irrespective of the VCLT. The CJEU has read Article 3(b) VCLT as meaning that the rules of the VCLT apply to international agreements between the EU and third states, insofar as these rules are an expression of general international customary law.[6] It may thus be concluded that the VCLT applies to the making of agreements by the EU either indirectly, as a matter of customary law (between the EU and third states), or directly (between the Member State and third states, in the context of mixity).[7]

The Lisbon Treaty defines the legal status of international agreements in the EU legal order and the tasks of each institution in the treaty-making process. Pursuant to Article 216(2) TFEU, agreements concluded by the EU are legally binding upon the EU institutions and the Member States. They thus form an integral part of the EU legal order.[8] Procedurally, the negotiation, signature, provisional application and conclusion of agreements by the EU are governed by Article 218 TFEU.[9] Article 207 TFEU further specifies these rules for the making of trade and investment agreements. Mixed agreements must also be ratified by all Member States in accordance with their constitutional requirements. Yet, as this chapter will demonstrate, national governments and parliaments are also involved in the process of making EU-only agreements, be that through the Council or in their own right. EU treaty-making remains a multi-level legal and institutional affair, irrespective of whether the character of the agreement is mixed or EU-only.

As was explained in Chapter 1, this book is about the making of bilateral trade and investment agreements up until their entry into force.[10] Against that background, this chapter examines the five main stages for making international (trade and investment) agreements under EU law, in view of the procedures set out in the VCLT: negotiations (section II), signature and conclusion (section III), provisional application (section IV) and entry into force (section V).

II. Negotiations

The negotiation of international agreements is generally a political affair. The negotiator must have a considerable amount of flexibility to react to the other side's demands.

See Joined Cases T-27/03, T-46/03, T-58/03, T-79/03, T-80/03, T-97/03 and T-98/03, *SP v Commission*, EU:T:2007:317, para 58.

[6] See especially Case C-162/96 (n 5), paras 24, 45, 46; and Case C-386/08, *Brita*, EU:C:2010:91, paras 40–41 See further J Odermatt, 'The Use of International Treaty Law by the Court of Justice of the European Union' (2015) 17 *Cambridge Yearbook of European Legal Studies* 121.

[7] Article 3(c) VCLT.

[8] See, eg, Case 181/73, *Haegemann*, EU:C:1974:41, para 5; Case 12/86, *Demirel*, EU:C:1987:400, para 7; or Opinion 1/91, *EEA I*, EU:C:1991:490, para 37. See further J Terhechte, 'Artikel 216 AEUV' in J Schwarze et al (eds), *EU-Kommentar*, 4th edn (Nomos, 2019) para 1; and K Schmalenbach, 'Artikel 216 AEUV' in C Calliess and M Ruffert (eds), *EUV/AEUV: Das Verfassungsrecht der Europäischen Union mit Europäischer Grundrechtecharta, Kommentar*, 6th edn (CH Beck, 2022) para 3.

[9] See further J Heliskoski, 'The Procedural Law of International Agreements: A Thematic Journey through Article 218 TFEU' (2020) 57 *Common Market Law Review* 79.

[10] See Chapter 1, section V.

However, international negotiations do not take place in a legal vacuum. Both international and EU law set out a procedural framework, which is then filled by practice.

The following will further explain the process of initiating the EU trade and investment treaty-making and the relevant actors involved. As a preliminary consideration, it examines the recent trend towards a more inclusive and transparent EU trade policy (section II.A). Thereafter, it assesses the authorisation (section II.B), representation (section II.C), participation (section II.D) and finalisation (section II.E) of negotiations.

A. Inclusivity and Transparency

Recent practice is especially focused on designing a more inclusive and transparent framework for negotiating EU trade and investment agreements.[11] Two principal reasons underpin this change in practice. First, and only after severe public pressure and the leakage of the TTIP negotiating directives, the Commission started a new transparency campaign: it called upon the Council to publish all negotiating directives of EU trade agreements[12] and began to transmit its recommendations for negotiating directives to national parliaments and to publish them online, alongside with the EU's draft textual proposals as well as reports of each negotiating round.[13] The campaign has allowed a public debate about matters that were previously classified, enabling the EP and national parliaments to address such matters directly in their respective resolutions.[14]

Second, it has become apparent that parliaments desire to use their newly gained information rights to participate actively in the negotiations of EU trade and investment agreements. Arguably, the early involvement of parliaments is equally important for the making of EU-only and mixed agreements.[15] For EU-only agreements, the involvement of national parliaments in the process of negotiations may partially compensate them for their loss of veto powers over the outcome of that process. For mixed agreements,

[11] See V Abazi, 'How Confidential Negotiations of the TTIP Affect Public Trust' (2016) 7 *European Journal of Risk Regulation* 247; M Cremona, 'Guest Editorial: Negotiating the Transatlantic Trade and Investment Partnership (TTIP)' (2015) 52 *Common Market Law Review* 351, 361; LM Marceddu, 'Implementing Transparency and Public Participation in FTA Negotiations: Are the Times A-Changin'?' (2018) 21 *Journal of International Economic Law* 681; S Boysen, 'Das System des Europäischen Außenwirtschaftsrecht' in A von Arnauld and M Bungenberg (eds), *Europäische Außenbeziehungen*, Enzyklopädie Europarecht, vol 12, 2nd edn (Nomos, 2020) 557, 566.

[12] The Council has so far refrained from answering that call. As much as that decision is arguably regrettable from a political perspective, it is lawful. The Treaties do not stipulate a legal obligation to publish negotiating directives. See further Opinion of Advocate General Wathelet, Case C-425/13, *Australia ETS*, EU:C:2015:174, para 67.

[13] Commission Communication, 'A Balanced and Progressive Trade Policy to Harness Globalisation' (2017) COM/2017/0492 final. See further C Herrmann, "Transleakancy' in C Herrmann et al (eds), *Trade Policy between Law, Diplomacy and Scholarship: Liber Amicorum in Memoriam Horst G. Krenzler* (Springer, 2015) 39: and A Marx and G Van der Loo, 'Transparency in EU Trade Policy: A Comprehensive Assessment of Current Achievements' (2021) 9 *Politics and Governance* 261.

[14] Although the EP was fully informed about EU trade and investment treaty negotiations in accordance with Article 218(1) TFEU, it was previously limited in what it was able to write in its resolutions because that information was classified. Interview with an EP official, 7 November 2018.

[15] See also Chapter 5, section I.

the involvement of parliaments in the negotiation process forestalls such agreements from being merely 'rubber-stamped' at the ratification stage. Moreover, it lowers the risk of non-ratification. Parliaments are more likely to consent to the conclusion of a mixed agreement if their demands were heard at the negotiation stage.

There are various ideas for increasing parliamentary participation in EU trade policy. Cottier, for instance, has suggested the establishment of an EU Trade Policy Act.[16] The adoption of such an act certainly bears potential 'to enhance inclusiveness and thus democratic legitimacy' of EU trade policy more generally.[17] Yet, a 'one-off' delegation of power by parliaments is arguably insufficient for guaranteeing parliamentary oversight of EU trade policy. In order to move away from a practice of 'rubber-stamping' to a culture of active national parliamentary participation, parliaments need to be involved in the formation of external trade policy.[18] The following outlines that the EP and national parliaments are increasingly involved in negotiations of EU trade agreements, albeit often through informal channels of communication. There is hence room to formalise inter-institutional dialogue, especially between the Commission, as the negotiator of EU trade and investment agreements, and national parliaments. Moreover, as Chapter 5 will show, national government could significantly enhance the role of national parliaments in EU treaty-making though national law and practice.

B. Authorisation and Opening

Pursuant to Article 207(3) TFEU, the Commission recommends the opening of trade and investment negotiations to the Council[19] and – after receiving formal authorisation – negotiates the agreement on behalf of the EU.[20] Before the official opening of negotiations, the Commission usually enters into exploratory talks with its trading partner to confirm the mutual desire to and benefits of enhancing their external trade relations ('scoping').[21] Given the broad and flexible nature of exploratory talks, the Commission

[16] T Cottier, 'Front-Loading Trade Policy-Making in the European Union: Towards a Trade Act' in M Bungenberg et al (eds), *European Yearbook of International Economic Law 2017* (Springer, 2017) 35.

[17] ibid.

[18] See also D Kleimann and G Kübek, 'The Signing, Provisional Application, and Conclusion of Trade and Investment Agreements in the EU: The Case of CETA and Opinion 2/15' (2018) 45 *Legal Issues of Economic Integration* 13, 44–45.

[19] Provided that the envisaged trading relations are part of a broader agreement that includes CFSP matters, the Commission and the High Representative recommend the opening of negotiations jointly. See, eg, Joint Recommendation for a Council Decision authorising the European Commission and the High Representative of the Union for Foreign Affairs and Security Policy to open negotiations and negotiate a modernised Association Agreement with the Republic of Chile, JOIN/2017/019 final. See also Annex to Council Decision authorising the opening of negotiations with the United Kingdom of Great Britain and Northern Ireland for a new partnership agreement, Directives for the Negotiations of a New Partnership with the United Kingdom of Great Britain and Northern Ireland [2020] Council doc 5870/20 ADD 1 REV 3, Addendum, para 172. On the latter, see further Chapter 8, section II.

[20] In case of mixity, the Member States might participate in the negotiations in their own right, via the Presidency or as part of a joint delegation under the 'Rome formula'. See further section II.C below. On the Commission as a negotiator, see also Y Devuyst, 'European Union Law and Practice in the Negotiation and Conclusion of International Trade Agreements' (2013) 12 *Journal of International Business and Law* 259, 293.

[21] See, eg, M Gatti and M Manzini, 'External Representation of the European Union in the Conclusion of International Agreements' (2012) 49 *Common Market Law Review* 1703, 1707.

is arguably neither legally obliged to obtain the consent of the Council to commence these talks nor to inform the Council and the EP about their content.[22] However, in recent practice, such information is often made public. CETA is a case in point: Prior to the start of the negotiations, a Joint Study by the Commission and the Government of Canada entitled 'Assessing the Costs and Benefits of a Closer EU-Canada Economic Partnership'[23] and a Joint Report on the EU-Canada scoping exercise for a potential trade agreement[24] were published. Moreover, the Commission held public consultations on the content and options of a comprehensive trade agreement with Canada[25] and conducted a sustainable impact assessment (SIA).[26] In light of the overall positive evaluation of the report, public opinion, the scoping exercise and SIA, the EU and Canada publicly announced at a summit meeting on 6 May 2009 their endeavour to negotiate a comprehensive trade and investment agreement.[27]

The opening of trade and investment negotiations by the Commission must be authorised by the Council (Article 207(3) TFEU). The Council generally attaches so-called negotiating directives to its decision authorising the opening of negotiations. The Commission should conduct the negotiations within the framework of the negotiating directives and in consultation with a special committee appointed by the Council, the Trade Policy Committee (TPC), which may also adjust and expand the negotiating directives.[28] The Commission's recommendation for opening the trade and investment treaty negotiations includes draft negotiating directives. However, a literal reading of Article 207(3) TFEU suggests that the Commission's right of initiative is limited to the authorisation of negotiations. The power to draft and adopt negotiating directives is granted to the Council alone. The practice of merging the authorisation of negotiations and the first set of negotiating directives into a single decision thus expands the Commission's right of initiative under Article 207(3) TFEU: the Commission not only initiates the treaty-making procedure but also provides a first sketch of the agreement's material scope. The Council may, of course, amend the Commission's recommendation, notably by QMV.[29]

[22] See also M Bungenberg, 'Artikel 218 AEUV' in H von der Groeben et al (eds), *Europäisches Unionsrecht: EUV/AEUV/GRC*, 7th edn (Nomos, 2015) para 33.

[23] Joint Study by the European Commission and the Government of Canada, 'Assessing the Costs and Benefits of a Closer EU-Canada Economic Partnership' (2008).

[24] Joint Report on the EU-Canada Scoping Exercise of 5 March 2009.

[25] Since then, civil society meetings and stakeholder consultations have become a more regular feature during trade and investment treaty negations. In 2021, the Commission organised 22 Civil Society Dialogue meetings and four events with stakeholders to update on ongoing negotiations. See European Commission, 'Transparency in EU Trade Policy: 2021 Statistics for DG TRADE' (2021), policy.trade.ec.europa.eu/eu-trade-relationships-country-and-region/transparency-eu-trade-negotiations/transparency-eu-trade-policy-2021-statistics-dg-trade_en.

[26] C Kilpatrick et al, 'Trade Sustainability Impact Assessment (SIA) on the Comprehensive Economic and Trade Agreement (CETA) between the EU and Canada: Final Report', Final Report (2011).

[27] EU-Canada Summit Declaration Prague [2009] 9547/09 (Presse 120).

[28] See further, eg, M Bungenberg, 'Artikel 207 AEUV' in M Pechstein et al (eds), *Frankfurter Kommentar zu EUV, GRC und AEUV*, 2nd edn (Mohr Siebeck, 2023) para 215; W Weiß, 'Artikel 207 AEUV' in E Grabitz et al (eds), *Das Recht der Europäischen Union: EUV/AEUV*, Stand: Mai 2023, 79 Erg.-Lfg. (CH Beck, 2023) para 96; R Leal-Arcas, *EU Trade Law* (Edward Elgar, 2009) 174 et seq.

[29] Commission recommendations are not formal proposals. Hence, the unanimity requirement contained in Article 293(1) TFEU does not apply. See further PJ Kuijper, 'Post-CETA: How We Got There and How to Go On' (2017) 53 *Revue trimestrielle de droit* européen 181. However, the Council acts unanimously

The negotiating directives outline the proposed material scope of the agreement. They should arguably be silent about the character of the envisaged agreement.[30] Whether or not the agreement is mixed can only be determined on the basis of the final text of the agreement. Yet, in some instances, the Council expressly authorised the Commission to negotiate a mixed agreement. The 2011 negotiating directives of CETA, for example, specified that the parties sought to include 'areas of mixed competence' into the investment chapter.[31] The same clause was inserted in the 2011 supplementary negotiating directives for the EUSFTA. In its written observations in *Opinion 2/15*, the Council suggested that the Commission had breached Article 207(3) TFEU in conjunction with Article 13(2) TEU by negotiating an 'EU-only' agreement against the explicit instructions of the TPC and, subsequently, the Committee of the Permanent Representatives of the Governments of the Member States to the European Union (COREPER).[32] Neither Advocate General Sharpston nor the CJEU further addressed this argument because they assessed the character of the EUSFTA on the basis of the final text of the agreement.[33] Indeed, preparatory acts, such as negotiating directives, are rarely brought before the CJEU. In the event that inter-institutional disputes about mixity come to light prior to or during the negotiations of an agreement, the Commission usually informally notifies the Council about its legal view through the TPC.[34] The CJEU is generally consulted in cases where disputes cannot be solved on the basis of the final treaty text. Exceptionally, however, the Commission has brought agreements that were in the process of being negotiated before the CJEU because it contested the Member States' intention to become contracting parties in their own right.[35]

In practice, negotiating directives are often referred to as 'mandates'. Arguably, the term mandate is ill-suited, as it wrongfully suggests that negotiating directives are legally binding.[36] Yet, the negotiating directives adopted by the Council pursuant to Article 207(3) TFEU do not legally prescribe the Commission to achieve a specific result in the negotiations.[37] Even the Council has asserted that negotiating directives and positions 'cannot be understood as implying an obligation for the Commission to

for agreements where this is legally required, such as Association Agreements (Article 218(8) TFEU). See further, eg, S Lorenzmeier, 'Artikel 218 AEUV' in E Grabitz, M Hilf, and M Nettesheim (eds), *Das Recht der Europäischen Union: EUV/AEUV*, Stand: Mai 2023, 79 Erg.-Lfg. (CH Beck, 2023) paras 34, 44b.

[30] See also Opinion of Advocate General Sharpston, Case C-114/12, *Neighbouring Rights*, EU:C:2014:224, paras 171 et seq.

[31] Paragraph 26(a) of the Recommendation from the Commission to the Council on the modification of the negotiating directives for an Economic Integration Agreement with Canada in order to authorise the Commission to negotiate, on behalf of the Union, on investment [2015] 12838/11.

[32] The negotiating directives for the FTA with Singapore are classified. But see Observations of the Council in Opinion 2/15, SGS16/00027 [2016] on file with the author, 4–7.

[33] See especially Opinion of Advocate General Sharpston, Opinion 2/15, *FTA with Singapore*, EU:C:2016:992, paras 83–84.

[34] Interview with a Commission official, 9 November 2018; interview with two Commission officials, 9 November 2018.

[35] See, eg, Case 114/12, *Neighbouring Rights*, EU:C:2014:2151; or Case C-389/15, *Revised Lisbon Agreement*, EU:C:2017:798.

[36] See, eg, Bungenberg (n 28) para 214: 'Die Kommission ist an die durch den Rat festgelegten Verhandlungsrichtlinien gebunden.' ('The Commission is *bound by* the negotiating directives adopted by the Council' (translation by the author and emphasis added)).

[37] See also JP Terhechte, 'Artikel 218 AEUV' in J Schwarze et al (eds), *EU-Kommentar*, 4th edn (Nomos, 2019) para 13.

achieve the recommended result'.[38] The CJEU similarly concluded that 'it is contrary to Article 218(4) TFEU for the positions established by the special committee or, as the case may be, the Council itself to be binding'.[39] Indeed, an obligation to precisely follow the Council's demands would disregard the mutual character of negotiations. The negotiator needs a certain degree of flexibility to facilitate compromise solutions with third states. Since the agreement can only be signed and concluded with the consent of the Council, the Commission's leeway to deviate from negotiating directives in practice is limited. Moreover, the Commission may withdraw its recommendation for opening the negotiations, provided that the Council's changes to it are contrary to the objectives originally pursued by the Commission.[40] In the spirit of institutional balance, both institutions must therefore cooperate sincerely in the conduct of international treaty negotiations (Article 13(2) TEU).[41]

It is contested whether the Council may sign and conclude an agreement whose negotiations it has not formally authorised. This question arose in *Opinion 3/94*, although this was subsequently withdrawn and therefore was never answered by the CJEU.[42] In *Opinion 3/94*, Germany argued that the Commission had no authority to negotiate an agreement with Colombia, Costa Rica, Nicaragua and Venezuela, known as the Framework Agreement on Bananas. The Commission was authorised to negotiate the WTO Agreements in the framework of the Uruguay Round and, in that context, to begin negotiations pursuant to Article XXVIII:5 GATT on the compensation to be offered by the (then) Community to certain GATT contracting parties in exchange for the abolition of a bound import duty on bananas. However, the Framework Agreement essentially precluded Colombia, Costa Rica, Nicaragua and Venezuela from adopting a Panel Report against the Community's banana import regime and fixed the applicable tariff rate quotas. In view of the fact that the Framework Agreement on Bananas did not aim at achieving further trade liberalisation, Germany argued that its negotiation was neither authorised by the Council's decision to open the Uruguay Round negotiations, nor its decision to open negotiations under Article XXVIII GATT. Therefore, Germany asserted that the Council's decision to sign the Framework Agreement on Bananas breached what is now Article 207(3) TFEU and that the Framework Agreement could not be lawfully adopted. Against this background, the Council maintained that: 'The decision to sign an agreement negotiated by the Commission implies approval of its contents and makes good any irregularity during the course of the negotiations.'[43]

[38] Case C-425/13, *Australia ETS*, EU:C:2015:483, para 87. Yet, the CJEU underlined that the negotiating directives may include rules of a procedural nature, eg, on information rights and channels between the Commission and the Council (para 78).

[39] ibid para 88.

[40] Case C-409/13, *Commission v Council*, EU:C:2015:217.

[41] See further, eg, M Chamon, 'The Institutional Balance, an Ill-Fated Principle of EU Law?' (2015) 21 *European Public Law* 371; M Chamon, 'Institutional balance and Community method in the implementation of EU legislation following the Lisbon Treaty' (2016) 53 *Common Market Law Review* 1501; C Hillion, 'Conferral, Cooperation and Balance in the Institutional Framework of EU External Action' in M Cremona (ed), *Structural Principles in EU External Relations Law* (Hart Publishing, 2018) 117; JP Terhechte, 'Im Dienste der Demokratie? – Das institutionelle Gleichgewicht in der Gemeinsamen Handelspolitik der EU' in C Herrmann (ed), *Die Gemeinsame Handelspolitik im europäischen Verfassungsverbund* (Nomos, 2020) 153.

[42] Opinion 3/94, *Framework Agreement on Bananas*, EU:C:1995:436, Opinion withdrawn.

[43] ibid, at V(c)2.

In other words, the Council contended that it may authorise the negotiations of an agreement implicitly and *ex post facto* by deciding to sign and conclude that agreement. There is arguably nothing in Article 207(3) TFEU that would legally preclude the Council from accepting an agreement negotiated by the Commission without proper authorisation, provided that the Member States in the Council are satisfied with the final outcome of the negotiation process.[44] In reality, it appears much more likely that such a scenario would result in inter-institutional disputes. It is precisely with a view to avoiding such conflicts that Article 207(3) and (4) TFEU actively involves the Commission and the Council in the negotiations of EU trade and investment agreements and that both institutions increasingly seek to include the EP, national parliaments and the general public: transparency, inclusiveness and cooperation at the start of the treaty-making process significantly increase the chances of reaching an outcome on which all decision-makers and veto-players can agree.

C. Capacity and Representation

International law is largely silent on treaty negotiations. Yet, it specifies rules regarding the capacity of states to make international agreements. That question must be clarified at the start of the treaty-making process and is thus relevant at the negotiation stage. The choice as to who may conduct negotiations on behalf of a state or an international organisation is left to their internal laws and practices alone.

International law assumes that every state has the capacity to enter into treaty negotiations (Article 6 VCLT). However, the same assumption cannot be made for international organisations such as the EU. Article 6 VCLTIO underlines that the treaty-making capacity of an international organisation is governed by the rules of that organisation. International law is thus not blind to the fact that international organisations are highly individual entities and, unlike states, do not possess full treaty-making powers.[45] The EU's treaty-making power is conferred by its constituent yet sovereign Member States and thus limited. It must ensure, on the basis of its internal laws, that it has the capacity to conclude an international agreement or, alternatively, include the Member States as independent contracting parties. International law, in turn, ensures that internal laws cannot be used as a pretext for non-compliance once a treaty has been ratified. Pursuant to Article 46(1) VCLT, a state may not invoke a violation of its internal legal rules as a ground for invalidating its consent 'unless that violation was manifest and concerned a rule of fundamental importance'. Pursuant to Article 46(2) VCLT, a violation is only manifest 'if it would be objectively evident to any State conducting itself in the matter'. In view of the complexity of the allocation of treaty-making power between the EU and the Member States, it is unlikely that a breach thereof would be considered 'objectively evident'. It is thus for the EU and the Member States to ensure that their internal rules are duly followed.[46] Precisely for this reason, Article 207(3) TFEU prescribes that both

[44] Interview with a Commission official, 9 November 2018; interview with two Commission officials, 9 November 2018.

[45] See also N Levrat, 'Article 6 VCLTIO' in Corten and Klein (n 2) 117.

[46] See also J Bäumler, 'Vom Vertragstext zum Inkrafttreten: Das Vertragsschlussverfahren im Mehrebenensystem am Beispiel CETA' (2016) 51 *Zeitschrift Europarecht* 607.

the Commission and the Council must ensure that the procedure and content of trade and investment agreements comply with EU internal policies and rules.

Provided that an agreement (also) concerns trade and investment, the EU generally has (some) treaty-making power. As mentioned above, the Commission represents the EU in trade negotiations (Article 17(1) TEU and Article 207(3) TFEU). In the case of mixity, the Member States sometimes want to participate in the negotiations alongside the Commission and negotiate alone the parts of the agreement falling within their competence.[47] Articles 207(3) and 218(3) TFEU do not principally preclude the Member States' participation in the negotiations, as long as the EU remains capable of representing its own interests in fields where it has and exercises competence. Whether the EU is represented by the Commission alone or the Commission and the Member States in treaty negotiations does not legally determine the character of the international agreement. As mentioned above, the choice between EU-only and mixity is made on the basis of the material content of the final agreement. The Commission and the Member States may thus form joint negotiating teams, provided that the agreement is expected to contain shared competence, even if the agreement is ultimately concluded under the EU-only procedure. By inference, agreements that were negotiated by the EU alone can be of a mixed character, provided that the final agreement falls partially outside the EU's exclusive competence.

Provided that a strong case for mixity can be made at the negotiating stage, the Member States' individual bargaining power increases. By emphasising vis-a-vis the third state that the envisioned agreement cannot be signed and ratified without their individual consent, the Member States have a greater degree of leverage to insist on non-negotiable national interests.[48] Mixity therefore adds a challenge to the third state's bargaining position, who is suddenly not only confronted with the EU's common position but also faces specific national demands.[49] In some situations, mixity therefore increases the EU's collective bargaining power, as individual Member States can extract further concessions.[50] Yet, the Member States' elevated individual roles simultaneously weaken the unity of the EU's external representation and the Commission's bargaining

[47] See further J Groux, 'Mixed Negotiations' in D O'Keeffe and HG Schermers (eds), *Mixed Agreements* (Kluwer, 1983) 87; T Cottier, 'Gemischte Abkommen der Europäischen Union: Grundlagen und Alternativen' in M Bungenberg and C Herrmann (eds), *Die gemeinsame Handelspolitik der Europäischen Union: Fünf Jahre nach Lissabon – Quo Vadis?* (Nomos, 2016) 11; M Demper, *Kooperationsstrukturen und Kooperationsvereinbarungen zwischen der EU und den Mitgliedstaaten im Rahmen gemischter Abkommen* (Nomos, 2018) 55 et seq.

[48] Interview with a Council official, 7 November 2018. See also S Bolaert, 'Mixity versus Unity: A View from the Other Side of the Rue de la Loi' in M Chamon and I Govaere (eds), *EU External Relations Law Post-Lisbon: The Law and Practice of Facultative Mixity* (Brill/Nijhoff, 2020) 251.

[49] See also Cottier (n 47) 24–25. On the third parties' perspective on mixity, see further J Heliskoski, *Mixed Agreements as a Technique for Organizing the International Relations of the European Community and its Member States* (Kluwer Law International, 2001) 121 et seq; PM Olson, 'Mixity from the Outside: The Perspective of a Treaty Partner' in C Hillion and P Koutrakos (eds), *Mixed Agreements Revisited: The EU and its Member States in the World* (Hart Publishing, 2010) 331; and J Odermatt, 'Facultative Mixity in the International Legal Order: Tolerating European Exceptionalism?' in Chamon and Govaere (n 48) 291.

[50] As was noted by TC Schelling, '[t]he well-known principle that one should pick good negotiators to represent him and then give them complete flexibility and authority – a principle commonly voiced by negotiators themselves – is by no means as self-evident as its proponents suggest; the power of a negotiator often rests on a manifest inability to make concessions and to meet demands'. See TC Schelling, *The Strategy of Conflict* (Harvard University Press, 1960), 19. The so-called 'Schelling conjecture' suggests that bargaining power can precisely result from domestic ratification constraints.

power and position. It is thus unclear whether the recourse to mixity at the negotiation stage strengthens or weakens the EU's bargaining power.[51] The choice as to who represents the EU and, potentially, the Member States – that is, the organ or persons performing the negotiations – thus remains a balancing exercise between unity and individual power assertion that can only be made on a case-by-case basis.

There are several strands of practice relating to the representation of the EU and/or the Member States in trade and investment treaty negotiations. The first and most common strand consists of entrusting the Commission to represent the EU (and the Member States) alone in the negotiations. The Commission is conferred the task of conducting the negotiations on behalf of the EU by the Council decision opening the negotiations.[52] In case the agreement at issue includes national competence, the Commission may further be authorised by the representatives of the governments of the Member States to act on their behalf.[53] In the event that the Member States' power is exclusive, such an authorisation is legally mandatory.[54]

The second strand is mixed negotiations.[55] Mixed negotiations are most common in the context of multilateral treaties and may take various forms.[56] In the context of multilateral trade negotiations, the EU and the Member States generally form a single negotiating team composed of representatives of the Commission and national government officials that is led by the Commission (the so-called Rome formula).[57] The Rome formula was, for example, used in the negotiations of the Uruguay round, leading to the WTO Agreements.[58] Alternatively, the Member States may also participate in their own right in mixed negotiations, with each Member State having its own delegation alongside the EU delegation.[59] This is currently the case for the negotiations conducted

[51] See also S Meunier and K Nicolaïdis, 'Who Speaks for Europe? The Delegation of Trade Authority in the EU' (1999) 37 *Journal of Common Market Studies* 477, 482.

[52] See, eg, Article 1(1) of the Council Decision of 9 April 2019 authorising the opening of negotiations with the United States of America for an agreement on the elimination of tariffs for industrial goods [2019] 6052/19.

[53] See, eg, Decision of the Representatives of the Member States meeting within the Council authorising the European Commission to negotiate, on behalf of the Member States, the provisions of a comprehensive trade and investment agreement with the United States of America that fall within the competences of the Member States' [2013] Council Doc No 7399/13; or Decision of the Representatives of the Governments of the Member States, meeting within the Council, authorising the European Commission to negotiate, on behalf of the Member States, the provisions of a Framework Agreement between the European Union and its Member States, of the one part, and Canada, of the other part, that fall within the competences of the Member States [2010] Council Doc No 17037/10.

[54] See further Opinion of Advocate General Jacobs, Case C-316/91, *Parliament v Council*, EU:C:1993:872, para 82.

[55] Groux (n 47).

[56] See especially ibid 92–93. See also Demper (n 47) 111 et seq; and F Kaiser, *Gemischte Abkommen im Lichte bundesstaatlicher Erfahrungen* (Mohr Siebeck, 2012) 57 et seq.

[57] Groux (n 47) 93; Cottier (n 47) 24.

[58] See, eg, P Van den Bossche, 'European Community in International Economic Relations: The Bittersweet Experience of the Uruguay Round' in JH Jackson and AO Sykes (eds), *Implementing the Uruguay Round* (Oxford University Press, 1997) 23, 57; and M Hilf, Negotiating and Implementing the Uruguay Round: The Role of EC Member States – the Case of Germany' in JH Jackson and AO Sykes (eds), *Implementing the Uruguay Round* (Oxford University Press, 1997) 121, 123–24.

[59] There are three main formulas of 'mixed negotiations': (1) the EU and the Member State holding the Presidency (bicephalous); (2) the EU and all the Member States (multicephalous), (3) the above-mentioned 'Rome formula'. In practice, various (other) constructions are possible. See further Groux (n 47) 92–93.

under the auspices of the UNCITRAL Working Group III on the MIC. The EU has reinforced observer status and acts along the 12 Member States that are full members of UNCITRAL as well as (most) of the remaining Member States, who are able to attend the negotiation sessions. Despite the high coordination costs,[60] the mixed negotiation technique works generally well in the context of UNCITRAL, as the EU and the Member States can re-state and re-emphasise points of particular importance to them, giving these points more weight in a large group setting.[61] The unity of the EU and the Member States in the conduct of these negotiations is also visible in the issuing of joint submissions.[62]

Mixity is rare in the context of bilateral negotiations. When negotiating in a bilateral setting, it is usually not beneficial to maintain a large group of representatives. There is no longer a benefit to outnumbering the other party, and the coordination costs for reaching a single voice are higher in case of mixed than in case of pure Commission negotiations. Nevertheless, mixed negotiations have occurred in the context of bilateral trade and investment treaties, albeit rarely. TTIP and CETA are two examples for bilateral mixed negotiations. For TTIP, the Member States authorised the Commission to negotiate on their behalf in areas concerning their competence;[63] however, the Member States attended negotiating sessions concerning their competence and were consulted through the TPC with regard to the establishment of negotiating documents.[64] The Member States' decision authorising the Commission to negotiate TTIP on their behalf did not further define the scope of 'provisions … that fall within the competence of the Member States', equipping the Member States with broad discretion to decide when to individually attend negotiation sessions.[65] For CETA, the Commission was generally authorised to negotiate on behalf of the EU and the Member States. However, the 2009 negotiating directives set out that the Member States shall be individually represented by the Presidency for negotiations concerning criminal sanctions and other infringements of intellectual property rights.[66] In practice, however, the role of the Presidency

[60] The coordination costs may be reduced by establishing a code of conduct before entering into the negotiations that determines when the EU and when the Member States may speak. So far, such a code of conduct has not been integrated into the negotiating directives of EU FTAs. But see, for example, Title II, paragraph 3(d) of the gentlemen's agreement annexed to the negotiating directives of the Convention on Navigation on the Danube, which provides that 'the Commission shall be the spokesman during the negotiations, and the representatives of the Member States shall speak only if requested to do so by the Commission' and that 'the representatives of the Member States must take no action which is likely to handicap the Commission in its work'. See Case C-433/03, *Commission v Germany*, EU:C:2005:462, para 70.

[61] Interview with a Commission official, 19 February 2019.

[62] See, eg, Submission from the European Union and its Member States, 'Possible Reform of Investor-State Dispute Settlement (ISDS)', United Nations Commission on International Trade Law Working Group III (Investor-State Dispute Settlement Reform), 39th session [2020] A/CN.9/WG.III/WP.159/Add.1.

[63] Article 1 of Council Doc No 7399/13 (n 53). On the TTIP negotiations, see further S Meunier, 'What Single Voice? European Institutions and EU–US Trade Negotiations' (2000) 54 *International Organization* 103; E Fahey, 'On the Benefits of the TTIP Negotiations for the EU Legal Order: A Legal Perspective' (2016) 43 *Legal Issues of Economic Integration* 327. On EU-US transatlantic trade relations more generally, see E Fahey, *The EU as a Global Digital Actor: Institutionalising Global Data Protection, Trade, and Cybersecurity* (Hart Publishing, 2022) 126 et seq.

[64] Article 3 of Council Doc No 7399/13 (n 53).

[65] ibid.

[66] Paragraph 47(3) of the Recommendation from the Commission to the Council in order to authorize the Commission to open negotiations for an Economic Integration Agreement with Canada [2009] 9036/09, partially declassified in 2015.

in the negotiations was limited and principally concerned only a single provision of CETA.[67] The subsequent FTAs with Singapore, Vietnam and Japan were then negotiated by the Commission alone.[68] CETA was therefore potentially the last EU trade and investment agreement where the Member States were involved in their own right in the negotiations. In the future, the Commission will act as the sole representative of the EU and the Member States in the negotiations of FTAs and IPAs.[69]

D. Conduct and Participation

Trade and investment treaty negotiations are conducted in 'rounds', ie, regular meetings between the negotiating teams of the EU and the third state. The EU's negotiating team is generally led by a senior official from the Directorate-General (DG) for Trade, usually the head of unit responsible for the respective geographical region of the trading partner.[70] The negotiations are in most cases based on textual proposals submitted by the EU.

Pursuant to Article 207(3) TFEU, the Commission must regularly report to the TPC on the progress of negotiations. In practice, the Commission negotiators and the TPC convene regularly, especially prior and after negotiation rounds have taken place. In addition, there are so-called technical meetings on, for example, certain quotas or geographical indications. The Commission may also meet informally with representatives of the Member States. In the context of mixed negotiations, informal meetings often take place before the start of each negotiating round in order to align negotiation positions and tactics.[71]

Pursuant to Articles 207(3) and 218(10) TFEU, the EP must be informed at all stages of the treaty-making process. The CJEU has confirmed that the requirement to inform the EP does not end with communicating the opening of negotiations, but includes a requirement to inform Parliament about 'the intermediate results reached by the negotiations'.[72] The 2010 Framework Agreement between the Commission and the EP stipulates that the Commission shall provide the EP, through its Committee on International Trade (INTA), the same information that it provides to the TPC for agreements that require the EP's consent.[73] This includes in particular information regarding draft amendments to adopted negotiating directives, draft negotiating texts and agreed articles, as well as any relevant documents received from third parties, subject to the

[67] Interview with a Commission official, 19 February 2019.

[68] ibid.

[69] See further Chapter 7, section IV.A.

[70] See, eg, European Commission, 'Report of the First Round of Negotiations for a Free Trade Agreement between the European Union and New Zealand' (2018).

[71] Interview with a Commission official, 19 February 2019.

[72] See Case C-263/14, *Tanzania*, EU:C:2016:435, para 77; see also Case C-658/11, *Mauritius*, EU:C:2014:2025. The *Mauritius* and *Tanzania* judgments of the CJEU had a significant practical impact on the institutional compliance of the duty to inform the EP. In the field of trade, the EP is generally informed more thoroughly than in other fields (interview with an EP official, 7 November 2018).

[73] Paragraphs 1 and 5 of Annex III of the Framework Agreement on Relations between the European Parliament and the European Commission [2010] OJ L304/47.

originator's consent.[74] The Commission shall provide the information to INTA in sufficient time, so that the EP may express its views and the Commission is able to take them into account.[75]

In the early post-Lisbon years, the EP made sure that the Commission and the Council would respect its newly gained information and veto rights in practice.[76] In early 2010, it rejected the SWIFT interim agreement on the processing and transfer of financial data between the EU and the US for the purposes of the Terrorist Finance Tracking Program,[77] amid concerns for privacy, proportionality and reciprocity.[78] Moreover, the EP strongly criticised the failure of the Commission and the Council to provide it with full information, and claimed a breach of the principles of institutional balance and sincere cooperation (Article 13(2) TEU).[79] The Council had authorised the Presidency to sign the SWIFT interim agreement on 30 November 2009 – the day before the entry into force of the Lisbon Treaty. Pursuant to Article 218(5) TFEU, the Council may decide to sign and provisionally apply international agreements without obtaining the EP's consent. However, and in contrast to its predecessors, the Lisbon Treaty prescribes that the EP must consent to the conclusion of the majority of EU international agreements, including the SWIFT interim agreement (Article 218(6)(a) TFEU).[80] However, the EP only gained access to the last declassified annex of the SWIFT interim agreement on 8 February 2010, two days prior to the EP's scheduled vote. In view of the limited timeframe to come up with a report – and with no possibility for the

[74] ibid para 23 in conjunction with Annex III, at 5.

[75] ibid para 24.

[76] On the EP's strengthened role in EU decision-making post-Lisbon, see generally C Eckes, 'How the European Parliament's Participation in International Relations Affects the Deep Tissue of the EU's Power Structures' (2014) 12 *International Journal of Constitutional Law* 904; R Passos, 'The European Union's External Relations a Year after Lisbon: A First Evaluation from the European Parliament' in P Koutrakos (ed), *The European Union's External Relations a Year after Lisbon* (2003) 3 *CLEER Working Paper* 49; and R Passos 'Mixed Agreements from the Perspective of the European Parliament' in Hillion and Koutrakos (n 49) 269. On trade specifically, see M Krajewski, 'External Trade Law and the Constitution Treaty: Towards a Federal and More Democratic Commercial Policy?' (2005) 42 *Common Market Law Review* 91, 125–26; Y Devuyst, 'The European Parliament and International Trade Agreements: Practice after the Lisbon Treaty' in I Govaere et al (eds), *The European Union in the World: Essays in Honour of Professor Marc Maresceau* (Nijhoff, 2014) 171; G Rosén, 'The Impact of Norms on Political Decision-Making: How to Account for the European Parliament's Empowerment in EU External Trade Policy' (2017) 24 *Journal of European Public Policy* 1450; or M Krajewski, 'Die neue handelspolitische Bedeutung des Europäischen Parlaments' in M Bungenberg and C Herrmann (eds), *Die gemeinsame Handelspolitik der Europäischen Union nach Lissabon* (Nomos, 2011) 53.

[77] Agreement between the European Union and the United States of America on the Processing and Transfer of Financial Messaging Data from the European Union to the United States for Purposes of the Terrorist Finance Tracking Program [2010] OJ L8/11.

[78] See European Parliament Press Release, 'SWIFT: European Parliament Votes down Agreement with the US' [2010] Reference No 20100209IPRs68674.

[79] The EP's rationale for and willingness to withdraw consent if access to classified information was denied in case of the SWIFT agreement was already noted by Passos (n 76) 53. For a subsequent account of the entire 'SWIFT affair', see R Passos, 'The External Powers of the European Parliament' in P Eeckhout and M López Escudero (eds), *The European Union's External Action in Times of Crisis* (Hart Publishing, 2016) 85, 88 et seq; D Galloway, 'Classifying Secrets in the EU' (2014) 52 *Journal of Common Market Studies* 668; and A Maurer, 'Comparative Study on Access to Documents (and Confidentiality Rules) in International Trade Negotiations', Study for the *European Parliament's Committee on International Trade* (2015). On the EU's broader legal framework and practice regarding secrecy and classified information, see especially V Abazi, *Official Secrets and Oversight in the European Union: Law and Practices of Classified Information* (Oxford University Press, 2019).

[80] See further section III.

Commission to take that report into account at negotiation stage – the EP's Committee on Civil Liberties, Justice and Home Affairs (LIBE) suggested making full use of the EP's post-Lisbon parliamentary prerogatives and recommended the rejection of the agreement. The Plenary voted to reject the agreement on 11 February 2010.

Inter-institutional information, cooperation and participation have faced a steep learning curve since 'the SWIFT affair'.[81] The EP in general and the INTA committee specifically have installed various means to keep informed about and impact the conduct of trade negotiations beyond access to documents. INTA has, for example, established monitoring groups for each trade and investment agreement under negotiation composed of a standing rapporteur and up to seven shadow rapporteurs from the different political groups. The EU chief negotiator and/or the Director-General for Trade regularly debriefs the responsible monitoring committee at INTA and attends INTA meetings if the respective trade and investment agreement is on the agenda.[82] These meetings are generally web-streamed. Yet, the chief negotiator and/or Director-General may also debrief the INTA committee or monitoring groups through in camera meetings on sensitive or confidential information.[83] Individual members of the EP can submit written questions regarding the conduct of trade and investment treaty negotiations to the Commission, which will be answered by the chief negotiator.[84] Overall, the EP has created a tight information network and monitoring system of trade and investment treaty negotiations. It may use the information it receives to issue resolutions that outline – more or less explicitly – the conditions for its consent. As a result, the EP's resolutions on EU trade and investment agreements have become very important for the Commission in the conduct of its negotiations.

Indeed, the EP, through its resolutions, has had a decisive influence on the procedure and design of new generation EU trade and investment agreements. To name but a few examples: the EP requested from the Council not to open the negotiations of the FTA with Japan before it had stated its opinion on the negotiating directives, and the Council followed that request.[85] It insisted on the inclusion of human rights clauses as essential elements and a monitoring system including civil society in the FTA with Peru and Colombia.[86] It ensured the protection of specific sectorial economic interests, such as the general carve-out of audiovisual and cultural services[87] or, in the case of the FTA with Korea, the inclusion of a bilateral safeguard clause.[88] It also advocated for

[81] Galloway (n 79) 670 et seq.

[82] See also D Kleimann, 'The Legitimacy of "EU-Only" Preferential Trade Agreements' in M Hahn and G Van der Loo (eds), *Law and Practice of the Common Commercial Policy* (Brill/Nijhoff, 2021) 461, 481, who mentions that between 2009 and 2013, the DG Trade held 155 informal technical briefings and gave more than 50 presentations to the INTA committee/monitoring groups/political groups/members.

[83] Interview with a Commission official, 19 February 2019.

[84] See, eg, Parliamentary question [2019] No E-002502-19.

[85] See European Parliament resolution of 13 June 2012 on EU trade negotiations with Japan [2012] P7_TA(2012)0246. See also E Fahey and I Wieczorek, 'The European Parliament as a Defender of EU Values in EU-Japan Agreements: What Role for Soft Law and Hard Law Powers?' (2022) 47 *European Law Review* 331.

[86] See, eg, Article 1 of the EU-Peru/Colombia FTA. On this, see European Parliament resolution of 13 June 2012 on the EU trade agreement with Colombia and Peru [2012] P7_TA(2012)0249.

[87] See, eg, European Parliament resolution of 23 May 2013 on EU trade and investment negotiations with the United States of America [2013] P7_TA(2013)0227, 11.

[88] See also D Kleimann, 'Taking Stock: EU Common Commercial Policy in the Lisbon Era' (2011) *CEPS Policy Brief* 21.

the formulation of separate TSD Chapters, which have since become a precondition for the EU to enter into trade negotiations.[89] The EP's most impactful resolution to date was arguably the resolution adopted on 8 July 2015 on TTIP,[90] which involved, in addition to INTA, the opinions of 13 other committees.[91] The resolution outlined several recommendations on precise material standards that the EP requested the Commission to include in the final agreement, concerning, for example, the scope of market access commitments, competition rules, procurement, regulatory cooperation, data privacy, TSD, transparency and civil society involvement.[92] It also requested the Commission to abolish ISDS and to develop a new court system.[93] Although TTIP never became reality, many of its demands have been incorporated into the ensuing EU trade and investment agreements and notably CETA, including the systemic change from ISDS to the ICS.[94] The EP has therefore not only legally enforced its post-Lisbon information and participatory rights, but has also anchored its new role in inter-institutional practice. In doing so, it has become an influential actor during EU trade and investment treaty negotiations.

However, for certain agreements, the EP has decided *not* to issue resolutions. This has, for instance, been the case with the opening of negotiations for a MIC. The Commission therefore lacks formal information about the EP's position on the UNCIRAL Working Group III negotiations. As it is difficult for the Commission to address a position it has formally not received, the EP's inaction reduces its influence on the formation of trade and investment policy, potentially to a mere 'take it or leave it' decision over the final output. The EP also decided not to submit observations on *Opinion 1/17*, although it had already voted in favour of concluding CETA. These instances suggest that trade and investment matters have become more contentious within the EP, making it more difficult to form an opinion in plenary.[95]

National governments and parliaments also participate in the EU treaty-making process, irrespective of the character of the agreement at issue, be that mixed or EU-only.

[89] See especially European Parliament resolution of 8 June 2011 on EU-Canada trade relations [2011] P7_TA(2011)0257. See also, eg, European Parliament resolution of 8 July 2015 containing the European Parliament's recommendations to the European Commission on the negotiations for the Transatlantic Trade and Investment Partnership (TTIP) [2015] P8_TA(2015)0252; European Parliament resolution of 5 July 2016 on a new forward-looking and innovative future strategy for trade and investment [2018] OJ C101/30; European Parliament non-legislative resolution of 13 February 2019 on the draft Council Decision on the conclusion of the Free Trade Agreement between the European Union and the Republic of Singapore [2019] P8_TA(2019)0093.

[90] EP resolution on TTIP (n 89).

[91] See further especially Passos (n 79) 105 et seq. The number of internal EP committees giving their respective opinions on EU FTAs depends on the material content of the agreement and the political desire of the respective committee to submit observations. In the case of CETA, for example, the Committee on Transport and Tourism (TRAN) decided not to submit observations on the parts of CETA concerning its competence for political reasons. The responsible committee (here INTA) must give an opinion before the vote in plenary. Interview with an EP official, 7 November 2018.

[92] See similarly the EP resolutions on CETA (n 89), at 2.

[93] EP resolution on TTIP (n 89), at 2(a)(xv).

[94] The Commission finalised its proposal for the ICS only two months after the EP's resolution on TTIP. See European Commission, Press Release, 'EU Finalises Proposal for Investment Protection and Court System for TTIP' [2015] IP/15/6059. The shift from ISDS to ICS was of course a result of several political forces and not only the EP resolution. On the evolution of ISDS/ICS, see T St John, *The Rise of Investor-State Arbitration: Politics, Law, and Unintended Consequences* (Oxford University Press, 2018); and H Lenk, *The Investment Court System: A Viable Reform Initiative?* (Handelshögskolan vid Göteborgs Universitet, 2019).

[95] Interview with an EP official, 7 November 2018.

National governments (usually via the responsible ministry) are regularly informed about the state of play of the negotiations, be that through their representative in the Council or the Commission. For example, between 2016 and 2017, the Commission met more than 30 times with national government officials dedicated to the negotiations of the EU-Japan FTA (an EU-only agreement).[96] As mentioned above, the Commission transmits its recommendation to open negotiations and the attached negotiating directives to national parliaments and to the EP at the same time as they are submitted to the Council.[97] In recent years, it has also become more common for Commission officials to visit national parliamentary debates and/or to informally debrief the responsible national parliamentary committees about the state of play of EU trade and investment negotiations.[98] There is nonetheless room to further expand and institutionalise the exchanges of views between the Commission and national parliaments. This is all the more important in view of the fact that the procedures foreseen in Protocols 1 and 2 TEU are not applicable as negotiations on international agreements are not conducted on the basis of draft EU legislation.[99] One example for a more formal inter-institutional dialogue structure is the so-called Barroso Initiative, which national parliaments may also use to state their views on the opening of trade and investment treaty negotiations, the proposed negotiating directives and the conduct of the negotiations.[100] They have indeed filed several opinions on the negotiations of EU trade and investment agreements.[101] During the CETA negotiations, national parliaments have further addressed the Commission through a concerted letter.[102]

EU citizens have a number of limited options to participate directly in the treaty negotiation process at the EU level. First, as was explained above, the Commission conducts public consultations prior to recommending the opening of trade and investment negotiations.[103] Second, EU citizens may voice their opinion through European Citizenship Initiatives (ECIs). In the *Stop TTIP* case,[104] the CJEU confirmed that ECIs may also concern preparatory acts, such as the Commission's recommendation to

[96] Meetings were held at a political or technical level or within the TPC. See further, policy.trade.ec.europa.eu/eu-trade-relationships-country-and-region/countries-and-regions/japan/eu-japan-agreement/negotiation-process_en.

[97] See section II.A above.

[98] Interview with a Commission official, 19 February 2019.

[99] See further D Jančić, 'TTIP and Legislative–Executive Relations in EU Trade Policy' (2017) 14 *West European Politics* 202, 213. Damestroy and Levrat have suggested the establishment of an 'early warning mechanism' for mixed agreements. However, anchoring such a mechanism in EU law would require amending Article 218 TFEU. See further M Damestoy and N Levrat, 'The Mixed Nature of the EU-Canada FTA: Between Competences Distribution and Democratic Legitimacy' in N Levrat et al (eds) *The EU and its Member States' Joint Participation in International Agreements* (Hart Publishing, 2022) 77, 84.

[100] On the Barroso initiative, see D Jančić, 'The Barroso Initiative: Window Dressing or Democracy Boost?' (2012) *Utrecht Law Review* 78; and, in the context of TTIP, Jančić (n 99) 213.

[101] See, eg, Assemblée National, 'Résolution Européene pour un debat sur l'accord économique et commercial global (CETA)' [2017] Text adopté n. 906. National parliamentary opinions and Commission replies can be found on the website of the Commission. See further, https://ec.europa.eu/dgs/secretariat_general/relations/relations_other/npo/index_en.htm.

[102] Tweede Kamer der Staten-Generaal, 'Letter in the Framework of the Political Dialogue: The Role of National Parliaments in Free Trade Agreements' (2014).

[103] See section II.A above.

[104] Case T-754/14, *Stop TTIP*, EU:T:2017:323. See also E Fahey, 'European Citizens Initiative 'STOP TTIP' Can Proceed Says General Court' (2017) 8 *European Journal of Risk Regulation* 787; and M Wendel, 'Demokratische Teilhabe und Freihandel – Zur Rolle von Bürgerinitiative und Transparenz bei der Entstehung eines transatlantischen Wirtschaftsvölkerrechts' in M Bungenberg and C Herrmann (eds), *Die gemeinsame Handelspolitik der Europäischen Union: Fünf Jahre nach Lissabon – Quo Vadis?* (Nomos, 2016) 93.

open or withdraw from the negotiations of an international (trade and investment) agreement.[105] In doing so, the *Stop TTIP* case has significantly increased EU citizens' ability to participate in the treaty-making process from the very beginning. The ECI in the *Stop TTIP* case essentially proposed that the Commission should recommend that the Council withdraws its decision to negotiate TTIP pursuant to Article 207(3) TFEU. Yet, ECIs are non-binding on the Commission. Should the Commission decide not to follow an ECI, it must duly justify its course of action.[106] In doing so, ECIs facilitate institutional and public debate, 'which is the primary objective of all ECIs'.[107]

E. Finalisation and Initialling

The negotiation process is finalised by the adoption and authentication of the text of the treaty by the parties. Pursuant to Article 9(1) VCLT, the adoption of a treaty text takes place by the consent of all parties that participated in its drawing up. The text is then established as 'authentic and definite'. Article 10 VCLT leaves it up to the drafters to determine how they want to denote a text as authentic and definite. Suggested instruments include signature, signature ad referendum, or initialling by the representatives of those states of the text of the treaty.

Pursuant to Article 7(1) VCLT, the text of a treaty can only be adopted and authenticated by a person who is considered as representing the respective state. The provision thus intends to forestall that the adoption of a treaty will not subsequently be declared ineffective by one party because of a lack of authority.[108] A person is considered as representing a state if they produce 'full powers'.[109] Alternatively, a person is considered as representing a state if practice or circumstances indicate that it was the intention of the respective state to consider that person as its representative without having to produce full powers.[110] In principle, the VCLT thus leaves it to the internal laws of states to designate their respective representative as well as the scope of their powers.[111]

Pursuant to Article 17(1) TEU, the Commission represents the EU in its external relations. In *IMO II*, the CJEU underlined that the 'Commission's competence to represent the European Union in the latter's exercise of its external competence does not depend on the exclusive or shared nature of that external competence'.[112] However, in that case, the CJEU also underlined that Article 17(1) TEU only empowers the Commission to ensure the external representation of the EU, and not the external

[105] *Stop TTIP* (n 104) para 49. The Commission argued that ECIs could only concern formal 'proposals', such as its proposals to sign and conclude an FTA (Article 218(5), (6) TFEU), but not preparatory acts such as its decision to recommend the opening of negotiations (Articles 207(3) and 218(3) TFEU). The CJEU dismissed the Commission's argument and held that ECIs may concern the whole treaty-making process.
[106] Article 10(1)(c) of Regulation (EU) No 211/2011 of the European Parliament and of the Council on the citizens' initiative [2011] OJ L065/1.
[107] *Stop TTIP* (n 104) para 14.
[108] See further Council of Europe, *Treaty-Making: Expression of Consent by States to Be Bound by a Treaty* (Brill, 2001) 5 et seq.
[109] Article 7(1)(a) VCLT.
[110] ibid Article 7(1)(b).
[111] F Hoffmeister, 'Article 7 VCLT' in Dörr and Schmalenbach (n 2) 129, 133.
[112] Case C-161/20, IMO II, EU:C:2022:260, para 52.

representation of the Member States, including in situations where the latter act jointly in the interests of the EU.[113]

The negotiations of EU trade and investment agreements are typically finalised by initialling. The Commission – as the EU's external representative pursuant to Article 17(1) TEU and lead negotiator pursuant to Article 207(3) TFEU – takes the decision to initial the text in consultation with the Council (specifically the TPC) and the EP (specifically INTA). In practice, it is usually the Commission chief negotiator who initials the text on the EU side. Provided that the Member States negotiate the treaty text in their own capacity with a view to becoming parallel contracting parties besides the EU (eg, in the multilateral context), they must pursuant to Article 9(1) VCLT adopt the text in their own right. This is generally not the case for bilateral agreements, even if the Member States negotiate some provisions themselves, because the EU and the Member States form a joint negotiating team and a composite contracting party. After the text has been initialled, the EU Commissioner for trade, together with a political leader of the third state (eg, a trade minister), usually announce the completion of the text at a summit meeting.

After the negotiations are officially announced to be completed, the Commission sends the Council, the EP, and national governments and parliaments (through the Council) the agreed text of the agreement irrespective of the character of that agreement (mixed or EU-only). The agreement in principle and its text is also published online. The adopted text is then subjected to 'legal scrubbing' (ie, legal review and – if necessary – correction). Although the process of 'legal scrubbing' is set out to achieve terminological consistency, it may at times lead to significant substantive changes to the agreed text. The agreed text of CETA was, for example, 'scrubbed' for almost two years. During that time, the replacement of the ISDS mechanism by the ICS was decided.[114] The agreements with Singapore and Vietnam were 'split' after they had been agreed upon in principle.[115]

III. Signature and Conclusion

The VCLT stipulates six main procedural means to express the consent to be bound by a treaty: signature, exchange of instruments constituting a treaty, ratification, acceptance, approval or accession.[116] The parties to an agreement may also agree on an alternative procedural way.[117] Some EU trade and investment agreements suggest 'approval' for expressing consent to be bound[118] and thus a two-stage ratification process.[119] The details for expressing consent to be bound are left to the internal requirements of

[113] ibid paras 76–77.
[114] See European Commission, Press Release, 'CETA: EU and Canada Agree on New Approach on Investment in Trade Agreements' [2016] IP/16/399.
[115] See further Chapter 7, section III.A.
[116] Article 11 VCLT.
[117] ibid.
[118] See, eg, Article 15.10(1) of the EU-Korea FTA; Article 16.13(1) of the EUSFTA; Article 17.16(1) of the EU-Vietnam FTA (hereinafter 'EUVFTA'); Article 30.7(1) CETA.
[119] Pursuant to Article 14(2) VCLT, '[t]he consent of a State to be bound by a treaty is expressed by acceptance or approval under conditions similar to those which apply to ratification'.

the parties.[120] EU law generally foresees a two-step process for the ratification of international agreements: signature and conclusion.[121] Accordingly, signature is a means of authentication (Art. 10 VCLT) qualifying the EU to proceed with treaty conclusion, which culminates in an expression to be bound by the treaty (Art. 11 VCLT). A treaty then enters into force in accordance with the specific terms provided therein. The following discusses the procedural modalities (section III.A) and applicable voting majorities in the Council (section III.B) that underpin the EU's ratification of trade and investment agreements.

A. Procedural Modalities

Pursuant to Articles 218(5) and (6) TFEU, the Council adopts a decision on the signature and conclusion of an international agreement on behalf of the EU, following a proposal by the Commission.[122] As was explained above, Article 7(1) VCLT deals with the power to represent states, including for the purpose of authenticating the text of or expressing the consent to being bound by a treaty, with a view to ensuring that the participating representatives have proper representational power.[123] Article 7(2)(a) VCLT mentions some examples of persons that by virtue of their functions are considered as representing their states, including heads of states, heads of governments or foreign ministers. Famously, identifying the leader of the EU is less obvious than it is for most sovereign states.[124] EU law does not explicitly designate the person representing the EU for the purpose of signing or expressing consent to be bound by international agreements. Article 17(1) TEU sets out the competence of the Commission, as an institution, to represent the EU externally. At the same time, Article 218 TFEU leaves the last word in taking an internal decision on treaty signature and conclusion with the Council. In past practice, the Council had used its 'last word' to authorise its President, via the signature or conclusion decision, to designate the person empowered to sign a treaty or give notification on the completion of the applicable legal requirements and procedures for entry into force on behalf of the EU. However, following the Commission's successful challenge of the Council's practice to mandate the signing by a representative through the signature decision, it will in the future be for the Commission to ensure the actual signing of trade and investment agreements (following the adoption of a signature decision by the Council).[125] By inference, it will also be for the Commission to designate the person empowered to give notification on behalf of the EU about the completion

[120] See, eg, Article 30.7(1) CETA.
[121] Article 218 (5), (6) TFEU.
[122] The Council usually adopts a single signature and conclusion decision, respectively. However, in *Opinion 1/19*, the CJEU held that a single Council decision can be divided into two separate decisions if there is an 'objective need' to do so – for instance, to take account of Ireland's specific position under Protocol No 21. See further Opinion 1/19, *Istanbul Convention*, EU:C:2021:832, para 332.
[123] Hoffmeister (n 111).
[124] Henry Kissinger supposedly once asked: 'Who do I call if I want to call Europe?'
[125] Case C-551/21, *Commission v Council*, ECLI:EU:C:2024:281. For an example of past practice see eg, Article 2 of Council Decision (EU) 2017/37 of 28 October 2016 on the signing on behalf of the European Union of the Comprehensive Economic and Trade Agreement (CETA) between Canada, of the one part, and the European Union and its Member States, of the other part [2017] OJ L11/1; or Art. 5 of the Council

of the applicable legal requirements and procedures for entry into force (following the adoption of a conclusion decision by the Council). Provided that the agreement at issue is mixed, it must also be signed and ratified by all Member States individually in accordance with their own legal constitutional requirements.[126] In the case of mixity, the signature and conclusion by the EU pursuant to Article 218(5), (6) TFEU relates only to the parts of the agreement that fall within a competence held and exercised by the EU.[127] By inference, the signature and conclusion of a mixed agreement by each Member State relates only to the parts of the agreement that fall within a competence held and exercised by the Member States. Unfortunately, the EU's and the Member States' ratification acts do usually not indicate the limits of their respective competence, suggesting that they each ratify the entire mixed agreement. This creates numerous legal problems, including with regard to democratic oversight (with national parliaments encroaching on the EP's competence and, potentially, vice versa), and the extent to which national governments and parliaments can reject a mixed agreement.[128]

The signature of an international agreement initiates the ratification process. Signature does not imply that the parties are bound by a treaty. Yet, pursuant to Article 18(a) VCLT, parties are obliged to refrain from adopting acts defeating a treaty's object and purpose after signature. Pursuant to Article 218(5) TFEU, the signature decision can be adopted by the Council alone. The consent of the EP is not required at this stage. This is not unusual in a two-stage ratification process: the executive first commits to the objectives of the agreement by signature, but allows time to obtain parliamentary consent before agreeing to being bound by the treaty. Pursuant to Article 218(10) TFEU, the EP must be informed about the Council's decision to sign a treaty. The failure to duly inform the EP constitutes an 'infringement of an essential procedural requirement' within the meaning of Article 263(2) TFEU and may invalidate the respective legal act.[129] The CJEU confirmed that the duty to inform the EP prescribed by Article 218(10) TFEU implies that the EP must not be put before a fait accompli, but must be given sufficient time to express its opinions before the Council makes its decision.[130]

Article 14 VCLT stipulates when the consent of a state to be bound by the treaty is established by ratification. This is, inter alia, the case where the international treaty so provides or where the representative of a state has signed the treaty subject to ratification. The same conditions apply with regard to the acceptance and approval of treaties (Article 14(2) VCLT). As stated above, some EU trade and investment agreements suggest approval as a means for the parties to express their consent to be bound. The EU decides to approve a trade and investment agreement by means of a Council decision on the conclusion of an international agreement (Article 218(6) TFEU). In contrast to the signature, there are numerous circumstances where the conclusion of international agreements requires the consent of the EP, including for Association Agreements,[131] and agreements covering fields where the ordinary legislative procedure applies.[132]

Decision (EU) 2018/1907 of 20 December 2018 on the conclusion of the Agreement between the European Union and Japan for an Economic Partnership [2018] OJ L 330/1.

[126] See further Chapter 5, section V.

[127] Chapter 6, section II.

[128] See further Chapter 6, section IV.

[129] Case 138/79, *Roquette Frères v Council*, EU:C:1980:249, para 33.

[130] See especially *Tanzania* (n 72); and *Mauritius* (n 72). See also section II.D above.

[131] Article 218(6)(a)(i) TFEU.

[132] ibid Article 218(6)(a)(v).

As EU trade and investment agreements are largely covered by material fields where the ordinary legislative procedure applies internally,[133] they cannot be concluded without the EP's consent. It may be noted that Article 218(6)(a) TFEU must also be followed for agreements that may – under international law – be adopted by signature (Article 12 VCLT). In other words, the EU may not express its consent to be bound by signature to an international agreement without obtaining the consent of the EP where that consent is required pursuant to Article 218(6)(a)(i)–(v) TFEU, even though Article 218(6) TFEU refers to treaty 'conclusion'. It is the expression of the consent to be bound that is relevant.

Since the entry into force of the Lisbon Treaty, the EP has demonstrated that its newly gained veto powers for the conclusion of international agreements are not merely declaratory. Besides the above-mentioned 'SWIFT incident', the EP's rejection of the Anti-Counterfeiting Trade Agreement (ACTA) after 'unprecedented direct lobbying by thousands of EU citizens' is the main case in point.[134] The EP's rejection of ACTA underlines once more the importance of involving the EP as well as national parliaments and citizens at the negotiation stage.

National parliaments are informed about the Commission's proposals to sign and conclude international (trade and investment) agreements. They can impact their Member State representative in the Council through different national (constitutional) channels.[135] At the EU level, national parliaments can voice their opinions, including on Commission proposals to sign and conclude trade and investment agreements, through the above-mentioned Barroso initiative. The Commission will reply to these opinions.[136]

B. Voting Majorities in the Council: From Common Accord to QMV

Articles 218(8) and 207(4) TFEU stress that the Council must generally act by a qualified majority throughout the treaty-making process, that is, for adopting its decisions on the opening of treaty negotiations, signature and conclusion. For EU trade and

[133] The ordinary legislative procedure applies for unilateral trade measures (Article 207(2) TFEU); the harmonisation of the internal market (Article 114(1) TFEU); the free movement of capital (Article 63(1), 64(2) TFEU); transport (Article 91(1), 100(2) TFEU)); and for environment (Article 192(1) TFEU) and labour rights protection (Article 152(2) TFEU). FTAs are thus largely covered by material fields where the ordinary legislative procedure applies internally. Even if an agreement were to include a limited number of fields where the special legislative procedure would apply internally, these areas would be ancillary and hence would not change the applicability of Article 218(6)(a)(v) TFEU. See especially Case C-300/89, *Titanium Dioxide*, EU:C:1991:244, para 20; and Case C-130/10, *Parliament v Council*, EU:C:2012:472, paras 79 et seq.

[134] European Parliament, Press Release, 'European Parliament Rejects ACTA' [2012] Reference No 20120703IPR48247. The EP also rejected the second protocol annexed to the Fisheries Partnership Agreement with Morocco. See European Parliament legislative resolution on the draft Council decision on the conclusion of a Protocol between the European Union and the Kingdom of Morocco setting out the fishing opportunities and financial compensation provided for in the Fisheries Partnership Agreement between the European Community and the Kingdom of Morocco [2011] doc P7_TA(2011)0569. On the rejection of ACTA, see, eg, K Meissner, 'Democratizing EU External Relations: The European Parliament's Informal Role in SWIFT, ACTA, and TTIP' (2016) 21 *European Foreign Affairs Review* 269; and C Eckes, *EU Powers under External Pressure: How the EU's External Actions Alter its Internal Structures* (Oxford University Press, 2019) 161 et seq.

[135] See further Chapter 5, sections II and III.A.

[136] See, eg, Resolution of the Bundesrat [2014] Document 295/14, and the Commission's reply thereto (C(2015) 1665 final). See generally (n 101).

investment agreements (other than Association Agreements),[137] unanimity voting is hence the exception rather than the rule.

In past practice, the Member States in the Council nevertheless retained de facto veto powers over the decisions to sign and conclude EU trade and investment agreements because these agreements were concluded as mixed agreements by default.[138] It is an established practice in the Council to wait for the common accord of all Member States before taking a decision on the signature or conclusion of a mixed agreement. The practice of common accord originated under Article 133(6) EC, which, as previously explained, subjected the ratification of certain trade agreements to the 'common accord' of Member States.[139] The search for a common accord amongst Member States then became an established practice for the ratification of all types of mixed agreements, even after Article 133(6) EC was overhauled by the Lisbon Treaty reform. For the signature and conclusion of mixed agreements, the Council considered it 'necessary to ensure that all the Member States concerned consent to being bound as regards their national competences before proceeding to adopt, by the requisite majority (i.e., by qualified majority or unanimity), the Council Decision pursuant to the competences of the Union'.[140] Despite not constituting a formal voting rule, the practice of common accord thus established a de facto unanimous voting requirement, as the Member States' consent was sought before the Council took action.[141]

The practice of common accord was challenged by the EP, the Commission, Austria and Finland in *Opinion 1/19*. In essence, they asserted that the practice of common accord breached EU law because it added an extra step to the decision-making procedure that was not foreseen by the Treaties. The Commission argued that the Council (re-)introduced hybridity by subjecting the application of Article 218 TFEU to the prior search for a common accord amongst Member States, thereby disregarding the gist of the CJEU's finding in *Hybrid Acts*. Advocate General Hogan disagreed with this legal view. After noting that EU law does not set down any time limits for the Council to take a decision on the signature or conclusion of an international agreement, he found that the 'Council may postpone its decision for as long as it deems necessary in order to take an informed decision'.[142] The CJEU largely agreed with the Advocate General in this point. It held that insofar the Council 'acts in accordance with its Rules of Procedure and the effectiveness of Article 218(2), (6) and (8) TFEU is guaranteed, nothing precludes the Council from extending its discussions in order to achieve, inter alia, the greatest possible majority with a view to concluding an international agreement … which

[137] Pursuant to Article 218(8) TFEU, the Council acts unanimously for Association Agreements.

[138] *cf* Chapter 1, section III.

[139] *cf* Chapter 2, section III.A.

[140] The Member States remained free to decide on the practicalities for expressing their individual consent. Past practice ranges from separate decisions by Government Representatives at Council meetings, or joint entries in the Council or COREPER minutes, to implicit consents. See further Written Observations of the Council in Opinion 1/19, version with all clerical errors corrected [2019] SGS19/9241, on file with the author, 69.

[141] To be precise, there is a (marginal) difference: unanimity voting allows Member States to abstain without blocking an action, whereas common accord requires agreement between all Member States. See Written Observations of the Council (n 140) 69.

[142] Opinion of Advocate General Hogan, Opinion 1/19, *Istanbul Convention*, EU:C:2021:198, para 200.

may involve waiting for the "common accord" of the Member States'.[143] Yet, the CJEU held that the 'effectiveness' of Article 218 TFEU would be undermined if the search for a common accord were to be understood as a legal prerequisite by the Council and the Member States. Such an understanding would establish a 'hybrid decision-making process' which is incompatible with Article 218 TFEU and the CJEU's findings in *Hybrid Acts*.[144] Yet, as Chamon rightly observed, by ruling out 'common accord' as a legal prerequisite, the CJEU made a statement of principle that is of limited practical significance, as 'it merely means that the Council has to avoid referring to a lack of common accord among Member States when it is asked to explain why it does not conclude a mixed agreement'.[145] The CJEU further underlined that in accordance with Article 11 of the Council's Rules of Procedure, the Commission or a single Member State can initiate a vote in the Council, provided that a majority of Member States agrees to holding a vote.[146] In doing so, the CJEU underlined that a vote in the Council cannot be held back by a minority of Member States. As things currently stand, the decision to stop waiting for a common accord remains within the political discretion of the Council, its Member States and the Commission. Yet, the Council can always amend its rules of procedure, which may in practice caution the Commission's interference with the Council's internal decision-making processes.

Prior to *Opinion 1/19*, the Council had considered that the search for a common accord was a legal prerequisite for the ratification of the investment agreements with Canada, Vietnam and Singapore.[147] While the Council can now no longer use the lack of a common accord as a reason not to ratify EU IPAs, it appears to wait to take a decision on the conclusion of these agreements until they have been ratified by all Member States. The EP agreed to ratify CETA in 2017,[148] the IPA with Singapore in 2019[149] and the IPA with Vietnam Singapore in 2020.[150]

[143] Opinion 1/19 (n 122) para 253. See also G Kübek, 'Facing and Embracing the Consequences of Mixity: Opinion 1/19, *Istanbul Convention*' (2022) 59 *Common Market Law Review* 1465.

[144] Opinion 1/19 (n 122) para 246.

[145] M Chamon, 'Op-Ed: The Court's Opinion in Avis 1/19 Regarding the Istanbul Convention', *EU Law Live*, 12 October 2021, eulawlive.com/op-ed-the-courts-opinion-in-avis-1-19-regarding-the-istanbul-convention-by-merijn-chamon.

[146] Opinion 1/19 (n 122) para 255.

[147] Observations de la Commission Européene sur la demand d'Avis 1/19, *Convention d'Istanbul* [2019] sj.i.dir(2019)8875307, on file with the author, 31–32. Outside the context of trade policy, the Council has publicly stated that the adoption of signature or conclusion decisions were 'withheld after a common accord of the Member States to be bound by the Convention with respect to their national competences could not be established at COREPER'. See, for the Council of Europe Convention on the Manipulation of Sports Competitions [2014] CETS No 215, Council of the European Union, 'International Agreements That Concern EU Competences in the Area of Criminal Law – Inventory' [2017] 6892/17, 8.

[148] European Parliament legislative resolution of 15 February 2017 on the draft Council decision on the conclusion of the Comprehensive Economic and Trade Agreement (CETA) between Canada, of the one part, and the European Union and its Member States, of the other part [2017] P8_TA(2017)0030.

[149] European Parliament legislative resolution on the draft Council decision on the conclusion on behalf of the European Union of the Investment Protection Agreement between the European Union and its Member States, of the one part, and the Republic of Singapore, of the other part [2019] P8_TA(2019)0090.

[150] European Parliament legislative resolution of 23 January 2020 on the draft Council decision on the conclusion, on behalf of the Union, of the Investment Protection Agreement between the European Union and its Member States, of the one part, and the Socialist Republic of Viet Nam, of the other part [2020] P9_TA(2020)0028.

For the ratification of EU trade and investment agreements that are to be concluded by the EU alone, the waiting for a common accord of the Member States in the Council would arguably undermine the effectiveness of Articles 207 and 218 TFEU, provided that none of the unanimity exceptions apply. The search for the largest possible majority of Member States in the Council would circumvent the general requirement for QMV set out in Articles 207(4) and 218(8) TFEU. In such a situation, it also appears more likely for the Commission or a Member State to call for a vote, once it is apparent that a qualified majority of Member States in the Council supports the signature or conclusion of a given EU-only trade and investment agreement. As a result, the question arises as to whether EU trade and investment agreements must indeed be concluded by QMV or whether any of the unanimity exceptions in Articles 207 and 218 TFEU take effect.

C. Unanimity and Parallelism

Article 218(8) TFEU establishes a parallelism between internal and external voting rules in the Council: as soon as unanimity is required for the adoption of an internal EU act, it is also required for the adoption of international agreements in the same field. For the adoption of trade and investment agreements, Article 207(4) TFEU specifically dictates the need for such a parallelism in the fields of trade in services, commercial aspects of IPRs, and FDI. The wording of Articles 207(4) and 218(8) TFEU suggests that the requirement for the Council to vote unanimously on the opening of negotiations, signature and conclusion of EU (trade and investment) agreements is already triggered if only some provisions fall within the listed unanimity exceptions.[151] In doing so, these provisions ensure that EU external action is not used as a means to circumvent stricter internal voting requirements in the Council.

The Treaty of Lisbon no longer contains any relevant unanimity requirements for the adoption of internal EU acts in the fields of services and commercial aspects of IPRs. Internal EU acts in these fields are now adopted by QMV.[152] In this regard, Article 207(4) TFEU may be regarded as a relic of the pre-Lisbon period. However, the Treaties contain an internal unanimity requirement with regard to measures on the movement of capital to or from third countries involving direct investment. Pursuant to Article 64(3) TFEU, such measures must be adopted unanimously 'if they constitute a step backwards in Union law as regards the liberalisation of the movement of capital to or from third countries'. As previously explained, the EU's new generation trade and investment agreements automatically supersede and, as a consequence, terminate the Member States' existing BITs with the same trading partner.[153] Some authors have argued that the termination of the Member States' BITs would constitute a 'step

[151] Pursuant to Article 207(4) TFEU, it suffices that the agreement contains '*provisions* for which unanimity is required for the adoption of internal rules'. Article 218(8) TFEU stipulates that unanimity is required as soon as the agreement at issue covers '*a* field for which unanimity is required for the adoption of a Union act' (emphasis added).

[152] The requirement for QMV in the Council results from Article 62 in conjunction with Article 53(1) TFEU (services); from Article 64(2) TFEU (FDI); and from Article 118 TFEU (commercial aspects of IPRs).

[153] *cf* Chapter 2, section III.A.

backwards' within the meaning of 64(3) TFEU.[154] Yet, Article 64(3) TFEU specifically relates to EU law and not Member State law. The making of uniform rules on the liberalisation of capital with third countries via an international agreement adopted by the EU as a whole is arguably always a 'step forward' in the development of EU law, even if one were to assume that a pre-existing Member State BIT had achieved a higher degree of capital market liberalisation. In any event, the EU's new generation trade and investment agreements generally increase the liberalisation and protection of FDI as compared to the existing (older) Member State BITs.

Some authors have further claimed that the Council must vote unanimously for the conclusion of EU trade and investment agreements on the basis of Article 218(8) TFEU, read in conjunction with Article 113 TFEU,[155] because EU trade and investment agreements generally touch on the taxation of imports or exports for fiscal purposes and tax avoidance.[156] However, a closer look at the relevant provisions in EU trade and investment agreements shows that these agreements merely reiterate the prohibition of fiscal discrimination expressed in Article VIII GATT[157] or carve out taxation from their scope altogether.[158] It is also undisputed that the TSD Chapters of EU trade and investment agreements do not touch upon any of the existing internal unanimity requirements with regard to social protection[159] and environmental rights.[160]

In sum, new generation EU trade and investment agreements do not cover a field for which unanimity is required for the adoption of an internal EU act. Thus, unanimity does not arise as a matter of parallelism for the making of EU trade and investment agreements, be that on the basis of Article 207(4) or Article 218(8) TFEU.

D. Unanimity and Sensitive Service Sectors

Article 207(4) TFEU stipulates that the Council must also act unanimously for the making of trade and investment agreements 'in the field of trade in cultural and audiovisual services, where these agreements risk prejudicing the Union's cultural and linguistic diversity' (Article 207(4)(a) TFEU) and 'in the field of trade in social, education and health services, where these agreements risk seriously disturbing the national organisation of such services and prejudicing the responsibility of Member States to

[154] See especially B Schiffbauer, 'Mehrheitserfordernisse für Abstimmungen im Rat über TTIP, CETA & Co' (2016) 27 *Europäische Zeitschrift für Wirtschaftsrecht* 252. He further claimed that unanimity was required on the basis of Article 19(1) TFEU read in conjunction with Article 207(4) TFEU, as EU investment agreements would internally discriminate against EU investors (at 256). However, this claim has been nullified by the CJEU in Opinion 1/17, *Comprehensive Economic and Trade Agreement with Canada*, EU:C:2019:341, paras 180–83.

[155] See, eg, Schiffbauer (n 154); W Weiß, 'Verfassungsprobleme des Abschlusses und der vorläufigen Anwendung des CETA Freihandelsabkommens mit Kanada'. *Stellungnahme zur Öffentlichen Anhörung des Wirtschaft und Energie des Deutschen Bundestages* (2016).

[156] See, eg, Articles 1.4, 2.4(a), 2.9(2), 2.12 and 2.16 of the EU-Japan FTA.

[157] See, eg, Article 2.9 CETA; Article 2.10 of the EUSFTA; Article 2.8 of the EU-New Zealand FTA.

[158] See, eg, Article 1.4(3), (6) of the EU-Japan FTA; Article 16.6 of the EUSFTA; Article 17.7 of the EUVFTA; Article 10.42, Footnote 1 and Article 25.3(2),(3),(4) EU-New Zealand FTA.

[159] Article 153 1(c), (d), (f) and (g) TFEU; in conjunction with para 2 fourth sentence of the same provision.

[160] Article 192(2) TFEU.

deliver them' (Article 207(4)(b) TFEU). Simply put, Article 207(4) TFEU requires the Council to vote unanimously in particularly sensitive service sectors. Internally, these sectors generally fall within the realm of supporting competences, ie, in fields where the harmonisation of the Member States' laws and regulation by the EU is prohibited.[161] Consequentially, Article 207(4) TFEU ensures that the EU may only make external rules in areas of supporting competence if all the Member States in the Council so desire.

To trigger Article 207(4)(a), (b) TFEU, two cumulative criteria must be fulfilled: first, an agreement must include provisions on trade in the listed sensitive service sectors; and, second, the agreement must have an appreciable negative effect within the EU (indent (a)) or a Member State (indent (b)).[162] Unanimity is thus not automatically required if an EU trade and investment agreement touches on one of the sensitive service sectors listed in Article 207(4)(a), (b) TFEU. It is the effect of the international agreement on the EU's or a Member State's internal legal framework that is decisive for the application of Article 207(4)(a), (b) TFEU. The threshold for triggering Article 207(4)(a), (b) TFEU is therefore high, as tangible adverse effects on EU or Member State law need to be proven. The burden of proof lies with those Member States that wish to rely on Article 207(4)(a), (b) TFEU.

The EU's latest trade and investment agreements touch on the sensitive service sectors listed in Article 207(4)(a), (b) TFEU. CETA is a case in point. Although CETA does not apply to trade in audiovisual services,[163] it does not fully carve out trade in cultural services[164] and trade in social, education and health services.[165] Yet, CETA arguably does not have an appreciable negative effect on the EU's or a Member State's internal legal framework. In the field of trade in culture, the obligations enshrined in CETA do not principally exceed the EU's existing obligations within the framework of the GATS.[166] Therefore, CETA's effects on the EU's legal framework on trade in culture – if any – are marginal. This is also the case for CETA's provisions on trade in social, education and health services. As these areas are largely exempted from the scope of CETA, they will not cause serious disturbances of the national organisation of such services. The ensuing new generation FTAs all follow the blueprint of CETA and dealt with sensitive service sectors in the same manner.[167] Therefore, neither indent (a) nor (b) of Article 207(4) TFEU applies to the signature and conclusion of the EU's latest new generation trade and investment agreements.

[161] Article 6(a), (c) and (e) TFEU in conjunction with Article 2(5) TFEU.

[162] See further Bäumler (n 46).

[163] See, eg, Articles 7.7, 8.2, 9.2 and 12.2 CETA.

[164] Canada has broader exemptions for cultural services (eg, Articles 7.7 and 12.2(b)(i) CETA). However, some carve-outs only apply to Canada and not the EU (eg, Articles 8.2(3) and 9.2(2)(c) CETA).

[165] Trade in social, education and health services is exempted from Chapter 12 on 'domestic regulations' pursuant to Article 12.2(b)(ii) CETA and subject to each party's 'right to regulate' (Article 8.9 CETA); further carve-outs are enshrined in the country-specific schedules attached to CETA. Yet, there is no clause in CETA that exempts these fields from the agreement's entire scope.

[166] See also Bäumler (n 46) 612.

[167] These FTAs have similar carve-out clauses for trade in audiovisual and cultural, and social, health, educational services to CETA. See, eg, Articles 8.3(a), 8.9(c) and 8.21(4) in conjunction with fn 23 of the EUSFTA; Articles 8.3(2)(a), 8.9 and 8.22(4) in conjunction with fn 28 of the EUVFTA; Articles 4.2.(4)(b) and 12.3(1) in conjunction with fn 1, Article 12.3(7) of the EU-Japan FTA, or Articles 10.1(2) or 12.3 of the EU-New Zealand FTA.

In contrast to other new generation EU trade and investment agreements, the FTA with South Korea contains a protocol on cultural cooperation.[168] The protocol applies in the fields of cultural and audiovisual cooperation.[169] Although most of its clauses merely incentivise the parties to cooperate with 'best endeavours',[170] some provisions mandate active cooperation.[171] It arguably cannot be excluded that the link between the EU's and South Korea's cultural industries could risk linguistic diversity within the EU, as English is the *lingua franca* for global cultural projects. Moreover, in view of the object and purpose of Article 207(4)(a), (b) TFEU – that is, increased Member State control in the Council for the making of agreements in fields where the EU has supporting competence only – the attachment of an entire protocol on culture to an FTA justified unanimity voting in the Council. Yet, the Council decisions on the signature and conclusion of the FTA with Korea do not list Article 207(4)(a) TFEU as a legal basis.[172] The Council nevertheless voted unanimously as the FTA with Korea was concluded as a mixed agreement.

None of the ensuing trade and investment agreements followed the EU-Korea template and attached a specific protocol on cultural cooperation.[173] Therefore – with the exception of the EU-Korea FTA – none of the specific requirements for unanimity voting in the Council provided by Articles 207 and 218 TFEU apply to the negotiation, signature and conclusion of the EU's new generation trade and investment agreements. These agreements may be adopted by QMV in the Council.

IV. Provisional Application

The provisional application of treaties pending their entry into force is a long-standing practice under international law that is recognised in Article 25 VCLT.[174] Accordingly, a treaty or a part of a treaty may be applied provisionally if the treaty itself so provides

[168] EU-Korea FTA, Protocol on Cultural Cooperation [2011] OJ L127/1418.

[169] ibid Article 1(1).

[170] eg, ibid Articles 1(3), 4(1), 6(1), (3)–(5).

[171] The Protocol, for example, prescribes the mandatory setting-up of committees, exchange and dialogues on relevant subject matters (Articles 2 and 3 of the EU-Korea Protocol on Cultural Cooperation (n 168)). Moreover, pursuant to Article 3*bis*, a modified state-to-state dispute settlement mechanism applies to the Protocol.

[172] Council Decision (EU) 2011/265 of 16 September 2010 on the signing, on behalf of the European Union, and provisional application of the Free Trade Agreement between the European Union and its Member States, of the one part, and the Republic of Korea, of the other part [2011] OJ L127/1; Council Decision (EU) 2015/2169 of 1 October 2015 on the conclusion of the Free Trade Agreement between the European Union and its Member States, of the one part, and the Republic of Korea, of the other part [2015] OJ L307/2.

[173] Other forms of trade agreements at times annex a cultural cooperation protocol. See, eg, the Economic Partnership Agreement with the CARIFORUM states [2008] OJ L289/3.

[174] On the concept and practice of provisional application in public international law, see, eg, D Azaria, 'Provisional Application of Treaties' in DB Hollis (ed), *The Oxford Guide to Treaties*, 2nd edn (Oxford University Press, 2020) 229; D Mathy, 'Article 25 VCLT' in Corten and Klein (n 2) 639; R Lefeber, 'The Provisional Application of Treaties' in J Klabbers and R Lefeber (eds), *Essays on the Law of Treaties: A Collection of Essays in Honour of Bert Vierdag* (Brill/Nijhoff, 1998) 81; HG Krenzler, *Die vorläufige Anwendung völkerrechtlicher Verträge* (1964); A Quast Mertsch, *Provisionally Applied Treaties: Their Binding Force and Legal Nature* (Brill/Nijhoff, 2012).

or the negotiating parties have in some other manner so agreed.[175] Provisional application thus describes a situation where the contracting parties decide to give legal effect to a treaty as a whole or in parts, upon signature or on an agreed date, pending its entry into force. The ratification of most international agreements is subject to the consent of the national legislature and/or citizens. Especially in a multilateral context, the time between a treaty's signature and entry into force may thus take years or even decades. In the field of trade, the most well-known example is the GATT 1947, which was provisionally applied for over 47 years before the founding of the WTO in 1994.[176] In practice, provisional application is thus a useful tool for bridging the time between a treaty's signature and entry into force.

The EU usually decides to use provisional application in case of mixity. In the field of trade and investment, the mixed procedure requires around 40 affirmative national parliamentary votes and potentially national referenda.[177] Mixed agreements thus significantly prolong the duration of a treaty's ratification process. A classic example is the Agreement on Cooperation and Customs Union between the (then) EEC and San Marino, which took over 11 years to enter into force.[178] The ratification period of the FTA with Korea lasted no less than five years[179] and the ratification process of the FTA with Peru and Colombia has been ongoing since 2012.[180] Provisional application has therefore been an effective mechanism to mitigate the problems that arise from the lengthy ratification process of mixed agreements by ensuring immediate (market access) benefits for all parties after signature. At the same time, provisional application has been contentious in the context of mixity for two main reasons. First, requests to ensure democratic legitimacy of provisionally applied agreements have become louder in recent years. Second, the Commission and the Council have had frequent disagreements about the scope of provisional application because mixed agreements concern competences exercised by the Member States.

Despite its frequent use in practice, provisional application thus presents numerous theoretical and practical difficulties under international and EU law. The following sections explain some of these difficulties by first assessing the legal effect of provisional

[175] Article 25(1) VCLT. See also Guideline 3 and the ensuing commentary of the draft guidelines and draft annex constituting the Guide to Provisional Application of Treaties, with commentaries thereto [2021] *Yearbook of the International Law Commission*, vol II, part two.

[176] F Roessler, 'The Provisional Application of the GATT' (1985) 19 *Journal of World Trade* 289.

[177] See Chapter 5, section I.

[178] The agreement was signed in 1991 and concluded in 2002. *cf* Council Decision (EC) 2002/245 of 28 February 2002 on the conclusion of an agreement on co-operation and customs union between the European Economic Community and the Republic of San Marino and of the Protocol thereto following the enlargement which took effect on 1 January 1995 [2002] OJ L84/41. See further A Rosas, 'Mixed Union: Mixed Agreements' in M Koskenniemi (ed), *International Law Aspects of the European Union* (Kluwer Law International, 1998) 125, 134.

[179] Council of the European Union, Press Release, 'EU-South Korea Free Trade Agreement Concluded' [2015] 691/15.

[180] Council Decision (EU) 2012/735 of 31 May 2012 on the signing, on behalf of the Union, and provisional application of the Trade Agreement between the European Union and its Member States, of the one part, and Colombia and Peru, of the other part [2012] OJ L354/1. Ecuador joined the agreement in 2016; the agreement has since been applied provisionally with regard to Ecuador. See Council 2016/2369 of 11 November 2016 on the signing, on behalf of the Union, and provisional application of the Protocol of Accession to the Trade Agreement between the European Union and its Member States, of the one part, and Colombia and Peru, of the other part, to take account of the accession of Ecuador [2016] OJ L356/1.

application (section IV.A) and, second, the law and practice of provisionally applying mixed EU trade and investment agreements (sections IV.B, IV.C and IV.D).

A. Legal Effect

A precise definition of the term 'provisional application' is neither contained in Article 2 VCLT on the use of terms nor in Article 25 VCLT itself. Clearly, provisional application takes place before a treaty enters into force. It is thus something short of entry into force as stipulated in Article 24 VCLT.[181] As such, the terms 'provisional application' and 'provisional entry into force' refer to different legal concepts.[182] The latter implies that a treaty has obligatory force prior to entry into force; the former makes no presumption on the legal effects of a treaty's application. Indeed, in view of its broad wording, Article 25 VCLT could be interpreted as implicating that provisional application does not have binding legal effect, but merely expresses a party's intention to apply a treaty in good faith.[183]

Yet, states have apparently accepted the premise that the provisional application of treaties has legal effects in practice. Most states have advanced a synonymous understanding of provisional application and entry into force, the only difference being the more flexible termination process of provisional application.[184] This view was also expressed in several arbitration decisions on the ECT. The ECT must generally be applied provisionally unless provisional application contradicts with national constitutional rules or a party has expressly opted out from provisional application.[185] In *Kardassopoulos v Georgia*, a tribunal considered that although provisional application is 'not the same as entry into force', the 'ECT's provisional application is a course to which each signatory "agrees" in Article 45 (1): it is … thus a matter of legal obligation'.[186] As a result, the tribunal concluded that 'the language used in Article 45(1) is to be interpreted as meaning that each signatory State is obliged, even before the ECT has formally entered into force, to apply the whole ECT as if it had already done so'.[187] In *Yukos v Russian Federation*,[188] *Veteran Petroleum Ltd v Russian Federation*[189] and *Hulley*

[181] Mathy (n 174) 641–42.

[182] See especially JM Gómez-Robledo, 'First Report on the Provisional Application of Treaties', International Law Commission, Sixty-Fifth Session [2013] UN Doc A/CN.4/664, 84; G Gaja, 'Provisional Application of Treaties', Report of the International Law Commission, Sixty-Third Session [2011] UN Doc A/66/10, Annex C.

[183] In such a scenario, there would be a general understanding that the other party reciprocates the application of the treaty. Yet, non-compliance would not incur international responsibility. The lack of reciprocity could then lead to the termination of provisional application by the first party. See further Gaja (n 182) 198.

[184] JM Gómez-Robledo, 'Second Report on the Provisional Application of Treaties', International Law Commission, Sixty-Sixth Session [2014] UN Doc A/CN.4/675, 5 et seq. This understanding is echoed in the academic literature: see, eg, Lefeber (n 174) 16; Mathy (n 174) 25 et seq; Quast Mertsch (n 174) 236.

[185] Article 45(1), (2)(a) of the Energy Charter Treaty [1994] UNTS Vol. 2080, 95. See also Gaja (n 182) 332 et seq.

[186] *Ioannis Kardassopoulos v Republic of Georgia*, ICSID Case No ARB/05/18, para 209.

[187] ibid para 211.

[188] Permanent Court of Arbitration, *Yukos Universal Limited (Isle of Man) v Russian Federation*, PCA Case No AA 227, para 314.

[189] Permanent Court of Arbitration, *Veteran Petroleum Limited (Cyprus) v Russian Federation*, PCA Case No AA 228, para 314.

Enterprises Ltd v Russian Federation,[190] arbitral tribunals also held that the 'provisional application of a treaty creates binding obligations'.

The EU has a synonymous understanding of provisional application and provisional entry into force. The clauses on provisional application in EU trade and investment agreements generally stipulate that 'the Parties shall understand the term "entry into force of this Agreement" as meaning the date of provisional application'.[191] In doing so, the EU eradicates any doubt about the obligatory legal effect it wishes to confer upon trade and investment agreements that are being applied provisionally. Once a treaty enters into force – including in situations where provisional application is understood as entry into force – the *pacta sunt servanda* principle implies that the agreement is legally binding and that the parties must perform it in good faith (Article 26 VCLT).

B. EU Procedure

In the EU, provisional application has been regularly used, even before it was provided for in the Treaties.[192] The Treaty of Amsterdam inserted a specific provision stipulating that the signature of an agreement may be accompanied by its provisional application.[193] Pursuant to what is now Article 218(5) TFEU, the Council, acting on a proposal by the Commission, 'shall adopt a decision authorising the signing of the agreement and, if necessary, its provisional application before entry into force'. The Council usually adopts a single decision on the signature and provisional application of international agreements. However, in some situations, separate Council decisions on signature and provisional application may be required. This would, for example, be the case if the EU only decides to provisionally apply a small part of the envisaged agreement and, as a result, the decision on provisional application requires a different legal basis than the decision on signature. In practice, the Council has adopted separate decisions on the provisional application and signature of CETA, which allowed it to adopt the decisions by a different voting majority.[194] As was discussed above, the Council considered a common accord necessary for the conclusion of CETA because of its mixed character.[195] As the decision on provisional application only concerned

[190] Permanent Court of Arbitration, *Hulley Enterprises Limited (Cyprus) v Russian Federation*, PCA Case No AA 226, para 314.

[191] See, eg, Article 30.7(3)(d) CETA.

[192] Between 1976 and 1990, provisional application was used 200 times. See G Garzón Clariana, 'L'application provisoire des accords internationaux de la Communauté' in P Demaret et al (eds), *30 Years of European Legal Studies at the College of Europe: 30 ans d'e'tudes juridiques européennes au Collège d'Europe* (PIE-Peter Lang, 2005) 479, 482, as cited by R Passos, 'Some Issues Related to the Provisional Application of International Agreements and the Institutional Balance' in J Czuczai and F Naert (eds), *The EU as a Global Actor: Bridging Legal Theory and Practice: Liber Amicorum in Honour of Ricardo Gosalbo Bono* (Brill/Nijhoff, 2017) 380, 381, fn 4. Passos also notes that between 2004 and 2009, provisional application was provided for 80 times and that post-Lisbon, approximately every third EU international agreement is applied provisionally.

[193] Article 300(2) EC.

[194] Council Decision (EU) 2017/38 of 28 October 2016 on the provisional application of the Comprehensive Economic and Trade Agreement (CETA) between Canada, of the one part, and the European Union and its Member States, of the other part [2017] OJ L11/1080; Council Decision (EU) 2017/37 (n 125).

[195] *cf* section III.B above.

material areas that fell within the EU's exclusive competence, there was no rationale for applying the practice of common accord. QMV applied, at least formally.

Pursuant to Article 218(5) TFEU, the Council decision on the signature and provisional application of EU agreements may legally be taken without obtaining formal consent of the EP. This is not unusual: as it is the purpose of provisional application to give effect to an agreement without waiting for the completion of the formal ratification process, it is designed as an executive prerogative. As such, provisional application comes at the cost of bypassing democratic control processes. As will be further explained, several Member States do not recognise provisional application in their national constitutional law and only allow resorting to this practice after the completion of a treaty's formal ratification process.[196]

A similar practice was developed by the EU post-Lisbon. The EP is generally asked to give its formal consent to EU trade and investment agreements before such agreements are being applied provisionally.[197] This informal practice developed in the context of the ratification of the FTA with Korea. The former head of the Commission, Karel De Gucht, stressed in a speech before the EP that since new generation trade and investment agreements 'fundamentally define [the EU's] relationship to a third country for a long time ... it is politically warranted to involve the Parliament even before provisional application', promising that the FTA with Korea 'will *not* be provisionally applied before the Parliament has had a chance to give its consent' (emphasis in original).[198] Notably, the Council has not officially recognised the practice to ask for the EP's consent to a trade and investment agreement before the start of provisional application.[199] It is the Commission that awaits the EP's consent before proposing the provisional application of an EU trade and investment agreement.

The practice not to apply EU trade agreements before the EP has given its consent continued for the FTAs with Peru, Colombia and Ecuador, the Association Agreement with Latin America, and CETA.[200] Yet, the EP was merely informed about the provisional application of the Association Agreements with Georgia,[201] Moldova[202] and

[196] See Chapter 5, section VI.

[197] See also Kleimann and Kübek (n 18) 28.

[198] K De Gucht, 'The Implications of the Lisbon Treaty for EU Trade Policy', S&D seminar on EU Trade Policy, Oporto, 8 October 2010, 3–4. See also F Hoffmeister, 'The European Union's Common Commercial Policy a Year after Lisbon: Sea Change or Business as Usual?' in Koutrakos (n 76) 83, 92; Kleimann (n 88) 23; and A Suse and J Wouters, 'Exploring the Boundaries of Provisional Application: The EU's Mixed Trade and Investment Agreements' (2019) 53 *Journal of World Trade* 395.

[199] Interview with an EP official, 7 November 2018.

[200] As will be further explained in Chapter 7, provisional application is no longer relevant for most EU trade and investment agreements concluded under the new architecture, be that under the EU-only or the mixed procedure. See further Chapter 7, section IV.D.

[201] See European Parliament non-legislative resolution of 18 December 2014 on the draft Council decision on the conclusion, on behalf of the European Union, of the Association Agreement between the European Union and the European Atomic Energy Community and their Member States, of the one part, and Georgia, of the other part [2014] P8_TA(2014)0110; the agreement was applied provisionally in parts from 1 September 2014.

[202] See European Parliament non-legislative resolution of 13 November 2014 on the draft Council decision on the conclusion, on behalf of the European Union, of the Association Agreement between the European Union and the European Atomic Energy Community and their Member States, of the one part, and the Republic of Moldova, of the other part [2014] P8_TA(2014)0049; the agreement was applied provisionally in parts as of 1 September 2014.

Ukraine,[203] as well as the TCA with the UK.[204] The rationale for involving the EP prior to the provisional application of some EU trade agreements rather than others was outlined by the former head of DG Trade, Cecilia Malmström. In a 2014 hearing before the EP as a Commissioner candidate, she made the following political commitment:

> I am ready, when proposing decisions to sign politically important trade agreements which fall under my responsibility, to ask Council to delay provisional application until the European Parliament has given its consent. However, we need certain flexibility in applying such a practice as there will always be occasions where the urgency of a particular file, or its technical character, mean that it is unwarranted to delay its application pending the EP's consent.[205]

In her 'agenda for Europe', Ursula von der Leyen went a step further by promising that 'my Commission will always propose that provisional application of trade agreements take place only once the European Parliament has given its consent'.[206]

By emphasising that the EP will 'always' be asked to give its consent to EU trade and investment agreements prior to provisional application, von der Leyen suggested that there is no longer a need for 'certain flexibility in applying such a practice', as Malmström had maintained. However, by proposing the provisional application of the EU-UK TCA without awaiting the consent of the EP, the von der Leyen Commission showed that the need for flexibility apparently persists where particular situations of urgency make a delay of that treaty's provisional application unwarranted.[207]

The example of the TCA illustrates the fragility of the informal practice to ask for the EP's consent before provisionally applying an EU trade and investment agreement. Ultimately, the practice hinges on the discretionary powers of the Commission and the Council. In view of the increasing public interest in EU trade policy, the Commission's goal to strengthen its transparency and inclusiveness, and the imperative of involving all veto-players from the outset of the treaty-making process for the conclusion of such agreements, it would arguably be desirable to formalise the practice of not applying EU trade agreements provisionally before the EP has given its consent. This could best be achieved by amending Article 218 TFEU. As treaty change may not be feasible in the current political climate, the institutions could at least commit to this practice in an inter-institutional agreement, which according to the CJEU may have binding force.[208]

[203] The EP subsequently agreed to the provisional application of the EU-Ukraine Association Agreement for political reasons. See European Parliament resolution of 17 July 2014 on Ukraine [2014] P8_TA-PROV (2014)0009. See also Passos (n 192) 389.

[204] European Parliament resolution of 28 April 2021 on the outcome of EU-UK negotiations [2021] P9_TA(2021)0141, para 7.

[205] Answers to the European Parliament Questionnaire to the Commissioner-Designate Cecilia Malmström [2014]. In the context of CETA, see also European Parliament, Parliamentary Questions: Answer Given by Ms Malmström on Behalf of the Commission [2016] P-004200/2016.

[206] U von der Leyen, Candidate for President of the European Commission, 'A Union That Strives for More: My Agenda for Europe' (2019) 17.

[207] See further Chapter 8, section III.

[208] Article 295 TFEU. See also Case C-25/94, *Commission v Council (FAO)*, EU:C:1996:114.

C. Scope and Power

Pursuant to Article 25 VCLT, international treaties may be provisionally applied in full or in part. The possibility to resort to full or partial provisional application is usually re-iterated in EU trade and investment agreements.[209]

The provisional application of a treaty by the EU may encompass all areas of competence falling within the scope of the Treaties, ie, exclusive, shared, and supporting competences. The EU thus has the power to provisionally apply facultative mixed agreements alone and in full. The CJEU has underlined that there is no role for the Member States in the adoption of a Council decision on the signature and provisional application of an international agreement on the basis of Article 218(5) TFEU.[210] However, mandatory mixed agreements cannot be provisionally applied in full by the EU. International treaty provisions falling within the exclusive competence of the Member States cannot be exercised – even provisionally – by the EU.[211] Like any legislative act of the EU, the Council decision on provisional application must be substantively based on a competence-conferring Treaty provision. Reference to Article 218(5) TFEU alone is not enough; Article 218(5) TFEU is merely a procedural legal basis that must be cited in addition to a substantive legal basis (eg, Article 207 TFEU on the CCP). An exclusive Member State competence logically has no substantive legal basis in the TEU or the TFEU and can therefore not be included in the Council decision on provisional application. Unless the Member States decide to delegate their exclusive power to the EU level via Article 352(1) TFEU, they have to decide on the provisional application of the part of an agreement that falls within their exclusive prerogatives in their own right. In that case, the Council decision on provisional application would have to be accompanied by separate decisions on provisional application by each Member State. As Chapter 5 will show, this may be problematic, as some Member States only permit provisional application in exceptional circumstances, or not at all.[212] Consequentially, the parts of agreements falling within exclusive Member State competence are generally carved out from the scope of provisional application.

In practice, the scope of provisional application of new generation trade and investment agreements is largely confined to the EU's exclusive competence. As the CJEU concluded that all areas of new generation EU trade and investment agreements (other than, potentially, the ICS)[213] fall within EU exclusive and shared competence, they may largely (if not fully) be provisionally applied. The Commission has in the past frequently proposed the provisional application of EU trade and investment agreements in their

[209] See, eg, Article 30.7(3)(b) CETA.

[210] Case C-28/12, *Hybrid Acts*, EU:C:2015:282, para 44.

[211] See also C Herrmann, 'Unionsrechtliche und verfassungsrechtliche Fragen des Abschlusses und der vorläufigen Anwendung des Comprehensive Economic and Trade Agreement (CETA) zwischen der EU (inkl. Mitgliedstaaten) und Kanada', Stellungnahme für die Öffentliche Anhörung des Ausschusses für Wirtschaft und Energie des Deutschen Bundestages (2016) 9.

[212] See further Chapter 5, section V.

[213] It is not fully clear whether the EU may provisionally apply the ICS in full. See further Chapter 7, section IV.D.

entirety.[214] Yet, the Council generally carves out provisions falling within shared competence from the scope of provisional application.[215] In doing so, it may also seek to maintain a rationale for mixity. As was discussed in Chapter 2, mixity is usually facultative. In the context of facultative mixity, the inclusion of areas of shared competence (exercised by the Member States) is the basis for making the agreement mixed in the first place. In other words, the decision to conclude a mixed agreement in areas of shared competence presupposes that the Member States, and not the EU, exercise (at least part of) the shared competence. If the Council were to decide to apply provisionally aspects of a mixed agreement falling within the EU's shared competence, it could risk offsetting the very foundation for choosing to make a mixed agreement.[216] As a result, the Member States in the Council usually decide to apply only the parts of the mixed agreement provisionally that fall within EU exclusive competence. If they wish to apply the agreement provisionally in full, they decide to conclude the agreement under the EU-only procedure, as the case of the TCA demonstrates.[217]

D. EU Trade Practice

The Council has been reluctant to apply provisionally aspects of mixed (trade) agreements falling within the EU's shared competence.[218] The Council specifies the precise scope of provisional application in its decision on a treaty's signature and provisional application. Generally, these decisions indicate that areas (the Council considers as) falling outside the scope of EU exclusive competence are excluded from the scope of provisional application. In order to exclude certain provisions from the scope of provisional application, the Council used either a negative approach,[219] listing the specific treaty provisions that are exempted from provisional application, and/or a positive approach,[220] listing only those provisions that will be provisionally applied.[221]

Exceptionally, the Council decided to provisionally apply some areas of mixed trade and investment agreements it considered prior to *Opinion 2/15* as falling within shared competence. For the FTA with Korea, the Council decided to exempt the section on

[214] See, eg, Article 1 of the Proposal for a Council Decision on the provisional application of the Comprehensive Economic and Trade Agreement between Canada of the one part, and the European Union and its Member States, of the other part, COM (2016) 0470 final – 2016/0220 (NLE).

[215] See, eg, Council Decision (EU) 2017/38 (n 194).

[216] G Kübek and I Van Damme, 'Facultative Mixity and the European Union's Trade and Investment Agreements' in Chamon and Govaere (n 48) 661 et seq.

[217] See further Chapter 8, section IV.A.

[218] For a comprehensive analysis of the practice of provisionally applying EU FTAs, see also J Heliskoski, 'Provisional Application of EU Free Trade Agreements' in Hahn and Van der Loo (n 82) 586.

[219] See, eg, Article 3 of the Council Decision (EU) 2011/265 16 September 2010 on the signing, on behalf of the European Union, and provisional application of the Free Trade Agreement between the European Union and its Member States, of the one part, and the Republic of Korea, of the other part [2011] OJ L127/1.

[220] See, eg, Article 4 of the Council Decision (EU) 2014/295 of 17 March 2014 on the signing, on behalf of the European Union, and provisional application of the Association Agreement between the European Union and the European Atomic Energy Community and their Member States, of the one part, and Ukraine, of the other part, as regards the Preamble, Article 1, and Titles I, II and VII thereof [2014] OJ L161/1.

[221] The Council's decision on the provisional application of CETA combines the positive and negative approach. Compare Article 1(a) and 1(b) of the Council Decision (EU) 2017/38 (n 194). See also Kübek and Van Damme (n 216) 162.

criminal enforcement of intellectual property rights as well as parts of the protocol on cultural cooperation from the scope of provisional application.[222] However, it did not exclude the Protocol on Cultural Cooperation in its entirety from the scope of provisional application,[223] although the Protocol was the main reason for making the agreement mixed. Moreover, the Council decided to provisionally apply the FTA provisions on administrative proceedings,[224] maritime transport[225] and foreign non-direct investments[226] as well as the TSD Chapter,[227] although the Member States and the Council were of the legal opinion at the time that these fields qualify as shared competences.[228]

For the FTA with Peru and Colombia, the Council decided to exclude the 'essential elements' clause, provisions on administrative proceedings, review and appeal, as well as a clause re-affirming the party's existing rights and obligations in the field of IPRs under the Paris Convention and the TRIPS Agreement from the scope of provisional application.[229] The remaining parts of the treaty are being applied provisionally, including the FTA provisions on foreign non-direct investments[230] maritime transport,[231] TSD[232] and moral rights,[233] although the Council contended at the time that these fields fall within shared competence.

Against the backdrop of intense legal, political and public discussions, the Council confined the scope of provisional application of CETA more strictly to the realm of the EU's exclusive competence as compared to the provisional application of that agreement's predecessors.[234] The Council decided to exclude the majority of substantive investment protection disciplines[235] and the ICS from the scope of CETA's provisional application.[236] In addition, it carved out foreign non-direct investments. Chapter 8 CETA (investment) is therefore applied provisionally 'only in so far as foreign direct investment is concerned'.[237] Moreover, relevant provisions of Chapter 13 CETA (financial services) 'shall not be provisionally applied in so far as they concern portfolio investment, protection of investment or the resolution of investment disputes between investors and states'.[238] Third, individual provisions relating to camcording,

[222] See Article 3 of the Council Decision (EU) 2011/265 (n 219).

[223] Articles 1, 2, 3, 3*bis*, 4(1), (2), 5(1), (3)–(10), 6(2), (3) and 7 of the EU-Korea Protocol on Cultural Cooperation (n 168) are being applied provisionally. Remarkably, the scope of provisional application thus includes cultural dialogue and dispute settlement (Article 3 and 3*bis*).

[224] Article 12.5 EU-Korea FTA.

[225] ibid Article 7.47.

[226] ibid Article 8.2(2)(c).

[227] ibid Chapter 13.

[228] See also Kleimann and Kübek (n 18) 27–28.

[229] Article 3 of Council Decision (EU) 2012/735 (n 180).

[230] Article 152(b)(xi) of the EU-Peru/Colombia FTA.

[231] ibid Chapter 5, section 6.

[232] ibid Title IX.

[233] ibid Article 216.

[234] For an analysis of CETA's provisional application, see also L Pantaleo, 'The Provisional Application of CETA: Selected Issues' (2017) 41 *Questions of International Law* 59.

[235] In relation to Chapter 8 (Investment), solely Article 8.9 (Investment and regulatory measures), Article 8.10 (Treatment of investors and of covered investments), Article 8.11 (Compensation for losses) and Article 8.12 (Expropriation) are being applied provisionally, and only to the extent that they concern FDI. See Article 1(1)(a) of the Council Decision (EU) 2017/38 (n 194).

[236] Article 1(1)(a) Council Decision (EU) 2017/38 (n 194).

[237] ibid.

[238] ibid Article 1(1)(b).

administrative proceedings in the Member States and taxation are exempted from CETA's provisional application.[239] Yet, the Council continued its practice to apply provisionally some areas that it considered as falling within the realm of shared competence, such as maritime transport,[240] moral rights[241] and the TSD Chapters.[242] Moreover, the Council decided to provisionally apply the part of CETA that relates to the criminal enforcement of IPRs,[243] although the Member States indicated their strong insistence on mixity for this part in the course of the negotiations.[244]

Overall, the practice regarding the provisional application of the EU's new generation trade and investment agreements reveals some patterns. First, the Council consistently decided to provisionally apply some treaty provisions it considered as falling within shared competence because some Member States have had a particularly strong political and economic interest in these fields (maritime transport, sustainable development) or consider them of lesser importance (moral rights).[245] Here, the efficacy provided by the practice of provisional application – ie, immediate (market access) benefits – was considered more important by the Council than maintaining its legal stance in inter-institutional competence disputes. Second, prior to CETA and *Opinion 2/15*, the scope of provisional application generally included investment liberalisation disciplines as a whole. As EU trade and investment agreements use a broad asset-based definition of investment that covers both foreign direct and non-direct investments, this is arguably desirable.[246] The Council decision on the provisional application of CETA carves out foreign non-direct investments without qualifying the boundary between foreign 'direct' and 'non-direct' investments. In practice, this may cause significant legal uncertainties.[247] Third, some areas are consistently carved out from the scope of provisional application of mixed EU trade and investment agreements, such as 'essential elements' clauses and provisions relating to administrative proceedings in the Member States.[248] Fourth, there are some areas that are excluded only in the specific context of one agreement, but not generally for all of them, such as criminal IPRs enforcement, taxation or camcording.

Large parts of mixed trade and investment agreements are therefore applied provisionally by the EU, with the Council only carving out a few specific parts and/or provisions (it considers as) falling within shared competence. A recent – but increasingly common – variant of that practice is for the Council to subject the scope of a treaty's provisional application by the EU to different types of 'competence disclaimers'. For example, the preamble to the Council decision on the provisional application of the EU Association Agreement with Central America specifies that 'provisional application

[239] ibid Article 1(1)(c).
[240] Chapter 14 CETA.
[241] ibid Article 20.7(1)(a).
[242] ibid Chapters 22, 23, and 24.
[243] ibid Chapter 20, section C.
[244] See section II.C above.
[245] Interview with two Commission officials, 9 November 2018.
[246] Pursuant to Article 8(1) CETA, 'investment means every kind of asset that an investor owns or controls, directly or indirectly', including both direct and indirect investment flows.
[247] See also Kleimann and Kübek (n 18) 32.
[248] With the exception of the EU-Korea FTA, where the provisions on administrative proceedings are included within the scope of provisional application.

… does not prejudge the allocation of competences between the European Union and its Member States in accordance with the Treaties.'[249] Similarly, Article 1(d) of the Council decision on the provisional application of CETA qualifies that 'provisional application of Chapters 22, 23 and 24 of the Agreement shall respect the allocation of competences between the Union and the Member States.'[250] Article 4 of the Council decision on the provisional application of the Association Agreement with Ukraine authorises the provisional application of parts of the agreement 'only to the extent that they cover matters falling within the Union's competence.'[251] Even more specifically, the Council decision on the provisional application of the Strategic Partnership Agreement (SPA) between the EU and Japan qualifies that parts of the treaty may only be applied provisionally 'to the extent that [they] cover matters for which the Union has already exercised its competence internally.'[252]

In all these instances, the specific 'competence disclaimers' cannot be found in the Commission's proposal for the respective Council decisions on provisional application. The different qualifications were added by the Council. By adding these qualifications, the Council made the provisional application of an international agreement conditional upon EU constitutional requirements with which the EU's treaty partner might not be familiar. It is uncertain (and unlikely) that the EU itself would accept that the scope of provisional application is made dependent on a treaty partner's constitutional requirements.[253] In order to ascertain full legal certainty at the international stage, it would be beneficial to clearly list the provisions of an agreement that will (not) be applied provisionally in the relevant Council decision.

V. Entry into Force

Pursuant to Article 24 VCLT, the contracting parties to a treaty are generally free to specify the terms and conditions of entry into force. In the absence of such a specific clause, the treaty enters into force as soon as all negotiating parties have established their consent to be bound. Entry into force makes the treaty legally binding and obligates the parties to perform the agreement in good faith (*pacta sunt servanda*).[254]

EU trade and investment agreements generally specify that they 'enter into force on the first day of the second month following the date on which the Parties notify each

[249] Recital (6) of the preamble to the Council Decision (EU) 2012/734 of 25 June 2012 on the signing, on behalf of the European Union, of the Agreement establishing an Association between the European Union and its Member States, on the one hand, and Central America on the other, and the provisional application of Part IV thereof concerning trade matters [2012] OJ L2012/734/1. See also Recital (6) of the preamble to the Council Decision (EU) 2012/735 (n 180); or recital (4) of the preamble to the Council Decision (EU) 2014/295 (n 220).

[250] Council Decision (EU) 2017/38 (n 194).

[251] Council Decision (EU) 2014/295 (n 220).

[252] Article 4(b) of the Council Decision (EU) 2018/1197 on the signing, on behalf of the European Union, and provisional application of the Strategic Partnership Agreement between the European Union and its Member States, of the one part, and Japan, of the other part [2018] OJ L216/1.

[253] Kübek and Van Damme (n 216) 163.

[254] Article 26 VCLT.

other that their respective applicable legal requirements and procedures for entry into force of this Agreement have been completed, unless the Parties agree otherwise.'[255] The agreements usually further stipulate that the parties must notify each other in writing about the finalisation of their respective internal ratification processes. The EU's treaty partners must send such notifications to the General Secretariat of the Council.[256] The General Secretariat may also act as depositary for both parties. This is often the case for Association Agreements.[257]

The EU and each Member State ratify mixed agreements. In most cases, there is no legal requirement for them to complete the ratification process simultaneously. Some agreements, such as the United Nations Convention on the Law of the Sea (UNCLOS), stipulate that the EU may only deposit its ratification instrument if the majority of the Member States have deposited theirs.[258] It is nevertheless common practice that the EU and the Member States deposit their ratification instruments jointly.[259] As a general rule, the Council stalls its decision on the conclusion of EU mixed agreements until all the Member States have completed their internal ratification processes.[260] This is primarily done for political reasons: Member State governments do not wish to give their consent to a treaty in the Council before national parliaments have approved of the agreement. It remains to be seen whether the CJEU's conclusions in *Opinion 1/19* will change the Council's standard practice to await the deposition of ratification instruments by all the Member States before adopting a decision on the conclusion of a mixed agreement on behalf of the EU. As was mentioned above, the CJEU found in *Opinion 1/19* that a common accord between all the Member States cannot be regarded as a legal prerequisite for taking a decision on the conclusion of an agreement in the Council. Moreover, as was mentioned in Chapter 2, the CJEU recognised the practice of incomplete mixity (ie, the conclusion of a mixed agreement by the EU without some of its Member States) in that decision.[261] At least for multilateral mixed agreements that are politically contested but desired by a qualified majority of the Member States, such as the Istanbul Convention, the practice in the Council may therefore change. Bilateral mixed agreements, at least in their current form, require the consent of all contracting parties to be bound before they can enter into force.[262] The deposition of ratification instruments by the EU before (some of) the Member States would thus have no legal effects. Yet, an early deposition of the EU's ratification instrument could prevent it from being drawn into (sub-)national conflicts of interests.

[255] See, eg, Article 23.3 of the EU-Japan FTA, Article 30.7(2) CETA or Article 16.13(2) of the EUSFTA. A slightly different timeframe (60 days) was stipulated in Article 15.10(2) of the EU-Korea FTA.

[256] See, eg, Article 30.7(4) CETA. Yet, it is for the Commission to designate the person empowered to give notification on behalf of the EU. See section III.A above.

[257] See, eg, Article 486(1) of the EU-Ukraine Association Agreement.

[258] Article 3 of Annex IX of the United Nations Convention on the Law of the Sea [1982] UNTS Vol 1833, 3.

[259] K Schmalenbach, 'Artikel 218 AEUV' in Calliess and Ruffert (n 8) para 34.

[260] J Czuczai, 'Mixity in Practice: Some Problems and Their (Real or Possible) Solution' in Hillion and Koutrakos (n 49) 229, 233.

[261] *cf* Chapter 2, section III.

[262] See further Chapter 6, section VIII.

VI. Conclusion

The making of international (trade and investment) agreements by the EU is a complex affair, both procedurally and practically. The process may be divided in five steps: negotiations, signature, provisional application, conclusion and entry into force. For each of these steps, public international law provides a general framework that the EU, the third state(s) and the Member States are bound by. Under EU law, the making of trade and investment agreements is governed by the specific provisions stipulated in Articles 207 and 218 TFEU. Moreover, and irrespective of whether the agreement at issue is to be concluded under the mixed or EU-only procedure, the treaty-making process transcends national law and involves national governments, parliaments and citizens.

As was explained in Chapters 2 and 3, the procedure for making EU trade and investment agreements is, in the first instance, not a question of political preference, but a question of legal competence that was largely clarified by the CJEU in *Opinion 2/15*. The present chapter has shown that the procedural gap between EU-only treaty-making and mixity may not be as wide as it is often perceived. Mixity certainly increases the number of (sub-)national veto-players and, in doing so, makes the EU treaty-making process dependent on national constitutional ratification requirements (see further Chapter 5). However, this does not mean that EU-only treaty-making is not subject to (sub-)national influence and control.

In the post-Lisbon era, the participation of parliaments and citizens in the negotiations of trade and investment agreements alongside the 'traditional' EU actors – ie, the Commission and the Council – has noticeably increased. This development is arguably desirable and necessary to ensure support for the finalised agreement. Trade has become a topical issue in the public and political discourse within the Member States and raised concerns amongst EU citizens. It is important to react to these concerns in a representative, transparent and efficient manner through the continuous involvement of the EP, national parliaments and citizens from the beginning of the treaty-making process, ie, from the negotiation stage. None of these actors will be satisfied with a 'take it or leave it' option at the end.

Notably, the procedural technique for negotiating an EU agreement is not necessarily dependent on its prospective character ('mixed' or 'EU-only'). The character of an agreement is ultimately determined on the basis of the final text of the agreement, ie, at the signature stage. As a consequence, the Member States may be involved in the negotiations of EU-only agreements in their own right, provided the agreement is expected to contain shared competence. Conversely, the Commission may also negotiate mixed agreements on behalf of the Member States. In that respect, the Commission and the national governments must choose whether it is more effective to speak with a single voice (through the Commission) or divide the negotiation authority between them, giving the Member States a greater leverage to push for non-negotiable national interests. In the context of bilateral agreements, the benefits of unity in the external representation and the reduced coordination costs for maintaining a 'single voice' usually outweigh the benefits of having many representatives at the table (which may be more beneficial in the multilateral context). Under the new architecture, EU FTAs and IPAs will generally be negotiated by the Commission alone (see further Chapter 7).

The EP does not have the same legal right to consult with the Commission in the negotiation process as the Council. Yet, it has the same right to access to information. Post-Lisbon, the EP has addressed recommendations to the Commission that outline the conditions for its consent. Not least since the SWIFT and ACTA instances, it is clear that the EP will make use of its veto powers if it considers that parliamentary or public concerns were disregarded. The examples of the ICS and TSD Chapters show that the EP has indeed been highly influential in shaping the content of the EU's new generation trade and investment agreements.

The main differences between the mixed and the EU-only treaty-making procedure come to light at the stages of signing and concluding an agreement. Here, the procedural efficiency of the EU-only mode takes full effect: instead of having to await around 40 (sub-)national ratification processes (and endure the uncertainties about the outcome of national parliamentary votes and referenda), the agreement may enter into force after the Council and the EP have approved of its conclusion. The EP thus fulfils its constitutionally assigned role as the main democratic actor with regard to the EU's external trade policy. In the mixed scenario, by contrast, the EP becomes one of around 40 parliaments, and EU citizens are principally turned into national citizens. However, a move away from mixity reduces the ability of national parliaments to directly impact the course of EU trade policy. There are different avenues for national parliaments and citizens to nevertheless be involved in the making of EU trade agreements, eg, via their representative in the Council, oral and written exchanges with the Commission, public consultations or ECIs. At present, many of these avenues are informal (eg, Commission consultations with Member State governments and parliaments) and their frequency depends on the salience of the respective agreement. There is thus room for formalisation and consistency. Indeed, there is increasing awareness that an early involvement of national parliaments in the negotiation process of EU trade and investment agreements is essential for ensuring democratic participation and control, irrespective of an agreement's character. Democratic participation and control over mixed agreements cannot be obtained by merely asking national parliaments to rubber-stamp the final text of the agreement. Moreover, an early involvement of national parliaments reduces the risk of non-ratification. For EU-only agreements, the early involvement of national parliaments may partially compensate them for the loss of veto power at the ratification stage.

The extent to which a shift from the mixed to the EU-only procedure reduces the Member State governments' ability to veto the ratification of EU (trade and investment) agreements individually in the Council has been fiercely debated, including before the CJEU in *Opinion 1/19*. The CJEU held that finding a common accord amongst Member States cannot be understood as a legal prerequisite for taking a Council decision on the signature and conclusion of mixed agreements. At the same time, the CJEU's reply underlined that the timelines for taking a decision ultimately remain at the political discretion of the Council. The present chapter has argued that, as a matter of law, all of the EU's new generation trade and investment agreements could have been adopted by QMV in the Council except for the FTA with Korea. As will be shown in Chapter 7, the Council has generally accepted that new generation EU FTAs may be concluded by QMV, although it endeavours to reach consensus wherever possible.

Pending entry into force, treaties may be applied provisionally. For mixed agreements, provisional application is a pragmatic tool to overcome the increased duration of a treaty's ratification process. In recent practice, the EP has been asked to give its consent to EU trade and investment agreements prior to their provisional application so as to ensure that democratic control is not circumvented. Usually, the EU provisionally applies the part of a mixed agreement that falls within its exclusive competence, but that practice is not always consistent. At times, the Council decided, largely for practical reasons, to apply certain treaty aspects provisionally that (it considered to) fall within shared competence. The Council has further started a practice where it makes provisional application subject to certain types of 'competence disclaimers', which may cause legal uncertainty because the EU's treaty partner is unlikely to be aware of the attribution of competence within the EU.

The treaty-making process ends with entry into force. In case of mixity, the EU and the Member States generally seek to deposit their ratification instruments jointly so as to ensure that a treaty simultaneously takes effect in the territory of the EU. If the EU deposits its ratification instrument before (some of) the Member States deposit theirs, the agreement turns into an incomplete mixed agreement. It remains to be seen if, in the aftermath of *Opinion 1/19*, the Council will more frequently forgo the common practice of waiting for the common accord of all Member States before taking a conclusion decision on a mixed agreement – either by choice or after being 'forced' into a vote by a Member State or the Commission in accordance with its own Rules of Procedure. In the increasingly contentious (geo)political climate – both within and outside the EU – it has become difficult for the EU to counter fragmentation with integration. Against this background, it is arguably time to think about *moving beyond mixity*, especially in trade, where the EU's external power has become imperative not only for ensuring its economic position in times of geopolitical fragmentation but also for the promotion of its broader external relations objectives.

5

National Constitutional Law and National Parliaments

I. Introduction

In addition to the EU, the Member States must ratify mixed agreements in accordance with their respective national constitutional laws. The constitutional laws of almost all EU Member States make the ratification of international agreements conditional on national parliaments' consents. Malta is the only Member State where international agreements can be ratified by the executive alone. Mixity thus turns national governments and parliaments into veto-players. The precise number of (sub-)national parliaments that must consent to the ratification of mixed agreements is difficult to determine and varies by subject matter. A 2016 EP briefing illustrates that the ratification of mixed agreements must be authorised by 36 national parliaments (as many Member States have a bicameral legislature), in addition to the EP.[1] As the briefing does not account for sub-national parliaments (eg, the five regional/community parliaments of Belgium),[2] the number of veto-players appears to be even higher in the case of mixed EU trade and investment agreements. The briefing further shows that national referenda on mixed agreements are possible in the constitutional orders of 13 Member States.[3]

Since the entry into force of the Lisbon Treaty, the (desired) role of national parliaments in EU trade policy has been fiercely debated. In 2011, Krajeweski projected that 'the broadening of the scope of the common commercial policy by the Lisbon Treaty will lead to a disempowerment of the national parliaments'.[4] Woolkock noted that this development was aggravated by the perceived technocratic nature of EU trade policy at the time.[5] Indeed, mixed EU trade agreements were frequently 'rubber-stamped' by

[1] European Parliament, Directorate-General for the Presidency, 'National Parliaments Background Briefing: Procedures of Ratification of Mixed Agreements' (2016). The study is based on A Eschbach, *Die Ratifizierungsprozesse in den EU-Mitgliedstaaten: Eine Darstellung unter besonderer Berücksichtigung der Freihandelsabkommen TTIP und CETA* (2015).

[2] See further section IV.A.

[3] European Parliament (n 1). The number was adjusted to take account of the fact that since 2008 and at the point of writing this book, referenda on mixed agreements are no longer possible in the Netherlands. See further section V.E.

[4] M Krajewski, 'New Functions and New Powers for the European Parliament: Assessing the Changes of the Common Commercial Policy from the Perspective of Democratic Legitimacy' in C Herrmann and M Bungenberg (eds), *Common Commercial Policy after Lisbon*, Special Issue, *European Yearbook of International Economic Law* (Springer, 2013) 67, 81.

[5] S Woolcock, *European Union Economic Diplomacy: The Role of the EU in External Economic Relations* (Routledge, 2012) 54.

national parliaments with little discussion and/or without a formal vote.[6] This changed with the TTIP negotiations and the CETA with Canada. Jančić observed that the sudden salience of EU trade policy 'provoked a remarkable reaction in national parliaments'.[7] He considered that the designation of TTIP and CETA as mixed agreements was 'crucial' because it gave national legislatures 'the right to veto and to condition their consent with the attainment of certain goals'.[8]

Against this background, it was not surprising that the (future) role of national parliaments in EU trade policy took centre stage in the initial discussions on *moving beyond mixity*. In 2016, the representatives of 20 chambers of national parliaments, in a joint letter, urged the Commission to ratify TTIP and CETA as mixed agreements because of the 'important role national parliaments have in the democratic decision-making process of the EU'.[9] In the face of the initial rejection of CETA by the Walloon government at the end of 2016, Paul Magnette, Minister-President of Wallonia at the time, supported by 40 academics, published the 2017 'Namur Declaration', calling the EU to respect 'the civil society's legitimate demands for transparency and the democratic parliamentary control procedures'.[10] At the same time, opposing voices criticising the mixed procedure and its systemically inherent 'vetocracy' became louder.[11] The fact that the representatives of fewer than four million EU citizens almost stopped the signature of a trade agreement approved by the representatives of more than 440 million EU citizens questioned not only the effectiveness and credibility of the EU as an external trade actor but also the prevailing view that mixity is democratically more legitimate than EU-only treaty-making.[12] In response to the Namur Declaration, more than 60 academics adopted the 'Trading Together Declaration' in 2017, arguing that the insistence of (sub-)national governments to participate in their own name in the conclusion of EU trade agreements weakens the EU's position in international relations by 'allowing a particular local interest to veto the interests of all other EU citizens even in areas where EU Member States have decided to act collectively'.[13] The Declaration further claimed that 'these attempts undermine the role of the European Parliament, and by doing so weaken democratic legitimacy at the EU level'.[14]

[6] See, eg, the ratification of the EU-Korea free trade agreement by the Dutch Parliament, discussed further in section IV.E.

[7] D Jančić, 'TTIP and Legislative–Executive Relations in EU Trade Policy' (2017) 14 *West European Politics* 202, 209.

[8] ibid 216.

[9] Tweede Kamer der Staten-Generaal, 'Letter in the Framework of the Political Dialogue: The Role of National Parliaments in Free Trade Agreements' (2014).

[10] The text of the Namur Declaration is available at: ejiltalk.org/namur-declaration-of-5-december-2016-an-eu-values-driven-path-to-negotiating-and-concluding-economic-and-trade-agreements.

[11] FC Mayer, 'European Vetocracy? How to Overcome the Wallonian CETA Problem', *Verfassungsblog*, 24 June 2015, verfassungsblog.de/european-vetocracy-how-to-overcome-the-wallonian-ceta-problem.

[12] See D Kleimann and G Kübek, 'The Signing, Provisional Application, and Conclusion of Trade and Investment Agreements in the EU: The Case of CETA and Opinion 2/15' (2018) 45 *Legal Issues of Economic Integration* 13, 44–45.

[13] The text of the Trading Together Declaration is available at: https://ielp.worldtradelaw.net/2017/01/the-trading-together-declaration.html.

[14] On the Namur and Trading Together Declaration, see M Damestoy and N Levrat, 'The Mixed Nature of the EU-Canada FTA: Between Competences Distribution and Democratic Legitimacy' in N Levrat et al (eds), *The EU and its Member States' Joint Participation in International Agreements* (Hart Publishing, 2022) 77, 84.

The request for *Opinion 2/15* reminded all players at the time that the choice for or against mixity is a legal question that can only be answered on the ground of the division of external competence between the EU and the Member States (see Chapters 2 and 3). The CJEU's conclusions in *Opinion 2/15* enable the EU and its trading partners to balance the costs and benefits of confining the scope of an envisaged agreement to trade matters, or alternatively designing a comprehensive trade and investment protection agreement (see Chapter 1). The question of how national parliaments can be better integrated into the treaty-making process arises against the background of that substantive design choice and for mixed and EU-only agreements alike. As was mentioned in Chapter 4, there is an increasing awareness that national parliaments must be better integrated at the early stages of the treaty-making process and not only at the very end of it. For mixed agreements, the involvement of national parliaments in the negotiation of EU trade and investment agreements lowers their risk of being either rubber-stamped or rejected at the ratification stage. For EU-only agreements, the early involvement of national parliaments may partially compensate them for the loss of veto powers at the ratification stage.[15]

This chapter argues that in addition to increasing direct cooperation between EU and national institutions on the basis of EU law and practice, Member State governments can indirectly strengthen the involvement of their parliaments in EU treaty-making on the basis of national (constitutional) law and practice. Its aims are twofold: first, it seeks to highlight how EU-only and mixed agreements are made at the national level, thereby illustrating the legal complexity of multilevel treaty ratification processes, particularly for mixed agreements; and, second, it seeks to illustrate the role of national parliaments in EU foreign affairs under national constitutional law, thereby highlighting how the loss of direct parliamentary influence the *move beyond mixity* inevitably brings about can be partially mitigated by national constitutional laws and practices.

This chapter zooms in on the constitutional legal orders of five selected Member States: Belgium, Denmark, France, Germany and the Netherlands. These states have been chosen because they exemplify different modes of government (from centralised to federal states) and different legal, historical and practical views on involving subnational actors in foreign affairs. While these case studies cannot reflect the complexity of (mixed) treaty-making in 27 national legal orders, they thus serve to illustrate different approaches to institutional participation in foreign affairs by federated and/or multi-level legal systems, especially with a view to the role of national parliaments. In view of the main stages of treaty-making outlined in the previous chapter, this chapter hence analyses the procedure for negotiating (sections II and III) signing and concluding (sections IV and V), provisional applying (section VI) and judicially controlling (section VII) EU-only and mixed agreements, respectively, under the constitutional legal orders of selected Member States.

[15] See also G Van der Loo, 'Less is More? The Role of National Parliaments in the Conclusion of Mixed (Trade) Agreements' in J Santos Vara and S Rodriguez Sánchez-Tabernero (eds), *The Democratisation of EU International Relations through EU Law* (Routledge, 2018) 210; and D Kleimann, 'The Legitimacy of "EU-Only" Preferential Trade Agreements' in M Hahn and G Van der Loo (eds), *Law and Practice of the Common Commercial Policy* (Brill, 2021) 461.

II. Negotiations of EU-Only Agreements

As was explained in the previous chapter, EU-only trade agreements are made exclusively on the basis of EU law, in accordance with the procedure set out in Articles 207 and 218 TFEU. The Member States determine their position in the Council, and influence the negotiations of EU trade and investment agreements specifically through the Council's TPC. To understand the making of EU-only agreements, one therefore has to look also at how Member States take a position in the Council, and how their parliaments are involved in that process as a matter of national law.

The Member States have created different laws and practices for developing their representative's position in the Council. These laws and practices apply to EU affairs generally, and thus also to the making of international agreements by the EU. Many Member States require the involvement of national parliaments in that process as a matter of national (constitutional) law, with a view to compensating them for the loss of power that occurred as a result of the transfer of competence from the national to the supranational level. The information and participation rights national parliaments hold in EU affairs complement their more general participation rights, such as the right to debate, propose motions, issue resolutions, question the executive or hold expert meetings.

A. Belgium

Belgium is a specific case because it grants the governments of the federated entities a direct say in EU affairs.[16] Article 167(3) of the Belgian Constitution lays down a parallelism between internal and external competence. With a view to ensuring that parallelism in EU affairs, the federal government and the governments of the federated entities have concluded an inter-institutional agreement that sets out the procedure for Belgium's representation in the Council.[17] In contrast to other Member States, which are commonly represented in the Council by a federal/government minister, Belgium can, for certain subject matters, be represented by a minister of a federated entity.[18]

[16] Pursuant to Article 1 of the Belgian Constitution, the Belgian federal state is composed of three Regions (the Flemish Region, the Walloon Region and the Brussels-Capital Region) and three Communities (the Flemish Community, the French Community and the German-speaking Community). The distinction between Regions and Communities is not important here. For further details, see, eg, F Delpérée, *Le droit constitutionnel de la Belgique* (Bruylant, 2000) 305 et seq.

[17] Samewerkingsakkoord tussen de Federale Staat, de Gemeenschappen en de Gewesten, met betrekking tot de vertegenwoordiging van het Koninkrijk België in de Ministerraad van de Europese Unie [1994] Belgisch Stb. Nr 94, 2911 (Cooperation Agreement between the Federal State, the Communities and the Regions, regarding the representation of the Kingdom of Belgium in the Council of Ministers of the European Union, hereinafter 'EU Cooperation Agreement'). See further P Bursens and S Helsen, 'Multi-level governance in de praktijk: Strategieën ter optimalisering van de Belgische EU-Coördinatie' (2003) 56 *Studia Diplomatica* 3, 10; A Sepos, 'EU Policy-Making in Federal States: The Case of Belgium' (2003) 13 *Regional & Federal Studies* 57, 62; and T Verellen, *Foreign Relations Federalism: The EU in Comparative Perspective* (Oxford University Press, 2023) 46, 213.

[18] Article 7, in conjunction with Annex I, of the EU Cooperation Agreement (n 17). The minister of one of the regions or communities represents Belgium in its entirety. There is a rotation system in place that ensures equal representation between the federal and/or regional and community level, depending on the division of competence. See further B Kerremans, 'Determining a European Policy in a Multi-level Setting: The Case of Specialized Co-ordination in Belgium' (2000) 10 *Regional & Federal Studies* 36.

The Belgian position in the Council is determined in coordination meetings, which are organised and chaired by the foreign ministry, more specifically the Directorate-General for European Affairs and Coordination (DGE – hence 'DGE meetings').[19] DGE meetings are attended by representatives of the federal and federated governments. Positions are derived by consensus, and the Belgian representative in the Council can only take a position on matters that have been subject to coordination meetings.[20] If no consensus can be found,[21] the Belgian representative in the Council must abstain.[22]

The Belgian Constitution and the aforementioned intergovernmental agreement remain silent on the role of (sub-)national parliaments in EU decision-making.[23] Some parliamentary rights in EU affairs are set out in the Special Majorities Law on Institutional Reform, which has quasi-constitutional status.[24] Accordingly, 'proposals for regulations and directives and, as the case may be, other normative legal acts from the Commission' are sent to both Chambers of the Belgian Federal Parliament. The Chambers have the right to send a legally non-binding opinion on a proposed EU law to the King. The parliaments of the federated entities can send legally non-binding opinions to their governments.[25]

B. Denmark

Denmark has established one of the strongest parliamentary control systems over EU affairs on the basis of Article 6(2) of the 1972 Statute on Denmark's Accession to the (then) European Community, according to which the Danish government must inform Parliament's European Affairs Committee about proposed Council decisions which are directly applicable in Denmark or for the fulfilment of which the participation of Parliament is necessary. On the basis of that provision and as a result of long-standing practice, the Danish representative in the Council will not cast an affirmative vote if the European Affairs Committee of the Danish Parliament is against it (the so-called 'mandate procedure'; see further below).[26] The Danish Parliament's European Affairs Committee

[19] Article 2.2 of the EU Cooperation Agreement (n 17). Further information about the Directorate-General Coordination and European Affairs can be found at: diplomatie.belgium.be/en/policy/coordination-european-affairs/directorate-general-coordination-and-european-affairs/coordination.

[20] Article 2.5 and the explanation ('toelichting') of the EU Cooperation Agreement (n 17).

[21] There are several conflict resolution mechanisms, such as referring the matter to the inter-ministerial conference on foreign relations or the Coordination Committee (Article 2.4 of the EU Cooperation Agreement (n 17)). Ultimately, however, these mechanisms are all based on consensus between the federal and federated entities.

[22] See also Bursens and Helsen (n 17) 10. The 'Explanations' attached to the EU Cooperation Agreement (n 17) also note that abstentions in the Council are 'not neutral' in practice. Indeed, pursuant to Article 238(4) TFEU, abstentions do not prevent the adoption of a Council decision that requires unanimity (eg, Association Agreements).

[23] Article 168 of the Belgian Constitution only applies to the negotiation and revision of the EU founding treaties and not EU decision-making as such.

[24] Article 4 of the Belgian Constitution.

[25] Article 92*quater* of the Bijzondere Wet tot Hervorming der Instellingen [1980] Belgisch Stb, 9434 (hereinafter 'Special Law on Institutional Reform').

[26] See section IV.A. See also H Krunke and T Baumbach, 'The Role of the Danish Constitution in European and Transnational Governance' in A Albi and S Bardutzky (eds), *National Constitutions in European and Global Governance: Democracy, Rights, the Rule of Law: National Reports* (TMC Asser Press, 2019) 269, 275.

organises weekly meetings, where the relevant government minister presents the agenda for the upcoming Council meeting, on the basis of which negotiations on the government's negotiation position in the Council are being held. The government has made a commitment to provide the European Affairs Committee as early as possible (at the latest before a proposal has been subject to the agenda of COREPER) and on an ongoing basis with information on Commission proposals. Parliament is also informed about if and how a proposal changes along the way and can, on that basis, adjust its mandate.[27]

C. France

France's participation in the EU is governed by the Constitution itself (Title XV of the French Constitution entitled 'On the European Union'). Article 88-1 creates a legal obligation for the French Republic to 'participate in the European Union constituted by States which have freely chosen to exercise some of their powers in common'. Article 88-4 governs the procedure for participating in EU decision-making.[28] Accordingly, the government must 'lay before the National Assembly and the Senate drafts of European legislative acts as well as other drafts of or proposals for acts of the European Union as soon as they have been transmitted to the Council of the European Union'. As Article 88-4 is not confined to draft legislative acts, but expressly includes all types of proposed EU acts, it also includes draft negotiation directives circulated in the TPC. In its 2017 CETA Action Plan, the French government promised to involve the French Parliament ahead of the negotiations when 'mandates' are under discussion, to inform and discuss the course of the negotiations with relevant parliamentary committees, and to share its analysis of the impact assessment with Parliament.[29] A new Trade Policy Monitoring Committee, which brings together parliamentarians, professional associations, unions and NGOs, has been established for overseeing EU trade policy, which the government intends to turn into a standing body.[30] Pursuant to Article 88-4 of the French Constitution, the National Assembly and the Senate may pass legally non-binding 'European resolutions' on any document that has been issued by an EU institution.

[27] See Folketinget, 'EU-note: Europaudvalgets konsoliderede beretninger', Europaudvalget 2022–23 (2 samling), 4–5 (hereinafter 'Consolidated Reports of the EU Affairs Committee'). See also H Krunke, 'Memorandum on Denmark', evidence submitted to the House of Lord's Select Committee on European Union (2009).

[28] See in detail, for example, A Fuchs-Cessot, *Le Parlement à l'épreuve de l'Europe et de la Ve République* (Librairie générale de droit et de jurisprudence, 2004); H Roussillon (ed), *L'Article 88-4 de la Constitution française: le rôle du Parlement dans l'elaboration de la norme européenne* (Presses de l'Université des sciences sociales de Toulouse, 1995); J-D Nuttens, *Le Parlement français et l'Europe: L'article 88-4 de la Constitution* (Librairie générale de droit et de jurisprudence, 2001).

[29] French Government, 'Implementation of CETA: Government Action Plan' (2017), https://www.tresor.economie.gouv.fr/Articles/8930b45f-ccfd-499f-a7bb-d1f2c516ad91/files/a712fd2c-0f4d-40b0-a16d-d0958be5e135, 5.

[30] ibid.

D. Germany

The German Constitution[31] also includes a 'Europe clause' that requires the Federal Republic to 'participate in the development of the European Union' with 'a view to establishing a united Europe' (Article 23 of the German Constitution).[32] Germany's participation in EU decision-making and the role of the German Federal Parliament and the Federal Council in that process is further specified in Article 23(2)–(6) and in two acts of law.[33] Accordingly, the German Federal Parliament must be informed by the German government 'comprehensively, as early as possible and continuously of matters concerning the European Union'.[34] The German Federal Council has the same information rights for matters concerning the EU that could be of relevance for the federated entities.[35] In practice, all documents concerning the negotiations of EU trade and investment agreements, including all documents the German government receives from the TPC, such as position papers, textual proposals and written submissions by the Commission or any Member State, are forwarded to the Federal Parliament.[36] The information is deliberated by the EU committee of the Federal Parliament, whose establishment is explicitly foreseen in Article 45 of the German Constitution. Before taking a position in the Council, the German government must provide the Federal Parliament and, provided that the matter at issue falls within the interests of the German federated entities, the Federal Council, with an opportunity to issue an opinion. The government must take these opinions into account. Opinions of the Federal Council on matters falling within the exclusive competences of the federated entities must receive 'prime consideration'.[37] Should the German government deviate from the opinions of the Federal Parliament 'for good reasons of foreign or integration policy', it must invoke

[31] For the sake of simplicity, this chapter will also use the term 'Constitution' for countries whose constitution is entitled 'Basic Law', such as Germany or the Netherlands.

[32] Subject to the consent of the German Federal Parliament and the German Federal Council, possibly with a two-thirds majority (Article 79(2) of the German Constitution) and under the conditions of Article 79(3) of the German Constitution. On the evolution of the 'Europe clause' in the German Constitution, see especially K Schmalenbach, *Der neue Europaartikel 23 des Grundgesetztes im Lichte der Arbeit der Gemeinsamen Verfassungskommission: Motive einer Verfassungsänderung* (Duncker & Humblot, 1996). On Europe as a constitutional goal, see K-P Sommermann, 'Staatsziel "Europäische Union"' (1994) 47 *Die Öffentliche Verwaltung* 569. See generally also K-P Sommermann, 'Offene Staatlichkeit: Deutschland' in A von Bogdandy, P Villalón and PM Huber (eds), *Handbuch Ius Publicum Europaeum*, vol II (CF Müller, 2008) 3.

[33] Article 23(7) of the German Constitution. See further Gesetz über die Zusammenarbeit von Bundesregierung und Deutschem Bundestag in Angelegenheiten der Europäischen Union [2013] BGBl I, 2170 (Act on Cooperation between the Federal Government and the German Bundestag in Matters Concerning the European Union; hereinafter 'Act on EU Cooperation I'); Gesetz über die Zusammenarbeit von Bund und Ländern in Angelegenheiten der Europäischen Union [1993] BGBl I, 313; last amended by the Law of 22 September 2009 BGBl I, 3031 (Act on Cooperation between the Federation and the Federated Entities in Matters Concerning the European Union; hereinafter 'Act on EU Cooperation II'). See also, for example, F Brand, *Europapolitische Kommunikation zwischen Bundestag und Bundesregierung: Die Umsetzung der parlamentarischen Mitwirkungs- und exekutiven Kooperationspflicht nach Art. 23 Abs. 2 und Abs. 3 GG* (Duncker & Humblot, 2015).

[34] Article 23(2) of the German Constitution, read in conjunction with §§3 and 4 of the Act on EU Cooperation I (n 33).

[35] §2 of the Act on EU Cooperation II (n 33).

[36] This was clarified by the German government in a reply to a question from several members of the German Federal Parliament. See Deutscher Bundestag, Drucksache 19/6713 [2018].

[37] Article 23(5) in conjunction with § 5 of the Act on EU Cooperation II (n 33).

a parliamentary reservation in the Council with a view to seeking a consensus with the Federal Parliament.[38]

E. The Netherlands

The Netherlands has established parliamentary control mechanisms in EU affairs on the basis of Article 68 of the Dutch Constitution, which enshrines a general right for both Chambers of Parliament to be informed by the executive upon request. In practice, the Dutch government reports on a monthly basis, upon the request of a specially established working group, to the Second Chamber of the Dutch Parliament[39] on Commission proposals.[40] This is commonly known as the 'fiches procedure', as the government summarises the content of the Commission proposal, an assessment of its proportionality and subsidiary, and the Dutch negotiation position, on special forms called 'fiches'. Under what has become known as the 'agenda procedure', the Dutch government also sends an annotated agenda at least one week before every Council and European Council meeting to both Chambers of Parliament, which are deliberated in the Second Chamber in its weekly 'Europe deliberations'.[41] The Dutch Parliament does not have a constitutional right to state its opinion on proposed EU legal acts. However, Parliament makes use of its above-mentioned general rights to debate, pass motions, question the executive,[42] and hold expert meetings.[43] Parliamentary reservations are also known in Dutch legal practice, even though they are not formally regulated.[44] In the context of CETA, the Second Chamber of the Dutch Parliament has invoked a parliamentary reservation, asking the Dutch government not to decide on the provisional application of CETA without first giving Parliament an opportunity to discuss such a proposal. The Dutch government agreed thereto and informed the Council accordingly.[45]

[38] Article 23(3) of the German Constitution in conjunction with § 8(4) of the Act on EU Cooperation I (n 33).

[39] The first chamber used to rely on fiches but then changed its procedure. See also LFM Besselink and B van Mourik, 'The Parliamentary Legitimacy of the European Union: The Role of the States General within the European Union' (2012) 8 *Utrecht Law Review* 34.

[40] This is further described in the Dutch Rules on Legislation. *cf* Aanwijzingen voor de regelgeving, Aanwijzing 9.15. BNC-fiches.

[41] See also NY Del Grosso, *Parlement en Europese integratie* (Kluwer, 2000) 173 et seq; and Besselink and van Mourik (n 39) 36–37.

[42] An interesting practical example is the weekly 'questions hour' between members of the Dutch Parliament and the government enshrined § 12.2 of the Reglement van Orde van de Tweede Kamer, 2021, Kamerstukken II, 35322. Questions on EU trade policy have been raised in the question hour. See, eg, Stenogram vragenuur van 16 februari 2016, 2018D14384.

[43] In the context of trade policy, see, eg, Eerste Kamer der Staten-Generaal, Deskundigenbijeenkomst CETA 12 en 19 mei 2020.

[44] Notably, parliamentary reservations ('parlementair voorbehoud') are not the same as parliamentary scrutiny reservations ('parlementair behandelvoorbehoud'). The latter are only possible for legislative proposals. The practice in the context of CETA is thus a novelty.

[45] Kamerstuk II, 2015–2016, 21501-02 Nr 1615; and Aanhangsel van de Handelingen, Tweede Kamer der Staten-Generaal, 2015–2016, Nr 2702, Antwoord 3.

III. Negotiations of Mixed Agreements

As was explained in the previous chapters, mixed agreements are – for the part falling within national competence – made in accordance with national constitutional law. To understand the making of mixed agreements, one therefore has to also look at how international agreements are negotiated, signed and ratified under the constitutional laws of EU Member States (as it were, 'Member State-only agreements'). This section looks at the negotiations of treaties under national constitutional law; the stages of signature and ratification are further discussed below (see sections V and VI).

National constitutions typically contain a procedure for making international agreements that empowers the executive as the principal negotiator. In the case of Belgium and Denmark, this is formally the King. In France and Germany, the President formally makes international treaties.[46] In the Netherlands, the government is responsible for treaty negotiations.[47] In practice, it is usually the responsible ministry (typically the foreign affairs ministry for trade agreements and/or the ministry for economic affairs) that is put in charge of the negotiations. In sharp contrast to the national (constitutional) rules on the formation of EU (foreign) policy, the legal orders of most Member States do not foresee an active role for parliaments during the negotiation of international agreements. National parliaments can usually use their general rights, such as the right to debate, propose motions, pass non-binding resolutions, submit questions to the executive or hold expert hearings also in the context of national foreign policy. However, to make effective use of these rights, national parliaments need to be informed comprehensively and consistently about the state of play of ongoing treaty negotiations.

A. Belgium

As mentioned above, Article 167(3) of the Belgian Constitution establishes a parallelism between the division of internal and external competence. Accordingly, the federation and the federated entities can conclude international agreements alone or together ('Belgian mixed agreements') depending on the division of competence.[48] The procedure for making Belgian mixed agreements is set out in an intergovernmental agreement.[49] Under the agreement, a working group on mixed agreements has been established, which is composed of federal and federated government representatives.[50]

[46] Article 59(1) of the German Constitution; Article 52(1) of the French Constitution. Pursuant to Article 52(2) of the French Constitution, the President is informed about international agreements not subject to ratification ('accords'), which are negotiated by the Foreign Ministry.

[47] Article 90 of the Dutch Constitution.

[48] See further Verellen (n 17) 40 et seq. On mixed agreements made by federated entities of EU Member States, see JHH Weiler, 'The External Legal Relations of Non-Unitary Actors: Mixity and the Federal Principle' in D O'Keeffe and HG Schermers (eds), *Mixed Agreements* (Kluwer, 1983) 35.

[49] Samenwerkingsakkoord van 8 maart 1994 tussen de federale overheid, de Gemeenschappen en de Gewesten over de nadere regelen voor het sluiten van gemengde verdragen [1996] Belgisch Stb 17 (Cooperation agreement of 8 March 1994 between the Federal Government, the Communities, and the Regions on arrangements for concluding mixed agreements; hereinafter 'Cooperation Agreement Belgian Mixity').

[50] ibid Article 3.

The working group must make a recommendation on whether an agreement is mixed or not. The character of that agreement is ultimately decided by the intergovernmental conference on foreign relations.[51] Mixed EU trade and investment agreements are generally classified as Belgian mixed agreements,[52] as trade policy has been decentralised by the fifth state reform in 2001.[53] Once an agreement is classified as a Belgian mixed agreement, the representatives of the federated entities may participate in the negotiations alongside members of the federation as equal members of the delegation.[54] They must also consent to the negotiation directives and initial the finalised text. Federated governments thus have a decisive voice in the negotiations of Belgian mixed agreements. However, the same cannot be said about (sub-)national parliaments. Except for negotiations concerning a revision of the EU founding treaties,[55] there is no duty to inform the Belgian parliaments about the opening of treaty negotiations.

B. Denmark

Article 19(3) of the Danish Constitution stipulates that the government must consult the Foreign Affairs Committee of the Danish Parliament before making 'any decision of major importance to foreign policy'. The Danish government is thus legally obliged to keep Parliament informed about the developments of important treaty negotiations and the position of the Danish government in these negotiations.[56] On that basis, the Committee may, for instance, hold a debate, question the executive and adopt resolutions. As will be further discussed below, the Foreign Policy Committee has attempted to introduce a mandate procedure similar to the one established by the European Affairs Committee. Irrespective of the nature of these mandates (legally binding or not), there is empirical evidence that the Foreign Affairs Committee has had a significant influence on the conduct of Danish foreign policy.[57]

C. France

The Constitution of the Fifth French Republic has been established on the premise of the so-called *parlementarisme rationalisé* in order 'to put fetters on the omnipotent Parliaments of the Third and Fourth Republics and to entrench the pre-eminence of

[51] ibid Article 4.

[52] As, for example, confirmed by the Belgian State Council in its advice to the German Communities on the conclusion of CETA. *cf* Raad van State, afdeling Wetgeving [2018] advies 63.952/1/V, 4.

[53] See P Peeters, 'The Fifth Belgian State Reform ("Lambermont"): A General Overview (2003) 9 *European Public Law Review* 1, 4.

[54] Article 5 of the Cooperation Agreement Belgian Mixity (n 49). The Belgian delegation is coordinated by the Foreign Ministry and composed by the Intergovernmental Conference on Foreign Relations (Articles 4 and 5 of the Cooperation Agreement Belgian Mixity (n 49)).

[55] Article 168 of the Belgian Constitution and Article 16(2) of the Special Law on Institutional Reform (n 25).

[56] *cf* § 2 Lov om Det udenrigspolitiske Nævn [1954] LOV nr 54 (Law on the Foreign Policy Committee).

[57] See H Krunke, 'Developments in National Parliaments' Involvement in Ordinary Foreign and European Policy – Denmark' (2007) 13 *European Public Law Review* 335, 337.

the executive branch in French politics'.[58] Title XV of the French Constitution seeks to mitigate the effects of the *parlementarisme rationalisé* for EU matters. Conversely, in French foreign policy-making, the *parlementarisme rationalisé* is largely untouched. An involvement of the French Parliament in treaty negotiations is not foreseen by law. As a matter of practice, the French government hands over a list of signed agreements to the Commission on Foreign Affairs of the French Assembly and the Senate, respectively, every two or three months. The declaration of general policy, which the government may submit to Parliament with regard to internal policy matters, may also expand to foreign policy.[59]

D. Germany

In contrast to the 'Europe clause' (Article 23 of the German Constitution), Article 59(2) of the German Constitution does not stipulate any parliamentary rights during the negotiations of international agreements.[60] The German Constitutional Court has so far refrained from clarifying whether the Federal Government has any duties to involve Parliament during treaty negotiations conducted by Germany in its own right.[61] Several scholars have argued that basic parliamentary information rights can be derived from certain constitutional principles.[62] The extent of such rights remains unclear, but it is uncontested that they lag behind the information and participation rights of the German Federal Parliament and the German Federal Council in EU affairs.

E. The Netherlands

The Dutch law on the adoption and publication of international agreements provides that the Dutch foreign minister must periodically (in practice four times per year) provide the Dutch Parliament with a list of all draft agreements that are being negotiated by the Netherlands.[63] The list must contain a statement on the purpose, contracting parties, the name of the international organisation under which auspices the negotiations are conducted (if applicable) and the concerned ministries.[64] The

[58] D Jančić, 'The French Parliament: A European Scrutineer or National Actor?' (2013) 19 *European Public Law* 129, 131. See also P Avril, 'Le parlementarisme rationalisé' (1998) 114 *Revue du droit public* 1507.

[59] PM Eisemann and R Rivier, 'National Treaty Law and Practice: France' in D Hollis et al (eds), *National Treaty Law and Practice* (Brill/Nijhoff, 2005) 259.

[60] See generally C Tietje and K Nowrot, 'Parlamentarische Steuerung und Kontrolle des internationalen Regierungshandelns und der Außenpolitik' in M Morlok et al (eds), *Parlamentsrecht: Praxishandbuch* (Nomos, 2016) § 45.

[61] See especially *Bundesverfassungsgericht*, 2 BvE 4/11, DE:BVerfG:2012:es20120619.2bve000411, paras 92–93.

[62] See also, eg, R Poscher, 'Das Verfassungsrecht vor den Herausforderungen der Globalisierung' in C Hillgruber et al (eds), *Die Leistungsfähigkeit der Wissenschaft des Öffentlichen Rechts* (De Gruyter, 2008) 160, 186; and RA Lorz, *Interorganaspekt im Verfassungsrecht* (Mohr Siebeck, 2001) 301.

[63] See CB Modderman, *Parlementaire betrokkenheid bij de totstandkoming van verdragen* (Universiteit Utrecht, 2018) 111.

[64] The list must not include draft treaties where public disclosure would be detrimental to Dutch foreign policy interests. In these cases, Parliament may receive information confidentially.

Dutch government has also committed to informing Parliament about the opening of treaty negotiations it considers 'politically important' and, if possible, provides Parliament with an outline of the future agreement.[65] For 'less important' agreements, the periodic overview suffices. The Dutch government has broad discretion to determine which treaties are classified as 'politically important' and which are not.[66] The final text of agreements earmarked as 'politically important' will, if possible, be forwarded to Parliament for debate.

F. Mixity and the Parliamentary Information Gap: Does it Matter?

The extent to which national parliaments are involved in the negotiations of Member State-only agreements thus varies significantly between Member States, with Belgium, France and Germany situated on the lower end of the spectrum, the Netherlands in the middle and Denmark on the higher end. Overall, however, the information gap between governments and parliaments is greater in national foreign affairs than in EU (foreign) affairs.[67] National parliaments are usually not informed comprehensively and on a continuous basis about international agreements negotiated by their governments. Conversely, there is often a national (constitutional) law or practice in place that ensures that Member State parliaments are informed about discussions on proposed EU acts in the Council and are being forwarded relevant documents, including TPC documents on the EU's negotiation position on envisaged trade and investment agreements. On the basis of that information, parliaments can make more effective use of common participatory rights, such as the right to debate, issue opinions or question the executive.

For the negotiations of bilateral mixed EU agreements, it is in practice not noticeable that parliaments have fewer information and participation rights for the making of the 'Member State' part of the agreement than for the 'EU part'. Council documents that are being forwarded to national parliaments via their governments relate to the mixed agreement in its entirety. For the making of multilateral mixed agreements, this 'information gap' may well be an issue. For example, the Member States participate individually in the UNCITRAL negotiations on the MIC. At least in some Member States (eg, Germany and France), the executive is thus legally obliged to forward the EU negotiating directives and textual proposals to national parliaments and hear their opinion, but is under no similar legal obligation with regard to its own negotiating position.

[65] Draaiboek voor de regelgeving, Nr 226. See also the criteria for assessing international agreements adopted by the First Chamber of the Dutch Parliament. *cf* Eerste Kamer, Notitie 'Criteria voor de beoordeling van verdragen' [2009] 4–5 (hereinafter 'Assessment Criteria of the First Chamber').

[66] Modderman (n 63) 110.

[67] See especially R Golman and G Loewenstein, 'Information Gaps: A Theory of Preferences Regarding the Presence and Absence of Information' (2018) 5 *Decision* 143, who show that information gaps can negatively affect decision-making.

IV. The Signature and Conclusion of EU-Only Agreements

The signature and conclusion of EU-only trade and investment agreements is governed by EU law alone. Member State governments participate via the Council. The power and influence of national parliaments in that process hinges on their capacity to subject their government representative in the Council to their political will. The law and practice in the Member State in this regard varies considerably.

A. Belgium

Belgium is always represented by a federal minister in the Foreign Affairs Council. However, as discussed above, the Belgian position is established by consensus between the federal government and the governments of the federated entities if the content of the EU-only agreement touches on regional community and federal competences, as in the case of trade. In light of the complexity of this process, which already involves six veto-players,[68] it may not be desirable to give national and regional parliaments a decisive say on their governments' position in the DGE meetings. The federal government and the governments of the federated entities may of course, as a matter of political preference, stick to the opinions issued by their respective parliaments.[69]

B. Denmark

Around the time of Denmark's accession to the Community, on the basis of Article 6(2) of the Danish Act of Accession, a special practice emerged according to which the Danish representative in the Council only votes in favour of a proposal if the majority of the Danish Parliament's European Affairs Committee is not against it.[70] The practice is still applied today. Before the Danish government adopts a position in COREPER, the chair of the European Affairs Committee draws conclusions on the basis of the statements from the parties (usually the rapporteurs) by counting the number of seats the parties in question have in the Danish Parliament. Unless the rapporteurs representing a majority in the Danish Parliament oppose the government's negotiation proposal, the chair concludes that a majority against the government's negotiation proposal has not been established.[71] An approved negotiation proposal is often referred to as the negotiation mandate issued by the European Affairs Committee.[72] There is fierce scholarly debate as to whether such mandates are legally binding, because in Danish

[68] The federal government, the government of the Walloon region, the Flemish government, the government of the German-speaking community, the government of the Brussel-Capital region, the government of the French-speaking community. *Cf* the preamble to the EU Cooperation Agreement (n 17).

[69] Article 92*quater* of the Special Law on Institutional Reform (n 25).

[70] See further Krunke (n 57) 340.

[71] Consolidated Reports of the EU Affairs Committee (n 34) Bilag 2.

[72] ibid 5–7.

constitutional theory a practice can turn into a legally binding norm.[73] The practical relevance of this debate is rather limited, at least as long as Denmark continues to have minority governments. Pursuant to Article 15 of the Danish Constitution, a minister must not remain in office after Parliament has expressed a lack of confidence. Should government ministers not follow the 'mandate' they received from the European Affairs Committee, they risk facing a vote of no confidence in the Danish Parliament as a result of their position in the Council.

C. France

In sharp contrast to Denmark, parliamentary opinions on EU affairs are always legally non-binding in France. The introduction of a 'mandate procedure' would clash with the very idea of *parlementarisme rationalisé* in French constitutional law. The European resolutions issued by the French Parliament and the Senate pursuant to Article 88-4 of the French Constitution delicately balance the call for increased parliamentary involvement in EU affairs, on the one hand, and the powerful role of the executive in French legal tradition, on the other hand. Recent practice indicates that the French government strives to improve access to information and public discussion on EU trade policy.[74] Yet, there is no apparent desire to give Parliament control over the ultimate position taken by the French government in the Council on the signature and conclusion of EU trade and investment agreements.

D. Germany

German constitutional law makes the position of the German representative in the Council contingent on prior parliamentary approval in a limited number of cases, in accordance with the principle of 'responsibility for integration'. The principle of responsibility for integration emerged against the backdrop of the Lisbon judgment of the German Constitutional Court[75] and has since been anchored in secondary law.[76] Bearing responsibility for integration essentially implies that actions of the German

[73] See further Krunke (n 57) 340.

[74] *cf* French Government (n 29).

[75] *Bundesverfassungsgericht*, 2 BvE 2/08, DE:BVerfG:2009:es20090630.2bve000208, paras 236–38. See also, eg, M Nettesheim, 'Die Integrationsverantwortung – Vorgaben des BVerfG und gesetzgeberische Umsetzung' (2010) 63 *Neue Juristische Wochenzeitschrift* 177; JP Terhechte, *Europäische Verfassungsstudien* (Nomos, 2020) 469 et seq. For a broader overview, see, eg, A von Bogdandy, 'Prinzipien der Rechtsfortbildung im europäischen Rechtsraum – Überlegungen zum Lissabon-Urteil des BVerfG' (2010) 63 *Neue Juristische Wochenzeitschrift* 1, as well as the contributions in A Hatje and JP Terhechte (eds), *Grundgesetz und europäische Integration: Die Europäische Union nach dem Lissabon-Urteil des Bundesverfassungsgerichts* (Nomos, 2010). On the consequences for the CCP, see C Herrmann, 'Die gemeinsame Handelspolitik der Europäischen Union im Lissabon-Urteil' in A Hatje and JP Terhechte (eds), *Grundgesetz und europäische Integration: Die Europäische Union nach dem Lissabon-Urteil des Bundesverfassungsgerichts* (Nomos, 2010) 193.

[76] Integrationsverantwortungsgesetz [2009] BGBl I, 3022; last amended by Article 1 of the Law of 1 December 2009, BGBl I, 3822 (hereinafter 'Responsibility for Integration Act'). See further, eg, PM Huber, 'Die Integrationsverantwortung von Bundestag und Bundesregierung' (2017) 15 *Zeitschrift für Staats- und Europawissenschaften* 286.

representative in the Council facilitating a dynamic expansion of the EU's powers must be re-coupled to Parliament so as to ensure (national) democratic control. The German Constitutional Court listed three main cases where executive control must be re-coupled to Parliament, namely: (1) treaty amendments (special and simplified); (2) changes to the decision-making procedure in the Council (from special to ordinary legislative procedure and/or from unanimity to QMV); and (3) decisions expanding the competence of the EU (especially Article 352(1) TFEU).[77] The German representative in the Council may only consent to an action at the EU level in such cases if an internal legislative act pursuant to Article 23(1) of the German Constitution has been adopted or if the Federal Parliament has given its prior approval.[78] Notably, the Council decides unanimously in all of the aforementioned cases, so that the German Federal Parliament de facto holds veto powers over EU decision-making.

There have been frequent debates in Germany about strengthening parliamentary control over EU trade policy. Legally, it would arguably be possible to add the Council decisions on the signature and conclusion of EU-only FTAs to the list of cases where the government requires parliamentary consent before taking a position in the Council. However, this would require re-thinking the constitutional logic of the principle of 'responsibility for integration'. The German Constitutional Court established the principle of 'responsibility for integration' in order to control for the dynamic expansion of EU integration caused by a transfer of national power (eg, treaty amendments and the flexibility clause) or the surrender of national control (eg, Passerelle clauses). The making of EU-only FTAs is conceptually different: as EU-only FTAs fully fall within the EU's exclusive competence and the Council votes by QMV, the Member States have no individual power or control to lose to begin with. The rationale for requiring parliamentary responsibility for integration would thus not be the dynamic expansion of EU integration, but the political salience of the proposed legal act, and its relevance for national citizens. Moreover, if the Council decisions on the signature and conclusion of EU-only FTAs were to be added to the German secondary law on 'responsibility for integration',[79] parliamentary responsibility could only be asserted for the German position in the Council (participation in integration), but not for the decision taken by QMV in the Council (the outcome of integration). In practice, such a broader idea of 'responsibility for integration' has been employed only once by the former German Chancellor Angela Merkel, who was determined to involve the German Federal Parliament in the signature and conclusion decision of CETA irrespective of whether

[77] Bundesverfassungsgericht, 2 BvE 2/08 (n 75) paras 409 et seq.

[78] As set out in the Responsibility for Integration Act (n 76).

[79] As there is no transfer of sovereign power, such a decision could not be based on Article 23(1) of the German Constitution. Claims that the transfer of powers to treaty committees via Article 218(9) TFEU by EU trade and investment agreements requires recourse to Article 23(1) of the German Constitution are also misleading, as Article 218 TFEU is a procedural legal basis that can only be used in conjunction with a substantive legal basis to ensure that the EU acts within the realm of its conferred powers. See in more detail C Herrmann, 'Unionsrechtliche und verfassungsrechtliche Fragen des Abschlusses und der vorläufigen Anwendung des Comprehensive Economic and Trade Agreement (CETA) zwischen der EU (inkl. Mitgliedstaaten) und Kanada', *Stellungnahme für die Öffentliche Anhörung des Ausschusses für Wirtschaft und Energie des Deutschen Bundestages* (2016). It would nonetheless be possible to add EU trade and investment agreements to the existing law on responsibility for integration without referring to Article 23(1) of the Constitution. *cf*, for example, § 9(1) of the Responsibility for Integration Act (n 76)).

the agreement was classified as an EU-only or a mixed agreement, in view of CETA's political salience.[80]

E. The Netherlands

In the Netherlands, a so-called 'consent requirement' was introduced by the Dutch ratification act of the Maastricht Treaty with a view to subjecting EU decisions to national parliamentary control in all cases where the EP did not have veto powers.[81] At the time, the Dutch government had to obtain the consent of both Chambers of Parliament before taking a position in the Council on binding decisions in Title VI ('third pillar', justice and home affairs) and Title IV, provided the decisions were not taken under the co-decision procedure.[82] The consent requirement was also inserted into the Dutch approval acts of the Schengen Agreement and the ensuing Amsterdam and Nice Treaties.[83] According to Besselink and van Mourik, 'the major effect of the consent requirement has been that the Government has informed Parliament considerably more intensively about the state of negotiations' and was therefore able to influence the government's position in the Council.[84] An actual veto was never cast. With the Lisbon Treaty reform, the scope of the consent requirement has been greatly reduced. Today, the Dutch government must only obtain the consent of the Dutch Parliament before taking a position in the Council regarding matters falling within Articles 77(3), 87(3), and 89 TFEU.[85]

Similar to the case of Germany, it would arguably be legally possible to extend the 'consent requirement' to the Council decisions on the signature and conclusion of EU-only FTAs. This would once again require re-thinking the rationale for establishing the consent requirement in the first place. So far, the consent requirement has only been used in cases where the EP has no veto power. National parliamentary control has thus been viewed as an alternative, and not an addition, to EU parliamentary control. This logic could easily be transferred to the Council decision on the signing of EU FTAs, as that decision can be taken by the Council without obtaining the consent of the EP. However, subjecting the Dutch government's position on the conclusion decision to prior parliamentary consent would revert the rationale of the consent requirement, as

[80] Bundesregierung, 'Freihandelsabkommen CETA – Merkel: Bundestag muss zustimmen', 30 June 2016, https://www.bundesregierung.de/breg-de/service/archiv/alt-inhalte/merkel-bundestag-muss-zustimmen-437980.

[81] Amendment by van der Linden et al, Kamerstuk II, 1992–1993, 22 647 (R1437), Nr 20; and Articles 3 and 4 of the Rijkswet goedkeuring en bekendmaking verdragen [1992] (Kingdom Law on the Approval and Publication of Treaties; hereinafter 'Kingdom Law').

[82] See also Besselink and van Mourik (n 39) 37.

[83] *cf* Amendment by van Traa-de Hoop Scheffer, Kamerstukken II 1991–1992, 22 140, no 20 (for the Schengen Agreement); Articles 3 and 4 of the Rijkswet houdende goedkeuring Verdrag van Amsterdam houdende wijziging Verdrag betreffende … tot oprichting van de Europese Gemeenschappen, Trb 1998, 11 (for the Amsterdam Treaty); and Articles 3 and 4 of the Rijkswet houdende goedkeuring van het Verdrag van Nice, Trb. 2001, 47 (for the Nice Treaty).

[84] Besselink and van Mourik (n 39) 37.

[85] *cf* Article 3 of the Rijkswet houdende goedkeuring Verdrag van Lissabon tot wijziging van het Verdrag betreffende … tot oprichting van de Europese Gemeenschap, Trb 2008, 11.

the EP holds veto powers in accordance with Article 218(6)(a) TFEU. As in the case of Germany, the rationale for subjecting the Dutch representative's decision in the Council to prior parliamentary consent would instead be the increased political salience of EU trade and investment agreements.

V. The Signature and Conclusion of Mixed Agreements

The Member States sign and conclude mixed agreements in their own right, in addition to the EU and the third state(s). Under international law, both the EU and the Member States are thus viewed as contracting parties to mixed agreements. However, under EU law, the EU institutions and the Member States have to act within the boundaries of their respective competence when negotiating, signing and concluding a mixed agreement. For bilateral mixed agreements, this is underlined by the preamble, which designates the EU and the Member States as a composite contracting party ('the European Union and the Member States, of the one part').[86] Moreover, many mixed agreements define the 'EU party' as being composed of 'the Union, or its Member States, or the Union and its Member States, in accordance with their respective powers as derived from the Treaty on the Functioning of the European Union'.[87] This formulation makes it clear that mixity does not imply that the EU and the Member States exercise competence in parallel over the entire agreement, but that treaty-making power is divided as between them.

From an EU law perspective, the EU and the Member States must therefore act within the framework of their competences when signing and concluding a mixed agreement. While the limits of the EU's competences are at least implicitly indicated by the legal basis of the Council signature and conclusion decisions, the Member States typically do not set out the limits of their independent treaty-making powers in their national ratification instruments.[88] As a result, national governments and parliaments usually ratify mixed agreements in their entirety, thereby encroaching upon the EU's exclusive competence.[89] This further implies that national parliaments typically encroach upon the competences of the EP when reviewing mixed agreements. If the EU does not clearly indicate which competence it exercises, the same is true vice versa. A clearer indication of the scope of the EU's and the Member States' competence in their respective ratification instruments is therefore not only important for solving non-ratification dilemmas, as the next chapter argues; it is also important for ensuring that the EP and national parliaments can fully exercise their respective right to ensure democratic oversight over the ratification of mixed agreements, without encroaching on the legal prerogatives of the other.

Against this background, the following analyses the laws and practices for ratifying international agreements under national constitutional law. Hence, the following shows

[86] See further, in the context of the EEA Agreement, C Hillion, 'Brexit Means Br(EEA)xit: The UK Withdrawal from the EU and its Implications for the EEA' (2018) 55 *Common Market Law Review* 135, 139.

[87] *cf.*, eg, Article 482 EU-Ukraine Association Agreement. See also S Schaefer and J Odermatt, 'Nomen est Omen? The Relevance of "EU Party" in International Law' in Levrat et al (n 14) 131. See also Chapter 6, section III.

[88] For practical examples, see Chapter 6, section IV.

[89] Article 2(1) TFEU.

how the Member States ratify the part of a mixed agreement that falls within national competence. In doing so, it highlights pertinent constitutional debates about the procedure for ratifying mixed agreements under national law, especially with regard to the role of national parliaments in that process.

A. Belgium

Under Belgian constitutional law, external action falls within the King's exclusive powers. In practice, these powers are typically exercised by the foreign minister. According to Article 167(1) of the Belgian Constitution, the 'King directs international relations, notwithstanding the competence of Communities and Regions to regulate international cooperation, including the concluding of treaties, for those matters that fall within their competences in pursuance of or by virtue of the Constitution'. Pursuant to the second paragraph of Article 167, the King concludes international agreements, except for those falling within the exclusive prerogatives of the Belgian federated entities. The provision further dictates that agreements concluded by the King require the assent of the Chamber of Representatives. By inference, the negotiation and signature of international agreements remain executive prerogatives.

As mentioned earlier, mixed EU trade and investment agreements generally qualify as 'Belgian mixed agreements', as trade policy falls within the powers of the Belgian federated entities. Belgian mixed agreements are signed by the Belgian foreign minister as well as the ministers of the Belgian federated entities.[90] Legally, parliaments are not involved at this stage. However, the case of CETA has shown that the opinions of (sub-)national parliaments on the signature of Belgian mixed agreements can be politically decisive. On 14 October 2014, the Walloon Parliament issued a motion that called on the Walloon government to refuse to delegate full powers to the Belgian federal government for the signature of CETA.[91] Paul Magnette, the Walloon Prime Minister at the time, followed this recommendation and refused his consent to the signature of CETA, which initially left the Belgian federal government unable to sign the agreement.[92]

Pursuant to Article 167(2) of the Belgian Constitution, treaties concluded by the federal state require the consent of the Chamber of Representatives. The State Council provides an advisory opinion. The consent of the Belgian Senate is not required.[93] Yet, Belgian mixed agreements require the consent of the parliaments of the federated entities.[94] As trade policy falls within the competences of the federated entities, the consent of all five sub-national parliaments,[95] in addition to the Chamber of

[90] Article 8 of the Cooperation Agreement Belgian Mixity (n 49).

[91] Parlement Walloon, Motion déposée en conclusion du débat sur les projets de Traité CETA et de Déclaration interprétative du traité, 606 [2016–2017] No 2.

[92] See further Chapter 6.

[93] Since the 2014 Belgian state reform. *cf* Articles 77–78 of the Belgian Constitution. See also Verellen (n 17) 156; and, more generally, P Popelier, 'Bicameralism in Belgium: The Dismantlement of the Senate for the Sake of Multinational Confederalism' (2018) 10 *Perspectives on Federalism* 215.

[94] Article 167(3) of the Belgian Constitution; Article 9(1) of the Cooperation Agreement Belgian Mixity (n 49).

[95] The Flemish Parliament, the Walloon Region Parliament, the Brussels Region Parliament, the French Community Parliament, and the German-speaking Community Parliament. See M Uyttendaele, *Les institutions de la Belgique* (Bruylant, 2014) 95 et seq.

Representatives, is required for the conclusion of mixed EU trade and investment agreements.

B. Denmark

In accordance with Article 19(1) of the Danish Constitution, the King shall act on behalf of the realm in international affairs. 'Ordinary' international agreements must therefore formally be signed and concluded by the King. In practice, that power is vested with the government, most commonly the minister of foreign affairs.[96] Article 19(3) obliges the Danish government to consult the Foreign Affairs Committee of the Danish Parliament prior to the making of any decision of major importance to foreign policy. In the face of the political salience and economic importance of mixed EU trade and investment agreements, it is uncontested that the decision to sign the 'Danish part' thereof is of major importance to Danish foreign policy within the meaning of Article 19(3). As mentioned earlier, the Foreign Affairs Committee has been trying to establish a 'mandate procedure' similar to the one used by the European Affairs Committee. Whether the Danish government is legally obliged to follow the 'mandates' of the Foreign Affairs Committee is not clear, as practice can evolve into a binding legal norm under Danish constitutional law.[97] However, Article 19(3) of the Danish Constitution explicitly speaks of a duty to 'consult' Parliament. Therefore, it appears that the Danish government, as a matter of law, retains a final say on the decision to sign the 'Member State' part of mixed EU trade and investment agreements.

Pursuant to Article 19(1) of the Danish Constitution, the King must not enter into any international legal obligation which for the fulfilment requires the consent of the Danish Parliament or which is otherwise of major importance. Mixed EU trade and investment agreements require implementation at the national level and are arguably of major importance. As a result, the Danish Parliament must consent to the conclusion of mixed EU trade and investment agreements by Denmark. Consent may be given by statute or by parliamentary decision. A simple majority in Parliament suffices.[98]

Article 20 of the Danish Constitution sets out a 'special' procedure for ratifying international agreements that delegate sovereign power to international authorities. Such agreements can only be adopted by a supermajority in Parliament or a positive referendum. The threshold for using the Article 20 procedure is rather high. The Lisbon Treaty, for example, did not make the cut.[99] It has been argued that CETA, and more

[96] Council of Europe, Committee of Legal Advisers on Public International Law (CAHDI), Expression of Consent by States to Be Bound by a Treaty, Analytical Reports and Country Reports [2001] CAHDI (2000) 13 FINAL, Part II – Country Reports, Denmark, 119. See also P Svensson, 'Parliament and Foreign Policy Making in Denmark' (1998) 2 *Irish Studies in International Affairs* 19, 25.

[97] See further Krunke (n 57) 338.

[98] Yet, more than half the members must be present and take part in the voting. See Article 50 of the Danish Constitution.

[99] See further Højesteret, 199/2012, U.2013.1451H, as analysed by H Krunke, 'The Danish Lisbon Judgment – Danish Supreme Court, Case 199/2012, Judgment of 20 February 2013' (2014) 10 *European Constitutional Law Review* 542.

specifically the ICS, can only be ratified under the Article 20 procedure.[100] The Danish government rejected that argument, explaining that a transfer of sovereign power within the meaning of Article 20 does not automatically take place by agreements establishing a system for settling disputes between states and individuals, where the former act as respondents.[101] Indeed, Denmark commonly uses the Article 19 procedure for concluding such agreements (eg, the Rome Statute, the ECHR or BITs). The Danish Parliament ultimately gave its consent to CETA in June 2017 in accordance with the conditions set out in Article 19 of the Danish Constitution.[102]

Pursuant to Article 42 of the Danish Constitution, any legislative act – including the decision to conclude an international agreement – can be subjected to a referendum. Referenda can be requested by one-third of the members of Parliament within three weekdays of the date of approval of the legislative act. An act is deemed to be rejected if a majority of the electors participating in the referendum, comprising at least 30 per cent of all eligible voters, vote against it. There has been a proposal to adopt a parliamentary resolution on holding an indicative referendum on the conclusion of CETA by Denmark. However, that proposal did not obtain the required support in Parliament.[103]

C. France

Article 52(1) of the French Constitution prescribes that the President shall negotiate and ratify international treaties. In practice, the power is usually delegated to the government, more precisely the Ministry of Europe or the Ministry of Foreign Affairs.[104] Article 52(2) stipulates that the President must be informed of the negotiation and conclusion of international agreements that are not subject to ratification. Such agreements are negotiated by the government, and also approved by it, rather than ratified. The distinction between 'treaties' and 'agreements' drawn by Article 52 of the French Constitution has been widely discussed in the literature, although it appears to be largely formal in practice: under French constitutional law, the same conditions for parliamentary authorisation apply to treaties and agreements. Under international law, treaties and agreements have the same legal effect and consequences, as ratification and approval both express a consent to be bound.[105] There is broad discretion for

[100] See especially the opinion of the lawyer G Lett entitled 'Notat om, hvorvidt CETA-aftalen med Canada vil indeholde suverænitetsafgivelse i grundlovens forstand', 11 August 2016.

[101] *cf* Europaudvalget 2016-17 B 4 endeligt svar på spørgsmål 3 Offentligt [2016].

[102] Folketingsbeslutning 2016/1 BSV 74, adopted by the Danish Parliament at the second reading on 1 June 2017.

[103] *cf* Forslag til folketingsbeslutning om at afholde vejledende folkeafstemning om Danmarks tiltrædelse af den samlede økonomi- og handelsaftale mellem Den Europæiske Union og dens medlemsstater på den ene side og Canada på den anden side (CETA) [2017] Samling 2016–17, beslutningsforslag B 88.

[104] *cf* Ministère de l'Europe et des Affaires Étrangères, Guide des bonnes pratiques en matière de négociation et de conclusion des engagements internationaux de la France [édition 2020] 13 (hereinafter 'Treaty-Making Guide').

[105] R Le Boeuf, 'La double nature de la ratification des traités: observations sur les discordances entre les procédures constitutionelles et internationales' (2016) 107 *Revue française de droit constitutionnel* 601, 605 et seq. He points out that some authors argue that only treaties can be subjected to referenda in accordance with Article 11 of the French Constitution.

the executive to determine the form of an international treaty or agreement. Article 53 only prescribes the form in two instances, namely for peace treaties and commercial treaties.[106] Trade and investment agreements apparently qualify as 'commercial treaties' and must hence be ratified. Indeed, the French national parliaments were asked to authorise the 'ratification' of CETA.[107]

Treaties and agreements are signed by the President and the government, respectively. The President or the government may authorise representatives to act on their behalf.[108] If the President signs the agreement, the signature act must be countersigned by the Prime Minister in accordance with Article 19 of the French Constitution.[109] Parliaments are not involved in the signature process.

Article 53 of the French Constitution denotes the types of treaties and agreements that require parliamentary authorisation before being ratified by the executive. Amongst them are commercial treaties and treaties and agreements modifying provisions which are matters for statute. As stated above, mixed EU trade and investment agreements are apparently commercial in nature.[110] They also qualify as treaties 'modifying provisions which are matters for statute', as this criterion has been broadly interpreted by the French Constitutional Council. In a 1970 decision, the Constitutional Council found that all treaties and agreements concerning legislative matters (and thus not just those requiring the modification of existing legislation) fall within the scope of Article 53 of the French Constitution.[111] The French government has taken the position that CETA requires the approval of Parliament because it includes provisions of a legislative nature.[112]

Pursuant to Article 53, agreements requiring parliamentary consent can only be ratified by an Act of Parliament. The draft ratification act is adopted by the Council of Ministers,[113] after obtaining the (at this stage legally non-binding)[114] opinion of the Constitutional Council. The Assembly and the Senate must vote on an identical text of the draft act. A simple majority suffices for the adoption of the act. If both Chambers cannot agree on an identical text after two readings (or a single reading, under the accelerated procedure), a conciliation committee composed of an equal number of representatives of both Chambers may be tasked with proposing a joint text, which may then be submitted by the Government to both Chambers for approval. If this conciliation process fails, the Government may, after one more reading by both Chambers, ask the National Assembly to take a final decision (Article 45

[106] Circulaire du 30 mai 1997 relative à l'élaboration et à la conclusion des accords internationaux, JORF n° 0125 du 31 mai 1997.

[107] Projet de loi n°2107 autorisant la ratification de l'accord économique et commercial global entre l'Union européenne et ses Etats membres, d'une part, et le Canada, d'autre part, et de l'accord de partenariat stratégique entre l'Union européenne et ses Etats membres, d'une part, et le Canada, d'autre part [2019].

[108] Council of Europe (n 96) 130.

[109] See also Treaty-Making Guide (n 104) 20.

[110] See also Question de Mme Garriaud-Maylam Joëlle (Français établis hors de France – UMP) publiée le 17 juillet 2014, and the French Ministry of Foreign Affair's response thereto.

[111] Conseil constitutionnel, Décision n° 70-39 DC du 19 juin 1970. See also Eisemann and Rivier (n 59) 260.

[112] Projet de loi n°2107 (n 107) Exposé des Motifs.

[113] The French Council of Ministers is composed of the President and members of government.

[114] The State Council has both advisory and judicial powers. On the latter, see, eg, Article 54 of the French Constitution and section VII.B below.

of the French Constitution). In principle, mixed EU trade and investment agreements therefore need to be approved by the French Assembly and the Senate. However, in case of disagreement, the National Assembly has the last word. At the point of writing this book, the National Assembly and the Senate continue to search for a common text on the ratification of CETA. In March 2024, the Senate rejected the draft law on the conclusion of CETA by France at first reading. In accordance with the procedure set out in Article 45 of the French Constitution, the draft law will be reconsidered and, ultimately, may be decided upon by the National Assembly.[115]

In accordance with Article 11(1) of the French Constitution, the President, on a recommendation by the government or a joint motion by the Assembly and the Senate, may initiate a referendum on a draft ratification act of a treaty that would affect the functioning of the institutions without being contrary to the Constitution.[116] Article 11 further provides that a referendum might be initiated by one-fifth of the Members of Parliament, supported by one-tenth of all eligible voters. In such instances, the draft legislative act subject to the call for a referendum must be considered by both Chambers of Parliament. If Parliament fails to consider the act within the period of one month, the President must submit it to a referendum.

D. Germany

Pursuant to Article 59(1) of the German Constitution, the President signs and concludes international agreements. In practice, this power is delegated to the federal government or, more specifically, the federal cabinet.[117] There is no role foreseen for Parliament during the signature of international agreements. Treaty negotiation and signature thus remain executive prerogatives under German constitutional law.

In accordance with Article 59(2) of the German Constitution, the President must obtain parliamentary consent for the conclusion of two main types of international treaties. First are treaties that regulate the political relations of the Federation. According to the German Constitutional Court, treaties 'which seek to maintain, strengthen, or extend the power of a State in relation to other States are to be regarded as political treaties'.[118] The Court further held that trade agreements only establish such relations of power if they are used by states 'to strengthen their joint economic position in the competition between the states'.[119] The question of whether mixed EU trade and investment agreements qualify as 'political agreements' has been contested for some

[115] Texte n°95 (2023–2024) modifé par le Sénat le 21 mars 2024. On the power of the Senate in French lawmaking see further eg, J Money and G Tsebelis, 'The Political Power of the French Senate: Micromechanisms of Bicameral Negotiations' (1995) 1 *Journal of Legislative Studies* 192, 193 et seq.

[116] See further, eg, F Hamon and M Troper, *Droit constitutionnel* (Librairie générale de droit et de jurisprudence, 2018) 566.

[117] For example, the Federal Cabinet agreed on the signature of CETA on 19 October 2016. See also the 2022 Trade Agenda of the German Federal Cabinet, entitled 'Eckpunktepapier "Handelspolitik der Bundesregierung"', available at: bmwk.de/Redaktion/DE/Downloads/E/eckpunktpapier-handelsagenda.pdf?__blob=publicationFile&v=4.

[118] Bundesverfassungsgericht, 2 BvE 2/51, para 33. Translation by the author.

[119] ibid para 39.

time. In 2008, an inter-institutional conflict between the German Federal Parliament and the government arose precisely about that question in the context of the ratification of the economic partnership agreement (EPA) between the EU and certain West African states.[120] The German government sought that it could ratify the agreement without obtaining the prior consent of the Federal Parliament because the EPA largely fell within the EU's exclusive competence. In the eyes of the government, the agreement therefore did not have a political character.[121] Naturally, the Federal Parliament disagreed. Eventually, the government agreed to make the German ratification act of the EPA conditional on the Federal Parliament's approval, albeit without prejudice to legal constitutional necessity.[122] In view of the political salience of new generation EU trade and investment agreements, most German constitutional scholars nowadays argue that these agreements legally classify as political agreements within the meaning of Article 59(2) of the German Constitution.[123]

Article 59(2) of the German Constitution further specifies that international agreements, irrespective of their political relevance, have to be subjected to prior parliamentary consent if they relate to federal legislation. The German Constitutional Court clarified that an agreement relates to federal legislation if the implementation of that agreement requires the adoption of a federal law.[124] Accordingly, the criterion 'agreements relating to federal legislation' questions whether the German implementing act of an agreement would require the consent of the German legislature.[125] Notably, the German implementing act of mixed EU agreements can only cover material areas falling within a competence held and exercised by Germany. Most mixed EU trade and investment agreements indeed cover a matter that 'relates to' federal legislation because they terminate pre-existing BITs concluded by Germany. As these BITs were concluded with the consent of the German Federal Parliament, the new EU agreement can only be implemented by changing the existing federal law.[126] It has also been argued that ICS proceedings against Germany might cause an unforeseen change in the budget plan

[120] Economic Partnership Agreement between the West African States, the Economic Community of West African States (ECOWAS) and the West African Economic and Monetary Union (UEMOA), of the one part, and the European Union and its Member States, of the other part [2014] 13370/14, 2014/0265 (NLE).

[121] This becomes apparent from the debate in Parliament on the expert hearing on the matter. *cf* Deutscher Bundestag, Stenografischer Bericht 178. Sitzung [2016] 17543; Deutscher Bundestag, Wortprotokoll der 82. Sitzung Ausschuss für Recht und Verbraucherschutz [2016].

[122] See also B Grzeszick and J Hettche, 'Zur Beteiligung des Bundestages an gemischten völkerrechtlichen Abkommen: Internationale Freihandelsabkommen als Herausforderung des deutschen Europa- und Außenverfassungsrechts' (2016) 141 *Archiv des öffentlichen Rechts* 225, 227.

[123] See, eg, Grzeszick and Hettche (n 122) 252; TP Holterhus, 'Die Rolle des Deutschen Bundestages in der auswärtigen Handelspolitik der Europäischen Union – Insbesondere zu den parlamentarischen Einflussmöglichkeiten im völkerrechtlichen Vertragsschlussverfahren' (2017) 52 *Zeitschrift Europarecht* 231, 249; B Grzeszick, 'Völkervertragsrecht in der parlamentarischen Demokratie: CETA als Präzedenzfall für die demokratischen Anforderungen an völkerrechtliche Verträge', *Neue Zeitschrift für Verwaltungsrecht* 35 (2016) 1753; W Weiß, 'Informations- und Beteiligungsrechte des Deutschen Bundestags bei gemischten Abkommen wie TTIP' (2016) 16 *Die Öffentliche Verwaltung* 661, 666–67; R Streinz, 'Disputes on TTIP: Does the Agreement Need the Consent of the German Parliament' in C Herrmann et al (eds), *Trade Policy between Law, Diplomacy and Scholarship: Liber Amicorum in Memoriam Horst G. Krenzler* (Springer, 2015) 271.

[124] Bundesverfassungsgericht, 2 BvE 2/51 (n 118) para 65.

[125] See further, eg, F Schorkopf, *Staatsrecht der internationalen Beziehungen* (CH Beck, 2017) 179 et seq.

[126] See also Grzeszick and Hettche (n 122) 254–55.

originally adopted by Parliament, which would equally cause changes to the existing federal legislation.[127]

In sum, there is therefore little doubt that the Federal Parliament must, as a matter of law, consent to the conclusion of mixed EU trade and investment agreements by Germany. It is less clear whether the Federal Council is also legally required to approve of the German ratification act. The Federal Council must consent to the ratification of a treaty falling within the scope of Article 59(2) of the German Constitution if said treaty would internally – ie, assuming it were domestic law – require its consent to be adopted.[128] The instances in which the adoption of a law requires the consent of the Federal Council are exhaustively listed in the German Constitution. The question is thus whether the parts of mixed EU trade and investment agreements that fall within the competences of the Member States concern material aspects which fall within the legislative competences of the Federal Council. Some scholars have argued that mixed EU trade and investment agreements indeed touch upon a single legislative competence of the Federal Council, namely state liability,[129] which might result from ICS proceedings, a national competence.[130] In addition to these legal arguments, there has also been political pressure to subject mixed EU trade and investment agreements to the scrutiny and consent of both Chambers of Parliament, including from the Federal Council itself.[131] The involvement of both Chambers of Parliament may thus be as much of a political as a legal choice. In practice, BITs and mixed EU trade and investment agreements have indeed only been concluded by Germany after the Federal Parliament and the Federal Council have expressed their consent.[132]

E. The Netherlands

In accordance with Article 90 of the Dutch Constitution, the government signs and concludes international agreements. In practice, this task is usually assumed by the Prime Minister or the Foreign Minister. As in the case of Germany and France, the signature of international agreements remains an executive prerogative. However, for the conclusion of international agreements, the Dutch government must obtain parliamentary consent as a general rule.[133]

[127] See, eg, M Krajewski, 'Umweltschutz und internationales Investitionsschutzrecht am Beispiel der Vattenfall-Klagen und des Transatlantischen Handels- und Investitionsabkommens (TTIP)' (2014) 25 *Zeitschrift für Umweltrecht* 396, 400.

[128] See also Schorkopf (n 125) 182–83.

[129] *cf* Article 74 of the German Constitution.

[130] See, eg, Krajewski (n 127) 400; W Weiß, 'Verfassungsprobleme des Abschlusses und der vorläufigen Anwendung des CETA Freihandelsabkommens mit Kanada', *Stellungnahme zur Öffentlichen Anhörung des Ausschusses für Wirtschaft und Energie des Deutschen Bundestages* (2016) 29. *Contra*, see M Ruffert, 'Das CETA-Ratifikationsgesetz bedarf nicht der Zustimmung des Bundesrates!', *Verfassungsblog*, 31 October 2016, verfassungsblog.de/das-ceta-ratifikationsgesetz-bedarf-nicht-der-zustimmung-des-bundesrates.

[131] See, eg, 924. Sitzung des Bundesrates, 11 July 2014, Top 55.

[132] *cf* Articles 77(2a) and 78(1) of the German Constitution.

[133] Article 91(1) of the Dutch Constitution. Some exceptions to this general rule are, in accordance with Article 91(1), laid down in Article 7 of the Kingdom Law (n 81). However, these exceptions are not relevant to the study of trade and investment agreements.

After a treaty has been signed by the government, it must be forwarded to Parliament 'as soon as possible'.[134] The ratification act must be approved by both Chambers of the Dutch Parliament, and – in contrast to France – none of the Chambers has the power to override the other in the event of conflict. The Dutch Parliament can approve a proposed ratification act either explicitly, ie, by an Act of Parliament, or tacitly, after obtaining the opinion of the Council of States.[135] Approval is deemed to have been tacitly granted if the wish for explicit approval has not been expressed by one of the Chambers, by the Chair of each Chamber on their behalf or by one-fifth of the members of one of the Chambers, within 30 days after they received the signed text of the treaty for the purpose of tacit approval.[136] During the 30-day period, the government and Parliament may enter into informal discussions. The government has broad discretion to propose a ratification act to Parliament under the explicit or tacit procedure. In practice, the government chooses the former if the agreement requires constitutional change,[137] an implementing act, or if it is likely that Parliament wishes to express consent.[138] Mixed EU trade and investment agreements were generally proposed under the explicit procedure. However, consent was expressed with little parliamentary scrutiny. For example, neither the Second nor the First Chamber of the Dutch Parliament wished to hold a plenary debate about the EU-Korea FTA, and the Dutch ratification act was approved by both Chambers consecutively without voting.[139] This has changed with the ratification of CETA, which has been frequently debated in both Chambers of the Dutch Parliament.[140]

Article 91(3) of the Dutch Constitution sets out a special procedure for ratifying international agreements that deviate from the Constitution.[141] It requires, amongst other things, a four-fifths majority in Parliament. The procedure is rarely used in practice. It was, for example, never used for the ratification of the EU founding treaties.[142] Some have nevertheless argued that the procedure is required for the Dutch ratification act of CETA. Their argument is essentially based on Article 212 of the Dutch Constitution, which reserves judging disputes about civil claims and damages exclusively to the Dutch courts. Opponents have argued that CETA obligations originate and are based on international law, and therefore could not be based

[134] Article 2(1) of the Kingdom Law (n 81).

[135] Article 91(2) of the Dutch Constitution; Articles 3 and 6(1) of the Kingdom Law (n 81).

[136] Article 5(1) of the Kingdom Law (n 81).

[137] In such cases, the explicit procedure is mandatory. See Article 6(1) of the Kingdom Law (n 81).

[138] See Assessment Criteria of the First Chamber (n 65). Parliament's desire to express its consent may become apparent from its reaction to the list of draft treaties it received from the foreign ministry four times per year. See section IV.E above.

[139] Kamerstukken II, 2011–2012, 33 027, Nr 2. In both chambers, the law was adopted as a so-called 'Hamerstuk', ie, a proposed legislative act no one wishes to speak about during a plenary session and which is accepted without a vote.

[140] For practical examples, see, eg, nn 42 and 43.

[141] See also Staatscommissie Grondwet, Rapport Staatscommissie Grondwet [2010] 115–17; LFM Besselink and RA Wessel, *De invloed van ontwikkelingen in de internationale rechtsorde op de doorwerking naar Nederlands constitutioneel recht. Een 'neo-monistische' benadering* (Kluwer, 2009) 45 et seq; RA Wessel and WE van de Griendt, 'Offene Staatlichkeit: Niederlande' in von Bogdandy, Villalón and Huber (n 32) 177, 187.

[142] See further LFM Besselink and M Claes, 'The Netherlands: The Pragmatics of a Flexible, Europeanised Constitution' in Albi and Bardutzky (n 26) 179, 185.

on civil rights and resulting in claims under Dutch domestic law.[143] In practice, the Netherlands has never used the Article 91(3) procedure for the ratification of international investment agreements. Instead, Dutch BITs were frequently ratified under the tacit procedure.[144] CETA is proposed to be ratified under the express procedure, in accordance with Article 90 of the Constitution, by a simple majority in both Chambers of Parliament.[145]

The Dutch Constitution does not include a provision on referenda. Nonetheless, from July 2015 until February 2018, it was possible to hold consultative referenda on most legal acts, including on the Dutch ratification acts of mixed EU agreements.[146] A proposed law could be rejected by a majority of the votes cast if at least 30 per cent of eligible voters participated in the referendum. As will be further discussed in the next chapter, the Dutch citizens rejected the ratification of the EU-Ukraine Association Agreement in a 2016 consultative referendum by 61.1 per cent of the votes cast. With a turnout of 32 per cent, the required participation threshold was just reached.[147] In 2018, the Dutch Parliament repealed the law on consultative referenda. As a result, the Dutch citizens can no longer vote directly on the ratification of mixed EU trade and investment agreements. At the time of writing this book, there is political discussion to introduce legally binding referenda through constitutional change.

VI. The Provisional Application of Mixed Agreements

The provisional application of trade and investment agreements is usually an EU-only affair, even in the case of mixed agreements. As the scope of provisional application of mixed agreements is generally confined to matters falling within the EU's exclusive competence, the Member States must not authorise it in their own right.[148]

The Member States may decide to adopt an independent decision on the provisional application of a mixed agreement alongside the EU if the scope of provisional application comprises not only EU exclusive competence but also shared competence. Contrary to what has been argued by some, there is no legal necessity for the Member States to adopt such an independent decision if the agreement at issue is fully covered by EU exclusive and shared competence (facultative mixed agreement).[149] The CJEU confirmed that the EU may exercise shared competence alone for the implementation of a mixed

[143] Freya Baetens et al, 'Why the Netherlands Should Ratify CETA', *EJIL Talk!*, 30 June 2020, www.ejiltalk.org/why-the-netherlands-should-ratify-ceta.

[144] See, eg, the ratification notice of the BIT between Albania and the Netherlands, Kamerstukken II 1994–1995, 24 114 (R 1534), Nr 1.

[145] *cf* Kamerstukken, 2018–2019, 35 154, Nr 2.

[146] Wet raadgevend referendum, Stb 2015, 122 (Law on consultative referenda). The law expired on 12 July 2018, with retroactive effect until 10 July 2018.

[147] See RA Wessel, 'The EU Solution to Deal with the Dutch Referendum Result on the EU-Ukraine Association Agreement' (2016) *European Papers* 1305.

[148] See further Chapter 4, sections IV.C and IV.D.

[149] *Contra*, see, eg, B Kempen and B Schiffbauer, 'Die vorläufige Anwendung völkerrechtlicher Verträge im internationalen Mehrebenensystem' (2017) 77 *Zeitschrift für ausländisches öffentliches Recht und Völkerrecht* 95, 117; Weiß (n 123) 21.

agreement.[150] The same must by inference be true for the provisional application of a mixed agreement, implying that the EU may decide to provisionally apply a facultative mixed agreement alone and in full. Nevertheless, as was explained in the previous chapter, facultative mixed agreements are made on the premise that (part of the) shared competence is exercised by Member States.[151] If the EU were to exercise (all of the) shared competence alone in the course of provisional application, there may no longer be a reason for mixity. As a result, (some of) the Member States may wish to decide on the provisional application of a facultative mixed agreement in their own right.

In the past, the Council and the Representatives of the Governments of the Member States could avoid competence disputes by jointly adopting a decision on a mixed agreement's provisional application.[152] However, the CJEU held that such hybrid decisions violate EU law.[153] Individual Member States have – albeit rarely – decided to provisionally apply mixed agreements in their own right alongside the EU. This was notably the case for the Framework and Cooperation Agreement with Korea, which was provisionally applied by Slovakia, Finland, and Spain in their own right.[154] Germany declared 'that it can apply the Agreement on a provisional basis only in accordance with its national law'.[155]

The Member States would be legally required to adopt a decision on the provisional application of a mixed agreement in their own right if the scope of provisional application touched on exclusive national competence.[156] This may cause legal problems, as the practice of provisional application is not recognised in the domestic laws of all Member States. Indeed, the constitutional laws of Belgium, Denmark, France and Germany do not know provisional application. Article 167(2) and (3) of the Belgian Constitution even stipulates that international agreements can only 'take effect' after receiving the approval of the Chamber of Representatives and/or sub-national parliaments. Provisional application is therefore 'only allowed on an exceptional basis when the treaty contains no provisions which are binding on citizens or place a burden on the state budget'.[157] In Denmark, provisional application is possible if the treaty does not require further implementation or has already been implemented at an early stage, so that 'the treaty obligations can be fulfilled from the moment of provisional application'.[158] In France, provisional application is only exceptionally possible if the treaty itself provides for it. It is common practice to avoid provisional application for

[150] Case C-600/14, *COTIF I*, EU:C:2017:935.

[151] See Chapter 4, section IV.C. See also G Kübek and I Van Damme, 'Facultative Mixity and the European Union's Trade and Investment Agreements' in M Chamon and I Govaere (eds), *EU External Relations Law Post-Lisbon: The Law and Practice of Facultative Mixity* (Brill/Nijhoff, 2020) 661 et seq.

[152] See, eg, Decision 339/EC of the Council and the Representatives of the Governments of the Member States of the European Union, meeting within the Council of 25 April 2007 on the signature and provisional application of the Air Transport Agreement between the European Community and its Member States, on the one hand, and the United States of America, on the other hand [2007] OJ L134/1.

[153] Case C-28/12, *Hybrid Acts*, EU:C:2015:282.

[154] *cf* Council database of Treaties and Agreements, Framework Agreement between the European Union and its Member States, on the one part, and the Republic of Korea, on the other part, consilium.europa.eu/en/documents-publications/treaties-agreements/agreement/?id=2010020&DocLanguage=en.

[155] ibid.

[156] See in more detail Chapter 4, section IV.C.

[157] Council of Europe (n 96) Part II – Country Report, Belgium, 101.

[158] ibid 119, 121.

agreements that may affect the rights and obligations of individuals or that require parliamentary authorisation to be concluded.[159] In Germany, provisional application is only possible for treaties that can be concluded by the executive alone. For agreements that require parliamentary consent, provisional application is subject to the same procedural rules as treaty conclusion.[160] Conversely, provisional application is expressly permitted under Dutch law, unless the agreement conflicts with constitutional or secondary law.[161] Prior to deciding on the provisional application of an international agreement, the Dutch government must carefully balance the 'interest of the Kingdom' to give immediate effect to the agreement against Parliament's interest to express its prior consent and justify why the former interest outweighs the latter.[162]

As the domestic legal orders of some Member States only permit provisional application in exceptional circumstances, or not at all,[163] it would be legally difficult to provisionally apply mandatory mixed agreements in full. For this reason alone, the practice to match the scope of provisional application of mixed agreements with the scope of the EU's exclusive competence is a pragmatic solution that circumvents dealing with the diverging rules governing the practice of provisional application in EU Member States.[164]

VII. National Constitutional Review

In many Member States, national constitutional courts may review the constitutionality of EU law and, as a matter of last resort, declare EU law unconstitutional. The Netherlands, where the review of acts of parliaments and treaties by courts is prohibited by the Constitution, is a prominent exception.[165] Where national courts possess the power to declare EU legal acts unconstitutional, they may by inference rule on the constitutionality of EU international agreements. EU trade and investment agreements can become the subject of constitutional review by national constitutional courts irrespective of their character as EU-only or mixed agreements (see sections VII.A and VII.B, respectively). However, the scope of review of national constitutional courts depends on the division of competence between the EU and the Member States.

[159] Article VI.3 of the Circulaire du 30 mai 1997 (n 106).
[160] Article 59(2) of the German Constitution. See also German Federal Foreign Office, Comments and Observations by Germany on the Draft Guide to Provisional Application of Treaties, Adopted by the International Law Commission on First Reading (2019) paras 14–15.
[161] Article 15(1), (2) of the Kingdom Law (n 81).
[162] Permanent Mission of the Kingdom of the Netherlands to the United Nations, Comments to the International Law Commission on the Provisional Application of Treaties [2016] NYV/2016/391.
[163] A Quast Mertsch, *Provisionally Applied Treaties: Their Binding Force and Legal Nature* (Brill, 2012) 62–64, suggests that the national legal orders of Austria, Italy, Luxembourg and Portugal preclude provisional application. However, her findings were partially contested by JM Gómez-Robledo, Special Rapporteur, 'Third Report on the Provisional Application of Treaties', International Law Commission [2015] UN Doc A/CN.4/687, 62.
[164] See further Chapter 4, section IV.D.
[165] Article 120 of the Dutch Constitution.

A. EU-Only Agreements

EU legal acts, such as EU-only agreements, can be brought before national constitutional courts on two main grounds.[166] First, national constitutional courts may be asked to review whether the scope of an EU legal act falls within the EU's conferred competence (ultra vires review).[167] Second, national constitutional courts may be asked to review whether an EU legal act encroaches on the national constitutional identity of the Member States (constitutional identity review).[168] Before declaring an EU legal act invalid on the ground that it encroaches on the Member States' sovereign power and/or identity, national constitutional courts have to refer the matter to the CJEU for a preliminary ruling.[169]

In national practice, the ultra vires and constitutional identity challenges are frequently raised together. For example, the German Constitutional Court faced a citizen's complaint in 2020 about the constitutionality of the EU-Japan FTA.[170] The complainants contended that the conclusion of the agreement by the EU alone breached their right to democracy, which forms part of Germany's constitutional identity.[171] They essentially argued that the agreement in general, and the decision-making bodies created therein specifically, exceed the EU's conferred competence and should therefore not have been ratified without the consent of the German Federal Parliament and Council.[172] However, the German Constitutional Court did not accept the constitutional complaint for decision, as the complainants did not sufficiently substantiate their legal arguments.[173]

B. Mixed Agreements: The Case of CETA

For mixed agreements, the standard of review national constitutional courts apply is wider than for EU-only agreements. The part of the mixed agreement that falls within shared and/or exclusive Member State competence can be reviewed by national constitutional courts under the same procedures as Member State-only agreements. For example, CETA was brought before the French Constitutional Council in accordance with Article

[166] See A Schöpgens and G van Calster, 'Multilevel Constitutional Review and EU External Treaty Making after Opinion 2/15' (2018) 23 *European Foreign Affairs Review* 439; and JP Terhechte, '(National-) Verfassungsrechtliche Grenzen der Weiterentwicklung des europäischen Außenwirtschaftsrechts' in M Bungenberg and C Herrmann (eds), *Die gemeinsame Handelspolitik der Europäischen Union nach Lissabon* (Nomos, 2011) 25.

[167] Article 5(2) TEU.

[168] ibid Article 4(2). See further, for a national constitutional perspective, A Voßkuhle, 'Multilevel Cooperation of the European Constitutional Courts' (2010) 6 *European Constitutional Law Review* 175; and, for an EU constitutional perspective, K Lenaerts and JA Gutiérrez-Fons, 'To Say What the Law of the EU is: Methods of Interpretation and the European Court of Justice' (2013) 9 *EUI Working Paper AEL*.

[169] This is generally recognised by constitutional courts. See, eg, the Maastricht judgment of the Danish Constitutional Court (Højesteret, I 361/1997, U.1998.800H).

[170] Bundesverfassungsgericht, 2 BvR 183/19, DE:BVerfG:2020:rk20200123.2bvr018319. See similarly, with regard to the ratification of the EUSFTA, Bundesverfassungsgericht, 2 BvR 882/19, DE:BVerfG:2019:rk20191107.2bvr088219.

[171] Articles 38(1) 20(1),(2) in conjunction with Article 79(3) of the German Constitution.

[172] Bundesverfassungsgericht, 2 BvR 183/19 (n 170) para 6.

[173] ibid paras 10–14.

54 of the French Constitution.[174] The provision stipulates that France cannot ratify an international agreement that, in the eyes of the Constitutional Council, contains a clause contrary to the Constitution, unless the Constitution is amended beforehand. In its CETA judgment, the French Constitutional Council applied a different standard of review for the parts of the agreement that fall within EU exclusive competence than for the parts of the agreement that fall within shared competence, taking the CJEU's conclusions in *Opinion 2/15* as a baseline. For matters falling within shared competence, the Constitutional Council reviewed the compatibility with all norms of French constitutional law. For matters falling within the exclusive competence of the EU, it applied a narrower standard of review, checking whether the constitutional identity of France remained untouched.[175] Showing 'a strong attitude of deference' towards international and EU law, it concluded that CETA 'does not contain any provision contrary to the constitution'.[176]

Approximately one year before the French Constitutional Council gave its verdict on CETA, the German Constitutional Court had already rejected applications for a preliminary injunction against CETA.[177] The applicants had essentially claimed that CETA violates Germany's constitutional identity by breaching individual democratic rights as well as the German Federal Parliament's legislative discretion.[178] In contrast to the French Constitutional Council, the German Constitutional Court did not pay close attention to the division of legislative and judicial competences within the EU. As a result, its judgment was harshly criticised for not being consistent with the principles of primacy and exclusivity of EU law.[179] Indeed, the German Constitutional Court had – prior to the delivery of *Opinion 2/15* – taken it upon itself to delineate EU exclusive from shared competence in the context of CETA. On that basis, it requested the German government to ensure that the scope of CETA's provisional application was confined to the realm of EU exclusive competence and that Germany can unilaterally terminate provisional application.[180] However, as will be further explained in the next chapter, the termination of the provisional application of a mixed agreement by a Member State violates EU law if the scope of provisional application is confined to EU exclusive competence, as the German Constitutional Court had explicitly requested.[181] The demands of the German Constitutional Court were nevertheless anchored in the Council decision on the provisional application of CETA, illustrating that national constitutional courts can exert considerable political influence during

[174] Conseil constitutionnel, Décision n° 2017-749 DC, FR:CC:2017:2017.749.DC.

[175] ibid paras 13–14.

[176] ibid para 75, as analysed by J Larik, '*Prêt-à-ratifier*: The CETA Decision of the French *Conseil constitutionnel* of 31 July 2017' (2017) 13 *European Constitutional Law Review* 759, 769.

[177] Bundesverfassungsgericht, 2 BvR 1368/16, DE:BVerfG:2016:rs20161013.2bvr136816. In preliminary injunction proceedings, the German Constitutional Court does not rule on the substantive arguments, unless they are clearly inadmissible or unfounded. Instead, it balances the disadvantages that would arise if the preliminary injunction was not issued, but the applicant was successful in the main proceedings, against the disadvantages that would arise if the preliminary injunction sought was issued, but the applications in the main proceedings were unsuccessful (see further para 35 of the decision).

[178] Article 79(3) in conjunction with Articles 20(1), (2), 23(1) and 59(2) of the German Constitution.

[179] See especially K Nowrot and C Tietje, 'CETA an der Leine des Bundesverfassungsgerichts: Zum schmalen Grat zwischen Ultra-vires Kontrolle und Ultra-vires Handeln' (2017) 52 *Zeitschrift Europarecht* 137.

[180] Bundesverfassungsgericht, 2 BvR 1368/16 (n 177) paras 68, 72.

[181] See further Chapter 6, section III.

the mixed treaty-making process.[182] In 2021, the German Constitutional Court ultimately rejected the applicant's substantive arguments, thereby confirming that the signature and provisional application of CETA was neither ultra vires nor encroached on Germany's constitutional identity.[183]

In contrast to the highest French and German courts, the Irish Supreme Court upheld a constitutional challenge against the ratification of CETA. In a 2022 judgment, by a majority of four to three, the Irish Supreme Court held that CETA's ICS breached Ireland's judicial sovereignty.[184] In essence, the Supreme Court considered that the requirement to enforce certain ICS awards automatically, which follows from the Irish Arbitration Act 2010, interferes with the constitutional requirement that justice must be administered by judges appointed under the Irish Constitution.[185] This reasoning notably differs from the reasoning of the French Constitutional Council, which considered that the ICS does not interfere with the judicial sovereignty of France because arbitrators merely issue monetary awards and would thus not hold the power to interpret or annul decisions taken by the EU institutions or the Member States.[186] A similar reasoning was applied by the CJEU in *Opinion 1/17*.[187] Yet, the majority of Justices of the Irish Supreme Court, including the former Advocate General Hogan, were 'unpersuaded by aspects of the reasoning of the CJEU in *CETA Opinion 1/17* so far as it might be relied on as an authority in the particular and special *sphere of Irish constitutional law*' (emphasis in original).[188] The Supreme Court ultimately held that CETA can only be ratified by Ireland if the Arbitration Act 2010 is amended to allow Irish courts to refuse the enforcement of CETA awards where they consider that such awards breach the Irish constitutional identity or compromise Ireland's obligation to enforce EU law.[189] However, it remains unclear whether such amendments would be compatible with the ICSID Convention.[190]

VIII. Conclusion

The making of international agreements is traditionally a prerogative of the executive. With little influence at the outset of the treaty-making process, parliaments are typically

[182] The German Constitutional Court held in a subsequent decision that the commitments made by the Federal Government and the EU institutions at the point of signing and provisionally applying CETA sufficiently take account of its demands. See Bundesverfassungsgericht, 2 BvR 1444/16, DE:BVerfG:2016:rs20161207.2bvr144416.

[183] Bundesverfassungsgericht, 2 BvE 4/16, DE:BVerfG:2021:es20210302.2bve000416, para 84.

[184] Supreme Court of Ireland, *Costello v Government of Ireland, Ireland, and the Attorney General* [2022] IESC 44_5.

[185] To put it in the words of Justice Hogan, in the context of CETA, the Irish Arbitration Act 2010 'serves as a sort of makeshift pontoon bridge by which a CETA Tribunal award is enabled to cross that legal Rubicon from the realm of international law into an enforceable judgment recognised as such by our own legal system on a more or less automatic basis'. See ibid, Judgment of Mr Justice Gerard Hogan, para 84.

[186] Conseil constitutionnel (n 174) para 23.

[187] Opinion 1/17, *Comprehensive Economic and Trade Agreement with Canada*, EU:C:2019:341, para 144.

[188] *Costello* (n 184) Judgment of Mr Justice Gerard Hogan, para 107.

[189] See, eg, ibid paras 228 et seq.

[190] See P Leonard, 'Patrick Costello v the Government of Ireland, Ireland and the Attorney General: Obstacles to the Ratification of CETA in the Irish Constitutional Context' (2023) 38 *ICSID Review – Foreign Investment Law Journal* 286, 292.

left with either derailing the conclusion of an international agreement, thereby creating a foreign policy crisis, or (reluctantly) accepting the agreement as it is.[191] The balance between effectiveness and parliamentary involvement in foreign policy was re-thought in most Member States for a particular type of 'foreign' policy, namely supranational EU policy. With the establishment of the Community/Union, many Member States have created national (constitutional) laws that ensure that their parliaments are fully and continuously informed about proposed EU (foreign policy) acts and can weigh in on their government's position in the Council. In doing so, the Member States sought to compensate their national parliaments for the loss of direct decision-making powers that the transfer of competence from the national level to the supranational level inevitably brought about.

Similar debates about frontloading national parliamentary influence to the beginning of the treaty-making process in order to compensate them for the loss of veto powers over the outcome of that process are held in the context of *moving beyond mixity*, which highlights that mixity is indeed 'one of the defining questions of the constitutional life of the European Union'.[192] This chapter has shown that, as a result of the creation of parliamentary rights in EU matters in the national (constitutional) laws of the Member States, national parliaments tend to be informed more extensively and early about the making of EU-only agreements than they are about the making of international agreements by the Member States themselves. For the making of multilateral mixed agreements, where the EU and the Member States act in parallel, this can lead to the paradoxical situation that national governments are required, as a matter of national constitutional law, to forward the EU negotiating directives and positions to their parliaments, while they are under no similar obligation with regard to their own negotiating positions. With the increasing political salience of EU trade policy, national parliaments have – on the basis of the information they receive from the EU and their governments – become more vocal, through parliamentary questions, debates, expert hearings, opinions etc. The creation of standing bodies designated to EU trade policy, such as the French Trade Policy Monitoring Committee, could potentially ensure that national parliaments and other interested stakeholders become involved in the making of EU trade and investment agreements on a more continuous and structural basis, and not only (or primarily) for particularly contentious agreements, such as TTIP, CETA or Mercosur.

This chapter has also shown that the Member States can answer some of the calls for increased national parliamentary control over EU trade policy on the basis of national constitutional law. The example of Denmark – where the national parliament can mandate the representative in the Council to vote against a proposed EU act – shows that there are also ways to confer decision-making powers to national parliaments in the EU-only setting. The 'Danish model' could be implemented in some Member States with a few constitutional twists. However, despite calls to increase national parliamentary influence over the making of EU trade and investment

[191] The Dutch expression 'slikken of stikken' (swallow or choke) to describe this practice is very fitting.

[192] C Hillion and P Koutrakos (eds), *Mixed Agreements Revisited: The EU and its Member States in the World* (Hart Publishing, 2010) xix. See also RA Wessel and J Larik, 'The European Union as a Global Legal Actor' in RA Wessel and J Larik (eds), *EU External Relations Law: Text, Cases and Materials*, 2nd edn (Hart Publishing, 2020) 1, 26.

agreements, it is not clear whether many Member States would desire making the position of their representative in the Council subject to prior parliamentary approval. The practice would, for example, conflict with the French constitutional premise of *parlementarisme rationalisé*, while in Belgium, it would increase the already large number of actors (six in total) that must agree on the position taken by the Belgian representative in the Council.

The case of Belgium, where mixed EU trade and investment agreements are also classified as Belgian mixed agreements (a situation of double mixity, as it were), illustrates the complexity of the mixed procedure particularly well. No fewer than five subnational parliaments, in addition to the Federal Chamber of Representatives, must agree on the ratification of mixed agreements by Belgium. Mixity also raises constitutional debates in other Member States, for instance, about how many different (chambers of) parliament(s) are required, as a matter of law, to consent to the ratification of a mixed agreement or about the applicable voting rules. Differences between national constitutional legal rules, such as on the general acceptance of provisional application as a permitted practice, can cause additional legal hurdles. This added complexity, coupled with the allocation of numerous additional veto rights, takes an enormous toll on the effectiveness of EU foreign policy. Curbs on the effectiveness of EU external action are particularly impactful in the domain of trade policy, the 'centre-piece of the EU's external policies',[193] which is increasingly used as a 'unique lever' to achieve wider foreign policy goals.[194] Moreover, the fact that national parliaments usually ratify mixed agreements in full, thereby encroaching on the constitutional prerogatives of the EP, has noticeable effects on the practice of ensuring democratic oversight of the ratification of these agreements.

Ultimately, national constitutional courts retain the last word on EU trade and investment agreements. They may review the constitutionality of both EU-only and mixed agreements, although the scope of review is wider for the latter. In recent years, national constitutional courts were asked to review both EU-only and mixed EU trade and investment agreements. CETA has so far been reviewed by no fewer than three constitutional courts. While the highest French and German courts ultimately confirmed the constitutionality of CETA, the Irish Supreme Court concluded that the ratification of CETA by Ireland is unconstitutional without prior changes to the existing legislation. At the time of writing, the practical ramifications of that judgment on the ratification of EU IPAs and BITs by Ireland are not fully clear.

[193] P Eeckhout, *EU External Relations Law*, 2nd edn (Oxford University Press, 2011) 439.
[194] European Commission, Trade Policy Review: An Open, Sustainable and Assertive Trade Policy, COM (2021) 66 final, 1.

PART III

The Interrelationship between Treaty-Making Power and Procedure

6

The Non-ratification of Bilateral Mixed Trade and Investment Agreements

I. Introduction

The times where the EU's external trade policy was described as a purely technical domain that was distant from the public interest and eye are long gone. Since the TTIP negotiations at the latest, trade policy has become trade politics.[1] Both at the EU and at the national levels, the role and impact of parliaments in the treaty-making process have increased significantly. Chapters 4 and 5 showed that neither the EP nor (sub-)national parliaments will continue to 'rubber-stamp' the ratification of EU trade and investment agreements.

The choice between EU-only and mixity affects the way in which (sub-)national parliaments exert democratic control over EU trade policy. Under the EU-only procedure, national parliaments form part of a vertically integrated governance system. They mainly use the information and participation rights derived from national constitutional law to indirectly impact EU treaty-making through their government's action in the Council.[2] In addition, they may enter into a political dialogue with the EU institutions.[3] Under the mixed procedure, national parliaments directly impact the treaty ratification process as most Member State governments can, under national constitutional law, only conclude international agreements after obtaining the consent of their parliaments. Moreover, referenda about the ratification of mixed agreements are possible in several Member States.[4] Mixity thus grants (sub-)national parliaments and citizens de facto veto rights over the ratification of EU agreements. But what happens if a (sub-)national parliament rejects the ratification of a bilateral mixed trade and investment agreement? Or if citizens reject a bilateral mixed trade and investment agreement in a referendum? Does this mean that the agreement cannot be ratified by the EU and all the other Member States?

* Parts of this chapter are based on G Kübek, 'The Non-ratification Scenario: Legal and Practical Responses to Mixed Treaty Rejection by Member States' (2018) 23 *European Foreign Affairs Review* 21.

[1] See especially F De Ville and G Siles-Brügge, *TTIP: The Truth about the Transatlantic Trade and Investment Partnership* (Polity Press, 2016).

[2] See further Chapter 5, section II.

[3] See further Chapter 4, section II.D.

[4] See further Chapter 5, section V.

The non-ratification of mixed agreements by one or more Member States was not considered an actual problem for a long time.[5] Like Brexit, that scenario was simply not perceived as being realistic in practice. National treaty ratification was said to significantly prolong but not to stop the ratification process of mixed agreements. The infamous 'Grappa incident' began to challenge that assumption.[6] Italy threatened not to ratify the Association Agreement with South Africa because it was unhappy with the lack of protection of the denomination of 'Grappa' and contended that the EU should therefore stop the agreement's provisional application, which the EU and South Africa had already agreed upon. After Italy obtained last-minute concessions for 'Grappa' and Greece – which then also subjected its ratification to individual demands – for 'Ouzo', the agreement was concluded by all Member States and the EU in 2002.[7] A few years later, Germany barely escaped a non-ratification crisis: the FTA with Peru and Colombia only passed in the German Federal Council with 36 affirmative votes and abstentions (35 votes are required for passing the majority threshold).[8]

In 2016, the ratification of a mixed EU agreement (initially) failed for the first time in a Member State. On 6 April, 61 per cent of Dutch voters rejected their country's ratification act of the Association Agreement between the EU and Ukraine. As was explained in the previous chapter, between 2015 and 2018 the Netherlands had a law in place that allowed consultative referenda on most legislative acts.[9] With a turnout of 32 per cent, the referendum on the Dutch ratification of the EU-Ukraine Association Agreement just passed the 30 per cent participation threshold. Despite its consultative nature, the Dutch government felt obliged to act on the results of the referendum and so felt the agreement could not be ratified, thereby precluding its entry into force. After lengthy and difficult discussions, a 'Decision of the Heads of State or Government of the 28 Member States of the European Union' was adopted during a European Council meeting, which enabled the Dutch ratification of the EU-Ukraine Association Agreement after all.[10] Shortly afterwards, in October 2016, the regional Parliament of Wallonia voted against the Belgian signature of CETA. Under Belgian constitutional law, the ratification of CETA must be authorised by the governments of the Belgian federated entities ('Belgian mixed agreement').[11] The federated government of Wallonia decided to follow the opinion of its parliament and refused to give consent to the Belgian signature of CETA. Notwithstanding the Belgian federal government's approval of CETA, the

[5] Ehlermann's seminal work did, for example, not address the non-ratification of mixed agreements in any detail. See C-D Ehlermann, 'Mixed Agreements: A List of Problems' in D O'Keeffe and HG Schermers (eds), *Mixed Agreements* (Kluwer, 1983) 3.

[6] A Rosas, 'The Future of Mixity' in C Hillion and P Koutrakos (eds), *Mixed Agreements Revisited: The EU and its Member States in the World* (Hart Publishing, 2010) 367, 369–70.

[7] ibid.

[8] *cf* Deutscher Bundestag, Stenografischer Bericht 909. Sitzung [2013]. See further T Cottier, 'Gemischte Abkommen der Europäischen Union: Grundlagen und Alternativen' in M Bungenberg and C Herrmann (eds), *Die gemeinsame Handelspolitik der Europäischen Union: Fünf Jahre nach Lissabon – Quo Vadis?* (Nomos, 2016) 11, 17.

[9] See further Chapter 5, section V.E.

[10] Decision of the Heads of State or Government of the 28 Member States of the European Union, Meeting within the European Council, on the Association Agreement between the European Union and the European Atomic Energy Community and Their Member States, of the one part, and Ukraine, of the other part, Annex to the Conclusions of the European Council Meeting of 15 December 2016 [2016] EUCO 34/16.

[11] See further Chapter 5, section V.A.

EU's treaty-making capacity therefore hinged upon the Walloon veto. On 27 October 2016, the governments of the Belgian federal and federated entities reached an agreement on the conditions under which they may exercise their full authority to sign CETA, which paved the way for the agreement's subsequent signature by Canada and the EU.[12] However, the 'CETA saga' has not ended with the agreement's signature. In 2020, the Cypriot Parliament voted against the conclusion of CETA by Cyprus because it was unhappy with the protection and denomination of certain agricultural products, particularly Halloumi cheese.[13] In 2022, the conclusion of CETA by Ireland has been declared unconstitutional by the Irish Supreme Court without changes to Irish statutory law. And in 2024, the French Senate rejected the conclusion of CETA by France for reasons relating to trade in agricultural goods.[14]

The non-ratification scenario illustrates the volatility and uncertainty inherent in the system of mixity. As was explained in Chapter 1, most of the previously known problems of mixity can be shifted to the implementation stage where they can be resolved more easily by the main legal conflict resolution mechanisms in EU law, ie, primacy, pre-emption and sincere cooperation.[15] However, the non-ratification scenario occurs *before* a mixed agreement enters into force and becomes an integral part of the EU legal order pursuant to Article 216(2) TFEU. As a result, it is more intricate to use EU legal principles as a solution to the non-ratification crisis. This is all the more so for bilateral mixed agreements, as they require the consent of all contracting parties to enter into force.

Despite these added layers of complexity, this chapter seeks to point out different legal and practical solutions to the non-ratification of bilateral mixed trade and investment agreements by individual Member States. As a background for discussion, section II further explains why the underlying legal problems are exacerbated by the bilateral character of EU trade and investment agreements. Sections III–VIII offer concrete solutions to addressing the rejection of a bilateral mixed trade and investment agreement by a Member State under EU and national constitutional law.

II. Non-ratification and Bilateral Mixity

Although the EU and the Member States form a composite contracting party in bilateral mixed agreements ('the EU *and* its Member States, of the *one part*'), the Member States are contracting parties to such agreements under international law. As a consequence, the Member States must ratify such agreements under the rules of the VCLT in order to be bound by them in their own right. By inference, they have the right to reject to be bound by such agreements in their own right.

[12] Déclaration du Royaume de Belgique relative aux conditions de pleins pouvoirs par l'Etat fédéral et les Entités fédérées pour la signature du CETA (2016).

[13] See M Chamon and T Verellen, 'Whittling Down the Collective Interest: CETA, Facultative Mixity, Democracy and Halloumi', *Verfassungsblog*, 7 August 2020, verfassungsblog.de/whittling-down-the-collective-interest.

[14] On the Irish and French CETA crises see further Chapter 5, sections V.C and VII.B.

[15] See Chapter 1, section III. See also J Heliskoski, *Mixed Agreements as a Technique for Organizing the International Relations of the European Community and its Member States* (Kluwer Law International, 2001).

As they contain contractual obligations between two parties only, bilateral agreements can only enter into force after all negotiating states have expressed their consent to be bound. This is also the case for bilateral mixed EU agreements. The entry into force clause of bilateral mixed EU agreements typically stipulates that such agreements may only enter into force after 'the Parties … have completed their respective internal requirements and procedures'.[16] The univocal reference to the exchange of ratification instruments by all contracting parties implies that bilateral mixed agreements must be ratified by the EU, the Member States and the third state in order to enter into force. By inference, the refusal of a single party to ratify a bilateral mixed agreement prevents entry into force.

If a Member State rejects the ratification of a bilateral mixed agreement, it thus ends the ratification process for the 'EU party' as a whole, ie, for the EU and the remaining Member States.[17] In doing so, the rejecting Member State evidently breaches EU law. Pursuant to Article 2(1) TFEU, the Member States must refrain from acting in areas where the EU is exclusively competent – externally as well as internally.[18] The Member States can therefore only ratify – and, by inference, reject – the parts of a mixed agreement for which they hold and exercise competence. By inference, the EU can only ratify the parts of a mixed agreement for which it holds and exercises competence. In *Opinion 1/19*, the CJEU stressed that:

> [W]hen negotiating and concluding a mixed agreement, the European Union and the Member States must act within the framework of their competences, while respecting the competences of any other contracting party. It follows that the conclusion of a mixed agreement by the European Union and the Member States in no way implies that the Member States exercise, in that event, competences of the European Union or that the European Union exercises competences of those States; rather, each of those parties acts exclusively within its sphere of competence.[19]

The CJEU thus emphasised that the ratification of a mixed agreement by the EU and the Member States should be viewed as strictly separate and mutually independent processes. In *Opinion 1/19*, the CJEU confirmed that the rejection of a mixed agreement by one Member State does not preclude the conclusion of the same agreement by the EU.[20] Yet, *Opinion 1/19* concerned the ratification of a multilateral mixed agreement. As will be further explained below, multilateral mixed agreements usually enter into force after a majority (but not all) of the signatory states have completed their ratification processes.[21] Therefore, the rejection of a multilateral mixed agreement by a Member State usually does not preclude the EU and the remaining Member States from ratifying the agreement. Conversely, as was explained above, the refusal of a Member State to ratify a bilateral mixed agreement prevents its entry into force. The CJEU's demand that

[16] Article 30.7(1),(2) CETA. See similarly Article 4.15(1) EUSIPA or Article 4.13(1) EUVIPA.

[17] On the definition of 'EU party', see Chapter 5, section V; and section III below in this chapter.

[18] Article 2(1) TFEU in conjunction with Article 4(2) TEU. See also Case 45/07, *IMO*, EU:C:2009:81.

[19] Opinion 1/19, *Istanbul Convention*, EU:C:2021:832, paras 258–59. For an analysis, see G Kübek, 'Facing and Embracing the Consequences of Mixity: Opinion 1/19, Istanbul Convention' (2022) 59 *Common Market Law Review* 1465.

[20] Opinion 1/19 (n 19) para 257.

[21] See further section VII below.

the EU and the Member States must not encroach on each other's competences during the ratification and rejection of a mixed agreement is thus more difficult to realise in the bilateral than in the multilateral context.

This chapter argues that it is nonetheless possible to separate the EU's and the Member States' respective powers to ratify and reject bilateral mixed trade and investment agreements. The outcome of *Opinion 2/15* facilitates separating the parts of the agreements that fall within EU exclusive competence from the parts of the agreements that fall within a competence held and exercised by the Member States.[22] There are several ways in which this competence divide between the EU and the Member States can be reflected in the procedure for ratifying – and, by inference, rejecting – bilateral mixed trade and investment agreements. First, a bilateral mixed agreement can continue to be applied provisionally after a Member State rejects its conclusion (section III). This is more of a temporary solution that does not address the underlying legal problems that emerge after the rejection of a bilateral mixed agreement by a Member States. A starting point for finding a solution to this underlying problem is a clear(er) indication of the EU's and the Member States' respective competence to ratify and reject a mixed agreement in their respective ratification acts (section IV). The explicit rejection of only part of a mixed agreement by a Member State would arguably facilitate the EU, the remaining Member States and the rejecting Member State to cooperate loyally with a view to finding a way for the part of the agreement that falls within EU exclusive competence to enter into force if the EU and the remaining Member States so desire (section V). One way to practically ensure that a rejecting Member State can disapply the parts of the agreement that fall within a competence held and exercised by the Member States is reservations (section VI). Another way is incomplete mixity (section VII). Arguably, it may be time for the EU to embrace incomplete mixity as a 'built-in' mechanism to overcome the non-ratification scenario from the outset. Doing so would require re-designing the entry into force clause of bilateral mixed agreements (section VIII).

III. Provisional Application

Once a mixed agreement has been signed and provisionally applied, a Member State's refusal to ratify that agreement does not initially affect its provisional application. As was explained in Chapter 4, mixed trade and investment agreements are usually applied provisionally and the scope of provisional application is principally confined to areas falling within the exclusive competence of the EU.[23] It is therefore for the EU, and not for the individual Member States, to terminate the provisional application of a bilateral mixed agreement.

[22] The solutions proposed here may not be fully transferrable to other fields, where the division of competence between the EU and the Member States is less clear. Yet, there are generally good reasons to 'unmix' mixed agreements from the outset. See Y Kaspiarovich and RA Wessel, 'Unmixing Mixed Agreements: Challenges and Solutions for Separating the EU and its Member States in Existing International Agreements' in N Levrat et al (eds), *The EU and its Member States' Joint Participation in International Agreements* (Hart Publishing, 2022) 75.

[23] See Chapter 4, section IV.C. See also Chapter 5, section VI.

Article 25(2) VCLT stipulates that 'the provisional application of a treaty or a part of a treaty with respect to a State shall be terminated if that State notifies the other States between which the treaty is being applied provisionally of its intention not to become a party to the treaty'. International law therefore prescribes that provisional application can be terminated unilaterally by a party to the envisaged agreement if that party no longer wishes to ratify the agreement.[24] At first sight, it thus appears that the Member States – in their role as parties to mixed EU agreements – could simply terminate provisional application. However, as was explained in Chapters 4 and 5, the decision to provisionally apply a bilateral mixed agreement is usually taken by the Council alone because the scope of provisional application (largely) comprises exclusive EU competence. Decisions by the Council can only be terminated on the basis of an *actus contrarius* – ie, by the Council and, for EU trade and investment agreements, generally by QMV – and not by the Member States in accordance with their national constitutional rules.[25]

An opposite reading would imply that a Member State could, as it were, terminate the provisional application of a mixed agreement on behalf of the EU and the remaining Member States. Such a reading not only conflicts with EU law generally and Article 218 TFEU specifically, but also with the text of bilateral mixed agreements. For example, Article 30.7(3)(c) CETA stipulates that '*[a] Party* may terminate the provisional application of this Agreement by written notice to *the other Party*' (emphasis added). The use of the singular term 'party' underlines that the legal authority to denounce provisionally enforced treaties is ultimately vested in the EU or the third state and not the Member States individually. Indeed, mixed EU agreements typically define the 'EU party' as consisting of 'the European Union or its Member States or the European Union and its Member States within their respective areas of competence'.[26] Accordingly, in areas of exclusive EU competence, the exercise of competence by the EU excludes the Member States' status as a 'parties' to the agreement (the EU *or* the Member States). The Association Agreement with Ukraine specifies even more clearly that the Member States have nothing to do with provisional application, irrespective of their status as contracting parties. According to Article 486(3), '*the Union* and Ukraine agree to provisionally apply this Agreement in part, *as specified by the Union*' (emphasis added).[27] By inference, only the EU can terminate provisional application; the Member States have no individual role to play in that process.

As the Member States cannot terminate the provisional application of a bilateral mixed EU trade and investment agreement in their own right, the provisional application of that agreement can continue even after the agreement has been rejected by a Member State. There are no time limits to provisional application. The 1947 GATT had,

[24] The possibility of unilateral termination foreseen in Article 25(2) VCLT is of particular importance for states whose internal constitutional rules do not require parliamentary consent to decide on a treaty's provisional application. See, eg, H Krieger, 'Article 25' in K Schmalenbach and O Dörr (eds), *Vienna Convention on the Law of Treaties: A Commentary*, 2nd edn (Springer, 2018) 441, 452.

[25] See similarly G Van der Loo and RA Wessel, 'The Non-ratification of Mixed Agreements: Legal Consequences and Solutions' (2017) 54 *Common Market Law Review* 735.

[26] See, eg, Article 1.1 CETA.

[27] See, conversely, Article 486(1) of the EU-Ukraine Association Agreement regarding the agreement's ratification, which specifically relates to 'the Parties' instead of 'the Union and Ukraine'.

for example, been applied provisionally for almost 50 years. Pursuant to Article 25(2) VCLT, the Council must terminate provisional application only if has become clear that the EU *as a whole* no longer wishes to ratify the agreement in question. In response to the demands of the German Constitutional Court,[28] the Council has made the political promise to terminate provisional application, in accordance with the EU procedures, in case the ratification of a bilateral mixed agreement in a Member State has 'failed permanently and definitively'.[29] Given that the political views in the Member States frequently change (especially after elections), it is at the discretion of the EU institutions to assess at what point in time the ratification of a treaty in a Member State has 'failed permanently and definitely'.

IV. Separating National Ratification Procedures

By allowing the EU to continue to exercise its exclusive competence, provisional application offers a temporal way out of the non-ratification scenario. Yet, it does not offer a lasting solution ensuring that the Member States can use their right to reject the ratification of a bilateral mixed agreement in accordance with the terms of that agreement without automatically encroaching on the EU's exclusive external competence. A first step to aligning the Member States' right to reject the parts of a bilateral mixed agreement that fall within their competences without breaching Article 2(1) TFEU is arguably a clear separation of the EU's and the Member States' competences during the process of ratification. Advocate General Sharpston first attempted to draw such a dividing line by noting that:

> It is true that, in principle, each party (including the Member States) must – as matters stand – choose between either consenting to or rejecting the entire agreement. However, that choice must be made in accordance with the Treaty rules on the allocation of competences. Were a Member State to refuse to conclude an international agreement for reasons relating to aspects of that agreement for which the European Union enjoys exclusive external competence that Member State would be acting in breach of those Treaty rules.[30]

Indeed, should Cyprus or France, for example, ultimately reject CETA for reasons relating to trade in agricultural products and/or geographical indications, two aspects for which the EU enjoys exclusive competence, it would be possible to bring infringement proceedings against these Member States before the CJEU. In other situations, it may be more difficult to extract the true motives underlying a national rejection of a mixed agreement. The Member States' ratification instruments are not confined to the parts of a mixed agreement that fall within national competence. Instead, Member

[28] *Bundesverfassungsgericht*, 2 BvR 1368/16, DE:BVerfG:2016:rs20161013.2bvr136816, paras 68, 72. See further Chapter 5, section VII.B.

[29] Council of the European Union, Comprehensive Economic and Trade Agreement (CETA) between Canada, of the one part, and the European Union and its Member States, of the other part – Statements to the Council minutes [2016] 13239/16 WTO 288 SERVICES 25 FDI 21 CDN 21, 'Regarding the Termination of Provisional Application of CETA: Statement by Germany and Austria'.

[30] Opinion of Advocate General Sharpston, Opinion 2/15, *FTA with Singapore*, EU:C:2016:992, para 568.

State governments generally subject mixed agreements in their entirety to national or regional parliamentary consent.[31] The EU usually does not stipulate the precise limitations of its treaty-making powers either, although the legal basis of the Council conclusion decision offers some guidance in that regard.

Practice indicates that is it indeed possible to confine the scope of EU and national ratification acts to the areas in which the EU and the Member States, respectively, remain competent. The ratifications of the WTO Agreements by the (then) Community and Germany are a case in point. The WTO agreements were ratified by the Community only as regards 'matters within its competence', which the CJEU had previously pinpointed in *Opinion 1/94*. By inference, Germany separated its ratification instruments on the basis of the outcome of *Opinion 1/94*. The legislative acts relating to the conclusion of the GATS and the TRIPS Agreement were adopted pursuant to the procedure foreseen in Article 59 of the German Constitution and were thus approved by the German Federal Parliament and the German Federal Council.[32] Conversely, the German Parliaments were merely informed about the German government's decision to ratify the 1994 GATT, as that agreement fell within the EU's exclusive competence.[33] The Dutch ratification act of the EU-Ukraine Association Agreement followed a similar approach. The scope of the Dutch ratification act of the EU-Ukraine Association Agreement related to the agreement only as far as 'the Kingdom [of the Netherlands] can be bound thereto'.[34] In the referendum on the EU-Ukraine Association Agreement, the Dutch citizens were, in turn, asked to approve or reject the Dutch ratification act of the EU-Ukraine Association Agreement. As a consequence, the Dutch voters never rejected the EU-Ukraine Association Agreement in its entirety. Hence, the Dutch government would not have acted against the outcome of the referendum if it had ratified the EU-exclusive parts of the Association Agreement with Ukraine.[35]

As the vertical division of trade and investment competence has been clarified by the CJEU, it would be possible to expressly confine the EU's and the Member States'

[31] See, eg, Gesetz zu dem Assoziierungsabkommen vom 21. März 2014 und vom 27. Juni 2014 zwischen der Europäischen Union und der Europäischen Atomgemeinschaft und ihren Mitgliedstaaten einerseits und der Ukraine andererseits [2015] BGBl II, 530; or Loi n° 2015-823 du 7 juillet 2015 autorisant la ratification de l'accord d'association entre l'Union européenne et la Communauté européenne de l'énergie atomique et leurs Etats membres, d'une part, et l'Ukraine, d'autre part.

[32] *cf* Gesetz zu dem Übereinkommen vom 15. April 1994 zur Errichtung der Welthandelsorganisation und zur Änderung anderer Gesetze [1994] BGBl II, 1438.

[33] *cf* Deutscher Bundestag, 'Information über die multilateralen Übereinkommen der GATT-Uruguay-Runde, die nicht unter die nationale Gesetzgebungszuständigkeit fallen' [1994] Drucksache 12/7986. The Committee on Economic Affairs of the German Federal Parliament issued an opinion on both the law on the establishment of the WTO (n 32) and the information received about the conclusion of the 1994 GATT (see above), in line with Article 23(3) of the German Constitution (*cf* Beschlußempfehlung und Bericht des Ausschusses für Wirtschaft (9. Ausschuß) [1994] Drucksache 12/8122). On the general legal framework for involving the German Parliaments in the making of EU-only agreements (or the EU-only part of mixed agreements), see Chapter 5, sections II.D. and IV.D.

[34] Wet van 8 juli 2015, houdende goedkeuring van de op 27 juni 2014 te Brussel tot stand gekomen Associatieovereenkomst tussen de Europese Unie en de Europese Gemeenschap voor Atoomenergie en haar lidstaten, enerzijds, en Oekraïne, anderzijds, Stb 2015, 315. Translation by the author.

[35] See also P Van Elsuwege, 'What Will Happen if the Dutch Vote "No" in the Referendum on the EU-Ukraine Association Agreement?', *Verfassungsblog*, 10 February 2016, www.verfassungsblog.de/what-will-happen-if-the-dutch-vote-no-in-the-referendum-on-the-eu-ukraine-association-agreement.

ratification acts of mixed trade and investment agreements to the areas in which they hold and exercise competence. The most feasible solution in practice would be to confine the Member States' ratification acts to investment protection disciplines and the ICS, and to expressly exclude these areas from the Council decisions on the signature and conclusion of mixed EU trade and investment agreements. In doing so, the EU and the Member States would ensure that they do not encroach upon each other's (exclusive) competence. Likewise, as the previous chapter argued, the EU and the Member States would make sure that the EP and national parliaments do not encroach upon each other's competence to exercise democratic oversight over the ratification of mixed EU trade and investment agreements.[36]

V. Loyal Cooperation

Against the background of EU's and the Member States' obligation to act within the limits of their respective competence during the ratification of a mixed agreement (see the excerpt of *Opinion 1/19* above), a follow-up question arises, particularly in the context of bilateral mixity: is a Member State, when making use of its right to reject a mixed agreement for the parts falling within national competence, legally required to take measures to enable the EU to approve that agreement for the parts falling within EU exclusive competence?

As was explained in Chapter 2, Article 4(3) TEU requires the EU and the Member States to cooperate loyally – both internally and externally.[37] The second sentence of Article 4(3) TEU stipulates that: 'The Member States *shall take any appropriate measure*, general or particular, to ensure fulfilment of the obligations arising out of the Treaties or resulting from the acts of the institutions of the Union' (emphasis added). The duty of loyal cooperation thus requires the Member States to take action in their own right to ensure the 'fulfilment of the obligations arising out of the Treaties'. The principle of exclusivity enshrined in Article 2(1) TFEU doubtlessly qualifies as 'an obligation arising out of the Treaties'. Moreover, the Council decisions on the signature and conclusion of mixed agreements form 'acts of the institutions of the Union'. The conditions for triggering Article 4(3) TEU in the non-ratification scenario are thus fulfilled.[38]

The CJEU acknowledged the principle of loyal cooperation with regard to the ratification of mixed agreements in *Opinion 2/91*. Here, it held that the EU institutions and the Member States must 'take all the measures necessary' so as to best ensure loyal cooperation when ratifying mixed agreements.[39] The extent of that duty is not fully clear. It is largely uncontested that the principle of loyal cooperation can be invoked to 'set a deadline for the Member States within which they have to have completed (positively

[36] See Chapter 5, section V.

[37] See further Chapter 2, section V.A.

[38] See also D Kleimann and G Kübek, 'The Signing, Provisional Application, and Conclusion of Trade and Investment Agreements in the EU: The Case of CETA and Opinion 2/15' (2018) 45 *Legal Issues of Economic Integration* 13, 35.

[39] Opinion 2/91, *ILO Convention No 170*, EU:C:1993:106, para 38.

or negatively) their procedures for ratification'.[40] This technique was, for example, used in the ratification of the Vienna Convention for the Protection of the Ozone Layer[41] by the EU. Pursuant to Article 3(1) of the Council decision authorising that agreement's conclusion:

> Member States, which have not already done so, shall take, *at the latest by 31 October 1988*, the necessary steps to permit the deposit, as far as possible simultaneously, of the instruments of ratification, acceptance, approval or accession to the Vienna Convention by the Community and the Member States.
>
> Member States will inform the Commission, as soon as possible, of their decision to accede to or to ratify the Convention, as appropriate, or of the prospective date of finalization of those procedures. The Commission, in cooperation with Member States, shall arrange a date for the simultaneous deposit of the instruments, which shall *in any case be before 1 January 1989*. (Emphasis added)[42]

So far, the EU has not indicated a deadline for the Member States to complete the necessary steps to ratify a bilateral mixed trade and investment agreement, although such a ratification deadline would increase certainty about the state and duration of the ratification process.

Aside from ratification timelines, it is contested whether the duty of loyal cooperation can be invoked against the Member States during the ratification of mixed agreements, let alone to levy concrete obligations of result.[43] The right to approve or reject an international treaty is generally considered to be the constitutional prerogative of each contracting party under international law. According to Van der Loo and Wessel, the duty of cooperation can therefore not be stretched in such a way as to oblige a Member State to ratify a mixed agreement. If that were the case, 'one would fail to see the meaning of national ratification in the first place'.[44] They further argue that an obligation incumbent on the Member States to ratify a mixed agreement would constitute a potential violation of the fundamental notion under international law that 'consent to be bound' can only be expressed voluntarily.[45]

The CJEU has repeatedly held that the EU must observe international law when exercising its external competence,[46] which unquestionably entails respect for the Member States' right to approve and reject mixed agreements in their own right. However, the question remains whether the Member States' right to approve and reject a mixed agreement extends to the entire agreement or only to the parts that fall within their

[40] See P-J Kuijper, 'Of "Mixity" and "Double-Hatting": EU External Relations Law Explained' (2008) Oratiereeks, *Vossiuspers University of Amsterdam* 5, 20. See also M Klamert, *The Principle of Loyalty in EU Law* (Oxford University Press, 2014) 202; and, more critically, J Czuczai, 'Mixity in Practice: Some Problems and Their (Real or Possible) Solution' in Hillion and Koutrakos (n 6) 229, 244.

[41] Vienna Convention for the Protection of the Ozone Layer [1985] UNTS Vol 1513, 293.

[42] Council Decision (EEC) 88/540 of 14 October 1988 concerning the conclusion of the Vienna Convention for the protection of the ozone layer and the Montreal Protocol on substances that deplete the ozone layer [1988] OJ L297/8.

[43] See J Wouters et al, *The Law of EU External Relations: Cases, Materials, and Commentary on the EU as an International Legal Actor* (Oxford University Press, 2021) 121.

[44] Van der Loo and Wessel (n 25) 744.

[45] ibid.

[46] See, eg, Joined Cases C-402/05 P und C-415/05 P, *Kadi*, EU:C:2008:461, para 291; Joined Cases C-626/15 and C-659/16, *Antarctic MPAs*, EU:C:2018:925, para 127.

competence. Indeed, an obligation incumbent on a Member State to apply the parts of a mixed agreement that fall within EU exclusive competence cannot be viewed as an expression of non-voluntary consent. Otherwise, the conclusion of an 'EU-only' agreement by QMV would similarly constitute a violation of international law.

The CJEU, albeit in a multilateral context, found that the EU neither infringes international nor EU law when acceding to a mixed agreement against the will of some of its Member States with regard to its exclusive competence.[47] In a bilateral context, it is not possible for the EU to simply accede to an agreement without some of its Member States. As bilateral mixed agreements require the deposition of ratification instruments by all parties, the EU cannot exercise its exclusive competence without its Member States. Against that background, the question arises if the principle of loyal cooperation could be invoked to require a rejecting Member State to conclude *only those parts of a bilateral mixed agreement that fall within EU exclusive competence.* National governments, parliaments and citizens would retain their right to approve and reject the parts of a bilateral mixed agreement they remain competent to review. In practice, this may require reservations that carve out the application of certain treaty provisions to the rejecting Member State's territory and thus the consent of all contracting parties (Article 20(2) VCLT – this is further explained in the next section).

Arguably, the CJEU's case law does not contradict a broad reading of the duty of loyal cooperation as an active duty of the Member States to enable the EU to exercise its exclusive competence during the ratification of a bilateral mixed agreement. In the recent *COTIF II* case, the CJEU found that Germany breached Article 4(3) TEU because its conduct harmed the 'effectiveness of the international action of the European Union, as well as the latter's credibility and reputation on the international stage'.[48] The non-ratification of a bilateral mixed agreement by a Member State causes considerable harm to the EU's international credibility and reputation. Against that background, it could be argued that a rejecting Member State is required to 'take any appropriate measure, general or particular'[49] to enable the EU and the remaining Member States to approve a bilateral mixed agreement with regard to their respective competence.

Such a broad reading of the duty of loyal cooperation would ensure that Article 2(1) TFEU does not lose its effectiveness during the ratification process of bilateral mixed agreements. EU exclusive competences remain outside the reach of national legal acts, including treaty ratification instruments. It is for the EP – and not for national parliaments – to ensure democratic oversight of the parts of mixed agreements that fall within EU exclusive competence. Moreover, the national government of a rejecting Member State does not breach national constitutional law when ratifying, in the spirit of loyal cooperation, only the parts of a bilateral mixed agreement that fall within EU exclusive competence after the EP authorised the conclusion of that agreement. The previous section illustrated, using the example of the Dutch ratification act of the EU-Ukraine Association Agreement, that it is possible to carefully draft national ratification instruments so as to enable national governments to respect the principle of exclusivity, on

[47] Opinion 1/19 (n 19) paras 264–65, 271–73.
[48] Case C-620/16, *COTIF II*, EU:C:2019:256, para 98.
[49] Article 4(3) TEU.

the one hand, and national parliaments' and citizens' constitutional right to approve or reject the parts of the agreement they are legally competent to review, on the other hand. (Sub-)national actors may thus continue to refuse the application of a mixed agreement, provided they remain the competent decision-makers.

VI. Reservations

In a scenario where a Member State rejects the part of a bilateral mixed agreement relating to national competence, but the EU, the remaining Member States and the third state nevertheless wish to conclude that agreement, a practical solution must be found for making sure that the parts of the agreement falling within national competence are not applied to and in the rejecting Member State.

The VCLT provides for such a solution. Pursuant to Article 19 VCLT, a party to an agreement may generally formulate reservations when signing, ratifying, accepting, approving or acceding to a treaty.[50] For bilateral agreements, the other contracting party must accept the reservation.[51]

It may not always be practical for individual Member States to 'opt out' of the parts of a bilateral mixed agreement that fall within national competence.[52] For EU trade and investment agreements, it would, for example, be difficult to opt out of only the provisions relating to foreign non-direct investment protection, as international investment agreements do not distinguish between direct and non-direct investments.[53] Yet, a practical solution could be found where a rejecting Member State issues a reservation for the entire chapter on investment protection, including the ICS. The chapter on investment protection could nonetheless be applied between the EU and the remaining Member States on the one hand, and the third state, on the other hand, on the territories of the remaining Member States and the third state.

VII. Incomplete Mixity

In the wake of the EU-Ukraine Association Agreement and CETA crises, incomplete mixity has been suggested as another solution to address the non-ratification of bilateral mixed agreements by Member States.[54] Incomplete mixity has the advantage that

[50] The provision stipulates three exceptions, namely where: (a) the reservation is prohibited by the treaty; (b) the treaty provides that only specified reservations, which do not include the reservation in question, may be made; or (c) the reservation is incompatible with the object and purpose of the treaty. Mixed EU trade and investment agreements do not preclude reservations. The non-application of the provisions on investment protection and ICS by one Member State also does not go against the object and purpose of the treaty as such. Therefore, these exceptions do not appear to be relevant in the context of this chapter. On (exceptions) to reservations, see, eg, C Walter, 'Artikel 19' in Dörr and Schmalenbach (n 24) 261.

[51] Article 20(2) and (5) VCLT.

[52] On opt-outs, see also Van der Loo and Wessel (n 25) 763.

[53] See H Lenk, 'More Trade and Less Investment for Future EU Trade and Investment Policy: CJEU, Opinion 2/15, *Free Trade Agreement between the European Union and Singapore*, 16 May 2017, EU:C:2017:376' (2018) 19 *Journal of World Investment and Trade* 305, 318.

[54] Van Elsuwege (n 35); Kleimann and Kübek (n 38) 26; and Van der Loo and Wessel (n 25) 746–49.

the rejecting Member State does not have to agree in its own right to the ratification of the parts of a bilateral mixed agreement that fall within EU exclusive competences. The rejecting Member State would simply be deleted as a contracting party altogether. The agreement could nonetheless be ratified as a bilateral mixed agreement between the EU and some of its Member States, on the one part, and the third state, on the other part. Irrespective of being deleted as an independent contracting party, the rejecting Member State is bound by the EU's decision to conclude the agreement (Article 216(2) TFEU). The resulting incomplete mixed agreement applies to the rejecting Member State to the extent that it falls within EU exclusive competence. All areas that fall within national competence would, in turn, not apply to the rejecting Member State.

In *Opinion 1/19*, the CJEU expressly acknowledged incomplete mixity as a solution to the non-ratification scenario.[55] The Council subsequently adopted decisions on the signature and conclusion of the Istanbul Convention,[56] even though several Member States have stated their intention not to ratify the Convention in their own right.[57] The ratification of the Istanbul Convention as an incomplete mixed agreement bears the risk that the EU will be held liable internationally for the rejecting Member States' non-compliance with the Convention. The Council decisions on the conclusion of the Istanbul Convention are explicitly confined to the reach of the EU's exclusive competence while emphasising that the 'Union's accession to the Convention shall be without prejudice to the Member States' competence as regards the ratification of the Convention on matters falling within their national competences'.[58] It is not yet clear if third parties will accept the 'partial' accession of the EU to the Convention, as the latter does principally not allow reservations.[59] However, for bilateral mixed trade and investment agreements, incomplete mixity would not raise the same legal concerns as it is, as mentioned above, practically feasible to carve out the application of the investment protection chapter and specifically the jurisdiction of the ICS to a rejecting Member State's territory. Moreover, reservations are not principally precluded.

[55] Opinion 1/19 (n 19) para 260. See also Kübek (n 19) 1482. See subsequently also Case C-621/21, *Women who are Victims of Domestic Violence*, EU:C:2024:47, para 46, which confirms that all EU Member States are bound by the EU's ratification of the Istanbul Convention, to the extent that the matter falls within EU competence.

[56] Council of Europe Convention on Preventing and Combating Violence Against Women and Domestic Violence [2014] CETS No 210. As the first gender-specific and legally binding instrument on the violation against women in Europe, the accession of the EU to the Istanbul Convention is of exceptional legal and political importance. See S Prechal, 'The European Union's Accession to the Istanbul Convention' in K Lenaerts et al (eds), *An Ever-Changing Union? Perspectives on the Future of EU Law in Honour of Allan Rosas* (Hart Publishing, 2019) 279.

[57] Council Decision 2023/1075 of 1 June 2023 on the conclusion, on behalf of the European Union, of the Council of Europe Convention on preventing and combating violence against women and domestic violence with regard to institutions and public administration of the Union [2023] OJ L143l/1; and Council Decision 2023/1076 of 1 June 2023 on the conclusion, on behalf of the European Union, of the Council of Europe Convention on preventing and combating violence against women and domestic violence with regard to matters related to judicial cooperation in criminal matters, asylum and non-refoulement [2023] OJ L143l/4.

[58] Article 1(2) of Council Decision 2023/1075 (n 57); and Article 1(2) of Council Decision 2023/1076 (n 57). The EU ratified the Convention only for 'matters related to judicial cooperation in criminal matters, asylum and non-refoulement' and 'with regard to institutions and public administration of the Union'. The Council decisions on the conclusion of the Istanbul Convention are thus another example of ratification acts that are confined to the scope of competence of the EU. See section IV above.

[59] Article 78(1) of the Istanbul Convention. As a result, it is not clear if the EU can adopt a declaration of competence. See the Opinion of Advocate General Hogan, Opinion 1/19, *Istanbul Convention*, EU:C:2021:198, paras 207 et seq.

In practice, a 'complete' bilateral mixed agreement could be turned into an 'incomplete' one with few adjustments to its text and substance. A simple solution to implement those changes would be the adoption of an Adjustment Protocol by the remaining contracting parties. This has been done before by the EEA Member States after Switzerland rejected the agreement in the 1990s.[60] The remaining EEA Member States signed the Adjustment Protocol to the EEA as a new agreement under international law – without Switzerland. The Protocol deleted Switzerland from the preamble to the EEA and modified material provisions where required.[61]

After a Member State rejects the ratification of a bilateral mixed agreement, the conclusion of an Adjustment Protocol between the EU, the remaining Member States and the third state could enable the agreement's entry into force as an incomplete mixed agreement. The rejecting Member State may certainly cast a negative vote in the Council. It may therefore veto the adoption of an Adjustment Protocol for agreements that must be concluded unanimously, such as Association Agreements (Article 218(8) TFEU). Yet, if the envisaged agreement is subject to QMV, a rejecting Member State may be overruled by the remaining Member States as represented in the Council and subsequently be bound by the EU's conclusion of the resulting incomplete mixed agreement.

VIII. Re-designing Entry into Force Clauses

In contrast to bilateral agreements, multilateral agreements commonly do not require the deposition of ratification instruments by all contracting parties before the agreement can enter into force. Instead, the entry into force of multilateral treaties is typically triggered by meeting a ratification threshold. For the EU, the use of ratification thresholds implies that incomplete mixity is factored into the design of the agreement. It is possible for the EU to submit its ratification documents without some of the signatory Member States and for that agreement to nevertheless enter into force once the ratification threshold is met.

In multilateral treaty-making practice, the EU has used the 'built-in' possibility to resort to incomplete mixity to deliberately trigger an agreement's entry into force. A case in point is the ratification of the Paris Agreement on Climate Change by the EU.[62] The Paris Agreement entered into force after 55 parties accounting for 55 per cent of the global greenhouse gas emissions deposited their ratification instruments.[63] In line with its standard practice,[64] the EU initially sought to await the completion of the Member States' national ratification processes before concluding the Paris Agreement in its own right. At the end of September 2016, approximately one month prior to the US election, only seven Member States had ratified the Paris Agreement individually and it

[60] Van Elsuwege (n 35).
[61] Protocol Adjusting the Agreement on the European Economic Area [1994] OJ L001/572.
[62] Paris Agreement [2016] UNTS Vol 3156.
[63] Article 21(1) of the Paris Agreement.
[64] See Chapter 4, section V.

became clear that it was unfeasible for the other Member States to complete their ratification processes until the beginning of November. At the time, 61 countries had ratified the agreement (including the US), but they accounted for only 48 percent of global emissions.[65] As the EU accounted for all emissions made in its territory, its ratification implied meeting the 55 per cent threshold and triggering entry into force. Indeed, the Member States in the Council decided to 'speed up' the ratification process at the EU level, even though some of them had not ratified the Paris Agreement in their own right.[66] On 4 October 2016, the EU concluded the Paris Agreement.[67] On 4 November 2016 – four days prior to the US presidential election – the agreement entered into force.[68] As a party may only withdraw from the agreement three years after its entry into force, the newly elected US President Trump could not initially terminate the Paris Agreement.[69] The remaining EU Member States subsequently ratified the agreement in their own right.

The case of the Istanbul Convention showed that the use of ratification thresholds can enable the EU to overcome the non-ratification scenario. The Istanbul Convention entered into force on 1 August 2014, after 10 signatories, including eight Member States of the Council of Europe, had expressed their consent to be bound.[70] Notably, five EU Member States had expressed their consent to be bound by 1 August 2014, thereby triggering the Convention's entry into force.[71] The decision of the Council, by a qualified majority, to ratify the Convention in 2023 implied that the EU could accede to an agreement that was already in force, despite the decision of some of the signatory EU Member States not to ratify the Convention in their own right.

It remains to be seen whether the EU will in the future also embrace incomplete mixity in the design of bilateral mixed agreements. For 'typical' (ie, non-mixed) bilateral agreements, ratification thresholds make no sense because these types of agreements contain substantive obligations between two parties only. The situation is arguably different and more complex for bilateral mixed EU agreements. Substantively, these agreements contain commitments between two parties only, namely the 'EU party' and the third state. They do not set out material obligations between the EU and the Member States inter se. Yet, bilateral mixed EU agreements need to be signed and ratified by 27 Member States, the EU and the third state before they can enter into

[65] European Commission, Directorate-General for Climate Action, 'Ministers Approve EU Ratification of Paris Agreement' (2016).

[66] Council of the European Union, press release, 'Climate Change: Council Speeds up Process for EU Ratification of Paris Agreement' [2016] 541/16.

[67] Council Decision (EU) 2016/1841 of 5 October 2016 on the conclusion, on behalf of the European Union, of the Paris Agreement adopted under the United Nations Framework Convention on Climate Change [2016] OJ L282/1.

[68] United Nations, Depository Notification Paris Agreement, Reference: C.N.735.2016.TREATIES-XXVII.7.d.

[69] Article 28 of the Paris Agreement.

[70] Article 75(3) of the Istanbul Convention (n 56).

[71] By ratifying to the Convention in full, these Member States breached the EU's exclusive competence over parts of the Convention as confirmed by the CJEU in Opinion 1/19 (n 19). The fact that the Commission never initiated infringement proceedings against these Member States suggests that the EU institutions implicitly supported the Member States' independent external action at a time where the EU was paralysed to act in its own right. Nonetheless, it would have been legally advisable for the Member States to clearly indicate the limits of their external competence in their ratification instruments (see section IV above).

force. From a procedural perspective, the classification of any type of mixed agreement as 'bilateral' is thus paradoxical. Ratification thresholds would acknowledge that the procedure for making bilateral mixed agreements involves more than two parties and would address the uncertainty for their entry into force brought about by a multitude of veto players.

In practice, the entry into force of bilateral mixed agreements could, for example, be made conditional on the deposition of the ratification instruments by two-thirds of their contracting parties, which must necessarily include the EU and the third party. Notably, ratification thresholds would not 'end mixity'. Bilateral mixed agreements, with or without a ratification threshold, cannot be concluded by the EU alone. The size of the threshold would determine how many Member States would have to ratify the agreement in addition to the EU to prompt entry into force. Therefore, the use of thresholds would not deprive the requirement for national ratification of its effect, as a group of Member States could still veto the conclusion of a mixed agreement for the EU in its entirety. However, by re-designing of the entry into force clause of bilateral mixed agreements, it would become impossible for a Member State to derail the entry into force of an agreement desired by the EU, the majority of Member States and a third state.

IX. Conclusion

For a long time, the non-ratification of mixed agreements by a Member State was not assumed to be a realistic scenario. This has changed rapidly in recent years, especially when it comes to bilateral mixed trade and investment agreements. The politicisation of EU external trade policy caused (sub-)national parliaments and citizens to revamp their role in the (mixed) treaty-making process. Parliaments will no longer 'rubber-stamp' EU trade and investment agreements, but will seek to be more actively involved in the early stages of the treaty-making process. In the case of mixity, (sub-)national parliaments can use the threat of casting a veto as leverage to ensure that national governments and the EU institutions carefully consider and address their concerns. Yet, there is also a threat that (sub-)national parliaments will not use their veto rights as a measure of last resort, but to extract individual concessions by paralysing EU international action. The recent rejection of CETA by the Cypriot Parliament because it was unhappy with the denomination of Halloumi cheese is a case in point.

For bilateral mixed agreements, the non-ratification scenario is particularly complex and challenging. Because these agreements enter into force only after all parties have deposited their respective ratification instruments, the non-ratification by a Member State derails the ratification process for the EU, the remaining Member States and the third state. This raises both legal and political concerns. Politically, the non-ratification of a bilateral mixed agreement by a Member State questions the assumption that mixity always increases democratic legitimacy as an agreement approved by the representatives of the vast majority of the EU's population would be rejected by the representatives of just a fraction thereof (eg, 0.3 per cent in the case of Wallonia).[72] Legally, a conflict

[72] See also Kleimann and Kübek (n 38).

arises between the Member States' right to terminate the ratification of an agreement which they conclude in their own right and the principle of exclusivity enshrined in Article 2(1) TFEU. It appears that by exercising their right reject a mixed agreement, the Member States cannot avoid encroaching upon the EU's exclusive competence.

The present chapter has outlined how the EU and the Member States can implement the CJEU's request to 'act within the framework of their competences, while respecting the competences of any other contracting party' when ratifying a bilateral mixed trade and investment agreement.[73] Because the division of competences is sufficiently clear and stable after *Opinion 2/15*, one can think of several ways to separate the EU's and the Member States' respective ratification competence. A first step is indicating the scope of the EU's and the Member States' treaty-making powers clearly in their respective ratification acts. Confining the scope of national ratification acts, specifically, to the areas of the agreements that fall within the Member States' competences makes it clear that national parliaments and citizens only have the power to approve or reject parts of the agreement. In the event that a national parliament rejects the ratification of a bilateral mixed agreement, the government of that Member State could, in the spirit of loyal cooperation, agree to implement the parts of the agreement that fall within EU exclusive competence while respecting its parliament's choice not to be bound individually by the parts of the agreement falling within Member State competence. In practice, the government of the rejecting Member State could, for example, issue a reservation that precludes the application of treaty provisions on investment protection and investor-state dispute settlement to and in that Member State.

Another option would be to turn the originally 'complete' bilateral mixed agreement into an 'incomplete' mixed agreement after it has been rejected by a Member State. This chapter has argued that it may be time to embrace incomplete mixity in the design of the entry into force clauses of bilateral mixed trade and investment agreements from the outset. It is true that incomplete mixity may cause problems on the international level, especially when it comes to the assumption of international responsibility. However, for trade and investment agreements, it is possible to mitigate these problems because the division of competence between the EU and the Member States is sufficiently clear and it is practically feasible to exclude Member States from the parts of the agreements that fall within their competence (investment protection and the ICS). In practice, incomplete mixity could be embraced as a solution to the non-ratification scenario in the design of bilateral mixed trade and investment agreements by stipulating that these agreements enter into force after the EU, the third state and a large majority (but not all) of the Member States deposit their respective ratification instruments. The introduction of ratification thresholds would acknowledge that there are actually more than two players involved in the ratification process of 'bilateral' mixed agreements.

In the future, the EU, its Member States and the third state should arguably consider the threat of non-ratification of mixed trade and investment agreements during the treaty negotiations. *Moving beyond mixity* does not necessarily entail a choice against mixity, but a deliberate choice of the treaty-making procedure and a careful

[73] Opinion 1/19 (n 19).

consideration of the consequences that stem from that choice. The mixed ratification process casts significant doubts on entry into force and thus comes with considerable procedural costs. These costs should be carefully balanced against the benefits of designing trade and investment agreements that exceed the realm of the EU's exclusive competence. In the event that mixity is the preferred option, the EU institutions and the Member States should arguably consider how the non-ratification scenario could best be forestalled, possibly through the design of the agreement. Otherwise, the EU and the Member States risk being trapped in internal decision-making preoccupations without being able to conduct – joint or individual – external relations.

7

The New Architecture

I. Introduction

The Lisbon Treaty reform significantly increased the exclusive reach of the CCP, questioning the need for mixity in the field of trade (see Chapter 3). At the same time, the problems associated with mixity intensified in recent years with the near-rejection of mixed agreements by national parliaments and citizens (see Chapter 6), and the resulting quest for more public and parliamentary participation in EU commercial decision-making – both at the EU level (see Chapter 4) and at the national level (see Chapter 5).

Opinion 2/15 was requested by the Commission with the clear intention to *move beyond mixity*.[1] While the outcome of the Opinion did not fully support EU-only treaty-making in the field of trade and investment, it provided impetus for practical change. On 8 May 2018, the Council largely approved a proposal of the Commission establishing a new architecture for making EU trade and investment agreements.[2] Most importantly, the new architecture supports splitting FTAs and IPAs into separate agreements. Through the split, the EU can conclude FTAs alone, while IPAs remain mixed agreements. In doing so, the EU counters the growing trend in international economic law towards comprehensive trade and investment protection agreements, adjusting the design of such agreements to the scope of its own conferred – and therefore limited – powers. In implementing the new architecture, the Council also reflected on finer points in law concerning future EU trade and investment practice. On 30 April 2019, the new architecture cleared the final hurdle with the CJEU confirming the compatibility of the ICS in *Opinion 1/17*, thereby facilitating the making of stand-alone EU IPAs.[3]

This chapter examines the legal and practical implications of the new architecture. It assesses the practice of splitting FTAs and IPAs into separate agreements, how that split affects the procedure for making EU trade and investment agreements, and whether the new architecture provides a way out of the non-ratification scenario described in the previous chapter. In essence, therefore, this chapter aims to find out how the new

[1] Opinion 2/15, *FTA with Singapore*, EU:C:2017:376.
[2] Council of the European Union, Draft Council conclusions on the negotiation and conclusion of EU trade agreements – Adoption [2018] 8622/18.
[3] Opinion 1/17, *Comprehensive Economic and Trade Agreement with Canada*, EU:C:2019:341. The ICS is the cornerstone of current stand-alone EU IPAs and the main trigger of mixity.

architecture works, what it changes, and to what extent these changes solve the emerging problems brought about by mixity in the field of trade and investment.

The chapter is structured as follows: section II explains the contours of the new architecture. Section III assesses the practice of splitting EU FTAs and IPAs. Section IV examines the effects of the new architecture on the procedure for making EU trade and investment agreements. Section V considers the extent to which the new architecture provides a solution to the non-ratification scenario. Section VI concludes.

II. The General Formula

The near-rejection of CETA by the Walloon Parliament in October 2016 increased the anticipation of *Opinion 2/15*, which was delivered approximately six months later, and added impetus for using the outcome of the CJEU's decision to initiate policy change. The added value of mixity in the field of trade and investment was re-considered in light of the instances where EU external action was paralysed by (sub-)national players. Several academics suggested a clearer distinction between EU-only and mixed agreements in the field of trade and investment.[4] In their view, instead of making trade and investment agreements 'artificially mixed', separate agreements ought to be concluded for material issues falling within EU exclusive and shared competence, respectively.

The practicality of this plan was dependent on the balance struck by the CJEU in *Opinion 2/15*. It would, for example, have been difficult to separate comprehensive trade and investment protection agreements if the CJEU had followed Advocate General Sharpston's Opinion and found that the TSD Chapters fall within shared competence.[5] The CJEU's decision in *Opinion 2/15* may therefore also be valued for its inherent pragmatism. The finding that all areas comprised by 'new generation' FTAs fall within EU exclusive competence apart from foreign non-direct investments and ISDS practically and politically allows these agreements to be split into separate EU-only trade and mixed investment protection agreements.

After the delivery of *Opinion 2/15*, the Commission quickly initiated policy change. At the end of August 2017, the Commission published a proposal for a 'new architecture for splitting EU FTAs and EU investment agreements'.[6] According to this new architecture, negotiations of EU-only trade agreements covering all areas confirmed in *Opinion 2/15* as falling within the EU's exclusive competence are to occur separately from those of mixed investment protection agreements covering substantive standards and an ICS.[7] Practice also shows that trade agreements and investment

[4] See especially the 'Trading Together Declaration', which was further explained in Chapter 5, section I.

[5] Opinion of Advocate General Sharpston, Opinion 2/15, *FTA with Singapore*, EU:C:2016:992, paras 490 et seq.

[6] Available at: politico.eu/wp-content/uploads/2017/08/COM-proposal-splitting-trade-deals.pdf.

[7] See also J Brauneck, 'Abgetrennte Handelsabkommen ohne Beteiligung der Mitgliedstaaten?' (2018) 29 *Europäische Zeitschrift für Wirtschaftsrecht* 796; and P Conconi et al, 'EU Trade Agreements: To Mix or Not to Mix, That is the Question' (2021) 55 *Journal of World Trade Law* 231, 239.

protection agreements will be accompanied by a third type of agreement, a Partnership Agreement,[8] comprising broader socio-economic and environmental cooperation aims between the parties.[9]

On 8 May 2018, the Council adopted conclusions on the negotiation and conclusion of EU trade agreements.[10] Accordingly:

> The Council notes that in the future the Commission intends to recommend draft negotiating directives for FTAs covering exclusive EU competence on the one hand and separate mixed investment agreements on the other, with a view to strengthening the EU's position as a negotiating partner. It is for the Council to decide whether to open negotiations on this basis. It is equally for the Council to decide, on a case-by-case basis, on the splitting of trade agreements. Depending on their content, association agreements should be mixed. The ones that are currently being negotiated, such as with Mexico, Mercosur and Chile, will remain mixed agreements.[11]

The Council therefore principally approved the Commission's plan to make separate EU-only FTAs and mixed IPAs. By emphasising that the new architecture is introduced on a case-by-case basis, the Council ensured that it retains some discretion to maintain the 'old' comprehensive trade and investment protection agenda for certain trading partners, such as Canada and, potentially, the US. Likewise, by adding the qualification 'depending on their content', the Council ensured that it retains some discretion to act contrary to its principled position that Association Agreements 'should' be mixed agreements, as the case of the EU-UK TCA illustrates.[12] The political rationale for designing some EU new generation trade and investment agreements with non-neighbouring countries as part of a wider Association Agreement (eg, those with Mexico, Mercosur, and Chile), while designing others as separate FTAs and/or IPAs accompanied by Partnership Agreements (eg, those with Canada, Singapore, Japan) is not fully clear. It appears to be partly a matter of path-dependency, as the EU has had mixed Cooperation, Partnership or Association Agreements in place with Mercosur, Mexico and Chile since the late 1990s and early 2000s.[13]

[8] The term 'Partnership Agreement' is here used as an umbrella term to cover both Strategic Partnership Agreements and Partnership and Cooperation Agreements.

[9] On the composition of new architecture, see also G Kübek and I Van Damme, 'Facultative Mixity and the European Union's Trade and Investment Agreements' in M Chamon and I Govaere (eds), *EU External Relations Law Post-Lisbon: The Law and Practice of Facultative Mixity* (Brill/Nijhoff, 2020) 137, 158.

[10] Council of the European Union (n 2).

[11] ibid para 3.

[12] See further Chapter 8, section II.C.

[13] Interregional Framework Cooperation Agreement between the European Community and its Member States and the Southern Common Market and its Member Countries [1996] OJ C14/4; Economic Partnership, Political Coordination and Cooperation Agreement between the European Community and its Member States, of the one part, and the United Mexican States, of the other part [2000] OJ L276/45. Agreement establishing an association between the European Community and its Member States, of the one part, and the Republic of Chile, of the other part [2002] OJ L352/3.

Figure 7.1 The new architecture

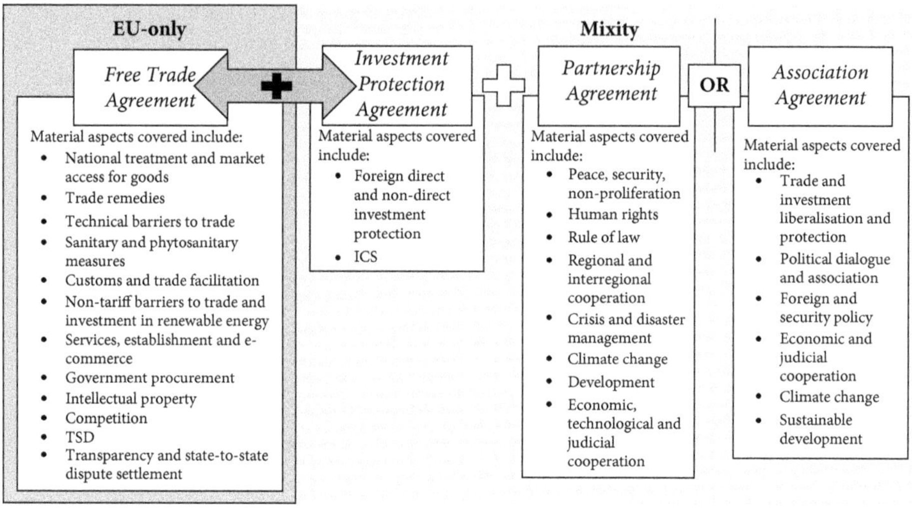

Figure 7.1 illustrates the general formula of the new architecture, as outlined by the Council in its conclusions of 8 May 2018.

Since the adoption of the new architecture, the EU has negotiated and/or concluded EU-only FTAs with multiple trading partners, including Japan,[14] Singapore,[15] Vietnam,[16] New Zealand and Australia. Yet, as has been projected,[17] the EU's external investment agenda began to dwindle after *Opinion 2/15*. So far, the EU has only signed stand-alone IPAs with Singapore[18] and Vietnam,[19] even though, as Figure 7.1 shows, it principally aims to negotiate FTAs and IPAs in parallel under the new architecture. The reasons for the reduced focus on making IPAs, as compared to FTAs, are complex and context-specific. The ratification process of the finalised EU-China IPA will not commence for political reasons in the foreseeable future. The investment treaty negotiations between the EU and Japan failed because Japan opposed turning ISDS into an ICS. Australia and New Zealand generally oppose investor-state dispute settlement and were therefore not interested in negotiating an IPA with the EU. It remains to be seen whether the growing political and public opposition against investor-state dispute settlement, which also informed the EU's

[14] Agreement between the European Union and Japan for an Economic Partnership [2018] OJ L330/3.

[15] Free Trade Agreement between the European Union and the Republic of Singapore [2019] OJ L294/3.

[16] Free Trade Agreement between the European Union and the Socialist Republic of Viet Nam [2020] OJ L186/3.

[17] H Lenk, 'More Trade and Less Investment for Future EU Trade and Investment Policy: CJEU, Opinion 2/15, *Free Trade Agreement between the European Union and Singapore*, 16 May 2017, EU:C:2017:376' (2018) 19 *Journal of World Investment and Trade* 1660.

[18] Council Decision (EU) 2018/1676 of 15 October 2018 on the signing, on behalf of the European Union, of the Investment Protection Agreement between the European Union and its Member States, of the one part, and the Republic of Singapore, of the other part [2018] OJ L279/1.

[19] Council Decision (EU) 2019/1096 of 25 June 2019 on the signing, on behalf of the Union, of the Investment Protection Agreement between the European Union and its Member States, of the one part, and the Socialist Republic of Viet Nam, of the other part [2019] OJ L175/1.

planned exit from the ECT, will change its external investment ambition and agenda, or whether the latter will gain new impetus through the eventual establishment of the MIC.

III. The New Architecture in Practice

This section analyses how the general formula of the new architecture depicted in Figure 7.1 is put into practice. This raises two main questions. First, how are formerly comprehensive trade and investment agreements legally disentangled (section III.A)? Second, what legal connections remain between the newly separated but geographically and substantively interwoven treaty regimes (sections III.B and III.C)? Focus is placed on the agreements with Singapore and Vietnam, as the EU has signed and/or concluded both FTAs and IPAs with these countries. In the future, these agreements will serve as blueprints for separating and re-entangling contractual trade and investment protection relations.

A. Splitting Free Trade and Investment Protection Agreements

The EU originally negotiated comprehensive trade and investment protection agreements under the 'old' formula with both Singapore and Vietnam. The negotiations were finalised prior to *Opinion 2/15*, but – in contrast to CETA – the Commission had not yet proposed the signature of either agreement. Therefore, the formerly comprehensive trade and investment agreements with Singapore and Vietnam could be split in hindsight, ie, *after* the institutions agreed on implementing the new architecture. The application of the new architecture thus resulted in stand-alone FTAs (the EUSFTA and the EUVFTA, respectively) and stand-alone EU IPAs (the EUSIPA and the EUVIPA, respectively). In that process, the originally envisaged ISDS system was turned into the ICS.

The process of splitting trade and investment disciplines was guided by the competence divisions established by the CJEU, on the one hand, and practical feasibility, on the other. The EUSFTA and the EUVFTA cover areas that the CJEU confirmed as exclusive EU competences (see Figure 7.1). The two main material issue areas the CJEU confirmed as falling outside the EU's exclusive competence, namely ISDS/ICS and foreign non-direct investments, are covered by the separate IPA. Yet, as was explained in Chapter 3, the distinction between 'direct' and 'non-direct' investments is artificial and difficult to implement in practice.[20] The FTAs with Singapore and Vietnam are principally confined to investment liberalisation and thus establishments. Yet, they do not fully carve out non-direct investments from the definition of financial services.[21] Nonetheless, the EU-only character of the EUSFTA and the EUVFTA has not been put into question by the EU institutions or the Member States.[22] One reason for the absence of inter-institutional conflict could be that IPAs with Singapore and Vietnam are not fully confined to shared

[20] *cf* Chapter 3, section IV.A.
[21] Article 8.49(2)(a)(ii)(9) EUSFTA; Article 8.41(2)(a)(ii)(I) EUVFTA.
[22] Legally, the reference to non-direct investments in the EUSFTA and the EUVFTA are arguably incidental to the main objective of financial service liberalisation, implying that they cannot trigger mixity. See further Chapter 3, section II.C.

competences either. The EUSIPA and EUVIPA also cover the protection of FDI, an exclusive EU competence, as the artificial separation of direct and indirect investment protection and the exclusion of FDI protection from the ICS was considered unnecessarily complicated.[23] The process of splitting FTAs and IPAs into separate agreements was thus as much guided by pragmatism and compromise as it was by the division of treaty-making powers within the EU.

B. Linking Investment Protection and Free Trade Agreements

Under the new architecture, there will be a significant time gap between the entry into force of the FTA and IPA (see section IV.C). Even assuming a smooth ratification process for either agreement, the EU-only FTA will enter into force a lot earlier than the mixed IPA. As a result, the IPA is typically linked to the FTA and not vice versa. According to their preambles, the EUSIPA and the EUVIPA, for example, recognise and build on the EUSFTA and the EUVFTA, respectively, and re-affirm the commitments made to sustainable development therein. The EUSIPA and the EUVIPA are thus designed to enter into force *after* the EUSFTA and EUVFTA, respectively. The cross-reference to the FTA's TSD Chapters is important here, as the IPAs do not include their own TSD Chapters.

There is a limited material overlap between the scope of the separated FTAs and the IPAs under the new architecture. In particular, both types of agreements include rules on the national treatment of establishments.[24] In case of a conflict of rules between the FTA and the IPA, the FTA (ie, the treaty that enters into force first) generally takes precedence over the ensuing IPA. The IPAs with Singapore and Vietnam stipulate that the parties may adopt or maintain an IPA-inconsistent measure 'with respect to the operation, management, conduct, maintenance, use, enjoyment and sale or other disposal of an establishment' if that measure is compatible with the terms of the related FTA, provided that: (a) it has been adopted before the entry into force of the IPA; or (b) is continued, replaced or amended after the entry into force of the IPA and is made less inconsistent with the terms of the IPA.[25] Yet, there is one exception: a party to the IPA cannot invoke the related FTA to prevent the other party from taking appropriate temporary remedies in the case of non-compliance.[26]

C. Linking Trade, Investment Protection and Partnership Agreements

The interconnected treaty network established under the new architecture includes not only FTAs and IPAs but also Partnership Agreements (see Figure 7.1). Partnership Agreements provide an overarching political and structural framework. They are also used to create institutional links between the individual agreements of the new

[23] Interview with two Commission officials, 9 November 2018.
[24] Article 8.11 EUSFTA, Article 8.5 EUVFTA; Article 2.3(1) EUSIPA; Article 2.3(1) EUVIPA.
[25] Articles 2.3(2) EUSIPA; Article 2.3(2) EUVIPA.
[26] Article 3.45(4) EUSIPA; Article 3.24(4) EUVIPA.

architecture. For example, pursuant to Article 43(3) of the EU-Singapore Partnership and Cooperation Agreement (PCA), 'the Parties may also complement this Agreement by concluding specific agreements in any area of cooperation falling within its scope. Such specific agreements shall be *an integral part of the overall bilateral relations as governed by this Agreement* and shall *form part of a common institutional framework*' (emphasis added).[27] The EUSFTA and the EUSIPA as well as the EUVFTA and the EUVIPA expressly stipulate that they shall be regarded as integral parts of their respective PCAs (the EUSPCA and the EUVPCA, respectively).[28]

The common institutional framework of the three agreements is created by interlinking the treaty bodies established under each agreement. The Joint Committee established under the respective PCAs takes on the main coordinating role.[29] Pursuant to Article 16.1(5) EUSFTA and 17.1(5) EUVFTA, respectively, the trade committee established under these FTAs must regularly report to the PCA joint committee on its activities and the activities of the FTA sub-committees. Notably, the committees set up under Article 4.1 EUSIPA and Article 4.1 EUVIPA, respectively, are not obliged to report to the EUSPCA's or the EUVPCA's Joint Committee. Nevertheless, the fact that all three agreements will form part of a common institutional structure will likely increase the coherence of the EU's bilateral trade and investment relations with Singapore and Vietnam, respectively.

Furthermore, and in contrast to the EUSIPA, the EUVIPA links its enforcement mechanism to the EUVPCA. Pursuant to Article 4.16(2) EUVIPA: 'If either Party considers that the other Party has committed a material breach of the Partnership and Cooperation Agreement, it may take appropriate measures with respect to this Agreement.'[30] In other words, the EUVPCA is enforceable through the EUVIPA. IPAs do not only entail a mechanism for solving disputes between individuals (ie, investors) and states, but also an arbitration mechanism to solve state-to-state disputes,[31] with the possibility to resort to financial compensation if the final report of the arbitral tribunal is not followed by a party.[32] Article 4.16(2) EUVIPA expands the jurisdiction of the arbitral tribunal to disputes between the parties arising under the EUVPCA. This might have far-reaching legal consequences. Although PCA provisions are broadly worded, serious and obvious treaty violations could be enforceable via the state-to-state dispute settlement mechanism set out in the IPA. This might be especially relevant for the provisions of the EUVPCA relating to sustainable development, as the TSD Chapter of the EUVFTA is excluded from that agreement's state-to-state dispute settlement mechanism.

IV. Procedural Adjustments

Chapter 4 explained the legal rules underpinning the making of EU trade and investment agreements. The new architecture does not change these rules. Nevertheless, it

[27] See similarly Article 55(3) EUVPCA.
[28] Article 16.18(1) EUSFTA; Article 4.12(1) EUSIPA; Article 17.22 EUVFTA; Article 4.20(2) EUVIPA.
[29] Article 41 EUSPCA; Article 52 EUVPCA.
[30] The measures must be in accordance with Article 57 EUVPCA. However, that provision generally does not preclude the enforcement of the EUVPCA through the EUVIPA.
[31] Chapter 3 section A of the EUVIPA.
[32] Articles 3.15 and 3.16 EUVIPA.

implies various practical changes with regard to the negotiations (section IV.A), signature and conclusion (sections IV.B and IV.C), and provisional application (section IV.D) of EU FTAs and IPAs. In view of the findings of Chapters 4 and 5, the present section outlines what these changes imply for the EU and the Member States.

A. Negotiations

The new architecture ensures certainty regarding the EU-only or mixed character of an international agreement at an early stage in the negotiations.[33] For FTAs, the EU-only procedure poses limits to the substantive reach of an agreement. These limits are already enshrined in the negotiating directives of FTAs made under the new architecture. For example, the negotiating directives of the FTAs with Australia and New Zealand stipulate that these agreements shall 'exclusively contain provisions on trade and foreign direct investment related areas'.[34] In doing so, any attempts to artificially create mixity are forestalled from the outset.[35]

Although the future character of EU FTAs and IPAs is clear, it will not necessarily be reflected in the representation of the EU and/or the Member States during treaty negotiations. The Commission will act as the sole negotiator of both FTAs and stand-alone IPAs, although the latter will be concluded as mixed agreements. So-called mixed negotiations will generally not occur under the new architecture.[36] As was explained in Chapter 4, the Member States were occasionally – through the Presidency – involved in the negotiations of specific FTA provisions, for example, regarding the criminal protection of intellectual property rights (notably for CETA).[37] Yet, there have never been mixed negotiations in the field of investment, at least not for bilateral trade and investment agreements. Some of the Member States do not have the (human) resources to be involved in their own right in the negotiations of such a comprehensive part of EU trade and investment agreements and it was therefore decided that the Commission should act on behalf of all the Member States.[38] The practice that the Commission negotiates bilateral trade and investment agreements on behalf of the Member States therefore already developed in the context of TTIP, CETA, as well as the (former) comprehensive trade and investment protection agreements with Singapore and Vietnam.

Nevertheless, the Council remarked in its conclusions of 8 May 2018 that EU IPAs should 'in principle be negotiated in parallel to FTAs' because 'negotiating EU-only trade agreements should not lead to a loss of negotiation leverage for the EU to obtain ambitious stand-alone investment agreements'.[39] Hence, the Council seeks to establish

[33] See also Kübek and Van Damme (n 9) 159.

[34] Negotiating Directives for a Free Trade Agreement with Australia [2018] 7663/18 ADD 1 RESTREINT UE/EU RESTRICTED; Negotiating Directives for a Free Trade Agreement with New Zealand [2018] 7661/18 ADD 1 RESTREINT UE/EU RESTRICTED.

[35] On the political strategy to 'infect' trade agreements with mixity, see Chapter 2, section III.B.

[36] J Groux, 'Mixed Negotiations' in D O'Keeffe and HG Schermers (eds), *Mixed Agreements* (Kluwer, 1983) 87.

[37] See further Chapter 4, section II.C.

[38] Interview with a Commission official, 19 February 2019.

[39] Council of the European Union (n 2) para 4.

a political link between FTA and IPA negotiations. Such a political link might present the Member States with the opportunity to extrapolate their veto powers in the field of investment to the field of trade, allowing the Member States to push for individual concessions in the FTA negotiations.[40] As was explained in Chapter 4, that strategy might at times play out well for the EU as a whole because non-negotiable Member State interests can strengthen the Commission's bargaining position.[41] However, such a political link between the FTA and the IPA would shift political weight from the EU to the Member States, and institutional control from the Commission to the Council, which would likely impact the negotiation power and position of the EU vis-a-vis the third state.

In its conclusions of 8 May 2018, the Council noted that although the 'legitimacy and inclusiveness of the adoption process' of EU-only FTAs is ensured by the Council and the EP, the 'Member States' parliaments, as well as civil society and other interested stakeholders, should be kept duly informed from the beginning of the process of preparation for negotiating trade agreements'.[42] The Council acknowledged that it is the task of both national governments and the EU institutions to provide information about the EU's trade and investment policy to national parliaments and citizens. Yet, the new architecture does not include any new avenues for integrating national parliaments into the process of designing EU FTAs and IPAs. The Council merely recognised the Commission's recent efforts to increase the transparency of treaty negotiations, while underlining that the decision to make public negotiating directives 'is exclusively for the Council to make, on a case-by-case basis'.[43] National parliaments will therefore continue to be principally involved in the EU-only treaty-making process through their governments, in accordance with national constitutional law.[44]

B. Signature, Conclusion and Voting Requirements

EU FTAs falling fully within the EU's competence will now be concluded by the EU alone. Although FTAs therefore no longer require ratification by Member States, the Council has underlined that the 'decisions on signature and conclusion are taken by the Council; this process allows Member States' governments to consult their national parliaments and other stakeholders'.[45] The Council therefore actively encourages the Member States to involve national parliaments, stakeholders and citizens in the EU decision-making process through national law.[46]

[40] Interview with a Commission official, 9 November 2018.

[41] See also T Cottier, 'Gemischte Abkommen der Europäischen Union: Grundlagen und Alternativen' in M Bungenberg and C Herrmann (eds), *Die gemeinsame Handelspolitik der Europäischen Union: Fünf Jahre nach Lissabon – Quo Vadis?* (Nomos, 2016) 11, 24–25; and S Bolaert, 'Mixity versus Unity: A View from the Other Side of the Rue de la Loi' in Chamon and Govaere (n 9) 251.

[42] Council of the European Union (n 2) para 8.

[43] ibid.

[44] *cf* Chapter 5, section II.

[45] Council of the European Union (n 2) para 7.

[46] See further Chapter 5, sections II and IV.

For the signature and conclusion of EU FTAs under the new architecture, the Council may generally vote by QMV.[47] However, the Council expressed its intention to 'continue endeavouring to obtain, to the greatest extent possible, a consensus in order to ensure that all Member States' interests and concerns are adequately respected in trade agreements.'[48] That explains why the EU-Japan FTA was concluded unanimously by the Council.[49] Nevertheless, the endeavour of the Council to seek decision-making by consensus can only be understood as a political desire to create the broadest possible basis for making decisions.[50] Legally, the Council may not deviate from the voting rules set out in the Treaties. The CJEU confirmed that 'the rules regarding the manner in which the EU institutions arrive at their decisions are laid down in the Treaties and are not at the disposal of the Member States or of the institutions themselves'.[51] It added that insofar that the practice to obtain a consensus in the Council 'is a prerequisite, in the Council's view, for initiating the conclusion procedure laid down in Article 218(2), (6) and (8) TFEU, it results in the addition to that procedure of a step which is not provided for in the Treaties' and is therefore contrary to EU law.[52]

Practice has already shown that political disputes might cause the Member States in the Council to vote by QMV. Against the background of ongoing trade wars, the Council decided in January 2019 to open negotiations for trade agreements with the US on the elimination of tariffs for industrial goods and conformity assessments for goods, respectively.[53] France voted against the adoption of these decisions and Belgium abstained. Although preparatory acts such as negotiating directives can generally be adopted by QMV, this was the first time the Council deviated from the practice of voting by consensus.[54] It remains to be seen whether the Council will in the future resort to QMV voting more often to overcome political conflict between Member States about the making of FTAs.

Legally, the Council can also vote on the conclusion of the parts of IPAs that fall within a competence exercised by the EU by QMV. However, the process of concluding the IPAs with Singapore and Vietnam indicates that the Council continues to await the deposition of ratification instruments by all Member States before taking a decision on the conclusion of these IPAs on behalf of the EU.[55] As a result, the conclusion decisions in the Council will, as a matter of practice, likely be taken by unanimity.

[47] See further Chapter 4, sections III.B–III.D.

[48] Council of the European Union (n 2) para 1.

[49] Interview with two Commission officials, 9 November 2018; interview with a Council official, 7 November 2018.

[50] Interview with a Council official, 7 November 2018.

[51] Case C-28/12, *Hybrid Acts*, EU:C:2015:282, para 42; Case C-68/86 *United Kingdom v Portugal*, EU:C:1988:85, para 38; Case C-133/06, *Parliament v Council*, EU:C:2008:257, para 54. See also Kübek and Van Damme (n 9) 165.

[52] Opinion 1/19, *Istanbul Convention*, EU:C:2021:832, para 245.

[53] Council Decision of 9 April 2019 authorising the opening of negotiations with the United States of America for an agreement on the elimination of tariffs for industrial goods [2019] 6052/19; Council Decision of 9 April 2019 authorising the opening of negotiations with the United States of America for an agreement on conformity assessment [2019] 6053/19.

[54] Interview with a Commission official, 19 February 2019.

[55] The EP formerly approved of the conclusion of the IPAs with Singapore and Vietnam in 2019. The fact that the Council has not taken a conclusion decision by 2023 suggests that it awaits the Member States individual treaty ratifications. See further Chapter 4, section V.

C. Signature, Conclusion and Choice of Legal Basis

The new architecture might lead to a clearer choice of legal basis for the Council decisions on the signature and conclusion of EU FTAs and IPAs. Before the new architecture, legal uncertainty about the allocation of competence led the Council to use multiple separate legal bases listing all the areas it perceived as falling outside the scope of Article 207(1) TFEU on the CCP. The signature of CETA, for example, was based on Article 43(2), Article 91, Article 100(2), Article 153(2), Article 192(1) and the first subparagraph of Article 207(4), in conjunction with Article 218(5) TFEU.[56] Arguably, here the Council did not observe the 'basic principle that any unessential multiplication of legal bases is to be avoided'.[57] It listed any (perceived) shared competence as a separate legal basis, although it decided *not* to exercise that competence at the EU level in order to turn CETA into a mixed agreement. In the context of a facultative mixed agreement, there is no need to list shared competences exercised by the Member States as legal bases because the shared competences are exercised by the Member States in their own right. Since the introduction of the new architecture, the EU legislature only indicated provisions as a legal basis that fall within the EU's (implied) exclusive competence. Substantively, FTAs will be based on Articles 91, 100(2)[58] and 207 TFEU.[59] EU IPAs are substantively based on Article 207 TFEU alone, reflecting the exercise of competence for FDI protection by the EU.[60] As the competences for foreign non-direct investment protection and ICS are exercised by the Member States, the Council did not add additional legal bases to its decisions. The new architecture therefore enhances legal clarity by reducing the number of substantive legal bases to a minimum and, simultaneously, by identifying who exercises shared competence in case of the IPA.

D. Provisional Application

Provisional application has become a rarity in EU treaty-making practice under the new architecture. It will mainly be used in the context of Association Agreements or PCAs, but generally not for FTAs and IPAs.[61] In practice, the choice not to use provisional application for IPAs in particular results in a significant time gap between the entry into force of FTAs and IPAs.

[56] Council Decision (EU) 2017/37 of 28 October 2016 on the signing on behalf of the European Union of the Comprehensive Economic and Trade Agreement (CETA) between Canada, of the one part, and the European Union and its Member States, of the other part [2017] OJ L11/1.

[57] Advocate General Wahl in Opinion 3/15, *Marrakesh Treaty*, EU:C:2016:657, para 34.

[58] Articles 91 and 100 TFEU govern transport services, which are carved out from the CCP (Article 207(5) TFEU) and must therefore be listed as separate legal bases. The provisions on transport services fall within the EU's implied exclusive competence (*cf* Chapter 3, section III.E). Therefore, Articles 91 and 100 TFEU must be listed as separate legal bases in addition to Article 207 TFEU.

[59] See, eg, Council Decision (EU) 2018/1907 of 20 December 2018 on the conclusion of the Agreement between the European Union and Japan for an Economic Partnership [2018] OJ L330/1.

[60] See, eg, Council Decision (EU) 2018/1676 of 15 October 2018 on the signing, on behalf of the European Union, of the Investment Protection Agreement between the European Union and its Member States, of the one part, and the Republic of Singapore, of the other part of 15 October 2018 [2018] OJ L279/1.

[61] See also Kübek and Van Damme (n 9) 163–64.

Provisional application is particularly useful if the ratification process – ie, the duration between a treaty's signature and entry into force – takes a long time. This is especially the case for mixed agreements, where time has to be allowed for the EP and national parliaments to consent to the agreement. The ratification process of EU-only FTAs is a lot shorter because national parliaments are no longer required to consent to the agreement. The EU can therefore proceed to conclude EU-only agreements much faster than mixed agreements, making provisional application less relevant. The average time between signature and entry into force for EU-only FTAs concluded under the new architecture has been six months.[62]

Furthermore, provisional application is less relevant for EU-only FTAs because, as was explained in Chapter 4, EU trade and investment agreements are as a matter of general practice only applied provisionally after the EP has consented to the conclusion of the agreement.[63] For EU-only FTAs, the procedure for provisional application and treaty conclusion is therefore essentially the same. Consequentially, the provisional application of EU-only FTAs is only relevant if the constitutional ratification requirements of the EU's treaty partner are expected to delay entry into force or in the case of exceptional political circumstances.

The EU's first stand-alone IPAs with Singapore and Vietnam will not be applied provisionally either, although they are ratified under the mixed procedure. As was explained in Chapter 3, *Opinion 2/15* is read by some – including the Member States and the Council – as implicating that the competence for ISDS/ICS is not shared within the meaning of Article 4 TFEU, but remains in part an exclusive Member State competence.[64] As was explained in Chapter 4, the scope of a Council decision on the provisional application of an EU agreement may only comprise material aspects that fall within the EU's (exclusive or shared) competence.[65] Therefore, according to the reading of the Council and the Member States, the EU may not apply the provisions relating to ICS in EU IPAs provisionally; only the Member States may decide so in their own right and by means of separate national decisions. As was explained in Chapter 5, the constitutional laws of some Member States only permit provisional application in exceptional circumstances.[66] Because of the Council's legal opinion that the EU cannot provisionally apply IPA provisions relating to the ICS and the fact that some Member States' constitutional rules do not per se recognise provisional application, there is currently neither legal nor political support for applying IPAs provisionally, at least with regard to the ICS.[67] And the application of substantive investment protection standards without enforcement is currently not considered to be effective.[68]

[62] *cf* the FTAs with Singapore, Vietnam, and Japan: the EU-Japan EPA was signed on 17 July 2018 and entered into force less than seven months later, on 1 February 2019. The EUSFTA was signed on 19 October and entered into force on 21 November 2019. The EUVFTA was signed on 25 June 2019 and entered into force in August 2020.

[63] See Chapter 4, section IV.B.

[64] See further Chapter 3, section IV.B. See also Kübek and Van Damme (n 9) 164 et seq.

[65] See Chapter 4, section IV.B.

[66] See Chapter 5, section VI.

[67] Interview with a Council official, 7 November 2018.

[68] Interview with two Commission officials, 9 November 2018.

In this context, it may be noted that Article 4.15(4) EUSIPA suggests that provisional application is mandatory ('this agreement shall be provisionally applied' (indent (a))); only 'certain provisions' of the IPA may be excluded from the scope of provisional application (indent (b)). The Council has requested to change the wording of this provision because it considers that the ICS cannot legally be applied provisionally by the EU.[69] At least the publicly available text of the agreement has not been changed accordingly.[70] Yet, the Commission has not proposed the provisional application of either the IPA with Singapore or with Vietnam.

Provisional application has thus become a dying art under the new architecture, only relevant for the making of PCAs[71] and Association Agreements. The EU-UK TCA was a special case and will be dealt with separately in Chapter 8. However, in general, it is not likely that either EU-only FTAs or mixed IPAs will be provisionally applied under the new architecture. That causes a significant time gap between the entry into force of FTAs and IPAs: whereas the former may enter into force approximately six months after its signature, the ratification process of the latter is expected to take five years and more. It remains to be seen whether this 'ratification gap' has any adverse effects in practice.

V. Prospects of Non-ratification

As mentioned above, in the face of the Wallonia-CETA crisis, the splitting of comprehensive EU trade and investment protection agreements into separate EU-only FTAs and mixed IPAs was suggested as a means to thwart the non-ratification of these agreements by a Member State. Indeed, under the new architecture, vast parts of the 'old' comprehensive trade and investment protection agreements are shielded from the threat of non-ratification by a Member State because they form part of the EU-only FTA. In doing so, the new architecture largely forestalls the possibility of Member States blocking the EU from exercising its exclusive external competence. However, this does not mean that the ratification of EU FTAs or IPAs can no longer be rejected by parliaments under the new architecture.

As was explained in the previous section, the signature and conclusion of EU-only FTAs must be approved by the Council and the EP. In view of the Council's political intention to search for the broadest possible majority before deciding on the ratification of EU-only FTAs, the Member States de facto retain significant individual power in the Council. Moreover, the EP has veto powers over the ratification of EU FTAs and IPAs. In the past, the EP has been in principle in favour of agreements liberalising trade. Yet, recently, the interest in, debate about and critique against trade liberalisation increased and a 'very vocal minority' formed in Parliament opposing the conclusion of EU FTAs

[69] Interview with a Council official, 7 November 2018.

[70] According to a Commission official (interview, 19 February 2019), the language of the provision has since been adjusted ('may' instead of 'shall').

[71] The EUSPCA and the EUVPCA were not applied provisionally. However, see Council Decision (EU) 2018/1197 of 26 June 2018 on the signing, on behalf of the European Union, and provisional application of the Strategic Partnership Agreement between the European Union and its Member States, of the one part, and Japan, of the other part [2018] OJ L216/1.

and IPAs.[72] So far, the impact of that minority is not visible in the manifestation of EP positions against trade, but in the absence of positions in favour of trade. For example, the EP decided not to submit observations in *Opinion 1/17* supporting the compatibility of CETA with EU law, although it had already given its consent to CETA. It has also not adopted resolutions on the negotiations of the MIC.[73] The EP has so far never rejected an EU FTA or IPA. A legally challenging situation would arise if the EP were to reject the ratification of an EU-only FTA whilst approving the ratification of the associated IPA. As was explained above, the FTA constitutes a self-standing agreement and is, at most, linked to the PCA. Conversely, the IPA is substantively linked to the FTA; it is not designed to function without the FTA. Moreover, the purpose to protect investments would be significantly hampered if trade and FDI were not simultaneously liberalised. So far, this concern has not arisen in practice. The FTAs and IPAs with Singapore and Vietnam, respectively, passed with similar majorities in the responsible committee (ie, the INTA committee)[74] and the EP plenary.[75]

EU IPAs and Association Agreements will generally be concluded as mixed agreements under the new architecture. As a result, national parliaments and citizens will continue to have veto powers for the ratification of these agreements. The MIC will also be ratified under the mixed procedure. As the Member States negotiate and thus design the MIC in their own right alongside the Commission within the framework of UNCITRAL, it is for Member State governments to defend their position on the MIC before parliaments and citizens.

VI. Conclusion

The new architecture puts the CJEU's legal conclusions in *Opinion 2/15* into practice: comprehensive EU trade and investment protection agreements will be split into standalone EU-only FTAs and mixed IPAs. FTAs principally contain all areas that fall within the EU's exclusive competence, as confirmed by the CJEU in *Opinion 2/15*. IPAs establish substantive investment protection standards and contain an ICS. Practice shows that the FTA and the IPA are accompanied by a third agreement, a mixed Partnership Agreement. The Council will decide on a case-by-case basis whether to accept the application of the new architecture. The Council therefore has discretion to return to the 'old' comprehensive trade and investment protection agenda for certain important trading partners, such as the US. At the same time, the Council has discretion to exceptionally conclude Association Agreements under the EU-only procedure, as the case of the EU-UK TCA illustrates (see Chapter 8). The Council has declared its intention to ratify

[72] Interview with an EP official, 7 November 2018.

[73] See also Chapter 4, section II.D.

[74] The final votes for the conclusion of respective agreements in the INTA committee were: (1) for the EUSFTA: 25 votes to 11, with 1 abstention; (2) for the EUSIPA: 11 votes to 7, with 6 abstentions; (3) for the EUVFTA: 11 votes to 7, with 6 abstentions; (4) for the EUVIPA: 11 votes to 7, with 6 abstentions.

[75] The final votes for the conclusion of the respective agreements in the EP plenary were: (1) for the EUSFTA: 425 votes to 186, with 41 abstentions; (2) for the EUSIPA: 436 votes to 203, with 30 abstentions; (3) for the EUVFTA: 401 votes to 192 votes, with 40 abstentions; (4) for the EUVIPA: 407 votes to 188, with 53 abstentions.

the EU's Association Agreements with Mexico, Mercosur and Chile under the mixed procedure.

The separate negotiation and ratification of EU-only FTAs and mixed IPAs marks a remarkable political compromise, possibly ending a decade-long inter-institutional conflict about mixity and the EU's post-Lisbon trade and investment agreements.[76] The desire to avoid future conflicts is embodied in the practical implementation of the new architecture. It is not about rigorously implementing the results of *Opinion 2/15*, but about finding a pragmatic and feasible solution that is acceptable to all parties and reflects the current competence divide between the EU and the Member States in the field of trade and investment.

Timing is essential with regard to the ratification of agreements under the new architecture. The FTA, as an EU-only agreement, will enter into force a lot earlier than the mixed IPA. That 'ratification gap' will not be closed by applying provisionally the IPA. As the Council and the Member States contend that the ICS cannot be applied provisionally by the EU and some Member States do not recognise provisional application in their national constitutional laws, there is currently neither the legal scope nor the political will to apply IPAs provisionally. The EU's IPAs with Singapore and Vietnam show that the negotiators sought to ensure that the 'ratification gap' does not cause legal uncertainty or conflict in practice by linking substantively the IPAs to their respective FTAs, and integrating mechanisms to solve a potential conflict of rules once both agreements are in force. The FTA and IPA are further linked to the PCA, which provides an overarching institutional structure for all agreements. The EUVIPA links its enforcement mechanism to the EUVPCA, which means that material breaches of the PCA may be enforced through the state-to-state dispute settlement mechanism included in the IPA. That may be particularly relevant for sanctioning material breaches of sustainable development obligations.

Procedurally, the new architecture simplified and clarified the making of both FTAs and IPAs. The Commission represents the EU in the negotiations of both FTAs and IPAs under the negotiations. The Member States are no longer individually represented through the Presidency. In addition, the new architecture streamlined the procedure for signing and concluding EU FTAs and IPAs by clarifying the decision-making modalities and voting majorities in the Council, as well as the choice of legal basis.

As it turns mixity into a deliberate substantive design choice, the new architecture connotes the practice of *moving beyond mixity*. The choice between making an EU-only or a mixed agreement is made at negotiation stage and is clearly reflected in the substantive scope of the envisaged agreement as set out in the negotiating directives. Before entering into treaty negotiations, the EU and the third state balance procedure (avoiding the complexity of mixed agreements) against substance (confining the scope of FTAs to trade and investment liberalisation, leaving out investment protection disciplines). The conclusion of EU-only FTAs increases the unity and power of the EU as an external trade actor, and makes EU trade and investment treaty-making significantly more effective. Moreover, (sub-)national players can no longer prevent the EU, as a whole, from exercising its exclusive competence in the field of trade. If mixity is deliberately

[76] See also Kübek and Van Damme (n 9) 167.

chosen as a treaty-making technique from the outset, the EU and its trading partners can consider addressing some of the problems of mixity in the design of that mixed agreement (see Chapter 6).

The new architecture does not elevate the role of national parliaments. The Council largely leaves it up to national governments to put their parliaments into a position where they can impact EU trade and investment policy. While it is unfortunate that the Council did not use the new architecture to increase public information rights (eg, a commitment to make public the final version of the negotiation directives), Chapter 5 has shown that the Member States themselves can ensure, via their national laws, that national parliaments have a decisive say on the formation of EU trade policy.

Lastly, the new architecture does not solve all problems associated with mixity. The non-ratification crisis might still arise in the future with regard to mixed Association Agreements. This may be one reason why the Member States in the Council did not follow the general formula of the new architecture for the EU-UK Association Agreement, which was concluded as a facultative EU-only agreement. The next and final chapter of this book highlights the legal, political, and practical rationale of the Member States in the Council for deviating from the new architecture for the special case of the TCA.

8

The EU-UK Trade and Cooperation Agreement

I. Introduction

On Christmas Eve 2020, the EU and the UK announced the end of the negotiations for a 'future relations' agreement. A 'hard Brexit' was looming at the end of the transition period on 31 December 2020, which the UK had refused to extend. The negotiations between the EU and the UK on their future relations resulted in three agreements: a Trade and Cooperation Agreement;[1] an Agreement between the EU and the UK concerning security procedures for exchanging and protecting classified information, which supplements the TCA;[2] and an Agreement between the UK Government and Euratom for Cooperation on the Safe and the Peaceful Uses of Nuclear Energy.[3] This chapter focuses on the first of these.

In view of its scope, depths and political relevance, the TCA is the most important trade agreement the EU has concluded in the last decade.[4] Its signature on 29 December 2020 and its provisional application as of 1 January 2021 prevented the significant disruption that a 'hard Brexit' would have had on the EU's and the UK's bilateral trade and foreign relations 'to the detriment of individuals, businesses and stakeholders'.[5]

The TCA entered into force on 1 May 2021, after receiving the consent of the EP in late April. The procedure for negotiating, signing, provisionally applying and concluding the TCA differed in several aspects from the general post-Lisbon practice for making trade and investment agreements described in Chapters 4, 5 and 7.

[1] Trade and Cooperation Agreement between the European Union and the European Atomic Energy Community, of the one part, and the United Kingdom of Great Britain and Northern Ireland, of the other part [2021] OJ L149/10. For an overview, see the contributions in G Kübek, CJ Tams and JP Terhechte (eds), *EU-UK Trade and Cooperation Agreement: A Handbook* (Nomos/Hart Publishing/CH Beck, 2024); F Fabbrini (ed), *The Framework of the New EU-UK Relations* (Oxford University Press, 2021); S Peers, 'So Close, Yet So Far: The EU/UK Trade and Cooperation Agreement' (2022) 59 *Common Market Law Review* 49.

[2] Agreement between the European Union and the United Kingdom of Great Britain and Northern Ireland concerning security procedures for exchanging and protecting classified information [2021] OJ L149/2540.

[3] Agreement between the Government of the United Kingdom of Great Britain and Northern Ireland and the European Atomic Energy Community for Cooperation on the Safe and Peaceful Uses of Nuclear Energy [2021] OJ L150/1.

[4] G Kübek, CJ Tams, and JP Terhechte, 'Introduction' in Kübek, Tams and Terhechte (n 1).

[5] European Commission, 'EU-UK Trade and Cooperation Agreement: Protecting European Interests, Ensuring Fair Competition, and Continued Cooperation in Areas of Mutual Interest', press release, 24 December 2020.

Its negotiations were intertwined with and influenced by the Withdrawal Agreement, which was concluded about one year before the TCA.[6] The EU and the Member States focused on maintaining unity and adjusted its standard negotiating practice for trade agreements in view of that goal. Moreover, the TCA was signed and concluded as an EU-only Association Agreement, although the Council had announced less than a year earlier that Association Agreements should remain mixed agreements under the new architecture.[7] The unusual process of negotiating and ratifying the TCA was justified by the EU institutions on grounds of the special circumstances that led to the making of a trade agreement with a country that has withdrawn from the EU.[8] The EU institutions and the Member States reiterated that the case of the TCA does not establish a legal precedent for their future external relations, be that joint or individually.

Without disputing the 'exceptional and unique character' of the TCA, this chapter argues that the procedure for making the agreement may nonetheless be viewed as an example for future trade practice in at least two ways. First, the negotiating process of the TCA showed how unity during the negotiation process can be reached through close cooperation between the EU institutions, on the one hand, and between the EU and the Member States, on the other hand. Second, the ratification of the TCA illustrated that the EU institutions and the Member States have begun to use the facultative mixed procedure more deliberately to determine the character of an agreement falling within shared competence on a case-by-case basis rather than opting for mixity purely as a matter of path-dependency and principle. The careful weighing and balancing of the costs and benefits of making either a facultative mixed or a facultative EU-only trade and investment agreement depending on the specific economic, political and legal circumstances is another stepping stone in the *move beyond mixity*, as it allows the EU and the Member States to make full use of the clarity, effectiveness and flexibility that the post-Lisbon legal order provides. As was argued in Chapters 4 and 5, the question of how national parliaments and citizens can be better integrated into the treaty-making process arises against the backdrop of the choice in favour or against mixity, and for mixed and EU-only agreements alike.

[6] Agreement on the Withdrawal of the United Kingdom of Great Britain and Northern Ireland from the European Union and the European Atomic Energy Community [2019] OJ C384l/1. On the agreement, see, eg, JP Terhechte, *Brexit-Abkommen: Vertragstext, Protokolle, Politische Erklärung* (Nomos, 2020); T Liefländer et al, *EU-UK Withdrawal Agreement: A Commentary* (Oxford University Press, 2021); F Fabbrini (ed), *The Withdrawal Agreement* (Oxford University Press, 2020); and JP Terhechte, 'Strukturen und Probleme des Brexit Abkommens' (2020) 7 *Neue Juristische Wochenzeitschrift* 425. On the negotiations specifically, see E Jones, 'The Negotiations' in F Fabbrini (ed), *The Withdrawal Agreement* (Oxford University Press, 2020) 37.

[7] *cf* Chapter 7, section II.

[8] Council Decision (EU) 2020/2252 of 29 December 2020 on the signing, on behalf of the Union, and on provisional application of the Trade and Cooperation Agreement between the European Union and the European Atomic Energy Community, of the one part, and the United Kingdom of Great Britain and Northern Ireland, of the other part, and of the Agreement between the European Union and the United Kingdom of Great Britain and Northern Ireland concerning security procedures for exchanging and protecting classified information [2020] OJ L444/2, indent 6; Council Decision (EU) 2021/689 of 29 April 2021 on the conclusion, on behalf of the Union, of the Trade and Cooperation Agreement between the European Union and the European Atomic Energy Community, of the one part, and the United Kingdom of Great Britain and Northern Ireland, of the other part, and of the Agreement between the European Union and the United Kingdom of Great Britain and Northern Ireland concerning security procedures for exchanging and protecting classified information [2021] OJ L149/2, indent 3.

This chapter is structured as follows. Section II examines the negotiations of the TCA. It explains how the EU and the Member States adjusted their negotiating practice with a view to ensuring unity. Section III explains the legal character of the TCA as an EU-only Association Agreement. It zooms in on the legal rationale of the Member States in the Council for opting against mixity, and explains the legal consequences of that choice. Section IV looks in more detail at the legal issues surrounding the TCA's provisional application and outlines why they were a key driver for the Council's choice to sign and conclude the TCA as an EU-only agreement. It also highlights the EP's position on these issues. Section V outlines the role of national parliaments. Section VI concludes.

II. Negotiations

Unlike other trade and investment treaty negotiations, the negotiations for the EU-UK TCA were deeply intertwined with the negotiations of a different agreement, namely the Withdrawal Agreement.[9] The UK government signalled early on in the Brexit process that it wished to leave the single market and customs union and instead wished to work towards 'a wide reaching, bold and ambitious free trade agreement'.[10] In its guidelines of 23 March 2018, the European Council 'confirm[ed] its readiness' to work towards an EU27-UK trade and investment agreement. In line with its approach to conduct sequential negotiations[11] – divorce first, future relations second – the Commission recommended on 3 February 2020 the opening of 'negotiations for a new partnership' with the UK.[12] The UK had formally withdrawn from the EU on 1 January 2020. By recommending the opening of negotiations one month later, the Commission followed the European Council's invitation to submit to the Council 'a draft comprehensive mandate for a future relationship with the United Kingdom immediately after its withdrawal'.[13]

The broader contours of what was to become the TCA had already been set out in a Political Declaration that accompanied the Withdrawal Agreement.[14] The Withdrawal Agreement further includes a 'best endeavour' clause inviting the EU and the UK to negotiate and ratify the agreements referred to in the Political Declaration 'with a view to ensuring that those agreements apply, to the extent possible, as from the end of the transition period'.[15]

[9] See n 6 above.

[10] HM Government, *The United Kingdom's Exit from and New Partnership with the European Union*, White Paper, 17 January 2017, Principle 8. See also European Council (Art 50) guidelines for Brexit negotiations of 29 April 2017, EUCO XT 20004/17, para 19.

[11] See, eg, European Council (n 10) paras 4 et seq.

[12] Recommendation for a Council Decision authorising the opening of negotiations for a new partnership with the United Kingdom of Great Britain and Northern Ireland, COM (2020) 35 final.

[13] European Council (Art 50) meeting – Conclusions, EUCO XT 20027/19, 13 December 2019, para 3.

[14] Political Declaration Setting out the Framework for the Future Relationship between the European Union and the United Kingdom [2020] OJ C34/1. Pursuant to Article 50(2) TEU, the Withdrawal Agreement shall take 'account of the framework for [the withdrawing state's] future relation with the Union'.

[15] Article 184 of the Withdrawal Agreement.

Procedurally, the negotiations of the TCA differed from the negotiations of comparable new generation EU trade and investment agreements in several aspects. While the Commission was still nominated as the EU negotiator, the chief negotiator was not from DG Trade, as is typically the case for EU trade and investment agreements. Instead, in view of its main goal to 'to maintain unity, act as one and approach the negotiations with unified positions', the EU institutions had decided to re-appoint Michel Barnier, who had previously led the withdrawal negotiations.[16] Moreover, the Commission was authorised to conduct the negotiations in cooperation with the High Representative and in agreement with him on CFSP matters.[17] Although provisions on political cooperation or CFSP matters ultimately did not make it into the final text of the TCA,[18] the obligation of the Commission to cooperate with the High Representative throughout the negotiations deviated from the EU's standard trade practice and underlined the envisaged broad scope of the TCA. In the Council, the General Affairs Council and COREPER, assisted by the Working Party on the UK, remained the designated committees in consultation with which the negotiations had to be conducted, rather than the TPC, which typically takes on this role in EU trade and investment treaty negotiations.[19] COREPER and the Working Party on the UK were (de-)brieved before and after each negotiation session, and forwarded all necessary information. The Working Party on the UK was consulted on all negotiating documents sent to the UK. Moreover, Member State governments were more closely involved in the TCA negotiations than they were during the negotiations of previous EU trade and investment agreements. In keeping with the structure of the withdrawal negotiations, the TCA negotiations were conducted in unity and transparency with the Member States, with a view to ensuring that the Member States did not conduct bilateral negotiations or raise individual claims vis-a-vis the UK.[20] In contrast to other EU trade and investment agreements, the EU was indeed highly successful in speaking with a single voice, suggesting that a close involvement of the Member States' governments - be that in via the Council and/or in their own right - and, by inference, their national parliaments can facilitate unity.[21]

[16] Statement by the Council and by the Representatives of the Governments of the Member States Meeting within the Council [2020] 6126/1/20 REV 1, Annex B. The document was seemingly adopted as Council doc. 6239/20. However, the latter is not publicly available. On unity in EU external relations, see especially C Herrmann, 'Much Ado about Pluto? The "Unity of the Legal Order of the European Union" Revisited' in M Cremona and B de Witte, *EU Foreign Relations Law: Constitutional Fundamentals* (Hart Publishing, 2008) 19.

[17] Annex to Council Decision authorising the opening of negotiations with the United Kingdom of Great Britain and Northern Ireland for a new partnership agreement, Directives for the Negotiations of a New Partnership with the United Kingdom of Great Britain and Northern Ireland [2020] Council Doc 5870/20 ADD 1 REV 3, Addendum, para 172 (hereinafter 'negotiating directives').

[18] See also P Van Elsuwege, 'A New Legal Framework for EU-UK Relations: Some Reflections from the Perspective of EU External Relations Law' (2021) 6 *European Papers* 785, 798.

[19] Statement by the Council and the Commission on working methods and role of the special committee (WP on the UK) in the negotiations of a new partnership agreement with the UK, 6126/1/20 REV 1 (n 16) Annex A. On the role of the TPC, see Chapter 4, section II.B.

[20] See European Council (n 13); Negotiating Directives (n 17) paras 169-170; and Statement by the Council and by the Representatives of the Governments of the Member States meeting within the Council (n 16).

[21] See, by contrast, the case of CETA. *cf* Chapter 6, section I.

The EP adopted a resolution on 'the proposed mandate for negotiations for a new partnership agreement with the [UK]' on 12 February 2020, ie, only nine days after the Commission recommended the opening of negotiations.[22] There was a notable degree of convergence between the negotiating objectives set out by the EP in its resolution of 12 February 2020 and the Council's negotiating directives, which the EP acknowledged in a follow-up resolution adopted on 18 June 2020.[23] The EP further acknowledged that it 'was able to express its opinion on a regular basis given the strong and frequent consultation and dialogue with the EU's Chief Negotiator and the Commission's UK Taskforce'.[24] As will be explained further below, the involvement of the EP in the finalisation of the negotiations was considerably hampered by the increasing time pressures.[25] Nonetheless, the negotiating objectives of the EP expressed in its resolutions of February and June 2020 are largely reflected in the final text of the TCA, which is likely a result of the close cooperation between the Commission and the EP, on the one side, and the Member States, the Council and the Commission, on the other side, throughout a majority of the negotiations.

Substantively, the TCA was conceptualised as an agreement reaching beyond the EU's exclusive trade and investment competences from the outset. The negotiation directives, inter alia, referred to 'trade and economic cooperation, law enforcement and judicial cooperation in criminal matters, foreign policy, security and defence and thematic areas of cooperation'.[26] In view of the objective of maintaining unity, the Member States had authorised 'the Commission to conduct negotiations in areas of the future relationship that fall within the competences of the Member States, in accordance with the negotiating directives'.[27] The fact that the Member States expressly authorised the Commission to act on their behalf suggests that they had envisioned the TCA as a (mandatory) mixed agreement. As was explained in Chapter 4, the Member States are only obliged to authorise the Commission to act on their behalf in areas of exclusive national competence.[28] However, the negotiating directives did not include any material issue area that apparently fell within the exclusive competence of the Member States. As such, it appears that the Member State had issued the authorisation as a hedging instrument with a view to granting maximum flexibility to the Commission. Questions about the division of competence between the EU and the Member States were deliberately postponed to the ratification stage. Notably, neither the negotiating directives of the EU nor the UK included a reference to investment protection and the establishment of an ICS. The TCA was thus substantively designed in such a way as to ensure that the Council retains political discretion over the agreement's character at the end of the

[22] European Parliament resolution of 12 February 2020 on the proposed mandate for negotiations for a new partnership with the United Kingdom of Great Britain and Northern Ireland [2020] P9_TA(2020)0033.

[23] European Parliament recommendation of 18 June 2020 on the negotiations for a new partnership with the United Kingdom of Great Britain and Northern Ireland [2020] P9_TA(2020)0152, para 5.

[24] European Parliament resolution of 28 April 2021 on the outcome of EU-UK negotiations [2021] P9_TA(2021)0141, para 7.

[25] See further section IV below.

[26] Negotiating directives (n 17) para 7.

[27] Statement by the Council and by the Representatives of the Governments of the Member States meeting within the Council (n 16).

[28] See Chapter 4, section II.C.

negotiating process. Indeed, the Council and the Member State governments underlined in a common statement that the character of the TCA was to be 'determined at the end of the negotiations'.[29]

III. Signature and Conclusion

The TCA was signed on 29 December 2020, only five days after the negotiations were officially finalised. It was concluded by the Council, after receiving the consent of the EP, on 29 April 2021. By signing and concluding the TCA as an Association Agreement (section III.A) under the EU-only procedure (section III.B), the Member States in the Council decided to break with past practice and the Council's vision for the new architecture. As a result, debates arose about the legal consequences of the Council's political choice to conclude the TCA as an EU-only agreement (section III.C).

A. The Character of the TCA as an Association Agreement

The Commission had proposed a comprehensive treaty from the outset, covering all areas originally envisaged in the political declaration. The UK had preferred the making of separate agreements and, in particular, a separate FTA, possibly in view of the new architecture.[30] However, as for the Withdrawal Agreement,[31] the EU institutions had insisted that 'all negotiations are indivisible'.[32]

In view of the 'comprehensive scope of the envisaged partnership [with the UK] and the ambitious and long-term relationship that it seeks to establish', Article 217 TFEU was envisaged by the EU from the outset of the negotiations as the substantive legal basis of the future partnership agreement with the UK.[33] Pursuant to Article 217(1) TFEU, the EU may 'conclude with one or more third countries or international organisations agreements establishing an association involving reciprocal rights and obligations, common action and special procedure'. The CJEU has confirmed that Article 217 TFEU 'empowers the European Union to guarantee commitments towards third countries in all the fields covered by the FEU Treaty'.[34] Pursuant to Article 218(6)(i) and (8) TFEU, Association Agreements must be concluded by the Council acting unanimously after obtaining the consent of the EP. Irrespective of whether Association Agreements are concluded under the EU-only or the mixed procedure, the Member States thus hold veto powers in the Council.

[29] Statement by the Council and by the Representatives of the Governments of the Member States meeting within the Council (n 16).

[30] See Chapter 7, section II.

[31] See, eg, European Council (Art 50) guidelines for Brexit negotiations, EUCO XT 20004/17, 29 April 2017, para 1.

[32] European Parliament recommendation of 18 June 2020 (n 23) para 2.

[33] Recommendation for a Council Decision (n 12) 5. See also Statement by the Council and by the Representatives of the Governments of the Member States meeting within the Council (n 16) 1.

[34] Case C-81/13, *United Kingdom v Council*, EU:C:2014:2449, para 61. See also Case 12/86, *Demirel*, EU:C:1987:400, para 9.

The EU's treaty-making practice under Article 217 TFEU is wide and not always cohesive. Association Agreements are used to establish privileged relations with third states.[35] As a result, they are frequently used in the context of the EU's neighbourhood and accession policy.[36] Yet, as was mentioned in Chapter 7, the EU has also concluded Association Agreements with countries located far beyond its geographical neighbourhood (eg, Chile).[37]

By signing and concluding the TCA as an Association Agreement, the EU treated the UK similarly to other neighbouring countries. Yet, the name and acronym of the Trade and Cooperation Agreement (TCA) appear to be inspired by new generation trade and investment agreements (eg, CETA, the EUSFTA or the Japan-EU Economic Partnership Agreement) and may politically serve to set the TCA apart from other Association Agreements with a DCFTA that mention the word 'association' in their title (eg, the EU-Ukraine Association Agreement). As was explained by Van Elsuwege, the absence of the word 'association' in the title and text of the TCA is of no legal relevance to the application of Article 217 TFEU.[38] It may ultimately be reflective of the fact that the TCA dissociates (rather than associates) a former Member State from the EU.

B. The Character of the TCA as a Facultative EU-Only Agreement

Association Agreements are usually concluded as mixed agreements. In fact, the very first mixed agreement concluded by the (then) Community with Greece was an Association Agreement. Since then, the (now) EU has deviated from its established practice to make Association Agreements as mixed agreements in less than a handful of instances.[39] In view of the vast scope of Association Agreements, which cover the entire breadth of the EU's conferred competence, the Council has (at least so far) principally decided to leave the exercise of non-exclusive competence with the Member States.[40] Despite being a legitimate policy choice from a legal perspective, mixity partially defies the logic of Article 217 TFEU. After all, the provision empowers the EU (and not

[35] See, eg, Case C-431/11, *United Kingdom v Council*, EU:C:2013:589, para 49. See also K Schmalenbach, 'Artikel 217 AEUV' in C Callies and M Ruffert (eds), *EUV/AEUV: Das Verfassungsrecht der Europäischen Union mit Europäischer Grundrechtecharta*, Kommentar, 6th edn (CH Beck, 2022) para 1; and S Vöneky and B Beylage-Haarmann, 'Artikel 217 AEUV' in E Grabitz et al (eds), *Das Recht der Europäischen Union: EUV/AEUV*, Stand: Mai 2023, 79 Erg.-Lfg. (CH Beck, 2023) para 3.

[36] See generally P Van Elsuwege and M Chamon, 'The Meaning of "Association" under EU law: A Study on the Law and Practice of EU Association Agreements', *Study for the Policy Department for Citizens' Rights and Constitutional Affairs of the European Parliament* (2019). On Association Agreements in the context of the EU's neighbourhood policy and accession, see also G Van der Loo, *The EU-Ukraine Association Agreement and Deep and Comprehensive Free Trade Area: A New Legal Instrument for EU Integration without Membership?* (Brill, 2016); D Phinnemore, 'Stabilisation and Association Agreements: Europe Agreements for the Western Balkans' (2003) 8 *European Foreign Affairs Review* 77; M Maresceau, 'Les accords d'intégration dans les relations de proximité de l'Union Europeénne' in C Blumann (ed), *Les frontiers de l'Union Européenne* (Bruylant, 2013), and M Kotzur, 'Europäische Nachbarschaftspolitik' in A von Arnauld and M Bungenberg (eds), *Europäische Außenbeziehungen*, Enzyklopädie Europarecht, vol 12, 2nd edn (Nomos, 2020) 401.

[37] See Chapter 7, section II.

[38] Van Elsuwege (n 18) 790.

[39] Examples include the 1971 Association Agreement between the Community and Malta; the 1973 Association Agreement between the Community and Malta; and the 2016 Stabilisation and Association Agreement between the EU and Kosovo. See further Chapter 1, sections III.A and III.B.

[40] On the legal rationale of facultative mixity, see Chapter 2, section IV.A.

individual Member States) to establish an association with third countries. Likewise, third countries seek to establish 'reciprocal rights and obligations' with the EU and not with individual Member States. Nonetheless, as was mentioned in Chapter 7, the Council announced in its 2018 conclusions on the new architecture that '[d]epending on their content, association agreements should be mixed'.[41]

The TCA is the first association agreement concluded under the new architecture and immediately breaks with the Council's principal opinion that these agreements 'should be mixed'.[42] On 29 December 2020, in its signature decision, the Council announced its political choice to ratify the TCA as an EU-only agreement 'in view of the exceptional and unique character of the Trade and Cooperation Agreement, which is a comprehensive agreement with a country that has withdrawn from the Union'.[43] Rather than following the new architecture, the ratification of the TCA mimics that of the Withdrawal Agreement, which had to be concluded by the EU alone in accordance with Article 50(2) TEU.[44] This shows once again that the procedure for making the 'divorce' and 'future relations' agreements with the UK were deeply intertwined.

The decisions to sign and conclude the TCA as an EU-only agreement were taken by unanimity in the Council, in accordance with Article 218(8) TFEU. The Dutch government, in a letter to the Second Chamber of the Dutch Parliament, further elaborated on the rationale behind the Member States' decision in the Council.[45] Accordingly, the Council made a political choice to break with mixity because it considered that the ratification of the TCA as an EU-only agreement was the only way to ensure the application of the TCA in full at the end of the transition period. The Member States in the Council could not complete the ratification of a mixed agreement under national constitutional law before the end of the transition period. As will be further explained below,[46] the Member States also did not consider that a mixed agreement with provisional application was a feasible alternative to the EU-only mode, as some Member States were not in a position to provisionally apply the parts of the TCA that fall within shared competence in their own right in time. A mixed agreement with provisional application therefore would have led to 'a situation with the same effect as no deal in sub-areas'.[47] Against that background, the Council decided to exercise shared competence at the EU level for the signature and conclusion of the TCA.

Prior to casting their vote on the signature of the TCA in the Council, several Member States had asked the CLS to examine the legality of the political choice to conclude the TCA as an EU-only agreement.[48] In its opinion, the CLS first examined the

[41] Council of the European Union, Draft Council conclusions on the negotiation and conclusion of EU trade agreements – Adoption [2018] 8622/18. See further Chapter 7, section II.

[42] ibid.

[43] Council Decision (EU) 2020/2252 (n 8) indent 6.

[44] On Article 50 TEU, see especially P Eeckhout and E Frantziou, 'Brexit and Article 50 TEU: A Constitutionalist Reading' (2017) 54 *Common Market Law Review* 655. On the ratification of the Withdrawal Agreement, see P Craig, 'The Ratifications' in Fabbrini (n 6) 83.

[45] Kamerstukken II, 2020–2021, 35393, Nr 11.

[46] See section IV.A below.

[47] Kamerstukken II (n 45), translation by the author.

[48] Council Legal Service, Trade and Cooperation Agreement between the European Union and the European Atomic Energy Community, of the one part, and the United Kingdom of Great Britain and Northern Ireland, of the other part – EU-only agreement – Exercise by the EU of its potential competence [2021] 5591/21. The

scope of the TCA. It concluded that the TCA covered both exclusive and shared competence. It further underlined that the agreement contains no provision that falls within the exclusive competences of the Member States.[49] In light of the CJEU's established case law, it thus concluded that mixity was facultative, thereby confirming the legality of the Council's political discretion to determine the character of the TCA as either an EU-only or a mixed agreement. As the CLS opinion underlines, the Council explicitly indicated in its decision on the signature of the TCA that it wished 'to make use of the possibility for the Union to exercise its external competence with regard to the [UK]'.[50]

The CLS noted that some shared competences covered by the TCA had not yet been exercised internally by the EU. However, according to the CLS, this does not affect the facultative character of that agreement.[51] Indeed, the EU's choice not to exercise a shared competence internally does not affect its capacity to exercise that shared competence externally. In fact, facultative mixity usually arises with regard to non-exercised shared internal competences. Once a shared competence has been exercised internally, it often turns into an implied exclusive external competence and the agreement is no longer facultative.[52] The CJEU concluded in *Commission v Ireland* that the (then) Community can enter into agreements 'even if the specific matters covered by those agreements are not yet, or are only very partially, the subject of rules at Community level, which, by reason of that fact, are not likely to be affected'.[53] In *COTIF I*, the CJEU (re-)confirmed that 'the existence of an external European Union competence is not … dependent on the prior exercise, by the Union, of its internal legislative competence' and that the EU is competent to exercise shared competence that has not been the subject of internal legislation externally alone, if the Council so decides.[54] In the context of the TCA, the CLS concluded that 'Article 217 TFEU can be used whenever there is EU competence … even if that competence has not been exercised'.[55]

C. Consequences of the TCA's EU-Only Character

The fact that the TCA includes various material issue areas where the Member States remain the primary legislatures within the EU raised further questions about the consequences of the Council's decision to make an EU-only agreement. Some argued that it is problematic from a competence perspective that the Member States are required

text of the opinion is available at: eulawanalysis.blogspot.com/2021/01/the-brexit-deal-council-legal-service.html. For a critical analysis of the role of the Council Legal Service in EU decision-making, see P Leino-Sandberg, *The Politics of Legal Expertise in EU Policy-Making* (Cambridge University Press, 2021) 197 et seq.

[49] Council Legal Service opinion (n 48) para 28.

[50] Council Decision (EU) 2020/2252 (n 8) indent 6. See likewise Council Decision (EU) 2021/689 (n 8), indent 3. Council Legal Service opinion (n 48) para 9.

[51] The CLS describes areas of shared competence in which the EU has not (yet) adopted legislation as 'potential competences' (n 48). The notion 'potential competences' is arguably ill-suited. Pursuant to Article 4(2) TFEU, shared EU competence in several fields exists. The EU's choice not to make use of its shared competence does not make its existence any less tangible.

[52] On the so-called ERTA doctrine, see Chapter 3, sections II.E and III.E.

[53] Case C-459/03, *MOX Plant*, EU:C:2006:345, para 95.

[54] Case C-600/14, *COTIF I*, EU:C:2017:935, paras 66–68.

[55] Council Legal Service opinion (n 48) para 33.

to implement parts of the TCA.[56] Yet, it is common practice that the Member States implement EU acts, including in fields where the EU has exclusive competence.[57] If the EU concludes an agreement covering fields of shared competence, the Member States are bound by that agreement as a matter of EU law.[58] As a result, they may be required to exercise their retained shared internal competence in such a way as to comply with an agreement concluded by the EU. Concluding an international agreement under the EU-only instead of the mixed procedure does not imply that the Member States are not obliged to comply with the terms of that agreement in their own right and/or must not actively contribute to its implementation; it merely means that the Member States are bound to do so indirectly, as a matter of EU law, and not directly, as a matter of international law.

The Member States were further concerned about the effect of the TCA's EU-only conclusion on their future ability to make agreements with third states other than the UK in areas of shared competence.[59] In its signature decision, the Council stressed that its choice to make an EU-only agreement 'is without prejudice to the respective competences of the Union and of the Member States in relation to any ongoing or future negotiations for, or signature or conclusion of, international agreements with any other third country'.[60] Several Member States had asked the CLS to confirm that the conclusion of the TCA as an EU-only agreement does not establish a legal precedent. The CLS confirmed that the Council's decision to conclude the TCA as an EU-only agreement neither implies that future Association Agreements will be concluded by the EU alone, nor that the Member States are precluded from exercising shared external competence in areas covered by the TCA vis-a-vis other third states.[61] This is arguably correct. Contrary to what has been argued by some, the exercise of external competence by the EU does not 'deactivate' a corresponding shared internal competence.[62] When the EU concludes an agreement covering shared competence alone, it exercises the shared competence only in the context of that agreement. In accordance with Article 2(2) TFEU, the Member States can continue to exercise that shared competence internally and in relation to other third states, as long as they do not affect the functioning of the agreement concluded by the EU, and EU law more generally. The Member States' ability to act alone, internally or externally, in areas of shared competence governed by an EU-only agreement thus depends on the degree of substantive harmonisation brought about by that agreement. Most provisions of the TCA in fields of shared competence are specific to the relations between the EU and the UK, and should

[56] C Eckes and P Leino-Sandberg, 'The EU-UK Trade and Cooperation Agreement: Exceptional Circumstances or a New Paradigm for EU External Relations?' (2022) 85 *Modern Law Review* 164, 166, 182 et seq.

[57] Article 2(1) TFEU stipulates that the Member States may only act in areas of EU exclusive competence if so empowered by the EU or for the implementation of EU acts. See also Case 104/81, *Kupferberg*, EU:C:1982:362, paras 11–12.

[58] Article 216(2) TFEU.

[59] See, eg, Kamerstukken II, 2020–2021, 35393, Nr 13.

[60] Council Decision (EU) 2020/2252 (n 8) indent 15.

[61] Council Legal Service opinion (n 48) paras 37 et seq.

[62] Opinion of Cruz Villalón, Case C-414/11, *Daiichi Sankyo*, EU:C:2013:49, para 60. *Contra*, see opinion of Advocate General Wahl, Opinion 3/15, *Marrakesh Treaty*, EU:C:2016:657, para 148. See also Chapter 3, section III.A.

therefore not become an obstacle to the Member States' independent external relations with other third countries. The TCA even leaves some room for the Member States to make their own bilateral agreements with the UK. The precise conditions for making such 'top-ups' by the Member States are governed by the TCA itself.[63]

On request of the Member States in the Council, the Commission confirmed in a statement attached to the Council minutes that the exercise of shared competence by the EU in the context of the TCA does not constitute a legal restriction on the exercise of those powers in future agreements with third countries.[64] Although the statement itself remains confidential, one can infer from its existence and the CLS opinion that the institutions agree that the political choice to make an EU-only agreement does not establish a legal precedent and does not affect the Member States' independent external relations capacity with other third states. In the future, the statements and opinions made by the Commission and the Council in the context of the ratification of the TCA may well be drawn upon and could facilitate a more informed (inter-)institutional debate about making a facultative EU-only or a facultative mixed agreement on a case-by-case basis, rather than opting for mixity purely as a matter of principle. From that perspective, the conclusion of the TCA may well serve as a precedent, albeit a practical one.

IV. Provisional Application

The previous chapter explained that EU-only trade agreements concluded under the new architecture will generally not be applied provisionally.[65] The TCA is, once again, a special case. In accordance with Article 783(2) TCA, the EU and the UK decided to provisionally apply the TCA in full as of 1 January 2021. The choice against mixity facilitated the provisional application of the TCA in full, which in turn enabled the EU and the UK to avoid the consequences of a 'hard Brexit' in all areas covered by the agreement (section IV.A). The fact that the decision on signature and provisional application had to be taken in less than a week's time adversely affected the position of the EP in the final stages of the ratification process. Arguably, the EP nonetheless emerged empowered from the process of making the TCA (section IV.B).

A. Provisional Application and the Choice Against Mixity

As was mentioned in the previous section, the desire to provisionally apply the TCA in full was a key driver for the Council's political decision to make an EU-only and not a mixed agreement. As was explained in Chapter 5, the Member States may decide to adopt an independent decision on the provisional application of a mixed agreement alongside the EU if the scope of provisional application not only comprises EU-exclusive but also shared competences. However, in some Member States, provisional application

[63] See, eg, Article 419(4) TCA. See also Articles 6–8 of Council Decision (EU) 2020/2252 (n 8).
[64] The existence of the statement is noted in Kamerstukken II (n 59).
[65] *cf* Chapter 7, section IV.D.

is only possible in exceptional situations (eg, Belgium, Denmark and France), while in other Member States (eg, Germany), national parliaments are legally required to approve of the provisional application of an international agreement.[66] Therefore, it would have been legally and/or practically unfeasible for some Member States to adopt an individual decision on the provisional application of the parts of the TCA falling within shared competence in time. The Member States did also not desire to carve out the parts of the TCA that fall within shared competence from the scope of provisional application, as they had done for CETA, for example,[67] because of the severe economic and social effects of a 'hard Brexit' in these fields.[68] As facultative mixed agreements are made on the premise that the shared competence is exercised by the Member States, it would have been legally contradictory to sign and conclude the TCA as a mixed agreement, while allowing the EU to exercise the shared competence temporarily, as it were, during the provisional application of the agreement.[69] As a result, the Council decided to exercise shared competence at the EU level for the signature, provisional application and conclusion of the TCA.

B. The Role of the European Parliament

As mentioned above, the EP and the Commission cooperated closely during much of the negotiations, 'which ensured [that the EP's] positions were fully reflected in the EU's initial mandate and defended by the EU's Chief Negotiator during the course of negotiations'.[70] The inclusion of the EP in the making of the TCA significantly decreased during the final stages of the ratification process. In particular, the Commission did not await the EP's consent before proposing the Council decision on the signature and provisional application of the TCA. This was not the first time that the Commission deviated from its informal practice to ask the EP to give its formal consent to EU trade and investment agreements before such agreements are being applied provisionally. As was mentioned in Chapter 4, the EP was previously merely informed about the provisional application of the Association Agreements with Georgia, Moldova and Ukraine.[71] However, before voting on her candidacy, Ursula von der Leyen had promised the EP that her Commission will '*always* propose that provisional application of trade agreements take place only once the European Parliament has given its consent' (emphasis added).[72] The case of the TCA showed that 'always' apparently meant 'categorically, unless the matter is exceptionally timely or technical'. As the negotiators could only reach an agreement on the text of the TCA on 24 December 2020, the EP would have had only one week to issue its consent prior to the agreement's envisaged provisional application

[66] See further Chapter 5, section VI.
[67] See further Chapter 4, section IV.D.
[68] See Kamerstukken II (n 45).
[69] See further Chapter 4, section IV.C.
[70] EP resolution of 28 April 2021 (n 23) para 7.
[71] *cf* Chapter 4, section IV.B.
[72] U von der Leyen, Candidate for President of the European Commission, 'A Union That Strives for More: My Agenda for Europe' (2019), https://commission.europa.eu/system/files/2020-04/political-guidelines-next-commission_en_0.pdf, 17.

as of 1 January 2021. This would have implied rubber-stamping the agreement rather than thoroughly reviewing its content. In view of these time limits, the Commission and the Council made use of their legal prerogative to decide on the provisional application alone.[73] The EP, in turn, took its time to scrutinise the TCA. Article 783(2)(a) TCA envisioned the provisional application to end on 28 February 2021. However, the EP requested an extension of the duration of provisional application to allow sufficient time to review the text of the TCA. As the EP's consent is required for the conclusion of the TCA pursuant to Article 218(6)(a)(i) TFEU, the Commission, the Council and the UK government had no choice but to extend the provisional application of the TCA until 30 April 2021.[74] The EP formally approved the conclusion of the TCA on 28 April with a large majority (660 votes in favour, 5 against and 32 abstentions).[75]

In its resolution on the outcome of the EU-UK negotiations, the EP strongly criticised 'the extreme last-minute nature of the Agreements' which, inter alia, 'impacted Parliament's prerogatives to scrutinise and apply democratic oversight of the final text of the Agreements ahead of their provisional application'.[76] The EP stressed that 'agreements must not be applied provisionally without the consent of Parliament' and that the ratification process of the TCA can 'in no way … constitute a precedent for future trade agreements'.[77] In a subsequent statement, the Commission vowed to do better in the future and promised to involve the EP more closely in the implementation of the TCA.[78]

Against that background, Larik noted that the EP 'emerged as an even more empowered institution' from the ratification process of the TCA.[79] This observation is arguably correct for at least three reasons. First, the EP was actively involved in the majority of the negotiation process and its positions are largely reflected in the text of the TCA. Second, it sharply criticised the Commission and the Council for not involving it sufficiently during the ratification stages, and the former felt compelled to respond to the EP's critique. Third, the EP (in sharp contrast to the UK House of Commons) took sufficient time to scrutinise the final text of the TCA.[80] In doing so, the EP became the 'most

[73] Article 218(5) TFEU. See also Chapter 4, section IV.B.

[74] Decision No 1/2021 of the Partnership Council established by the Trade and Cooperation Agreement between the European Union and the European Atomic Energy Community, of the one part, and the United Kingdom of Great Britain and Northern Ireland, of the other part of 23 February 2021 as regards the date on which provisional application pursuant to the Trade and Cooperation Agreement is to cease (2021/356) [2021] OJ L68/227. See also M Chamon, 'Extending Provisional Application of the TCA: A Matter of Democracy', *DCU Brexit Institute News*, 24 February 2021, dcubrexitinstitute.eu/2021/02/extending-provisional-application-of-the-tca.

[75] European Parliament, 'Parliament Formally Approves EU-UK Trade and Cooperation Agreement', press release (2021).

[76] EP resolution of 28 April 2021 (n 23) para 7.

[77] ibid.

[78] Commission statement on the role of the European Parliament in the implementation of the EU-UK Trade and Cooperation Agreement (2021), available at: politico.eu/wp-content/uploads/2021/04/27/20210422-Statement-to-EP-renumbered.pdf. On the role of the EP in the implementation of the TCA, see G Kübek, 'Institutional Framework and Governance' in Kübek, Tams and Terhechte (n 1) para 44.

[79] J Larik, '"The Mother of All Parliaments"? How the Ratification of the Trade and Cooperation Agreement Boosts the European Parliament's Profile', *DCU Brexit Institute News*, 29 April 2021, dcubrexitinstitute.eu/2021/04/the-mother-of-all-parliaments-how-the-ratification-of-the-trade-and-cooperation-agreement-boosts-the-european-parliaments-profile.

[80] ibid.

important instance of democratic oversight' in the ratification process of the TCA.[81] The EP's resolution of 28 April 2021 shows that it will insist on maintaining such a prominent role during the negotiations and ratification of future EU trade and investment agreements.

V. The Role of National Parliaments

National parliaments were involved in the making of the TCA from the outset. Several of them adopted detailed positions on the negotiations of a future relations agreement with the UK, addressed to their Member State's representative in the Council. For example, the French Senate issued a 'European resolution' in accordance with Article 88-4 of the French Constitution, in which it underlined its expectations of the content of the future agreement, particularly with regard to fisheries, transport and judicial cooperation in criminal matters.[82] Similarly, the German Federal Parliament issued an opinion on the opening of negotiations for a partnership agreement with the UK in accordance with Article 23(3) of the German Constitution.[83] Aside from substantive matters, the opinion also discussed the character of the envisaged agreement. It noted that 'for reasons of time, solutions that make entry into force by 1 January 2021 feasible are to be preferred, such as a pure EU agreement that must on the side of the EU only be ratified by the European Parliament and the Council'.[84] The German Federal Parliament thus explicitly requested the EU-only conclusion of the TCA from the outset. This example shows that national parliaments may sometimes support the political choice against mixity.

Although national parliaments had access to (confidential) negotiating documents,[85] they had little time to scrutinise the outcome of the negotiations due to the last-minute signature and conclusion of the TCA. In several Member States, the foreign ministry and/or the European Affairs Committee of Parliament issued public summaries of the agreement.[86] The Danish Foreign Ministry invited the Danish Parliament to technical briefings both during and immediately after the finalisation of the negotiations.[87] Some national parliaments questioned senior members of the EU or the Member State executive on the outcome of the TCA negotiations. For instance, the

[81] ibid.

[82] Résolution n° 75 (2019-2020), devenue résolution du Sénat le 6 mars 2020. See Chapter 5, section II.C.

[83] Deutscher Bundestag, Drucksache 19/17122 [2020]. See Chapter 5, section II.D.

[84] ibid 2 (translation by the author).

[85] For example, the Dutch government involved the Dutch Parliaments in the following ways: (1) by forwarding the preparatory documents of the European Council and Council meetings; (2) through public and/or technical briefings; and (3) by continuing to use reading rooms for confidential documents. See Kamerstukken II, 2016–2017, 23987, Nr 173.

[86] See, eg, for Denmark, Notat til Folketingets Europaudvalg og Udenrigspolitisk Nævn, Aftalen mellem EU og Storbritannien om det fremtidige forhold, Europaudvalget 2020–21 EUU Alm.del – Bilag 207 Offentligt; or for France, Commission des Affaires Européennes, L'accord entre le Royaume-Uni et l'Union européenne Note d'information [2021].

[87] Europaudvalget 2019–20 EUU Alm.del – Bilag 702 Offentligt [2020]; Udenrigsministeriet, Notat, Handels- og samarbejdsaftalen mellem EU og Storbritannien, 2020-1125, EKN [2021] Europaudvalget 2020–21 EUU Alm.del – Bilag 207 Offentligt.

Federal Advisory Committee for European Affairs of the Belgian Senate organised an exchange of thoughts with the prime minister of Belgium, Alexander De Croo.[88] Similarly, the Second Chamber of the Dutch Parliament organised a special type of session ('notaoverleg') that enables its members to discuss policies with the responsible member of government (in casu, Stephanus A Blok, the Foreign Minister of the Netherlands at the time).[89] Others, such as the German Federal Parliament, organised a public expert hearing.[90]

The debates in most national parliaments focused on the scope and substance of the TCA. Debates on the treaty-making procedure arose in the Dutch and German Parliaments. The Second Chamber of the Dutch Parliament was generally concerned about the EU-only nature of the TCA.[91] A day before the TCA was signed, it voted in favour of a motion stating that the choice against mixity should 'not create a legal or political precedent'.[92] It called on the Dutch government to embed this in the Council decisions on signature and conclusion.[93] As was mentioned above, the Council decisions indeed exclude the precedential nature of the TCA explicitly. In the debate with Mr Block, Members of Parliament inter alia demanded sufficient time for national parliaments to scrutinise agreements made by the EU, to be more actively involved in the political choices about the character of such agreements in the Council, and to be more actively involved during their implementation.[94] Conversely, the German Federal Parliament supported the EU-only conclusion of the TCA.[95] After various experts confirmed the legality of the Council's political choice to make an EU-only agreement, it approved of the TCA's character in a subsequently adopted resolution.[96] It further emphasised the importance of its indirect involvement in the EU-only ratification process through the German government for ensuring responsibility for EU integration.[97]

VI. Conclusion

In view of its scope, reach and political significance, the TCA is the most important trade agreement that the EU has concluded in the last decade. The process of making

[88] Belgische Senaat, 'Gedachtewisseling over de handels- en samenwerkingsovereenkomst tussen de EU en het VK' (2021).

[89] Kamerstukken II, 2020–2021, 35393, Nr 30.

[90] Deutscher Bundestag, Europaausschuss, 82. Sitzung 25 Januar 2021 – Öffentliche Anhörung.

[91] See also Eckes and Leino-Sandberg (n 56) 173.

[92] Kamerstukken II, 2020–2021, 35393, Nr 22.

[93] ibid.

[94] Kamerstukken II (n 89). The general political preference for mixity in and by the Netherlands is well documented in the literature. See especially LA Campo et al, 'The Netherlands and (Facultative) Mixity: Pragmatism over Principle?' in M Chamon and I Govaere (eds), *EU External Relations Law Post-Lisbon: The Law and Practice of Facultative Mixity* (Brill/Nijhoff 2020) 317; and I van der Steen, 'A View from the Netherlands' in C Hillion and P Koutrakos (eds), *Mixed Agreements Revisited: The EU and its Member States in the World* (Hart Publishing, 2010) 294.

[95] Deutscher Bundestag, Drucksache 19/28793 [2021].

[96] ibid. See further n 90 above, especially the opinions by Professor Dr Daniel Thym, Professor Dr Holger Hestermeyer and Professor Dr Paulina Starski.

[97] Deutscher Bundestag (n 95). On the concept of responsibility for integration under German constitutional law, see Chapter 5, section IV.D.

the TCA has been unusual in many respects. It is an agreement concluded with a state that has withdrawn from the EU. It is tied to the Withdrawal Agreement in both form and procedure. It is, essentially, an agreement about dissociation rather than association. The 'exceptional and unique'[98] character of the TCA can be explained by politics and the progress of the negotiations. Its character as an Association Agreement results from the EU's insistence on the indivisibility of the negotiations, which in turn resulted in the design of a single comprehensive 'trade and …' agreement. Notably, investment protection and investor-state dispute settlement were carved out from the scope of the negotiating directives of the TCA. The TCA was thus deliberately designed to include only EU exclusive and shared competences, leaving the Member States in the Council with a political choice at the end of the negotiation process to sign and conclude either an EU-only or a mixed agreement. The Council ultimately chose the former option, as an agreement on the final text of the TCA could only be reached at the eleventh hour. Mixity would have, inter alia, implied that the Member States had to issue individual decisions on the provisional application of the TCA for the parts of the agreement falling within shared competence. In some Member States, that would have been practically unfeasible because of national constitutional law requirements. In view of the consequences of a 'hard Brexit' in sub-areas, the Council decided to exercise shared competence at the EU level for the signature, provisional application and conclusion of the TCA. The EU institutions and the Member States emphasised that the way in which the TCA was made does not establish a legal precedent for their joint and individual external relations.

This chapter has argued that the making of the TCA may nonetheless serve as a practical example in two main ways. First, the negotiations of the TCA exemplified how unity can be achieved through close cooperation between the EU institutions on the one hand, and between the EU institutions and the Member States on the other hand. Throughout much of the negotiations, there was frequent consultation between the Commission and the EP, and the latter was able to voice its opinions on a regular basis. The broad overlap between the EP's positions and the Council's negotiating directives were noteworthy even for Parliament,[99] and the resulting congruence between the EP's resolutions and the final text of the TCA may partially explain why the EP approved of the TCA with an overwhelming majority. The Member States were closely involved in the negotiations through the special Council Working Party on the UK, COREPER and in their own right, which by inference strengthened the position of national parliaments acting via their governments. This may explain why in the case of the TCA – in contrast to, for example, CETA – none of the Member States tried to use their veto rights in the Council as leverage to extract individual concessions or to make bilateral 'side-deals' with the UK. The case of the TCA thus outlined how EU trade and investment negotiations can be made inclusive and cooperative while reaching unity. That unity was threatened during the ratification stages of the TCA. The last-minute nature of the agreement particularly affected the position of the EP, as there was no time to await its consent before the agreement was applied provisionally. By insisting on having sufficient

[98] Council Decision (EU) 2020/2252 (n 8) indent 6.
[99] EP recommendation of 18 June 2020 (n 23) para 5; and EP resolution of 28 April 2021 (n 4) para 7.

time to scrutinise the agreement, the EP nonetheless emerged empowered from the ratification process of the TCA. Yet, as the EP itself stressed, the lack of involvement of the EP in the final stages of making the TCA cannot constitute a precedent for the making of future EU trade and investment agreements.

Second, the negotiations of the TCA exemplified that the EU institutions and the Member States are occasionally willing to determine the character of a facultative agreement on a case-by-case basis. The signature and conclusion of the TCA broke with the Council's principled opinion that Association Agreements should be mixed. The Member States in the Council balanced the benefits and costs of the EU-only and the mixed procedure, and decided that the former was more suitable for the special case of the TCA. The Council's political choice to conclude the TCA under the EU-only procedure facilitated its full provisional application and its swift entry into force. In view of the political and economic importance of the TCA, the risk of non-ratification inherent in the mixed procedure was apparently considered too high by Member State governments, which in any case held veto rights over the signature and conclusion of the TCA in the Council.[100] The CLS confirmed the legality of the Council's political choices and underlined that the use of the facultative EU-only procedure does not affect the Member States' ability to make agreements with other third states in fields of shared competence. The Commission re-iterated the latter in a separate statement. Noticeably, there was little backlash by national parliaments against the Council's political choice to ratify the TCA under the EU-only procedure. The discussions in national parliaments were largely focused on the substance of the TCA, with few exceptions. The German Federal Parliament advocated the use of the EU-only procedure from the outset of the negotiation process. It monitored the debate at the EU level and sought to influence the position of the German representative in the Council. The Second Chamber of the Dutch Parliament was more critical of the EU-only character of the TCA. Yet, it did not oppose the conclusion of the TCA as such. Overall, the legal views expressed by national governments, parliaments, the Commission and the Council indicate that they have come to understand the complexity of facultative mixity and have started to make use of the Council's discretion to determine the treaty-making procedure of agreements falling within shared competence more deliberately, depending on the specific legal, political and economic situation at hand. By making more deliberate choices about mixity, also in the facultative scenario, on the basis of an informed and public debate, the EU institutions and the Member States could make full use of the clarity, flexibility, effectiveness and inclusiveness that the post-Lisbon division of competences and resulting practice has to offer. In doing so, the EU would continue to *move beyond mixity*.

[100] Article 218(8) TFEU.

9

Conclusion

Moving Beyond Mixity

In the post-Lisbon era, the EU has begun to *move beyond mixity* for the making of trade and investment agreements. The CJEU illuminated a new division of commercial treaty-making powers between the EU and the Member States, and largely clarified who is competent to exercise these powers, which in turn affected the way in which trade and investment agreements are designed and concluded. By analysing the interrelationship between treaty-making power and procedure, this book has brought to light the legal, inter-institutional and practical consequences of *moving beyond mixity* for the making of EU trade and investment agreements post-Lisbon.

This volume has argued that for the specific case of the EU's trade and investment policy, mixity has become a substantive design choice, to be made at the outset of the treaty-making process. To make that choice, the EU institutions must carefully balance the costs and benefits of using either the EU-only or the mixed procedure for that agreement's content and ratification process. The adoption of the new architecture highlighted that in the field of trade, this balancing exercise principally tilts in favour of the procedural effectiveness, unity and certainty that the EU-only procedure provides. There is still room for mixity, albeit less so. The EU's treaty-making practice since *Opinion 2/15* suggests that the EU institutions have begun to make more deliberate design and/or political choices in favour or against mixity, rather than opting for mixity purely as a matter of path-dependency or principle. This is not to say that the EU's recent trade practice has always been consistent. Overall, however, the EU managed to link substance to procedure more carefully. Room for improvement remains, especially when it comes to anticipating and addressing the consequences of using either the EU-only or the mixed procedure in both EU and national constitutional law and practice head-on.

Against this background, this concluding chapter systematically summarises the main themes and findings of this book.

I. Mixity as a Substantive Design Choice

The practice of mixity is complex and intricate. It brings to the fore the essential features of the EU's integration process and structure. In doing so, it raises questions about power, procedure and public participation in EU external relations.

Despite their virtual absence in the EU's founding treaties, mixed agreements have become an established practice in EU external relations. Following Heliskoski's pioneering book, mixed agreements were generally justified for procedural reasons.[1] As a concrete attribution of competence between the EU and the Member States was lacking in most policy fields, mixity enabled legal flexibility at the start of the negotiation process. It allowed the EU and the Member States to enter into treaty negotiations jointly and without first solving lengthy competence disputes, including before the CJEU.

In the post-Lisbon era, that reasoning has been overhauled for the EU's external trade and investment policy.[2] *Opinion 2/15* provided an ex ante review of the reach and limits of the EU's exclusive competence in the field of trade and investment. As a result, there is no longer a need to use mixity as a technique to overcome legal uncertainties about competence disputes. *Opinion 2/15* illuminates with sufficient clarity which substantive issues areas included in (formerly) comprehensive trade and investment protection agreements (may) trigger mixity. Knowledge about the triggers of mixity enable the negotiators to deliberately design either EU-only or mixed trade and investment agreements. To do so, they must carefully weigh the benefits of mixity (eg, making more comprehensive agreements) against the costs of including a multitude of veto players (eg, increased uncertainty about entry into force). This analysis may well yield different results for different treaty partners and/or types of agreements. Under the new architecture, the EU has begun to consistently design EU-only FTAs, thereby shielding large parts of formerly comprehensive trade and investment protection agreements from the many problems caused by mixity.[3]

II. More Power, More Unity, More Effectiveness

The design of the (then) EEC as a customs union shows that the Member States intended, from the moment of the EEC's inception, to transfer all of their powers with regard to external trade to the supranational level. However, the international trade agenda soon expanded beyond the reduction of tariff barriers. With the inclusion of 'behind the border issues' in international economic law and policy, a gap between the scope of the (now) EU's constitutionally guaranteed trade powers and its external trade ambitions emerged – and with it a long-standing conflict between the EU institutions inter se, as well as between the EU and the Member States, including before the CJEU, about who is competent to make international agreements in the field of trade and investment.[4]

Opinion 2/15 delivered much-anticipated and needed clarity about the vertical division of competence over trade and investment post-Lisbon.[5] By concluding that all areas of EU new generation trade and investment agreements except foreign non-direct investments and ISDS fall within the EU's exclusive competence, the CJEU provided an

[1] J Heliskoski, *Mixed Agreements as a Technique for Organizing the International Relations of the European Community and its Member States* (Kluwer Law International, 2001).
[2] See Chapter 1, sections III and IV.
[3] See Chapter 7, section II.
[4] See Chapter 3, section I.
[5] Opinion 2/15, *FTA with Singapore*, EU:C:2017:376.

expansive approach to the scope of the CCP and the EU's otherwise implied exclusive competence.[6] In doing so, the CJEU linked the EU's trade policy back to its original purpose: an external policy of a supranational character that results as a logical consequence of a common internal market and customs union. Yet, adding a degree of flexibility to a methodological approach might come at the cost of reliability. From that perspective, further clarifications by the CJEU of the contours of its centre of gravity and ERTA tests would be desirable.[7]

Opinion 2/15 further set out the EU's capacity and mandate to pursue a value-driven trade policy. Following its reasoning in *Philippines Framework Agreement*,[8] the CJEU found that the express nexus between the EU's external (commercial) actions (especially Articles 205 and 207 TFEU), on the one hand, and its external relations objectives (especially Articles 3(5) and 21 TEU), on the other hand, connotates these objectives as an integral part of EU trade policy.[9] The CJEU's conclusions suggest that the pursuit of a value-driven trade policy is not merely a matter of political preference, but of law. However, in order to qualify as a CCP measure, value-driven EU trade instruments (like any other trade instruments) must display direct and immediate effects on international trade. Since *Opinion 2/15*, the EU has been more explicit about its strategy to use trade power as a lever to pursue wider external relations objectives.[10] Yet, this strategy only works if the EU can externally demonstrate its trade power through unified positions and actions.

The establishment of the new architecture aligns the EU's external power with its treaty-making capacity and ambition. As mentioned earlier, FTAs are now concluded as mandatory EU-only agreements.[11] As a result, individual Member State governments and/or parliaments can no longer legally prevent the EU from exercising its exclusive external trade competence. Provided that the Member States in the Council, per QMV, and the EP agree on signing and concluding an EU-only FTA, the threat of non-ratification by a single Member State – and the possibility for individual rent-seeking in that context[12] – disappears.[13] This increases the EU's international reputation, credibility and, ultimately, unity.

Aside from increasing unity, the *move beyond mixity* in the field of trade policy significantly increased the effectiveness of EU treaty-making. On the one hand, using the EU-only procedure streamlines the negotiation process.[14] The Commission negotiates trade and investment agreements on behalf of the EU. The Member States authorise and instruct the Commission jointly via the Council, but do not participate in the negotiations in their own right. On the other hand, using the EU-only procedure speeds up

[6] See Chapter 3, section III.
[7] See Chapter 3, sections II, III and V.
[8] Case C-377/12, *Philippines Framework Agreement*, EU:C:2014:1903.
[9] See Chapter 3, section III.C.
[10] See, eg, European Commission, Trade Policy Review: An Open, Sustainable and Assertive Trade Policy, COM (2021) 66 final, 1.
[11] See Chapter 2, section II.
[12] A case in point is the rejection of CETA by the Cypriot Parliament in order to extract increased protection for the denomination of Halloumi cheese. See further Chapter 6, section I.
[13] See Chapter 7, section V.
[14] See Chapter 4, section II.

the ratification process and enhances certainty over a signed treaty's entry into force.[15] Indeed, the complexity of mixed treaty ratification can hardly be overstated. Belgium, where mixed EU trade and investment agreements simultaneously classify as inner-Belgian mixed agreements (a case of double mixity, as it were), is a prime example.[16] No less than five sub-national parliaments, in addition to the Federal Chamber of Representatives, must agree on the ratification of mixed agreements by Belgium alone. The *move beyond mixity* implies that the EU can conclude trade agreements without its Member States, in accordance with the procedural rules set out in Articles 207 and 218 TFEU. As a result, agreements that previously took five years and more to ratify and whose entry into force was clouded with considerable uncertainty can now be applied within a few months after their signature on a permanent basis.[17]

In sum, the possibility of making EU-only FTAs enables the EU to (re-)assert its role as one of the most powerful and effective players on the global economic stage. It ensures a more unified position of the EU in favour or against external action in the field of trade – a field where the (sub-)national veto was never designed to exist in the first place.

III. Less Scope for Mixity

Opinion 2/15 and the resulting new architecture have considerably narrowed the scope for mixity. However, this does not imply that mixity is no longer relevant. Mixed agreements will continue to occur in practice, including in the field of trade and investment. *Opinion 2/15* outlined clear limits to the reach of EU exclusivity in the field of investment.[18] *Opinion 1/17* confirmed the compatibility of the ICS with EU law.[19] In the latter decision, the CJEU set out several conditions for the design of investment protection agreements that are met by the EU, but not by the Member States acting alone. In doing so, the CJEU pointed out that there is scope for further (mixed) integration through joint investment policy reform, such as the MIC.

In *Opinion 2/15*, the CJEU confirmed that ISDS/ICS and foreign non-direct investments fall within a competence shared between the EU and the Member States. In *COTIF I*, the CJEU clarified that mixity is facultative for the latter discipline.[20] It remains unclear if mixity is also facultative for agreements containing an ICS.[21] While it is clear that the competence for ISDS/ICS is shared, it is not clear whether the EU is capable of exercising that shared competence alone. Practice indicates ongoing inter-institutional disputes between the Commission and the Council on that very issue. The new architecture facilitated political compromise by establishing that

[15] See Chapter 4, sections III and V.
[16] See Chapter 5, section V. On Belgium specifically, see Chapter 5, section V.A.
[17] See Chapter 7, section IV.
[18] See Chapter 3, section IV.
[19] Opinion 1/17, *Comprehensive Economic and Trade Agreement with Canada*, EU:C:2019:341. See further Chapter 3, section IV.C.
[20] See Chapter 2, section IV.
[21] See Chapter 3, section IV.B.

EU IPAs will in practice be concluded as self-standing mixed agreements alongside EU-only FTAs.[22] For IPAs, mixity therefore continues to serve its 'original' purpose of overcoming legal uncertainties about inner-EU competence divides, thereby enabling the EU and the Member States to enter into treaty negotiations.[23] The new architecture further established that Association Agreements will principally be concluded as mixed agreements. However, the case of the TCA illustrated that there is some room for exceptions, at least for Association Agreements that deliberately carve out investment protection disciplines.[24]

While the new architecture principally sets out the choice in favour or against mixity in the field of trade and investment, it does not streamline the mixed procedure as such. The mixed procedure transcends international, EU and national constitutional legal orders, without being expressly recognised by either of them.[25] The law defines the contours of mixity, such as the vertical allocation of competence, but the specificities of using the mixed procedure largely emerge from practice. Indeed, the complexity of mixity can often only be managed by practical flexibility and pragmatism. For example, the choice of who represents the EU in treaty negotiations is rarely made on the basis of strict competence delineations, although – at least in the field of trade and investment – it is clear who has the power.[26] In the past, during so-called mixed negotiations, the Member States sometimes participated in their own right in the negotiations, including for bilateral agreements.[27] Under the new architecture, the Commission negotiates both EU-only FTAs and mixed IPAs alone because, in a bilateral setting, the costs of coordinating a large delegation are higher than the benefits of maintaining it.[28] The negotiations of the TCA have shown that close cooperation between the Commission and Member State governments does not have to come at a cost for the Commission as the sole negotiator of EU-only agreements, and may forestall conflicting positions or actions by the Member States in their own right.[29]

As the EU now makes a deliberate substantive design choice in favour of mixity for comprehensive trade and/or investment protection agreements, flexibility and pragmatism should in future practice be coupled with foresight to tackle the known problems of mixity head-on. The risk of non-ratification of mixed agreements could, for example, already be addressed during the treaty design stage, ie, before a non-ratification drama like CETA unfolds.[30] One solution would be to re-design the entry into force clause of 'bilateral' mixed agreements that, as a matter of procedure, include at least 29 parties. In doing so, incomplete mixity – ie, the ratification of an agreement by the EU and only some of its Member States – would become an integral part of the design of bilateral mixed agreements. In *Opinion 1/19*, the CJEU recognised the practice of incomplete

[22] See Chapter 7.
[23] See Chapter 1, section IV.A.
[24] See Chapter 8, sections I and III.B.
[25] See Chapter 2, section III; and Chapter 4, section I.
[26] The same is true for the design of separate EU FTAs and IPAs, which is as much informed by pragmatism as it is by competence allocations. See Chapter 7, section III.
[27] See Chapter 4, section II.C.
[28] See Chapter 7, section IV.A.
[29] See Chapter 8, section II.
[30] See Chapter 6.

mixity as a solution to the non-ratification scenario.[31] While that practice comes with its own challenges, it may at times be better to embrace these challenges than to not conclude the agreement at all, as the EU's accession to the Istanbul Convention in 2023 highlighted.

Provisional application is another valuable tool to tackle one of the main problems of mixity, namely the long duration between a mixed agreement's signature and entry into force.[32] Legal and practical problems have emerged in the context of the provisional application of facultative mixed agreements. In the context of facultative mixity, the inclusion of areas of shared competence (exercised by the Member States) is the basis for making the agreement mixed in the first place. If the Council were to decide to exercise the shared competence at the EU level during the period of provisional application, it could risk offsetting the very foundation for choosing to make a mixed agreement. As a result, the Council usually decides to carve out areas of shared competence from the scope of a mixed agreement's provisional application. Yet, the Council's practice is neither consistent nor fully clear, especially not for third states unfamiliar with the EU's internal competence divisions. Further problems emerge if the EU and the Member States wish to apply a facultative mixed agreement provisionally in full.[33] The national constitutional laws of several Member States do not recognise provisional application. Some Member States require prior parliamentary approval, while others only permit provisional application in exceptional circumstances or not at all. As a result, it would be difficult for all the Member States to adopt individual decisions on the provisional application of facultative mixed agreements for the parts falling within shared competence. Recent practice, such as ratification of the TCA, indicates that the EU exercises shared competence for the signature, provisional application and conclusion of agreements the Member States in the Council desire give full effect to before their entry into force.[34]

IV. More Deliberate Political Choices

The *COTIF I* judgment confirmed that mixity in areas of shared competence is facultative and therefore at the political discretion of the Council.[35] In past practice, it has rarely been relevant whether mixity was required as a matter of law or not, as the Council opted for mixity out of principle as soon as an agreement (also) covered areas of shared competence.[36] Furthermore, history showed that mixity has been path-dependent. Once mixity was chosen, it became the default option for making agreements in a given policy field.[37]

In future practice, the choice in favour or against mixity for facultative agreements may become more deliberate. This is, on the one hand, due to the fact that the law

[31] Opinion 1/19, *Istanbul Convention*, EU:C:2021:832, paras 258–59.
[32] See Chapter 4, section IV.
[33] See Chapter 5, section VI.
[34] See Chapter 8, section IV.
[35] Case C-600/14, *COTIF I*, EU:C:2017:935.
[36] See Chapter 2, sections III and IV.
[37] See Chapter 1, section III.

has drawn some contours around the Council's political choices. The CJEU clarified in *Antarctic MPAs* that mixity may be legally required in areas of shared competence for overriding reasons of international law.[38] Further legal limits to the Council's political choice arguably arise from the principle of sincere cooperation (Article 4(3) TEU) and for agreements that concern a single subject area falling within shared competence (hybridity).[39]

On the other hand, practice indicates that the Member States in the Council have begun to draw a distinction between mandatory and facultative mixed agreements, and to make use of the Council's discretion to determine the treaty-making procedure of agreements falling within shared competence more deliberately, depending on the specific legal, political and economic situation at hand.[40] The new architecture left some room to make EU trade agreements with important trading partners exceptionally under the mixed procedure.[41] On the flipside, as the agreements with the Kosovo and the UK demonstrate,[42] it leaves some room for concluding Association Agreements under the EU-only procedure. The various institutional statements issued in the context of the ratification of the EU-UK TCA may be drawn upon in future practice to inform the (inter-)institutional debate about making a facultative EU-only or a facultative mixed agreement on a case-by-case basis rather than opting for mixity purely as a matter of principle.[43]

V. More Parliamentary and National Constitutional Control

In the post-Lisbon era, the need to involve parliaments in the early stages of the treaty-making process has become evident in practice and has been frequently emphasised in scholarship.[44] Democratic control cannot be exercised by parliaments if they are merely being asked to rubber-stamp the final policy output. By integrating parliamentary views into the design of EU trade and investment agreements, the Commission and the Council can significantly reduce the risk of treaty rejection. This is particularly important for bilateral mixed agreements, which in the field of trade require the approval of around 40 (sub-)national parliaments before they can enter into force.[45] For EU-only agreements, the early involvement of national parliaments in the negotiating process may partially compensate the loss of parliamentary veto powers at the ratification stage and is therefore imperative. The question of how parliaments can be involved more closely in the process of making EU trade and investment agreements thus arises for

[38] Joined Cases C-626/15 and C-659/16, *Antarctic MPAs*, EU:C:2018:925. See further Chapter 2, section V.C.

[39] See Chapter 2, sections V.A and V.B.

[40] See Chapter 8.

[41] See Chapter 7, section II.

[42] Stabilisation and Association Agreement between the European Union and the European Atomic Energy Community, of the one part, and Kosovo, of the other part [2016] OJ L71/3; Trade and Cooperation Agreement between the European Union and the European Atomic Energy Community, of the one part, and the United Kingdom of Great Britain and Northern Ireland, of the other part [2021] OJ L149/10.

[43] See Chapter 8, section III.C.

[44] See Chapter 4, section II.A.

[45] See Chapter 5, section I.

EU-only and mixed agreements alike. Yet, the rationale for and the best way of doing so may differ depending on the character of the agreement.

For the making of EU-only agreements, the EP takes on its constitutionally assigned role as the main representative organ of EU citizens. In the post-Lisbon era, the EP has become a much more informed, effective and influential player in EU external relations in general, and for the making of trade and investment agreements specifically.[46] In the early post-Lisbon years, the EP has anchored its newly gained powers in institutional practice, including by successfully claiming breaches of procedural rules and the principle of institutional balance before the CJEU. In that early period, the EP also showed that it does not shy away from using its constitutionally assigned veto powers to forestall the ratification of EU agreements (eg, the SWIFT and ACTA cases). The EP has since demonstrated that it is capable of exercising its newly gained powers effectively and has exerted significant influence on the negotiations of EU trade and investment agreements. However, in recent years, the absence of certain actions by the EP, such as the decisions not to issue resolutions on the opening of negotiations for a MIC or the decision not to submit observations on *Opinion 1/17*, suggests that the EU's external trade and investment policy has become more controversial in the EP. As it is difficult for the Commission to address critique it has not formally received, the absence of an EP position reduces its influence on the policy design, potentially to a mere 'take it or leave it' decision. In other instances, the EP's position in the treaty-making process was reduced by the lack of informal inter-institutional cooperation. The signature and provisional application of the TCA is a case in point.[47] Contrary to established practice, the Commission did not await the EP's consent before proposing the Council decision on the signature and provisional application of the TCA. However, by aptly criticising the Commission and the Council while practically underlining the need for parliamentary involvement in the treaty-making process, the EP ensured that the TCA will not serve as a precedent in this respect.

Despite not having veto rights, national parliaments are involved in the making of EU-only trade and investment agreements. First, they can enter into dialogue with the EU institutions directly (eg, the Barroso initiative, visits by the Commission lead negotiators and joint letters addressed to the EU institutions).[48] These practices are largely informal and the extent to which they are used varies depending on the salience of the respective agreement. Thus, there is room for formalisation and consistency. Second, national parliaments can indirectly participate in the making of EU-only agreements through their representative in the Council.[49] Notably, the Member States re-thought the traditional prerogative of the executive in foreign policy for one particular type of 'foreign policy', namely EU policy. As the transfer of competence from the national to the supranational level took away powers from national parliaments, national constitutional laws and practices were established in most Member States to elevate the role of (sub-)national parliaments in EU matters. In particular, these national laws and practices enable national parliaments to be informed about and participate in the

[46] See Chapter 4, especially section II.D.
[47] See Chapter 8, section IV.B.
[48] See Chapter 4, sections II.D, III.A and VI.
[49] See Chapter 5.

formation of EU policies. As a result, national parliaments have access to the EU's negotiation positions for trade and investment agreements, and many have a formal right to issue an opinion on the position their government takes in the Council. In most Member States, national parliaments therefore have a greater say on the formation of EU foreign policy than they have on the formation of their own Member State's foreign policy.[50] The extent to which national parliaments have a decisive influence on their Member State's position on EU (external) matters varies significantly between the Member States.[51] By making their position in the Council conditional on prior parliamentary approval, national governments could significantly enhance the influence of (sub-)national parliaments on the formation of EU trade and investment policy. The Danish mandate procedure, according to which the Danish representative in the Council only votes in favour of a proposal if the majority of the Danish Parliament's European Affairs Committee is not against it, is a case in point. In some Member States, a similar practice could be adopted with a few constitutional twists. In others, it would be more complex. For example, the Belgian position in the Council on trade matters can only be established by consensus between six (sub-)federal entities. Giving (sub-)national parliaments a decisive say on the Belgian position in the Council on trade matters would further complicate the decision-making process.

Mixity downgrades the role of the EP and turns, as it were, EU citizens into national citizens. At the same time, it elevates the role of national parliaments, giving them a decisive say on the ratification of an agreement both within the Council (as a matter of practice) and by their Member State (as a matter of law). In recent years, mixity has also raised questions within the national constitutional legal orders of the Member States, particularly with regard to the mandatory participation of (sub-)federal chambers and the applicable voting rules in national parliaments.[52] The resulting debates made national parliaments more knowledgeable about mixity. Coupled with the increased political salience of trade policy, national parliaments have emerged as prominent actors in the making of EU trade and investment agreements post-Lisbon. Whereas national parliaments in the past approved mixed trade and investment agreements frequently without a formal debate or a vote, they have become much more vocal in recent practice. The veto rights allocated to (sub-)national parliaments under the mixed procedure significantly enhances their political leverage. However, the various CETA incidents showed that some national parliaments may use that leverage to extract individual concessions at the cost of paralysing EU external action.[53] These experiences may also explain why other national parliaments have requested a *move beyond mixity* in politically delicate circumstances (eg, the German Federal Parliament in the case of the TCA).[54]

Ultimately, national constitutional courts retain the final say on the conclusion of EU trade and investment agreements.[55] The scope of review of national constitutional courts is larger for mixed than for EU-only agreements. Yet, recent practice shows that

[50] See Chapter 5, section III.F.
[51] See Chapter 5, section IV.
[52] See Chapter 5, section V.
[53] See Chapter 6, section I.
[54] See Chapter 8, section V.
[55] See Chapter 5, section VII.

the ultra vires and constitutional identity review allow national courts to ensure the compatibility of EU trade and investment agreements with national constitutional law irrespective of their character. The CETA cases before the highest French, German and Irish courts demonstrate that national constitutional perspectives on EU trade and investment policy can differ fundamentally, posing unprecedented challenges to both the EU and the national legislature.

VI. Moving Beyond Mixity

Discussions about mixity largely centred on the question of 'who has power'. The answer to that question was rather simple: either the EU or the Member States. As soon as the Member States had some power, the agreement was principally concluded under the mixed procedure. Recent developments changed this rationale and practice for the making of EU trade and investment agreements. The division of competence between the EU and the Member States has been sufficiently clarified by the CJEU in *Opinion 2/15*. In the light of new case law (eg, *COTIF I, Opinion 1/19*) and practice (eg, the various CETA crises and the new architecture), the discussions about mixity began to shift from asking 'who has power?' to 'who should exercise that power?' While the answer to the latter question remains a binary choice (the EU acting alone or together with the Member States), it requires taking account of the broader effects of asserting power. Notably, the EU is now in a position to anchor these considerations in the substantive design of its trade and investment agreements.

The question of whether the EU should act with or without the Member States on the external plane is ultimately a question about the (desired) depth of supranational integration. It is about balancing the benefits of a more capable and unified EU against the costs of narrowing the Member States' independent scope of action in external relations. It is about considering the consequences of allocating a multitude of veto rights, and about the forms and modalities of parliamentary participation in external decision-making at the EU level and at the Member State level.

For agreements that principally fall within EU exclusive competence, such as EU trade and investment liberalisation agreements, the *move beyond mixity* through deliberate substantive treaty design is arguably the right one. The procedural effectiveness provided by the EU-only mode enables the EU to remain a power in and through trade in times of rising geopolitical instability. For other types of agreements, the decision to make an EU-only or a mixed agreement may not be as clear-cut. Yet, that decision should arguably remain a careful and deliberate one. Recent trade practice, such as the new architecture or the TCA, highlights that the EU and the Member States have begun to make more informed and intentional design and/or political choices in favour or against mixity. This change in practice and perspective is arguably imperative: in view of the threat of internal dis-integration and the trend towards global isolationism and protectionism, it is all the more important to carefully decide by whom, with whom and in what way external power should be exercised.

BIBLIOGRAPHY

I. Monographs and Edited Volumes

Abazi, V, *Official Secrets and Oversight in the European Union: Law and Practices of Classified Information* (Oxford, Oxford University Press, 2019)

Besselink, LFM and Wessel, RA, *De invloed van ontwikkelingen in de internationale rechtsorde op de doorwerking naar Nederlands constitutioneel recht. Een 'neo-monistische' benadering* (Deventer, Kluwer, 2009)

Bollrath, L, *Die Vertragsschlusskompetenz der Europäischen Gemeinschaft auf dem Gebiet der Gemeinsamen Handelspolitik* (Baden-Baden, Nomos, 2008)

Brand, F, *Europapolitische Kommunikation zwischen Bundestag und Bundesregierung: Die Umsetzung der parlamentarischen Mitwirkungs- und exekutiven Kooperationspflicht nach Art. 23 Abs. 2 und Abs. 3 GG* (Berlin, Duncker & Humblot, 2015)

Bungenberg, M and Herrmann, C (eds), *Common Commercial Policy after Lisbon*, Special Issue, *European Yearbook of International Economic Law* (Berlin, Springer, 2013)

Butler, G, *Constitutional Law of the EU's Common Foreign and Security Policy: Competence and Institutions in External Relations* (Oxford, Hart Publishing, 2019)

Corten, O and Klein, P (eds), *The Vienna Conventions on the Law of Treaties: A Commentary* (Oxford, Oxford University Press, 2011)

De Baere, G, *Constitutional Principles of EU External Relations* (Oxford, Oxford University Press, 2008)

De Ville, F and Siles-Brügge, G, *TTIP: The Truth about the Transatlantic Trade and Investment Partnership* (London, Polity Press, 2016)

Del Grosso, NY, *Parlement en Europese integratie* (Deventer, Kluwer, 2000)

Delgado Casteleiro, A, *The International Responsibility of the European Union: From Competence to Normative Control* (Cambridge, Cambridge University Press, 2016)

Delpérée, F, *Le droit constitutionnel de la Belgique* (Brussels, Bruylant, 2000)

Demper, M, *Kooperationsstrukturen und Kooperationsvereinbarungen zwischen der EU und den Mitgliedstaaten im Rahmen gemischter Abkommen* (Baden-Baden, Nomos, 2018)

Dimopoulos, A, *EU Foreign Investment Law* (Oxford, Oxford University Press, 2011)

Dörr, O and Schmalenbach, K (eds), *Vienna Convention on the Law of Treaties: A Commentary* (Berlin, Springer, 2012)

Eckes, C, *EU Powers Under External Pressure: How the EU's External Actions Alter its Internal Structures* (Oxford, Oxford University Press, 2019)

Eeckhout, P, *EU External Relations law*, 2nd edn (Oxford, Oxford University Press, 2011)

Fabbrini, F (ed), *The Withdrawal Agreement: The Law and Politics of Brexit, Volume II* (Oxford, Oxford University Press, 2020)

——. (ed), *The Framework of the New EU-UK Relations: The Law and Politics of Brexit, Volume III* (Oxford, Oxford University Press, 2021)

Fahey, E, *The EU as a Global Digital Actor: Institutionalising Global Data Protection, Trade, and Cybersecurity* (Oxford, Hart Publishing, 2022)

Fuchs-Cessot, A, *Le Parlement à l'épreuve de l'Europe et de la Ve République* (Paris, Librairie générale de droit et de jurisprudence, 2004)

Hamon, F, and Troper, M, *Droit constitutionnel* (Paris, Librairie générale de droit et de jurisprudence, 2018)

Hatje, A, *Loyalität als Rechtsprinzip in der Europäischen Union* (Baden-Baden, Nomos, 2001)

Hatje, A and Terhechte, JP (eds), *Grundgesetz und europäische Integration: Die Europäische Union nach dem Lissabon-Urteil des Bundesverfassungsgerichts*, Zeitschrift Europarecht, Beiheft 1/2010 (Baden-Baden, Nomos, 2010)

Heliskoski, J, *Mixed Agreements as a Technique for Organizing the International Relations of the European Community and its Member States* (The Hague, Kluwer Law International, 2001)

Herrmann, C (ed), *Die Gemeinsame Handelspolitik im europäischen Verfassungsverbund*, Zeitschrift Europarecht, Beiheft 2/2020 (Baden-Baden, Nomos, 2020)

Hillion, C and Koutrakos, P (eds), *Mixed Agreements Revisited: The EU and its Member States in the World* (Oxford, Hart Publishing, 2010)

Kaiser, F, *Gemischte Abkommen im Lichte bundesstaatlicher Erfahrungen* (Tübingen, Mohr Siebeck, 2012)

Kaspiarovich, Y, *L'UE et la protection des investissements internationaux: Une complexe articulation entre confiance mutuelle et réciprocité* (Zurich, Schulthess, 2022)

Klamert, M, *The Principle of Loyalty in EU Law* (Oxford, Oxford University Press, 2014)

Koutrakos, P, *EU International Relations Law*, 2nd edn (Oxford, Hart Publishing, 2015)

Krenzler, HG, *Die vorläufige Anwendung völkerrechtlicher Verträge* (Heidelberg, Universität Heidelberg, 1964)

Kube, V, *EU Human Rights, International Investment Law and Participation: Operationalizing the EU Foreign Policy Objective to Global Human Rights Protection* (Berlin, Springer, 2019)

Kübek, G, Tams, CJ, and Terhechte, JP (eds), *EU-UK Trade and Cooperation Agreement: A Handbook* (Baden-Baden, Oxford and Munich, Nomos, Hart Publishing and Beck, 2024)

Larik, J, *Foreign Policy Objectives in European Constitutional Law* (Oxford, Oxford University Press, 2016)

Leal-Arcas, R, *Theory and Practice of EC External Trade Law and Policy* (London, Cameron May, 2008)

Leal-Arcas, R, *EU Trade Law* (Cheltenham, Edward Elgar, 2009)

Leinarte, E, *Functional Responsibility of International Organizations: The European Union and International Economic Law* (Cambridge, Cambridge University Press, 2021)

Leino-Sandberg, P, *The Politics of Legal Expertise in EU Policy-Making* (Cambridge, Cambridge University Press, 2021)

Lenk, H, *The Investment Court System: A Viable Reform Initiative?* (Gothenburg, Handelshögskolan vid Göteborgs Universitet, 2019)

Liefländer, T, Kellerbauer, K, and Dumitriu-Segnana, E, *EU-UK Withdrawal Agreement: A Commentary* (Oxford, Oxford University Press, 2021)

Lonardo, L, *Russia's 2022 War against Ukraine and the EU's Foreign Policy Reaction: Context, Diplomacy, and Law* (London, Palgrave Macmillan, 2022)

Lorz, RA, *Interorganaspekt im Verfassungsrecht* (Tübingen, 2001)

Melo Araujo, BA, *The EU Deep Trade Agenda: Law and Policy* (Oxford, Oxford University Press, 2016)

Modderman, CB, *Parlementaire betrokkenheid bij de totstandkoming van verdragen* (Utrecht, Universiteit Utrecht, 2018)

Neframi, E, *Les accords mixtes de la Communauté européenne: aspects communautaires et internationaux* (Brussels, Bruylant, 2007)

Nuttens, J-D, *Le Parlement français et l'Europe: L'article 88-4 de la Constitution* (Paris, Librairie générale de droit et de jurisprudence, 2001)

Odermatt, J, *International Law and the European Union* (Cambridge, Cambridge University Press, 2021)

O'Keeffe, D and Schermers, HG (eds), *Mixed Agreements* (Deventer, Kluwer, 1983)

Pantaleo, L, *The Participation of the EU in International Dispute Settlement: Lessons from EU Investment Agreements* (The Hague, TMC Asser Press, 2019)

Quast Mertsch, A, *Provisionally Applied Treaties: Their Binding Force and Legal Nature* (Leiden, Brill/Nijhoff, 2012)

Roussillon, H (ed), *L'Article 88-4 de la Constitution française: le rôle du Parlement dans l'elaboration de la norme européenne* (Toulouse, Presses de l'Université des sciences sociales de Toulouse, 1995)

Schelling, TC, *The Strategy of Conflict* (Cambridge, MA, Harvard University Press, 1960)

Schmalenbach, K, *Der neue Europaartikel 23 des Grundgesetztes im Lichte der Arbeit der Gemeinsamen Verfassungskommission: Motive einer Verfassungsänderung* (Berlin, Duncker & Humblot, 1996)

Schorkopf, F, *Staatsrecht der internationalen Beziehungen* (Munich, CH Beck, 2017)

Schütze, R, *Foreign Affairs and the EU Constitution: Selected Essays* (Cambridge, Cambridge University Press, 2014)

Stegmann, PT, *Responsibility of the EU and the Member States under EU International Investment Protection Agreements: Between Traditional Rules, Proceduralisation and Federalisation* (Berlin, Springer, 2019)

Stein, KD, *Der gemischte Vertrag im Recht der Außenbeziehungen der Europäischen Wirtschaftsgemeinschaft* (Berlin, Duncker & Humblot, 1986)

St John, T, *The Rise of Investor-State Arbitration: Politics, Law, and Unintended Consequences* (Oxford, Oxford University Press, 2018)
Terhechte, JP, *Europäische Verfassungsstudien* (Baden-Baden, Nomos, 2020)
Thies, A, *International Trade Disputes and EU Liability* (Cambridge, Cambridge University Press, 2013)
Uyttendaele, M, *Les institutions de la Belgique* (Brussels, Bruylant 2014)
Van Damme, I, *Treaty Interpretation by the WTO Appellate Body* (Oxford, Oxford University Press, 2009)
Van der Loo, G, *The EU-Ukraine Association Agreement and Deep and Comprehensive Free Trade Area: A New Legal Instrument for EU Integration without Membership* (Leiden, Brill/Nijhoff, 2016)
Verellen, T, *Foreign Relations Federalism: The EU in Comparative Perspective* (Oxford, Oxford University Press, 2023)
Weiler, JHH, *The Constitution of Europe: 'Do the New Clothes Have an Emperor?' and Other Essays on European Integration* (Cambridge, Cambridge University Press, 1999)
Woolcock, S, *European Union Economic Diplomacy: The Role of the EU in External Economic Relations* (Abingdon, Routledge, 2012)
Wouters, J, Hoffmeister, F, De Baere, G, and Ramopoulos, T, *The Law of EU External Relations: Cases, Materials, and Commentary on the EU as an International Legal Actor*, 3rd edn (Oxford, Oxford University Press, 2021)

II. Journal Articles and Chapters in Edited Volumes

Abazi, V, 'How Confidential Negotiations of the TTIP Affect Public Trust' (2016) 7 *European Journal of Risk Regulation* 247
Adam, S, 'The Legal Basis of International Agreements of the European Union in the post-Lisbon era' in I Govaere, E Lannon, P Van Elsuwege and S Adam (eds), *The European Union in the World: Essays in Honour of Professor Marc Maresceau* (Leiden, Brill/Nijhoff, 2014) 65
Arena, A, 'Exercise of EU Competences and Pre-emption of Member States' Powers in the Internal and the External Sphere: Towards "Grand Unification"?' (2016) 35 *Yearbook of European Law* 28
Avril, P, 'Le parlementarisme rationalisé' (1998) 114 *Revue du droit public* 1507
Azaria, D, 'Provisional Application of Treaties' in DB Hollis (ed), *The Oxford Guide to Treaties*, 2nd edn (Oxford, Oxford University Press, 2020) 229
Baetens, F, 'The European Union's Proposed Investment Court System: Addressing Criticism of Investor-State Arbitration While Raising New Challenges' (2016) 43 *Legal Issues of Economic Integration* 367
Barav, A, 'The Division of External Relations Power between the European Economic Community and the Member States in the Case Law of the Court of Justice' in CWA Timmermans and ELM Völker (eds), *Division of Powers between the European Communities and their Member States in the Field of External Relations: Colloquium 30 and 31 May 1980, Amsterdam* (Deventer, Kluwer, 1981) 29
Bäumler, J, 'Should We Tame it, Cage it or Kill it? Past Criticisms, Present Developments, and Future Imperatives for Foreign Investment Protection in Light of the IPA-SA, TPP and CETA' (2016) 54 *Archiv des Völkerrechts* 261
——. 'Vom Vertragstext zum Inkrafttreten: Das Vertragsschlussverfahren im Mehrebenensystem am Beispiel CETA' (2016) 51 *Zeitschrift Europarecht* 607
Beaucillon, C, 'Opinion 2/15: Sustainable is the New Trade. Rethinking Coherence for the New Common Commercial Policy' (2017) 2 *European Papers* 819
Besselink, LFM and Claes, M, 'The Netherlands: The Pragmatics of a Flexible, Europeanised Constitution' in A Albi and S Bardutzky (eds), *National Constitutions in European and Global Governance: Democracy, Rights, the Rule of Law: National Reports* (The Hague, TMC Asser Press, 2019) 179
Besselink, LFM and van Mourik, B, 'The Parliamentary Legitimacy of the European Union: The Role of the Staten General within the European Union' (2012) 8 *Utrecht Law Review* 34
Bleckmann, A, 'The Mixed Agreements of the EEC in Public International Law' in D O'Keeffe and HG Schermers (eds), *Mixed Agreements* (Deventer, Kluwer, 1983) 155
Bolaert, S, 'Mixity versus Unity: A View from the Other Side of the Rue de la Loi' in M Chamon and I Govaere (eds), *EU External Relations Law Post-Lisbon: The Law and Practice of Facultative Mixity* (Leiden, Brill/Nijhoff, 2020) 251

Bosse-Platière, I and Cremona, M, 'Facultative Mixity in Light of the Principle of Subsidiarity' in M Chamon and I Govaere (eds), *EU External Relations Law Post-Lisbon: The Law and Practice of Facultative Mixity* (Leiden, Brill/Nijhoff, 2020) 49

Boysen, S, 'Das System des Europäischen Außenwirtschaftsrechts' in A von Arnauld and M Bungenberg (eds), *Europäische Außenbeziehungen*, Enzyklopädie Europarecht, vol 12, 2nd edn (Baden-Baden, Nomos, 2022) § 10

Brauneck, J, 'Abgetrennte Handelsabkommen ohne Beteiligung der Mitgliedstaaten?' (2018) 29 *Europäische Zeitschrift für Wirtschaftsrecht* 796

Broberg, M and Holdgaard, R, 'Demarcating the Union's Development Cooperation Policy after Lisbon: Commission v. Council (Philippines PCFA)' (2015) 52 *Common Market Law* Review 547

Bungenberg, M, 'Artikel 218 AEUV' in H von der Groeben, J Schwarze and A Hatje (eds), *Europäisches Unionsrecht: EUV/AEUV/GRC*, 7th edn (Baden-Baden, Nomos, 2015)

——. 'Artikel 207 AEUV' in M Pechstein, C Nowak, and U Häde, *Frankfurter Kommentar zu EUV, GRC und AEUV*, 2nd edn (Tübingen, Mohr Siebeck, 2023)

Bursens, P and Helsen, S, 'Multi-level governance in de praktijk: Strategieën ter optimalisering van de Belgische EU-Coördinatie' (2003) 56 *Studia Diplomatica* 3

Butler, G, 'Pinpointing the Appropriate Legal Basis for External Action' (2015) 6 *European Journal of Risk Regulation* 323

——. 'The EU's Flexibility Clause: Past, Present, and Future' in A Bakardjieva-Engelbrekt and X Groussot (eds), *The Future of Europe: Legal and Political Integration Beyond Brexit* (Oxford, Hart Publishing, 2019) 63

Butler, G, 'EU Customs Union, International Agreements of Member States and the Doctrine of Substitution: Nederlandse Spoorwegen' G Butler and RA Wessel (eds), *EU External Relations Law: The Cases in Context* (Oxford, Hart Publishing, 2022) 57

Campo, LA, Ott, A and Wessel, RA, 'The Netherlands and (Facultative) Mixity: Pragmatism over Principle?' in M Chamon and I Govaere (eds), *EU External Relations Law Post-Lisbon: The Law and Practice of Facultative Mixity* (Leiden, Brill/Nijhoff 2020) 317

Cannizzaro, E, 'In Defence of Front Polisario: The ECJ as a Global Jus Cogens Maker' (2018) 55 *Common Market Law Review* 569

Chamon, M, 'The Institutional Balance: An Ill-Fated Principle of EU Law?' (2015) 21 *European Public Law* 371

——. 'Institutional Balance and Community Method in the Implementation of EU Legislation Following the Lisbon Treaty' (2016) 53 *Common Market Law Review* 1501

——. 'Constitutional Limits to the Political Choice for Mixity' in E Neframi and M Gatti (eds), *Constitutional Issues of EU External Relations Law* (Baden-Baden, Nomos, 2018) 137

——. 'Implied Exclusive Powers in the ECJ's Post-Lisbon Jurisprudence: The Continued Development of the ERTA Doctrine' (2018) 55 *Common Market Law Review* 1101

——. 'Verplicht gemengd optreden van de Unie en de lidstaten binnen de Canberra Conventie ondanks het bestaan van een gedeelde bevoegdheid' (2019) 67 *SEW: Tijdschrift voor Europees en economisch recht* 250

Chamon, M and Cremona, M, 'The Representation of the EU and its Member States in Multilateral Fora: The AMP Antarctique Effect' in N Levrat, Y Kaspiarovich, C Kaddous and RA Wessel (eds), *The EU and its Member States' Joint Participation in International Agreements* (Oxford, Hart Publishing, 2022) 97

Colas, D, 'Retour sur la compétence externe partagée de l'Union: L'arrêt COTIF et les conditions de sa mise en application' in M Chamon, and I Govaere (eds), *EU External Relations Law Post-Lisbon: The Law and Practice of Facultative Mixity* (Leiden, Brill/Nijhoff, 2020) 384

Conconi, P, Herghelegiu, C and Puccio, L, 'EU Trade Agreements: To Mix or Not to Mix, That is the Question' (2021) 55 *Journal of World Trade Law* 231

Contartese, C and Pantaleo, L, 'Division of Competences, EU Autonomy and the Determination of the Respondent Party: Proceduralisation as a Possible Way out?' in E Neframi and M Gatti (eds), *Constitutional Issues of EU External Relations Law* (Baden-Baden, Nomos, 2018) 409

Cottier, T, 'Gemischte Abkommen der Europäischen Union: Grundlagen und Alternativen' in M Bungenberg and C Herrmann (eds), *Die gemeinsame Handelspolitik der Europäischen Union: Fünf Jahre nach Lissabon – Quo Vadis?* (Baden-Baden, Nomos, 2016) 11

——. 'Towards a Common External Economic Policy of the European Union' in M Bungenberg and C Herrmann (eds), *Common Commercial Policy after Lisbon*, Special Issue, *European Yearbook of International Economic Law* (Berlin, Springer, 2013) 3

——. 'Front-Loading Trade Policy-Making in the European Union: Towards a Trade Act' in M Bungenberg, M Krajewski, C Tams and JP Terhechte, *European Yearbook of International Economic Law 2017* (Berlin, Springer, 2017) 35

Cottier, T and Trinberg, L, 'Artikel 206 AEUV' H von der Groeben, J Schwarze and A Hatje (eds), *Europäisches Unionsrecht: EUV, AEUV, GRC*, 7th edn (Baden-Baden, Nomos, 2015)

Craig, P, 'Competence: Clarity, Conferral, Containment and Consideration' (2004) 29 *European Law Review* 323

——. 'The Ratifications' in F Fabbrini (ed), *The Withdrawal Agreement: The Law and Politics of Brexit, Volume II* (Oxford, Oxford University Press, 2020) 83

Cremona, M, 'A Policy of Bits and Pieces? The Common Commercial Policy after Nice' (2001) 4 *Cambridge Yearbook of European Legal Studies* 61

——. 'The Union as a Global Actor: Roles, Models, Identity' (2004) 41 *Common Market Law Review* 553

——. 'Balancing Union and Member State Interests: Opinion 1/2008, Choice of Legal Base and the Common Commercial Policy under the Treaty of Lisbon' (2010) 35 *European Law Review* 678

——. 'The European Union and Regional Trade Agreements' in C Herrmann and JP Terhechte (eds), *European Yearbook of International Economic Law 2010* (Berlin, Springer, 2010) 245

——. 'Values in EU Foreign Policy' in M Evans and P Koutrakos (eds), *Beyond the Established Legal Orders: Policy Interconnections between the EU and the Rest of the World* (Oxford, Hart Publishing, 2011) 275

——. 'EU External Relations: Unity and Conferral of Powers' in L Azoulai (ed), *The Question of Competence in the European Union* (Oxford, Oxford University Press, 2014) 65

——. 'Guest Editorial: Negotiating the Transatlantic Trade and Investment Partnership (TTIP)' (2015) 52 *Common Market Law Review* 351

——. 'Distinguished Essay: A Quiet Revolution – The Changing Nature of the EU's Common Commercial Policy' in M Bungenberg, M Krajewski, CJ Tams, JP Terhechte and RA Ziegler (eds), *European Yearbook of International Economic Law 2017* (Berlin, Springer, 2017) 3

——. 'EU External Competence: Rationales for Exclusivity' in S Garben and I Govaere (eds), *The Division of Competences between the EU and the Member States: Reflections on the Past, the Present and the Future* (Oxford, Hart Publishing, 2017) 133

——. 'The Internal Market and External Economic Relations' in P Koutrakos and J Snell (eds), *Research Handbook on the Law of the EU's Internal Market* (Cheltenham, Edward Elgar, 2017) 479

——. 'Shaping EU Trade Policy Post-Lisbon: Opinion 2/15 of 16 May 2017' (2018) 14 *European Constitutional Law Review* 231

Czuczai, J, 'Mixity in Practice: Some Problems and Their (Real or Possible) Solution' in C Hillion and P Koutrakos (eds), *Mixed Agreements Revisited: The EU and its Member States in the World* (Oxford, Hart Publishing, 2010) 229

Damestoy, M and Levrat, N, 'The Mixed Nature of the EU-Canada FTA: Between Competences Distribution and Democratic Legitimacy' in N Levrat, Y Kaspiarovich, C Kaddous and RA Wessel (eds), *The EU and its Member States' Joint Participation in International Agreements* (Oxford, Hart Publishing, 2022) 77

Dashwood, A, 'Why Continue to Have Mixed Agreements at All?' in JHJ Bourgeois, J-L Dewost and M-A Gaiffe (eds), *La Communauté européenne et les accords mixtes: Quelles perspectives?* (Brussels, PIE-Peter Lang, 1997) 93

——. 'External Relations Provisions of the Amsterdam Treaty' (1998) 35 *Common Market Law Review* 1019

——. 'The Attribution of External Relations Competence' in A Dashwood and C Hillion (eds), *The General Law of E.C. External Relations* (London, Sweet & Maxwell, 2000) 115

——. 'The Relationship between the Member States and the European Union/European Community' in A McDonnell (ed), *A Review of Forty Years of Community Law: Legal Developments in the European Communities and the European Union* (The Hague, Kluwer Law International, 2005) 37

Dashwood, A and Heliskoski, J, 'The Classic Authorities Revisited' in A Dashwood and C Hillion (eds), *The General Law of E.C. External Relations* (London, Sweet & Maxwell, 2000) 3

De Búrca, G and Scott, J, 'The Impact of the WTO on EU Decision-Making' in G de Búrca and J Scott (eds), *The EU and the WTO: Legal and Constitutional Issues* (Oxford, Hart Publishing, 2001) 2

Delgado Casteleiro, A and Larik, J, 'The Duty to Remain Silent: Limitless Loyalty in EU External Relations?' (2011) 36 *European Law Review* 534

Devuyst, Y, 'European Union Law and Practice in the Negotiation and Conclusion of International Trade Agreements' (2013) 12 *Journal of International Business and Law* 259

——. 'The European Parliament and International Trade Agreements: Practice after the Lisbon Treaty' in I Govaere, E Lannon, P Van Elsuwege and S Adam (eds), *The European Union in the World: Essays in Honour of Professor Marc Maresceau* (Leiden, Brill/Nijhoff, 2014) 171

De Witte, B, 'Exclusive Member State Competences: Is There Such a Thing?' in S Garben and I Govaere (eds), *The Division of Competences between the EU and the Member States: Reflections on the Past, the Present and the Future* (Oxford, Hart Publishing, 2017) 59

Do Nascimento e Silva, GE, 'The 1986 Vienna Convention and the Treaty-Making Power of International Organizations' (1986) 29 *German Yearbook of International Law* 68

Douma, WT, 'The Promotion of Sustainable Development through EU Trade Instruments' (2017) *European Business Law Review* 197

Eckes, C, 'How the European Parliament's Participation in International Relations Affects the Deep Tissue of the EU's Power Structures' (2014) 12 *International Journal of Constitutional Law* 904

Eckes, C and Leino-Sandberg, P, 'The EU-UK Trade and Cooperation Agreement: Exceptional Circumstances or a New Paradigm for EU External Relations?' (2022) 85 *Modern Law Review* 164

Editorial Comments, 'The Aftermath of Opinion 1/94 or How to Ensure Unity of Representation for Joint Competences' (1995) 32 *Common Market Law Review* 385

——. 'Playing by the Rules: Free and Fair Trade' (2018) 55 *Common Market Law Review* 373

Eeckhout, P, 'Exclusive External Competences: Constructing the EU as an International Actor' in *The Court of Justice and the Construction of Europe: Analyses and Perspectives on Sixty Years of Case-law – La Cour de Justice et la Construction de l'Europe: Analyses et Perspectives de Soixante Ans de Jurisprudence* (The Hague, TMC Asser Press, 2013) 613

——. 'Linking Internal and External Trade in a Perfect Customs Union: Donderwolcke' in G Butler and RA Wessel (eds), *EU External Relations Law: The Cases in Context* (Oxford, Hart Publishing, 2022) 90

Eeckhout, P and Frantziou, E, 'Brexit and Article 50 TEU: A Constitutionalist Reading' (2017) 54 *Common Market Law Review* 695

Eeckhout, P and Tridimas, T, 'The External Competence of the Community and the Case-Law of the Court of Justice: Principle versus Pragmatism' (1994) 14 *Yearbook of European Law* 143

Ehlermann, C-D, 'Mixed Agreements: A List of Problems' in D O'Keeffe and HG Schermers (eds), *Mixed Agreements* (Deventer, Kluwer, 1983) 3

Eisemann, PM and Rivier, R, 'National Treaty Law and Practice: France' in D Hollis, M Blakeslee and B Ederington (eds), *National Treaty Law and Practice* (Leiden, Brill/Nijhoff, 2005) 259

Emiliou, N, 'Opening Pandora's Box: The Legal Basis of Community Measures before the Court of Justice' (1994) 19 *European Law Review* 488

Fahey, E, 'On the Benefits of the TTIP Negotiations for the EU Legal Order: A Legal Perspective' (2016) 43 *Legal Issues of Economic Integration* 327

——. 'European Citizens Initiative "STOP TTIP" Can Proceed Says General Court' (2017) 8 *European Journal of Risk Regulation* 787

Fahey, E and Wieczorek, I, 'The European Parliament as a Defender of EU Values in EU-Japan Agreements: What Role for Soft Law and Hard Law Powers?' (2022) 47 *European Law Review* 331

Fritzmaurice, M, 'Law of Treaties' in S Chesterman, D Malone and S Villalpando (eds), *The Oxford Handbook of United Nations Treaties* (Oxford, Oxford University Press, 2019) 493

Galloway, D, 'Classifying Secrets in the EU' (2014) 52 *Journal of Common Market Studies* 668

Garzón Clariana, G, 'L'application provisoire des accords internationaux de la Communauté' in P Demaret, I Govaere and D Hanf (eds), *30 years of European legal studies at the college of Europe: 30 ans d'études juridiques européennes au Collège d'Europe* (Brussels, PIE-Peter Lang, 2005) 479

Gáspár-Szilágyi, S, 'A Standing Investment Court under TTIP from the Perspective of the Court of Justice of the European Union' (2016) 28 *Journal of World Investment & Trade* 701

Gatti, M and Manzini, M, 'External Representation of the European Union in the Conclusion of International Agreements' (2012) 49 *Common Market Law Review* 1703

Gatti, M and Matera, C, 'Facultative Mixity in the Area of Freedom, Security and Justice' in M Chamon and I Govaere (eds), *EU External Relations Law Post-Lisbon: The Law and Practice of Facultative Mixity* (Leiden, Brill/Nijhoff, 2020) 187

Gilsdorf, P, 'Die Außenkompetenzen der EG im Wandel' (1995) 30 *Zeitschrift Europarecht* 145

Golman, R and Loewenstein, G, 'Information Gaps: A Theory of Preferences Regarding the Presence and Absence of Information' (2018) 5 *Decision* 143

Groux, J, 'Mixed Negotiations' in D O'Keeffe and HG Schermers (eds), *Mixed Agreements* (Deventer, Kluwer, 1983) 87

Gruni, G, 'Towards a Sustainable World Trade Law? The Commercial Policy of the European Union after Opinion 2/15 CJEU' (2018) 13 *Global Trade and Customs Journal* 4

Grzeszick, B, 'Völkervertragsrecht in der parlamentarischen Demokratie: CETA als Präzedenzfall für die demokratischen Anforderungen an völkerrechtliche Verträge' (2016) 35 *Neue Zeitschrift für Verwaltungsrecht* 1753

Grzeszick, B and Hettche, J, 'Zur Beteiligung des Bundestages an gemischten völkerrechtlichen Abkommen: Internationale Freihandelsabkommen als Herausforderung des deutschen Europa- und Außenverfassungsrechts' (2016) 14 *Archiv des öffentlichen Rechts* 225

Hahn, M, 'Auswärtige Annexkompetenzen interner Politiken' in A von Arnauld and M Bungenberg (eds), Europäische Außenbeziehungen, Enzyklopädie Europarecht, vol 12, 2nd edn (Baden-Baden, Nomos, 2022) § 15

——. 'Artikel 207 AEUV' in C Calliess and M Ruffert (eds), *EUV/AEUV: Das Verfassungsrecht der Europäischen Union mit Europäischer Grundrechtecharta, Kommentar*, 6th edn (Munich, CH Beck, 2022)

Heliskoski, J, 'Mixed Agreements: The EU Law Fundamentals' in R Schütze and T Tridimas (eds), *Oxford Principles of European Union Law*, vol I (Oxford, Oxford University Press, 2018) 1174

——. 'The Exercise of Non-exclusive Competence of the EU and the Conclusion of International Agreements' in K Lenaerts, J-C Bonichot, H Kanninen, C Naômé and P Pohjankoski (eds), *An Ever-Changing Union? Perspectives on the Future of EU Law in Honour of Allan Rosas* (Oxford, Hart Publishing, 2019) 293

——. 'The Procedural Law of International Agreements: A Thematic Journey through Article 218 TFEU' (2020) 57 *Common Market Law Review* 79

——. 'Provisional Application of EU Free Trade Agreements' in M Hahn and G Van der Loo (eds), *Law and Practice of the Common Commercial Policy* (Leiden, Brill/Nijhoff, 2021) 586

Heliskoski, J and Kübek, G, 'A Typology of EU Mixed Agreements Revisited' in N Levrat, Y Kaspiarovich, C Kaddous and RA Wessel (eds), *The EU and its Member States' Joint Participation in International Agreements* (Oxford, Hart Publishing, 2022) 23

Herrmann, C, 'Vom misslungenen Versuch der Neufassung der gemeinsamen Handelspolitik durch den Vertrag von Nizza' (2001) 12 *Europäische Zeitschrift für Wirtschaftsrecht* 269

——. 'Common Commercial Policy after Nice: Sisyphus Would Have Done a Better Job' (2002) 39 *Common Market Law Review* 7

——. 'Much Ado about Pluto? The 'Unity of the Legal Order of the European Union' Revisited' in M Cremona and B De Witte, *EU Foreign Relations Law: Constitutional Fundamentals* (Oxford, Hart Publishing, 2008) 19

——. 'Grenzen der Binnenmarktkompetenz in der Jüngeren Rechtsprechung des EuGH' in W Schroeder (ed), *Europarecht als Mehrebenensystem: Beiträge zum 7. Österreichischen Europarechtstag 2007* (Vienna, Facultas, 2008) 14

——. 'Bilateral and Regional Trade Agreements as a Challenge to the Multilateral Trading System' (2009) 63 *Aussenwirtschaft: Schweizerische Zeitschrift für internationale Wirtschaftsbeziehungen* 263

——. 'Die gemeinsame Handelspolitik der Europäischen Union im Lissabon-Urteil' in A Hatje and JP Terhechte (eds), *Grundgesetz und europäische Integration: Die Europäische Union nach dem Lissabon-Urteil des Bundesverfassungsgerichts*, Zeitschrift Europarecht, Beiheft 1/2010 (Baden-Baden, Nomos, 2010) 193

——. 'Die Zukunft der mitgliedstaatlichen Investitionsschutzpolitik nach dem Vertrag von Lissabon' (2010) 21 *Europäische Zeitschrift für Wirtschaftsrecht* 207

——. 'The Role of the Court of Justice of the European Union in the Emerging EU Investment Policy' (2014) 15 *Journal of World Investment & Trade* 570

——. '"Transleakancy"' in C Herrmann, B Simma and R Streinz (eds), *Trade Policy between Law, Diplomacy and Scholarship: Liber Amicorum in Memoriam Horst G. Krenzler* (Berlin, Springer, 2015) 39

Herrmann, C and Streinz, T, 'Die EU als Mitglied der WTO' in A von Arnauld and M Bungenberg (eds), *Europäische Außenbeziehungen*, Enzyklopädie Europarecht, vol 12, 2nd edn (Baden-Baden, Nomos, 2022) § 13

Hilf, M, 'Negotiating and Implementing the Uruguay Round: The Role of EC Member States – The Case of Germany' in JH Jackson and AO Sykes (eds), *Implementing the Uruguay Round* (Oxford, Oxford University Press, 1997) 121

Hillion, C, 'Mixity and Coherence in EU External Relations: The Significance of the "Duty of Cooperation"' in C Hillion and P Koutrakos (eds), *Mixed Agreements Revisited: The EU and its Member States in the World* (Oxford, Hart Publishing, 2010) 87

——. 'Conferral, Cooperation and Balance in the Institutional Framework of EU External Action' in M Cremona (ed), *Structural Principles in EU External Relations Law* (Oxford, Hart Publishing, 2018) 117

——. 'Brexit Means Br(EEA)xit: The UK Withdrawal from the EU and its Implications for the EEA' (2018) 55 *Common Market Law Review* 135, 139

Hillion, C and Chamon, M, 'Facultative Mixity and Sincere Cooperation' in M Chamon and I Govaere (eds), *EU External Relations Law Post-Lisbon: The Law and Practice of Facultative Mixity* (Leiden, Brill/Nijhoff, 2020) 86

Hoffmeister, F, 'Commission v. United Kingdom, Commission v. Denmark, Commission v. Sweden, Commission v. Finland; Commission v. Belgium, Commission v. Luxembourg; Commission v. Austria, Commission v. Germany' (2004) 96 *American Journal of International Law* 567

——. 'Curse or Blessing? Mixed Agreements in the Recent Practice of the European Union and its Member States' in C Hillion and P Koutrakos (eds), *Mixed Agreements Revisited: The EU and its Member States in the World* (Oxford, Hart Publishing, 2010) 249

——. 'Article 7 VCLT' in O Dörr and K Schmalenbach (eds), *Vienna Convention on the Law of Treaties: A Commentary* (Berlin, Springer, 2012) 129

——. 'Bilateral Developments in EU Trade Policy Seven Years after Lisbon: A Look into the Spaghetti-Bowl à la Bruxelloise (2010–2016)' in M Bungenberg, M Krajewski, C Tams, JP Terhechte and AR Ziegler (eds), *European Yearbook of International Economic Law 2017* (Berlin, Springer, 2017) 411

——. 'The EU's Trade and Investment Agreements: European Convergence with World Trade Law?' in E Fahey (ed), *Framing Convergence with the Global Legal Order* (Oxford, Hart Publishing, 2020) 25

Holdgaard, R, 'The European Community's Implied External Competence after the Open Skies Cases' (2003) 8 *European Foreign Affairs Review* 365

Holterhus, TP, 'Die Rolle des Deutschen Bundestags in der auswärtigen Handelspolitik der Europäischen Union – Insbesondere zu den parlamentarischen Einflussmöglichkeiten im völkerrechtlichen Vertragsschlussverfahren' (2017) 52 *Zeitschrift Europarecht* 234

Huber, PM, 'Die Integrationsverantwortung von Bundestag und Bundesregierung' (2017) 15 *Zeitschrift für Staats- und Europawissenschaften* 286

Jančić, D, 'The Barroso Initiative: Window Dressing or Democracy Boost?' (2012) *Utrecht Law Review* 78

——. 'The French Parliament: A European Scrutineer or National Actor?' (2013) 19 *European Public Law* 129

——. 'TTIP and Legislative-Executive Relations in EU Trade Policy' (2017) 40 *West European Politics* 202

Jones, E, 'The Negotiations' in F Fabbrini (ed), *The Withdrawal Agreement: The Law and Politics of Brexit, Volume II* (Oxford, Oxford University Press, 2020) 37

Kampf, R, 'Zwangslizenz-VO vor Art. 1 Erwägungsgründe' in HG Krenzler, C Herrmann and M Niestedt (eds), *EU-Außenwirtschafts- und Zollrecht*, 21st edn (Munich, CH Beck, 2023)

Kaspiarovich, Y and Wessel, RA, 'The Role of Values in EU External Relations: A Legal Assessment of the EU as a "Good" Global Actor' in E Fahey and I Mancini (eds), *The EU as a Good Global Actor* (Edward Elgar, 2022) 92

——. '"Unmixing" Mixed Agreements: Challenges and Solutions for Separating the EU and its Member States in Existing International Agreements' in N Levrat, Y Kaspiarovich, C Kaddous and RA Wessel (eds), *The EU and its Member States' Joint Participation in International Agreements* (Oxford, Hart Publishing, 2022) 75

Keller, M and Schmitt, M, '120. Verordnung 1219/2012' in HG Krenzler, C Herrmann and M Niestedt (eds), *EU-Außenwirtschafts- und Zollrecht*, 21st edn (Munich, CH Beck, 2023)

Kempen, B and Schiffbauer, B, 'Die vorläufige Anwendung völkerrechtlicher Verträge im internationalen Mehrebenensystem' (2017) 77 *Zeitschrift für ausländisches öffentliches Recht und Völkerrecht* 95

Kerremans, B, 'Determining a European Policy in a Multi-level Setting: The Case of Specialized Co-ordination in Belgium' (2000) 10 *Regional & Federal Studies* 36

Klamert, M, 'Conflicts of Legal Basis: No Legality and No Basis But a Bright Future under the Lisbon Treaty?' (2010) 35 *European Law Review* 497

Klamert, M and Mayell, N, 'Lost in Exclusivity: Implied Non-exclusive External Competences in Community Law' (2008) 13 *European Foreign Affairs Review* 493

Kleimann, D, 'The Legitimacy of "EU-Only" Preferential Trade Agreements' in M Hahn and G Van der Loo (eds), *Law and Practice of the Common Commercial Policy* (Leiden, Brill/Nijhoff, 2021) 461

Kleimann, D and Kübek, G, 'The Signing, Provisional Application, and Conclusion of Trade and Investment Agreements in the EU: The Case of CETA and Opinion 2/15' (2018) 45 *Legal Issues of Economic Integration* 13

Kotzur, M, 'Europäische Nachbarschaftspolitik' in A von Arnauld and M Bungenberg (eds), *Europäische Außenbeziehungen*, Enzyklopädie Europarecht, vol 12, 2nd edn (Baden-Baden, Nomos, 2022) § 7

Koutrakos, P, 'Legal Basis and Delimitation of Competences in EU External Relations' in M Cremona (ed), *EU Foreign Relations Law: Constitutional Fundamentals* (Oxford, Hart Publishing, 2008) 171

——. 'The Autonomy of EU law and International Investment Arbitration' (2019) 88 *Nordic Journal of International Law* 41

Krajewski, M, 'External Trade Law and the Constitution Treaty: Towards a Federal and More Democratic Commercial Policy?' (2005) 42 *Common Market Law Review* 91

——. 'Die neue handelspolitische Bedeutung des Europäischen Parlaments' in M Bungenberg and C Herrmann (eds), *Die gemeinsame Handelspolitik der Europäischen Union nach Lissabon* (Baden-Baden, Nomos, 2011) 53

——. 'New Functions and New Powers for the European Parliament: Assessing the Changes of the Common Commercial Policy from the Perspective of Democratic Legitimacy' in M Bungenberg and C Herrmann (eds), *Common Commercial Policy after Lisbon*, Special Issue, *European Yearbook of International Economic Law* (Berlin, Springer, 2013) 67

——. 'Umweltschutz und internationales Investitionsschutzrecht am Beispiel der Vattenfall-Klagen und des Transatlantischen Handels- und Investitionsabkommens (TTIP)' (2014) 25 *Zeitschrift für Umweltrecht* 396

Krenzler, HG, 'Die Reichweite der gemeinsamen Handelspolitik nach dem Vertrag von Amsterdam – eine Debatte ohne Ende?' (1998) 33 *Zeitschrift Europarecht* 223

Krieger, H, 'Article 25' in K Schmalenbach and O Dörr (eds), *Vienna Convention on the Law of Treaties: A Commentary*, 2nd edn (Dordrecht, Springer, 2018) 441

Krunke, H, 'Developments in National Parliaments' Involvement in Ordinary Foreign and European Policy – Denmark' (2007) 13 *European Public Law Review* 335

——. 'The Danish Lisbon Judgment – Danish Supreme Court, Case 199/2012, Judgment of 20 February 2013' (2014) 10 *European Constitutional Law Review* 542

Krunke, H and Baumbach, T, 'The Role of the Danish Constitution in European and Transnational Governance' in A Albi and S Bardutzky (eds), *National Constitutions in European and Global Governance: Democracy, Rights, the Rule of Law: National Reports* (The Hague, TMC Asser Press, 2019) 269

Kübek, G, 'The Non-ratification Scenario: Legal and Practical Responses to Mixed Treaty Rejection by Member States' (2018) 23 *European Foreign Affairs Review* 21

——. 'Redefining the Boundaries of the Common Commercial Policy and the ERTA Doctrine: Opinion 3/15, Marrakesh Treaty' (2018) 55 *Common Market Law Review* 883

——. 'Autonomy and International Investment Agreements after Opinion 1/17' (2020) *Europe and the World: A Law Review* 1

——. 'The European Union's External Trade and Investment Policy Post-Lisbon: Competence, Procedure and Scope of Action' in M Andenas, C Contartese, M Happold, and L Pantaleo (eds), *The European Union as an Actor in International Economic Law* (The Hague, TMC Asser Press, 2020) 93

——. 'The Concept of (Non-)Commerciality and the ERTA Doctrine Post-Lisbon: Opinion 3/15, Marrakesh Treaty' in G Butler and RA Wessel (eds), *EU External Relations Law: The Cases in Context* (Oxford, Hart Publishing, 2022) 851

——. 'Facing and Embracing the Consequences of Mixity: Opinion 1/19, Istanbul Convention' (2022) 59 *Common Market Law Review* 1465

——. 'Institutional Framework and Governance' in G Kübek, CJ Tams and JP Terhechte (eds), *EU-UK Trade and Cooperation Agreement: A Handbook* (Baden-Baden, Oxford and Munich, Nomos, Hart Publishing and Beck, 2024)

Kübek, G and Van Damme, I, 'Facultative Mixity and the European Union's Trade and Investment Agreements' in M Chamon and I Govaere (eds), *EU External Relations Law Post-Lisbon: The Law and Practice of Facultative Mixity* (Leiden, Brill/Nijhoff, 2020) 137

Kübek, G, Tams, CJ, and Terhechte, JP, 'Einleitung' in G Kübek, CJ Tams and JP Terhechte (eds), *EU-UK Trade and Cooperation Agreement: A Handbook* (Baden-Baden, Oxford and Munich, Nomos, Hart Publishing and Beck, 2024)

Kuijper, PJ, 'Of "Mixity" and "Double-Hatting": EU External Relations Law Explained' (2008) *Oratiereeks, Vossiuspers University of Amsterdam* 5

——. 'International Responsibility for Mixed Agreements' in C Hillion and P Koutrakos (eds), *Mixed Agreements Revisited: The EU and its Member States in the World* (Oxford, Hart Publishing, 2010) 208

——. 'Post-CETA: How We Got There and How to Go On' (2017) 53 *Revue trimestrielle de droit européen* 181
Kumin, AJ and Bittner, P, 'Die "gemischten" Abkommen zwischen der Europäischen Union und ihren Mitgliedstaaten einerseits und dritten Völkerrechtssubjekten andererseits' in W Oberwexer (ed), *Die Europäische Union im Völkerrecht* (Baden-Baden, Nomos, 2012) 75
Larik, J, 'Much More Than Trade: The Common Commercial Policy in a Global Context' in MD Evans and P Koutrakos (eds), *Beyond the Established Legal Orders: Policy Interconnections between the EU and the Rest of the World* (Oxford, Hart Publishing, 2011) 13
——. 'From Speciality to a Constitutional Sense of Purpose: On the Changing Role of the Objectives of the European Union' (2014) 63 *International and Comparative Law Quarterly* 935
——. 'No Mixed Feelings: The Post-Lisbon Common Commercial Policy in Daiichi Sankyo and Commission v. Council (Conditional Access Convention)' (2015) 52 *Common Market Law Review* 779
——. 'Prêt-à-ratifier: The CETA Decision of the French Conseil constitutionnel of 31 July 2017' (2017) 13 *European Constitutional Law Review* 759
——. '*Pars Pro Toto*: The Member States' Obligations of Sincere Cooperation, Solidarity and Unity' in M Cremona (ed), *Structural Principles in EU External Relations Law* (Oxford, Hart Publishing, 2018) 175
Lavranos, N, 'Opinion 1/03, Lugano Convention' (2006) 43 *Common Market Law Review* 1087
Le Boeuf, R, 'La double nature de la ratification des traités: observations sur les discordances entre les procédures constitutionelles et internationales' (2016) 107 *Revue française de droit constitutionnel* 601
Lefeber, R, 'The Provisional Application of Treaties' in J Klabbers and R Lefeber (eds), *Essays on the Law of Treaties: A Collection of Essays in Honour of Bert Vierdag* (Leiden, Brill/Nijhoff, 1998) 81
Leino, P, 'The Politics of Efficient Compromise in the Adoption of EU Legal Acts' in M Cremona and C Kilpatrick (eds), *EU Legal Acts: Challenges and Transformations* (Oxford, Oxford University Press, 2018) 30
Lenk, H, 'Prior Judicial Involvement in Investor-State Dispute Settlement: Lessons from the Court's Rhetoric in Opinion 2/15' (2018) 13 *Global Trade and Customs Journal* 19
——. 'Mixity in EU Foreign Trade Policy is Here to Stay: Advocate General Sharpston on the Allocation of Competence for the Conclusion of the EU-Singapore Free Trade Agreement' (2017) 2 *European Papers* 357
——. 'More Trade and Less Investment for Future EU Trade and Investment Policy: CJEU, Opinion 2/15, Free Trade Agreement between the European Union and Singapore, 16 May 2017, EU:C:2017:376' (2018) 19 *Journal of World Investment and Trade* 305
Leonard, P, 'Patrick Costello v the Government of Ireland, Ireland and the Attorney General: Obstacles to the Ratification of CETA in the Irish Constitutional Context' (2023) 38 *ICSID Review – Foreign Investment Law Journal* 286
Levrat, N, 'Article 6 VCLTIO' in O Corten and P Klein (eds), *The Vienna Conventions on the Law of Treaties: A Commentary* (Oxford, Oxford University Press, 2011) 117
Lorenzmeier, S, 'Artikel 218 AEUV' in E Grabitz, M Hilf and M Nettesheim (eds), *Das Recht der Europäischen Union: EUV/AEUV* (Munich, CH Beck, 2023)
Manin, P, 'The European Communities and the Vienna Convention on the Law of Treaties between States and International Organizations or between International Organizations' (1987) 24 *Common Market Law Review* 457
Marceddu, LM, 'Implementing Transparency and Public Participation in FTA Negotiations: Are the Times a-Changin'?' (2018) 21 *Journal of International Economic Law* 681
Maresceau, M, 'Typology of Mixed Bilateral Agreements' in C Hillion and P Koutrakos (eds), *Mixed Agreements Revisited: The EU and its Member States in the World* (Oxford, Hart Publishing, 2010) 11
——. 'Les accords d'intégration dans les relations de proximité de l'Union Europeénne' in C Blumann (ed), *Les frontiers de l'Union Européenne* (Brussels, Bruylant, 2013)
Mathy, D, 'Article 25 VCLT' in O Corten and P Klein (eds), *The Vienna Conventions on the Law of Treaties: A Commentary* (Oxford, Oxford University Press, 2011) 639
Mavroidis, PC, 'Doha, Dohalf, or Dohaha? The WTO Licks its Wounds' (2011) 3 *Trade, Law and Development* 367
Marx, A and Van der Loo, G, 'Transparency in EU Trade Policy: A Comprehensive Assessment of Current Achievements' (2021) 9 *Politics and Governance* 261
Meissner, K, 'Democratizing EU External Relations: The European Parliament's Informal Role in SWIFT, ACTA, and TTIP' (2016) 21 *European Foreign Affairs Review* 269

Mengozzi, P, 'The EC External Competencies: From the ERTA Case to the Opinion in the Lugano Convention' in P Poiares Maduro and L Azoulai (eds), *The Past and Future of EU Law: The Classics of EU Law Revisited on the 50th Anniversary of the Rome Treaty* (Oxford, Hart Publishing, 2010) 213

Meunier, S, 'What Single Voice? European Institutions and EU-US Trade Negotiations' (2000) 54 *International Organization* 103

Meunier, S and Czesana, R, 'From Back Rooms to the Street? A Research Agenda for Explaining Variation in the Public Salience of Trade Policy-Making in Europe' (2019) *26 Journal of European Public Policy* 1847

Meunier, S and Nicolaïdis, K, 'Who Speaks for Europe? The Delegation of Trade Authority in the EU' (1999) 37 *Journal of Common Market Studies* 477

Money, J and Tsebelis, G, 'The Political Power of the French Senate: Micromechanisms of Bicameral Negotiations' (1995) *The Journal of Legislative Studies* 192

Neframi, E, 'The Duty of Loyalty: Rethinking its Scope through its Application in the Field of EU External Relations' (2010) 54 *Common Market Law Review* 323

——. 'Vertical Division of Competences and the Objectives of the European Union's External Action' in M Cremona and A Thies (eds), *European Court of Justice and External Relations Law* (Oxford, Hart Publishing, 2014) 73

Nettesheim, M, 'Die Integrationsverantwortung – Vorgaben des BVerfG und gesetzgeberische Umsetzung' (2010) 63 *Neue Juristische Wochenzeitung* 177

——. 'Artikel 207 AEUV' in R Streinz (ed), *EUV/AEUV: Vertrag über die Europäische Union, Vertrag über die Arbeitsweise der Europäischen Union, Charta der Grundrechte der Europäischen Union*, 3rd edn (Munich, CH Beck, 2018)

Nowrot, K and Tietje, C, 'CETA an der Leine des Bundesverfassungsgerichts: Zum schmalen Grat zwischen Ultra-vires Kontrolle und Ultra-vires Handeln' (2017) 52 *Zeitschrift Europarecht* 137

Odermatt, J, 'The Use of International Treaty Law by the Court of Justice of the European Union' (2015) 17 *Cambridge Yearbook of European Legal Studies* 121

——. '*Council of the European Union v. Front Populaire pour la Libération de la Saguia-El-Hamra et Du Rio de Oro (Front Polisario)*' (2017) 111 *American Journal of International Law* 731

——. 'Facultative Mixity in the International Legal Order: Tolerating European Exceptionalism?' in M Chamon and I Govaere (eds), *EU External Relations Law Post-Lisbon: The Law and Practice of Facultative Mixity* (Leiden, Brill/Nijhoff, 2020) 291

O'Keeffe, D, 'Exclusive, Concurrent and Shared Competence' in C Hillion and P Koutrakos (eds), *Mixed Agreements Revisited: The EU and its Member States in the World* (Oxford, Hart Publishing, 2010) 179

Olson, PM, 'Mixity from the Outside: The Perspective of a Treaty Partner' in C Hillion and P Koutrakos (eds), *Mixed Agreements Revisited: The EU and its Member States in the World* (Oxford, Hart Publishing, 2010) 331

Ortino, F and Eeckhout, P, 'Towards an EU Policy on Foreign Direct Investment' in A Biondi, P Eeckhout, and S Ripley (eds), *EU Law after Lisbon* (Oxford, Oxford University Press, 2012) 312

Ott, A, 'EU External Competence' in J Larik and RA Wessel (eds), *EU External Relations Law*, 2nd edn (Oxford, Hart Publishing, 2020) 61

Pantaleo, L, 'The Provisional Application of CETA: Selected Issues' (2017) 41 *Questions of International Law* 59

Passos, R, 'Mixed Agreements from the Perspective of the European Parliament' in C Hillion and P Koutrakos (eds), *Mixed Agreements Revisited: The EU and its Member States in the World* (Oxford, Hart Publishing, 2010) 269

——. 'The External Powers of the European Parliament' in M López Escudero and P Eeckhout (eds), *The European Union's External Action in Times of Crisis* (Oxford, Hart Publishing, 2016) 85

——. 'Some Issues Related to the Provisional Application of International Agreements and the Institutional Balance' in J Czuczai and F Naert (eds), *The EU as a Global Actor: Bridging Legal Theory and Practice: Liber Amicorum in Honour of Ricardo Gosalbo Bono* (Leiden, Brill/Nijhoff, 2017) 380

Peers, S, 'So Close, Yet So Far: The EU/UK Trade and Cooperation Agreement' (2022) 59 *Common Market Law Review* 49

Peeters, P, 'The Fifth Belgian State Reform ("Lambermont"): A General Overview' (2003) 9 *European Public Law Review* 1

Pescatore, P, 'Les relations extérieures des Communautés européennes. Contribution à la doctrine de la personnalité des organisations internationales' (1961) 103 *Collected Courses of the Hague Academy of International Law* 1

——. 'External Relations in the Case-Law of the Court of Justice of the European Communities' (1979) 16 *Common Market Law Review* 615
Petti, A and Scott, J, 'International Agreements in the EU Legal Order: International Fruit' in G Butler and RA Wessel (eds), *EU External Relations Law: The Cases in Context* (Oxford, Hart Publishing, 2022) 21
Phinnemore, D, 'Stabilisation and Association Agreements: Europe Agreements for the Western Balkans' (2003) 8 *European Foreign Affairs Review* 77
Popelier, P, 'Bicameralism in Belgium: The Dismantlement of the Senate for the Sake of Multinational Confederalism' (2018) 10 *Perspectives on Federalism* 215
Poscher, R, 'Das Verfassungsrecht vor den Herausforderungen der Globalisierung' in C Hillgruber, U Volkmann, G Nolte and R Poscher (eds), *Die Leistungsfähigkeit der Wissenschaft des Öffentlichen Rechts*, Veröffentlichungen der Vereinigung der Deutschen Staatsrechtslehrer 56 (Berlin, De Gruyter, 2008) 160
Prechal, S, 'The European Union's Accession to the Istanbul Convention' in K Lenaerts, J-C Bonichot, H Kanninen, C Naômé and P Pohjankoski (eds), *An Ever-Changing Union? Perspectives on the Future of EU Law in Honour of Allan Rosas* (Oxford, Hart Publishing, 2019) 279
Prete, L, 'Facultative Mixity after the Singapore Opinion: Clarity or Fresh Doubts' in M Chamon and I Govaere (eds), *EU External Relations Law Post-Lisbon: The Law and Practice of Facultative Mixity* (Leiden, Brill/Nijhoff, 2020) 213
Roessler, F, 'The Provisional Application of the GATT' (1985) 19 *Journal of World Trade* 289
Rosas, A, 'Mixed Union: Mixed Agreements' in M Koskenniemi (ed), *International Law Aspects of the European Union* (The Hague, Kluwer Law International, 1998) 125
——. 'The European Union and Mixed Agreements' in A Dashwood and C Hillion (eds), *The General Law of EC External Relations* (London, Sweet & Maxwell, 2000) 200
——. 'The Future of Mixity' in C Hillion and P Koutrakos (eds), *Mixed Agreements Revisited: The EU and its Member States in the World* (Oxford, Hart Publishing, 2010) 367
——. 'Exclusive, Shared and National Competence in the Area of EU External Relations: Do Such Distinctions Matter?' in I Govaere, E Lannon, P Van Elsuwege and S Adam (eds), *The European Union in the World: Essays in Honour of Professor Marc Maresceau* (Leiden, Brill/Nijhoff, 2014) 17
——. 'Mixity Past, Present and Future: Some Observations' in M Chamon and I Govaere (eds), *EU External Relations Law Post-Lisbon: The Law and Practice of Facultative Mixity* (Leiden, Brill/Nijhoff, 2020) 8
Rosén, G, 'The Impact of Norms on Political Decision-Making: How to Account for the European Parliament's Empowerment in EU External Trade Policy' (2017) 24 *Journal of European Public Policy* 1450
Schaefer, S and Odermatt, J, 'Nomen est Omen? The Relevance of "EU Party" in International Law' in N Levrat, Y Kaspiarovich, C Kaddous and RA Wessel (eds), *The EU and its Member States' Joint Participation in International Agreements* (Oxford, Hart Publishing, 2022) 131
Schermers, HG, 'A Typology of Mixed Agreements' in D O'Keeffe and HG Schermers (eds), *Mixed Agreements* (Deventer, Kluwer, 1983) 23
Schiffbauer, B, 'Mehrheitserfordernisse für Abstimmungen im Rat über TTIP, CETA & Co' (2016) 27 *Europäische Zeitschrift für Wirtschaftsrecht* 252
Schill, S, 'Authority, Legitimacy, and Fragmentation in the (Envisaged) Dispute Settlement Disciplines in Mega-Regionals' in S Griller, W Obwexer and E Vranes (eds), *Mega-Regional Trade Agreements: CETA, TTIP, and TiSA: New Orientations for EU External Economic Relations* (Oxford, Oxford University Press, 2017) 111
Schmalenbach, K, 'Artikel 216 AEUV' in C Calliess and M Ruffert (eds), *EUV/AEUV: Das Verfassungsrecht der Europäischen Union mit Europäischer Grundrechtecharta, Kommentar*, 6th edn (Munich, CH Beck, 2022)
——. 'Artikel 217 AEUV' in C Calliess and M Ruffert (eds), *EUV/AEUV: Das Verfassungsrecht der Europäischen Union mit Europäischer Grundrechtecharta, Kommentar*, 6th edn (Munich, CH Beck, 2022)
——. 'Artikel 218 AEUV' in C Calliess and M Ruffert (eds), *EUV/AEUV: Das Verfassungsrecht der Europäischen Union mit Europäischer Grundrechtecharta, Kommentar*, 6th edn (Munich, CH Beck, 2022)
Schöpgens, A and van Calster, G, 'Multilevel Constitutional Review and EU External Treaty Making after Opinion 2/15' (2018) 23 *European Foreign Affairs Review* 439
Schütze, R, 'Lisbon and the Federal Order of Competences: A Prospective Analysis' (2008) 33 *European Law Review* 709
Sepos, A, 'EU Policy-Making in Federal States: The Case of Belgium' (2003) 13 *Regional & Federal Studies* 57
Sommermann, K-P, 'Staatsziel "Europäische Union"' (1994) 47 *Die Öffentliche Verwaltung* 596
——. 'Offene Staatlichkeit: Deutschland' in A von Bogdandy, P Villalón and PM Huber (eds), *Handbuch Ius Publicum Europaeum*, vol II (Heidelberg, CF Müller, 2008) 3

Streinz, R, 'Disputes on TTIP: Does the Agreement Need the Consent of the German Parliament' in C Herrmann, B Simma and R Streinz (eds), *Trade Policy between Law, Diplomacy and Scholarship: Liber Amicorum in Memoriam Horst G. Krenzler* (Berlin, Springer, 2015) 271

Suse, A and Wouters, J, 'Exploring the Boundaries of Provisional Application: The EU's Mixed Trade and Investment Agreements' (2019) 53 *Journal of World Trade* 395

Svensson, P, 'Parliament and Foreign Policy Making in Denmark' (1998) 2 *Irish Studies in International Affairs* 19

Szép, V and Chawla, K, 'The EU's 2022 Sanctions against Russia: External Shocks Altering EU Restrictive Measure Practices?' (2023) 16 *Hungarian Yearbook of International Law and European Law* 196

Temple Lang, J, 'The ERTA Judgement and the Court's Case Law on Competence and Conflict' (1986) 6 *Yearbook of European Law* 183

Terhechte, JP, '(National-)Verfassungsrechtliche Grenzen der Weiterentwicklung des europäischen Außenwirtschaftsrechts' in M Bungenberg and C Herrmann (eds), *Die gemeinsame Handelspolitik der Europäischen Union nach Lissabon* (Baden-Baden, Nomos, 2011) 25

——. 'Common Commercial Policy and External Trade' in HCH Hofmann, GC Rowe and AH Türk (eds), *Specialized Administrative Law of the European Union: A Sectoral Review* (Oxford, Oxford University Press, 2018) 60

——. 'Artikel 216 AEUV' in J Schwarze, U Becker, A Hatje and J Schoo (eds), *EU-Kommentar*, 4th edn (Baden-Baden, Nomos, 2019)

——. 'Artikel 218 AEUV' in J Schwarze, U Becker, A Hatje and J Schoo (eds), *EU-Kommentar*, 4th edn (Baden-Baden, Nomos, 2019)

——. 'Im Dienste der Demokratie? – Das institutionelle Gleichgewicht in der Gemeinsamen Handelspolitik der EU' in C Herrmann (ed), *Die Gemeinsame Handelspolitik im europäischen Verfassungsverbund*, Zeitschrift Europarecht, Beiheft 2/2020 (Baden-Baden, Nomos, 2020) 153

——. 'Strukturen und Probleme des Brexit Abkommens' (2020) 73 *Neue Juristische Wochenzeitschrift* 425

Tietje, C and Nowrot, K, 'Parlamentarische Steuerung und Kontrolle des internationalen Regierungshandelns und der Außenpolitik' in M Morlok, U Schliesky and D Wiefelspütz (eds), *Parlamentsrecht: Praxishandbuch* (Baden-Baden, Nomos, 2016) § 45

Timmermans, CWA, 'ECJ Doctrines on Competence' in L Azoulai (ed), *The Question of Competence in the European Union* (Oxford, Oxford University Press, 2014) 155

Titi, C, 'International Investment Law and the European Union: Towards a New Generation of International Investment Agreements' (2015) 26 *European Journal of International Law* 639

Tridimas, T and Eeckhout, P, 'The External Competence of the Community and the Case-Law of the Court of Justice: Principle versus Pragmatism' (1994) 14 *Yearbook of European Law* 143

Van Damme, I, 'Case C-414/11 Daiichi: The Impact of the Lisbon Treaty on the Competence of the European Union over the TRIPS Agreement' (2015) 4 *Cambridge Journal of International and Comparative Law* 73

Van den Bossche, P, 'European Community in International Economic Relations: The Bittersweet Experience of the Uruguay Round' in JH Jackson and AO Sykes (eds), *Implementing the Uruguay Round* (Oxford, Oxford University Press, 1997) 23

Van der Loo, G, 'Less is More? The Role of National Parliaments in the Conclusion of Mixed (Trade) Agreements' in J Santos Vara and S Rodriguez Sánchez-Tabernero (eds), *The Democratisation of EU International Relations through EU Law* (Abingdon, Routledge, 2018) 210

Van der Loo, G and Wessel, RA, 'The Non-ratification of Mixed Agreements: Legal Consequences and Solutions' (2017) 54 *Common Market Law Review* 735

Van der Steen, I, 'A View from the Netherlands' in C Hillion and P Koutrakos (eds), *Mixed Agreements Revisited: The EU and its Member States in the World* (Oxford, Hart Publishing, 2010) 294

Van Elsuwege, P, 'Legal Creativity in EU External Relations: The Stabilisation and Association Agreement between the EU and Kosovo' (2017) 22 *European Foreign Affairs Review* 393

——. 'Old Habits Die Hard: Questions of Facultative Mixity in Relation to the Common Foreign and Security Policy' in M Chamon and I Govaere (eds), *EU External Relations Law Post-Lisbon: The Law and Practice of Facultative Mixity* (Leiden, Brill/Nijhoff, 2020) 169

——. 'A New Legal Framework for EU-UK Relations: Some Reflections from the Perspective of EU External Relations Law' (2021) 6 *European Papers* 785

Verellen, T, 'The ERTA Doctrine in the Post-Lisbon Era: Note under Judgment in *Commission v Council* (C-114/12) and Opinion 1/13' (2015) 21 *Columbia Journal of European Law* 383

——. 'Opinion 3/15 on the Marrakesh Treaty: ECJ Reaffirms Narrow "Minimum Harmonisation" Exception to ERTA Principle' (2017) 42 *Revista General de Derecho Europeo* 160

Verellen, T, 'Het Hof van Justitie en het EU-Singapore handelsakkoord, of de kunst van het koorddansen' (2018) *SEW: Tijdschrift voor Europees en economisch recht* 31

——. 'Convergence and Divergence in EU External Action: The Very Slowly Emergent Doctrine of Shared Competence' in M Sahadžić, M Kos, J Kukavica, J Gašperin Wischhoff and J Scholtes (eds), *Accommodating Diversity in Multilevel Constitutional Orders: Legal Mechanisms of Divergence and Converge* (Abingdon, Routledge, 2023) 112

Von Bogdandy, A, Prinzipien der Rechtsfortbildung im europäischen Rechtsraum – Überlegungen zum Lissabon-Urteil des BVerfG' (2010) 63 *Neue Juristische Wochenzeitschrift* 1

Von Bogdandy, A and Bast, J, 'The Federal Order of Competences' in A von Bogdandy and J Bast (eds), *Principles of European Constitutional Law*, 2nd edn (Oxford, Munich and Baden-Baden, Hart Publishing, CH Beck and Nomos, 2009) 275

Vöneky, S and Beylage-Haarmann, B, 'Artikel 217 AEUV' in E Grabitz, M Hilf and M Nettesheim (eds), *Das Recht der Europäischen Union: EUV/AEUV*, Stand: Mai 2023, 79 Erg.-Lfg. (Munich, CH Beck, 2023)

Voßkuhle, A, 'Multilevel Cooperation of the European Constitutional Courts' (2010) 6 *European Constitutional Law Review* 175

Walter, C, 'Artikel 19' in K Schmalenbach and O Dörr (eds), *Vienna Convention on the Law of Treaties: A Commentary*, 2nd edn (Berlin, Springer, 2018) 261

Weiler, JHH, 'The External Legal Relations of Non-Unitary Actors: Mixity and the Federal Principle' in D O'Keeffe and HG Schermers (eds), *Mixed Agreements* (Deventer, Kluwer, 1983) 35

——. 'The Transformation of Europe' (1991) 100 *Yale Law Journal* 2405

Weiß, W, 'Informations- und Beteiligungsrechte des Deutschen Bundestags bei gemischten Abkommen wie TTIP' (2016) 16 *Die Öffentliche Verwaltung* 661

——. 'The Reception of EU Facultative Mixity in Germany's Constitutional Order' in M Chamon and I Govaere (eds), *EU External Relations Law Post-Lisbon: The Law and Practice of Facultative Mixity* (Leiden, Brill/Nijhoff, 2020) 363

——. 'Vertragliche Handelspolitik der EU' in A von Arnauld and M Bungenberg (eds), *Europäische Außenbeziehungen*, Enzyklopädie Europarecht, vol 12 (Baden-Baden, Nomos, 2022) § 12

——. 'Artikel 207 AEUV' in E Grabitz, M Hilf and M Nettesheim (eds), *Das Recht der Europäischen Union: EUV/AEUV*, Stand: Mai 2023, 79 Erg.-Lfg (Munich, CH Beck, 2023)

Wendel, M, 'Demokratische Teilhabe und Freihandel – Zur Rolle von Bürgerinitiative und Transparenz bei der Entstehung eines transatlantischen Wirtschaftsvölkerrechts' in M Bungenberg and C Herrmann (eds), *Die gemeinsame Handelspolitik der Europäischen Union: Fünf Jahre nach Lissabon – Quo Vadis?* (Baden-Baden, Nomos, 2016) 93

Wessel, RA, 'Revisiting the International Legal Status of the EU' (2000) 5 *European Foreign Affairs Review* 507

——. 'Dissolution and Succession: The Transmigration of the Soul of International Organizations' in J Klabbers and Å Wallendahl (eds), *Research Handbook on the Law of International Organisations* (Cheltenham, Edward Elgar, 2001) 342

——. 'Cross-Pillar Mixity: Combining Competences in the Conclusion of the EU International Agreements' in C Hillion and P Koutrakos (eds), *Mixed Agreements Revisited: The EU and its Member States in the World* (Oxford, Hart Publishing, 2010) 30

——. 'The EU Solution to Deal with the Dutch Referendum Result on the EU-Ukraine Association Agreement' (2016) *European Papers* 1305

Wessel, RA and Larik, J, 'The European Union as a Global Legal Actor' in RA Wessel and J Larik (eds), *EU External Relations Law: Text, Cases and Materials*, 2nd edn (Oxford, Hart Publishing, 2020) 1

Wessel, RA and van de Griendt, WE, 'Offene Staatlichkeit: Niederlande' in A von Bogdandy, P Villalón and PM Huber (eds), *Handbuch Ius Publicum Europaeum*, vol II (Heidelberg, CF Müller, 2008) 177

Wouters, J, Coppens, D, and De Meester, B, 'The European Union's External Relations after the Lisbon Treaty' in S Griller and J Ziller (eds), *The Lisbon Treaty: EU Constitutionalism without a Constitutional Treaty?* (Heidelberg, Springer, 2008), 143

III. Working Papers and Policy Analyses

Bhagwati, JN, 'US Trade Policy: The Infatuation with FTAs' (1995) 726 *Colombia University Discussion Paper Series*

Cremona, M, 'External Relations of the EU and the Member States: Competence, Mixed Agreements, International Responsibility, and Effects of International Law' (2006) 22 *EUI Working Paper Law*

——. 'A Constitutional Basis for Effective EU External Action? An Assessment of the Provisions on EU External Action in the Constitutional Treaty' (2006) 30 *EUI Working Paper Law*

——. 'Member States as Trustees of the Community Interest: Participating in International Agreements on Behalf of the European Community' (2009) 17 *EUI Working Paper Law*

Hoekman, B and Mavroidis, PC, 'Burning Down the House? The Appellate Body in the Centre of the WTO Crisis' (2019) 56 *EUI Working Paper RSCAS*

Hoffmeister, F, 'The European Union's Common Commercial Policy a Year after Lisbon: Sea Change or Business as Usual' in P Koutrakos (ed), *The European Union's External Relations a Year after Lisbon* (2011) 3 CLEER Working Paper 83

Kleimann, D, 'Taking Stock: EU Common Commercial Policy in the Lisbon Era', *CEPS Policy Brief* (2011)

——. 'Reading Opinion 2/15: Standards of Analysis, the Court's Discretion, and the Legal View of the Advocate General' (2017) 23 *EUI Working Paper RSCAS*

Kube, V, 'The European Union's External Human Rights Commitment: What is the Legal Value of Article 21 TEU?' (2016) 10 *EUI Working Paper Law*

Lenaerts, K and Gutiérrez-Fons, JA, 'To Say What the Law of the EU Is: Methods of Interpretation and the European Court of Justice' (2013) 9 *EUI Working Paper AEL*

Meunier, S, 'The End of Naivety: Assertiveness and New Instruments in EU Trade and Investment Policy (2022) 55 *Policy Brief, EUI Global Governance Programme*

Passos, R, 'The European Union's External Relations a Year after Lisbon: A First Evaluation from the European Parliament' in P Koutrakos (ed), *The European Union's External Relations a Year after Lisbon* (2011) 3 CLEER Working Paper 49

Vidal Puig, R, 'Investment Arbitration in the EU following Achmea and Opinion 1/17' (2019) 19 *ECB Legal Working Paper Series* 20

IV. Commissioned Studies and Evidence

Eschbach, A, *Die Ratifizierungsprozesse in den EU-Mitgliedstaaten: Eine Darstellung unter besonderer Berücksichtigung der Freihandelsabkommen TTIP und CETA* (2015)

Herrmann, C, 'Unionsrechtliche und verfassungsrechtliche Fragen des Abschlusses und der vorläufigen Anwendung des Comprehensive Economic and Trade Agreement (CETA) zwischen der EU (inkl. Mitgliedstaaten) und Kanada', *Stellungnahme für die Öffentliche Anhörung des Ausschusses für Wirtschaft und Energie des Deutschen Bundestages* (2016)

Herrmann, C and Rosenfeld, H, 'Europarechtliche Grundlagen und Grenzen der Errichtung eines einheitlichen Bankenabwicklungsmechanismus (SRM)', *Gutachten im Auftrag der Bundestagsfraktion Bündnis90/Die Grünen* (2014)

Kilpatrick, C et al, 'Trade Sustainability Impact Assessment (SIA) on the Comprehensive Economic and Trade Agreement (CETA) between the EU and Canada: Final Report' (2011)

Krunke, H, 'Memorandum on Denmark', evidence submitted to the House of Lord's Select Committee on European Union (2009)

Maurer, A, 'Comparative Study on Access to Documents (and Confidentiality Rules) in International Trade Negotiations', Study for the *European Parliament's Committee on International Trade* (2015)

Van Elsuwege, P and Chamon, M, 'The Meaning of 'Association' under EU law: A Study on the Law and Practice of EU Association Agreements', *Study for the Policy Department for Citizens' Rights and Constitutional Affairs of the European Parliament* (2019)

Weiß, W, 'Verfassungsprobleme des Abschlusses und der vorläufigen Anwendung des CETA Freihandelsabkommens mit Kanada', *Stellungnahme zur Öffentlichen Anhörung des Wirtschaft und Energie des Deutschen Bundestages* (2016)

V. Institutional Studies and Reports

Council of Europe, Committee of Legal Advisers on Public International Law, Expression of Consent by States to be Bound by a Treaty – Analytical Report and Country Reports [2000] CAHDI (2000) 13 FINAL

Council of Europe, *Treaty-Making: Expression of Consent by States to Be Bound by a Treaty* (Leiden, Brill/Nijhoff, 2001)

European Parliament, Directorate-General for the Presidency, National Parliaments Background Briefing: Procedures of Ratification of Mixed Agreements (2016)

Gaja, G, 'Provisional Application of Treaties', Report of the International Law Commission, Sixty-Third Session [2011] UN Doc A/66/10, Annex C

Gómez-Robledo, JM, 'First Report on the Provisional Application of Treaties', International Law Commission, Sixty-Fifth Session [2013] UN Doc A/CN.4/664

——. 'Second Report on the Provisional Application of Treaties', International Law Commission, Sixty-Sixth Session [2014] UN Doc A/CN.4/675

——. 'Third Report on the Provisional Application of Treaties', International Law Commission, Sixty-Seventh Session [2015] UN Doc A/CN.4/687

VI. Blog Posts

Baetens, F, Bronckers, M, Kuijper, PJ, Voermans, W and Wessel RA, 'Why the Netherlands Should Ratify CETA', *EJIL Talk!*, 30 June 2020, ejiltalk.org/why-the-netherlands-should-ratify-ceta

Chamon, M, 'Extending Provisional Application of the TCA: A Matter of Democracy', *DCU Brexit Institute News*, 24 February 2012, dcubrexitinstitute.eu/2021/02/extending-provisional-application-of-the-tca

——. 'Op-Ed: The Court's Opinion in Avis 1/19 regarding the Istanbul Convention', *EU Law Live*, 12 October 2021, eulawlive.com/op-ed-the-courts-opinion-in-avis-1-19-regarding-the-istanbul-convention-by-merijn-chamon

Chamon, M and Verellen, T, 'Whittling down the Collective Interest: CETA, Facultative Mixity, Democracy and Halloumi', *Verfassungsblog*, 7 August 2020, verfassungsblog.de/whittling-down-the-collective-interest

Kuijper, PJ, 'Case C-244/17 – *Commission v Council*: The Centre of Gravity Test Revisited in the Context of Article 218 (9) TFEU', *European Law Blog*, 26 November 2018, europeanlawblog.eu/2018/11/26/case-c-244-17-commission-v-council-the-centre-of-gravity-test-revisited-in-the-context-of-article-218-9-tfeu

Larik, J, '"The Mother of All Parliaments"? How the Ratification of the Trade and Cooperation Agreement Boosts the European Parliament's Profile', *DCU Brexit Institute News*, 29 April 2021, dcubrexitinstitute.eu/2021/04/the-mother-of-all-parliaments-how-the-ratification-of-the-trade-and-cooperation-agreement-boosts-the-european-parliaments-profile

Mayer, FC, 'European Vetocracy? How to Overcome the Wallonian CETA Problem', *Verfassungsblog*, 24 June 2015, verfassungsblog.de/european-vetocracy-how-to-overcome-the-wallonian-ceta-problem

Prete, L, 'Some Thoughts on Facultative and Obligatory Mixity after Singapore and COTIF, and before CETA', *Verfassungsblog*, 13 October 2018, verfassungsblog.de/some-thoughts-on-facultative-and-obligatory-mixity-after-singapore-and-cotif-and-before-ceta

Ruffert, M, 'Das CETA-Ratifikationsgesetz bedarf nicht der Zustimmung des Bundesrates!', *Verfassungsblog*, 31 October 2016, www.verfassungsblog.de/das-ceta-ratifikationsgesetz-bedarf-nicht-der-zustimmung-des-bundesrates

Thym, D, 'Mixity after Opinion 2/15: Judicial Confusion over Shared Competences' *Verfassungsblog*, 31 May 2017, verfassungsblog.de/mixity-after-opinion-215-judicial-confusion-over-shared-competences

Van Elsuwege, P, 'What Will Happen if the Dutch Vote "No" in the Referendum on the EU-Ukraine Association Agreement?', *Verfassungsblog*, 10 February 2016, www.verfassungsblog.de/what-will-happen-if-the-dutch-vote-no-in-the-referendum-on-the-eu-ukraine-association-agreement

INDEX

www.ingramcontent.com/pod-product-compliance
Ingram Content Group UK Ltd.
Pitfield, Milton Keynes, MK11 3LW, UK
UKHW020247290926
15470UKWH00002B/788